Justice in the Workplace
From Theory to Practice
Volume 2

Series in Applied Psychology
Edwin A. Fleishman, George Mason University, Series Editor

Gregory Bedny and David Meister • *The Russian Theory of Activity: Current Applications to Design and Learning*

Michael T. Brannick, Eduardo Salas, and Carolyn Prince • *Team Performance Assessment and Measurement: Theory, Research, and Applications*

Jeanette N. Cleveland, Margaret Stockdale, and Kevin R. Murphy • *Women and Men in Organizations: Sex and Gender Issues at Work*

Russell Cropanzano • *Justice in the Workplace: Approaching Fairness in Human Resource Management, Volume 1*

Russell Cropanzano • *Justice in the Workplace: From Theory to Practice, Volume 2*

James E. Driskell and Eduardo Salas • *Stress and Human Performance*

Sidney A. Fine and Steven F. Cronshaw • *Functional Job Analysis: A Foundation for Human Resources Management*

Sidney A. Fine and Maury Getkate • *Benchmark Tasks for Job Analysis: A Guide for Functional Job Analysis (FJA) Scales*

J. Kevin Ford, Steve W. J. Kozlowski, Kurt Kraiger, Eduardo Salas, and Mark S. Teachout • *Improving Training Effectiveness in Work Organizations*

Jerald Greenberg • *Organizational Behavior: The State of the Science*

Uwe E. Kleinbeck, Hans-Henning Quast, Henk Thierry, and Hartmut Häcker • *Work Motivation*

Martin I. Kurke and Ellen M. Scrivner • *Police Psychology Into the 21st Century*

Manuel London • *Job Feedback: Giving, Seeking, and Using Feedback for Performance Improvement*

Robert F. Morrison and Jerome Adams • *Contemporary Career Development Issues*

Michael D. Mumford, Garnett Stokes, and William A. Owens • *Patterns of Life History: The Ecology of Human Individuality*

Kevin R. Murphy and Frank E. Saal • *Psychology in Organizations: Integrating Science and Practice*

Ned Rosen • *Teamwork and the Bottom Line: Groups Make a Difference*

Heinz Schuler, James L. Farr, and Mike Smith • *Personnel Selection and Assessment: Individual and Organizational Perspectives*

John W. Senders and Neville P. Moray • *Human Error: Cause, Prediction, and Reduction*

Justice in the Workplace
From Theory to Practice
Volume 2

Edited by

Russell Cropanzano
Colorado State University

2001

LAWRENCE ERLBAUM ASSOCIATES, PUBLISHERS
Mahwah, New Jersey   London

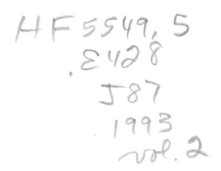

Lawrence Erlbaum Associates, Inc., Publishers
10 Industrial Avenue
Mahwah, NJ 07430

Cover design by Kathryn Houghtaling Lacey

Library of Congress Cataloging-in-Publication Data

Justice in the workplace : from theory to practice / edited by Russell Cropanzano—Volume 2.
      p. cm.
    Includes bibliographical references and index.
ISBN 0-8058-2694-7 (cloth : alk. paper)
ISBN 0-8058-2695-5 (pbk : alk. paper)
1. Employees rights. 2. Justice. 3. Personnel management.
    I. Cropanzano, Russell.
HF5549.5.E428 J87 2000
658.3'15—dc21

                           00-029367
                              CIP

Printed in the United States of America
10 9 8 7 6 5 4 3 2 1

Contents

Part II
The Practical Application of Organizational Justice

Part III
Looking to the Future

Series Foreword

Edwin A. Fleishman
George Mason University

There is a compelling need for innovative approaches to the solution of many pressing problems involving human relationships in today's society. Such approaches are more likely to be successful when they are based on sound research and applications. This Series in Applied Psychology offers publications that emphasize state-of-the-art research and its application to important issues of human behavior in a variety of social settings. The objective is to bridge both academic and applied interests.

It has been over seven years since volume one of *Justice in the Workplace* was published in our *Series in Applied Psychology*. That volume was among the very first books to take up the topic of organizational justice. In 1993 this was an unpretentious, fledgling. The moniker "organizational justice" had only been coined six years previously. Since publication of that 1993 volume, there have been many new developments in what has become a vigorous and expanding research field. As the papers in this second volume amply illustrate, justice research now touches virtually every aspect of organizational life—implementing performance appraisals, staffing firms, formulating strategic plans, achieving an optimal structure, promoting diversity, etc. Volume one was a first look at an emerging literature. Seven years later this second volume reviews a mature and influential, and still growing, area of inquiry.

Why has workplace justice become so important? No doubt there are myriad reasons. As a topic of inquiry, organizational justice in conceptually rich and integrative, as it borrows insights from other areas. Perhaps even more important, organizational justice has implications for how we treat others, and it holds some serviceable recommendations for practicing managers. To be sure, there are important strengths. Still, such things could be said of many research areas. So there must be more to the story. It could be that organizational justice captivates because it is so fundamental. Justice relates to how people assign tasks, bestow awards, and confer status. In doing so, justice research articulates the rules by which people organize themselves into entities as small as dyads or as large as multinational corporations. In the end, perhaps justice matters because it is about fairness, which has great personal resonance and makes it a story worth telling.

As we pointed out in the Foreword to volume 1, an organization's successes are usually social successes, just as it's failings tend to be social failings. Managers, as opposed to technicians, allocate the lion's share of their time to people: motivating them, rewarding them, coordinating them, and even removing them from their work units. The discipline of human resource management has a long history, coming of age as a set of sophisticated technical tools to help organizations deal with the ubiquitous concerns and complications involved in managing people. But like all technical tools, human resource interventions ultimately stand and fall on the people who administer them, and, in turn, on the people whom they administer. Although technical competence may be necessary, it is not a sufficient success. Human resource management must also attend to the concerns of the people being managed. It is here that research on organizational justice is so important. The justice perspective offers a complimentary view of the human resource enterprise. It offers us a look at the organization from the vantage point of personal concerns, wants, and needs. As such, it holds out the promise of both more effective and more humane organizations.

Russell Cropanzano is uniquely qualified to bring these developments together. He has been a key contributor to this area and as Editor of the first volume of *Justice in the Workplace* has a unique perspective on the field. Each of the contributors adds an important conceptual or practical perspective. This volume is comprehensive, diverse, and up to date in its treatment of this important topic. The book should be of interest to researchers, teachers, and managers interested in fairness, social justice, and more effective human resource management.

Preface

If you take Interstate 25 south from where I type these words, leave the highway just north of Trinidad, and take a reasonably good quality dirt road just far enough west, you'll reach the site of a small ghost town. This is (or was) Ludlow, Colorado. Ludlow is an inauspicious place, with only a few small structures, partially standing and safely fenced into a patch of private property. Unless you made a point of trying to find Ludlow, you wouldn't notice it. Although the countryside is beautiful, there are no residents in this abandoned coal town. Nor is Ludlow a stop on a byway to something more propitious. But whatever Ludlow lacks as a destination or a rest stop, the now barren site is an admirable beginning for a book on organization justice.

The event that defined Ludlow was a simple migration. In September 1913, roughly 9,000 miners gathered up their wives, children, and meager possessions and moved out of the squalid company town, setting up a tent colony as their new home. This act was symbolic as much as practical. As such, it touched off the strike against the Colorado Fuel and Iron Company that would be known to history as the Ludlow Massacre.

Owned by the wealthy John D. Rockefeller, the Colorado Fuel and Iron Company was a colossus that loomed over the individual workers. As historian Thomas Brooks (1971) observed, the company "controlled every aspects of their lives" (p. 129). In an era when being a miner was little better than a paid death sentence, workers certainly wanted better pay and working conditions. The Ludlow demands included a 10% pay increase, an 8-hour workday, and enforcement of state mining laws. But there were also concerns with personal dignity. The miners wanted to choose where they lived, select their own doctors, and spend their money in stores of their choosing. And perhaps most fundamentally, they wanted recognition of their union, the United Mine Workers, as a vehicle for ensuring that miners had a place at the decision-making table.

As the strike endured (it would eventually last 15 months), the company became impatient. Martial law was imposed, and the Colorado National Guard was dispatched. The militia occupied the commanding high ground, set up a machine gun, and exploded two warning bombs. In response, miners entrenched themselves in the local *arroyos,* affording themselves a measure of natural protection. As so often happens when nervous young men face each other with guns, someone fired a shot, and a day-long battle ensued. Although strong and brave, the miners were not an army. The militia eventually forced their way into the camp and, obeying the orders of their superiors, poured coal oil onto the tents. As a result of this conflagration, 13 women and 2 children died in a single tent. Meanwhile, discipline broke down among the militiamen, who rampaged through the camp, stealing valuables and even shooting three unarmed captives (Brooks, 1971; Gitelman, 1988). The Ludlow massacre was over.

From the vantage point of history, it is interesting to ask ourselves what those miners, their wives and children thought they were fighting for at Ludlow. It was probably not economic wealth. The risks were too great, and the probable pay-off too small (even had they gotten the 10% raise), to justify their obstinance. Nor is it likely, as Rockefeller argued, that the miners were simply deluded by unscrupulous and greedy union organizers. These workers were a practical lot, not given to flights of idealistic fancy. They *knew* the conditions of their lives. Besides, the United Mine Workers engendered such a depth of support and commitment from the workers that it is difficult to believe it was based on delusion.

A more likely explanation comes from taking unionized workers at their word. The miners were willing to risk death to achieve justice. The ideal of justice led them to confront the most powerful institution in their lives, to stand up to an advancing army, and even accept death. Ludlow is an especially poignant example of what this book is about—social justice in work organizations. In this sense, Ludlow is a morality tale. The story underscores the wages of industrial sin. Lacking fairness, the Colorado Fuel and Iron Company could maintain itself only by a tremendous cost in human suffering. The organization nearly ripped itself apart in a battle over justice. Justice is fundamental to the functioning of social systems, such as work organizations. To illustrate this point, let us see if we can understand the events leading to Ludlow from the perspective of an organizational justice researcher. As we see, Ludlow provides examples of the principle constructs about which this book is organized: distributive justice, procedural justice, and interactional justice.

Distributive justice refers to the fairness of the outcomes that are provided to workers. Outcomes are perhaps the most salient injustice at Ludlow. Miners were woefully underpaid and overworked. Additionally, their jobs were exceedingly difficult ("laborious labor" as one worker put it; Brooks, 1971, p. 131) and dangerous. Economically, they were bound to the company by expensive company stores that charged inflated prices and kept workers chronically in debt (Bettmann, 1974). Workers also lacked pension plans (Brooks, 1971) and workers compensation for disabilities (Bettmann, 1974).

Less obvious, but also apparent, were concerns over procedural justice—the fairness of the process by which outcomes are allocated. Workers at the Colorado Fuel and Iron Company had no formal representation to decision-making bodies. At the time of the strike they had no mechanism for appealing decisions made by company officials, nor could they organize themselves into an independent union. Indeed, the Colorado Fuel and Iron Company would eventually eliminate much of the industrial ill-will by providing workers with mechanisms for voice. For example, in the year after the Ludlow massacre, Rockefeller established a joint decision-making body composed of both managers and workers. Additionally, the United Mine Workers were eventually allowed to organize workers, and formal grievance systems have become standard practice in the unionized coal-mining industry (e.g., Gitelman, 1988; Ury, Brett, & Goldberg, 1989).

Interactional justice, the fairness of the interpersonal treatment that one receives, is perhaps the most subtle at all. Although such subtlety was missing at Ludlow. Rockefeller was so unconcerned with the Ludlow workers that he did not even bother to familiarize himself with their plight. According to the U.S. Commission on Industrial Relations (cited in Brooks, 1971): "Such details as wages, worker conditions, and the political, social, and moral welfare of the 15,000 or 20,000 inhabitants of his coal camps apparently held no interest for Rockefeller, for as late as April 1914, he professed ignorance of the details" (p. 128). Rather than considerately listening to worker concerns, the Colorado Fuel and Iron Company first employed armed goons to suppress the strike and, when they proved insufficient, supported the use of the Colorado Militia to restore the status quo ante. Significantly, after the Ludlow massacre Rockefeller attempted to restore interactional justice. Doing so involved face-to-face visits with workers, tours of the mines, even informal dances (Brooks, 1971; Gitelman, 1988). By the time of World War I, labor–management relations in the United States were beginning to improve (Painter, 1987).

Outcomes, processes, and interpersonal treatment form much of this book's content. These are three powerful tools for building and maintaining workplace justice. In Part I, these issues are discussed at a theoretical level. We begin historically. Chapter 1 traces the history of organizational justice from its inception in social psychology, to its current application in the organizational sciences. In preparing their history, Byrne and Cropanzano conducted extensive interviews with the major researchers in this area, including some of the authors of the present chapters. In chapter 2, Vermunt & Steensma apply organizational justice to the study of workplace stress. In so doing, they propose and review an expanded model of fairness. In chapter 3, van den Bos, Kind, and Wilke examine the cognitive processes by which people decide they are being treated fairly or unfairly. Using fairness heuristic theory as an organizing framework, they show how processes and outcomes are combined to make fairness judgments. Chapter 4 explores cross-cultural research on justice. McFarlin and Sweeney explore the application of organizational justice outside of North America. Chapter 5 takes up the issue of proactive justice, or the conditions, that spur a manger to treat a worker with fairness or unfairness. Folger and Skarlicki review evidence suggesting that a troubled business environment, as well as the intrinsic difficulty to being just, can cause managers to be unfair.

In Part II, these theories are applied to several issues important to both human resource management and society. In chapter 6, Bobocel, Davey, Hing, and Zanna examine affirmative action policies in the light of organizational justice. Bobocel and her colleagues find that a concern for social justice sometimes leads well-meaning people to oppose certain affirmative action programs. In chapter 7, Grandey explores family-friendly polices. Grandey reviews several possible programs and argues that they may be seen as fair or unfair, depending on the perspective taken by the observer. In chapter 8, Gilliland and Steiner propose a new paradigm for examining fairness in staffing decisions. Unlike traditional models of selection fairness, which focus on statistical issues, Gilliland and Steiner explore selection fairness from the perspective of the job candidate. They also discuss the consequences of these perceptions. The topic of chapter 9 is workplace revenge. Bies and Tripp discuss how revenge can often be seen as an act of "retributive justice." That is, retaliation for wrongdoing may be viewed as fair under some circumstances. In this way, injustice can create conflict and turmoil in work organizations. Closing out the section on practical applications, Korsgaard & Schweiger take a fairness perspective on strategic planning. These authors maintain that the fair processes can lead to more effective business plans.

In Part III, we come full circle. Whereas this book has begun with the Ludlow massacre early in the 20th century, we conclude with three looks at organizational justice in the years ahead. In chapter 11, Ambrose and Schminke take a look at organizations of the future. They suggest that formal procedures will be less useful tools for maintaining fairness. Instead, firms may need to rely on justice interpersonal relationships. Chapter 12 reviews the changing contract between workers and organizations. Cropanzano and Prehar both discuss these changes and then try to anticipate justice concerns that are likely to emerge in the future. Finally, in chapter 13, Greenberg and Wiethoff close the book by examining justice research more broadly. They consider both why people are unfair, as well as the consequences of such injustice.

—Russell Cropanzano

REFERENCES

Bettmann, O. L. (1974). *The good old days—They were terrible!* New York: Random House.
Brooks, T. R. (1971). *Toil and trouble: A history of American labor* (2nd ed.). New York: Delacorte.
Gitelman, H. M. (1988). *Legacy of the Ludlow massacre: A chapter in American industrial relations*. Philadelphia: University of Pennsylvania Press.
Painter, N. L. (1987). *Standing at armageddon: The United States, 1877–1919*. New York: Norton.
Ury, W. L., Brett, J. M., & Goldberg, S. B. (1989). *Getting disputes resolved: Designing systems to cut the costs of conflict*. San Francisco, CA: Jossey-Bass.

I

▼▼▼▼▼▼▼▼

THEORETICAL ADVANCES
AND NEW CONCEPTUAL DIRECTIONS

1

▼▼▼▼▼▼▼▼▼

The History of Organizational Justice:
The Founders Speak

Zinta S. Byrne
Russell Cropanzano
Colorado State University

This is a book about organizational justice. In the pages that follow we examine the current theoretical state of the field (chaps. 2 and 3), an assortment of practical applications of these theories (chaps. 4–7), and then we take an aspiring look into the future (chaps. 8–10). In this chapter the goals are simple and modest. We examine the past; beginning in the late 1970s and gaining considerable velocity in the 1980s, justice research roared through the social sciences. Not only were new theoretical positions proposed, debated, and reconstructed (for a sampling see Bies, 1987; Bies & Moag, 1986; Brockner & Wiesenfeld, 1996; Cropanzano & Folger, 1991; Folger, 1986; Greenberg, 1987a; Lind, 1995; Van den Bos, Lind, & Wilke, chap. 3, this volume), but few organizational practices escaped scrutiny from the lens of organizational justice. Such technical practices as performance evaluation (Folger, Konovsky, & Cropanzano, 1992), staffing (Gilliland, 1993; Gilliland & Steiner, chap. 8, this volume), strategic planning (Korsgaard, Sapienza, & Schweiger, chap. 10, this volume), pay systems (Alexander & Sinclair, 1995; Miceli, 1993), and downsizing (Folger & Skarlicki, chap. 5, this volume; Konovsky & Brockner, 1993) were reinvestigated under the magnifying glass of the justice paradigm. The result was an outpouring of new scholarship that continues today, highlighted by the appearance of several books (e.g., Cropanzano, 1993; Cropanzano & Kacmar, 1995; Folger & Cropanzano, 1998; Greenberg, 1996; Greenberg & Cropanzano, in press; Lind & Tyler, 1988; Sheppard, Lewicki, & Minton, 1993) and numerous review articles (e.g., Brockner & Wiesenfeld, 1996; Cropanzano & Folger, 1991; Cropanzano & Greenberg, 1997; Folger & Greenberg, 1985; Greenberg, 1990a, 1990b).

From all this attention it is easy to forget that organizational justice research is less than 15 years old. In fact, the very term *organizational justice* was only coined in 1987 by Greenberg in his *Academy of Management Review* paper (Greenberg, 1987a). Likewise, the chapter that is often credited with igniting this storm of interest, "Procedural Justice: An Interpretive Analysis of Personnel Systems," was published in 1985 by Folger and Greenberg. As shown, the emergence of organizational justice as a distinct area of psychological inquiry, as well as its explosive rise to prominence, was largely due to the aggregate efforts of five seminal researchers: Robert Bies, Robert Folger, Jerald Greenberg, Allan Lind, and Tom Tyler. To assist in the preparation of this manuscript, all five of these scholars consented to being interviewed by the senior author. The interviews took place by telephone in November of 1997. Although some specific questions were prepared in advance, the interviews were generally open-ended and accommodated a flexible structure allowing each interviewee to explore whatever issues he deemed important. This chapter is the result.

WHAT IS ORGANIZATIONAL JUSTICE?

At its most general level, organizational justice is an area of psychological inquiry that focuses on perceptions of fairness in the workplace. It is the psychology of justice applied to organizational settings (Lind & Tyler, 1988; Sheppard et al., 1992). In the beginning, organizational justice researchers borrowed heavily from existing social-psychological research on fairness. Bies echoed this in his interview, "justice originally came out of social psychology." In fact, Folger, Lind, and Tyler all received their original training in social psychology. Much, although by no means all, of the early social-psychology research was based on laboratory simulations (e.g., Folger, 1977), or surveys in legal environments (e.g., Tyler, 1984), although some important workplace studies were also conducted (Adams, 1965; Homans, 1965). In any case, although social-psychology research provided a useful tool for understanding work organizations, "borrowing" was not straightforward as we discuss in the next section. In the process of transforming social-psychological justice into *organizational justice* the new conceptual frameworks developed their own distinct stamp, hence shedding their borrowed look.

Defining organizational justice as the study of fairness perceptions at work is useful in that it captures the eclectic nature of justice as a research area. Organizational justice researchers have reached nearly universal consensus that fairness can plausibly be divided into at least two types (although other frameworks may also be reasonable; see Bies, in press; Greenberg, 1993). *Distributive justice*, or, the fairness of the outcomes received in a given transaction, is considered the first type. The second type is *procedural justice*, or, the fairness of the process that leads to those outcomes. These two types of justice are discussed later in this chapter and throughout this book. However, we should first examine the relation of distributive and procedural fairness to the colloquial definition of organizational justice.

From the start, organizational justice researchers have explicitly noted that both types of fairness are important. For example, Leventhal (1976a; 1976b; Leventhal, Karuza, & Fry, 1980) emphasized procedural fairness as well as distributive, recognizing that previous justice literature failed to acknowledge the importance of procedures in fair decisions. Additionally, Alexander and Ruderman (1987) examined both distributive and procedural justice in a study of federal government employees. Likewise, when Greenberg (1987a) coined the term *organizational justice*, he did so in the context of an article that reviewed both the distributive and procedural literature. Nevertheless, it is also true that organizational justice research has historically embodied more of a process-oriented flavor. This can be demonstrated by examining the titles of some of the seminal works in organizational justice. For example, Folger and Greenberg (1985) was titled *Procedural Justice: An Interpretative Analysis of Personnel Systems*. Likewise, an influential (and somewhat social psychological) book by Lind and Tyler (1988) was called *The Social Psychology of Procedural Justice*. Additionally, in two reviews of the organizational justice literature the authors devoted more space to procedural justice than distributive and claimed to do so because the literature on procedural justice was the larger of the two (Cropanzano & Greenberg, 1997; Greenberg, 1990a). Importantly, this procedural flavor should not be taken to suggest that distributive justice is unimportant to organizational justice researchers. As Greenberg so eloquently stated in his interview, "to study only one justice is like looking at only the left brain. When you study the entire brain, you can't ignore one half." Our only claim is that the more recent and current organizational justice research tends to emphasize the procedural aspects more than the distributive.

When these observations are considered, they complement the earlier definition of organizational justice. It is not simply the study of fairness perceptions at work; rather, it is the study of fairness perceptions given a particular paradigm with a certain emphasis. In particular, the character of organizational justice research owes its current shape to what Bies and Folger suggested in their interviews, "the influence of socio-political, cognitive, and legal sciences," while retaining its social psychological and procedural roots. It seems logical, at this point, to take a step back and first examine where organizational justice originated and then examine how it was shaped.

THE ORIGINS OF ORGANIZATIONAL JUSTICE

Although the history of organizational justice is short, it is also storied. A rich history of events have occurred in the short span of 20 years. During his interview, Tyler suggested that organizational justice research unfolded in at least three waves. These waves are also referred to in a recent book (Tyler, Boeckmann, Smith, & Huo, 1997). We use Tyler's ideas to structure this historical account. The first wave saw the rise of relative deprivation research. The second wave saw the coming of a distributive justice emphasis. And the third wave was dominated by the emergence of procedural justice.

First Wave: Relative Deprivation

> It was Joanne Martin, who was focused on relative deprivation, that offered me a revolutionary and radically different perspective for analyzing justice issues which had a big influence on me," recalled Bies during his interview. While referring to the base which relative deprivation research established Folger explained, "early in my graduate studies, I read a paper which talked about relative deprivation. It was from this compelling literature that I got the name "referent" for my Referent Cognition Theory.

As demonstrated by these quotes, the interviews attested to the foundation provided by the relative deprivation (RD) tradition. However, to understand *why* relative deprivation research was so influential we have to take a closer look at *what* this research communicated. As discussed by Crosby (1976), the term *relative deprivation* has two meanings. First, it refers to negative feelings that can result when an individual compares his or her own state of affairs to a more advantageous alternative. Secondly, RD refers to various theories that articulate how these comparisons take place, as well as the consequences of such comparisons.

The early RD theories had something approximating the following form: (a) The individual receives or anticipates receiving some outcome; (b) the individual ascertains the worth of this outcome by comparing it to some standard, usually an outcome obtained by a similar other; (c) if the obtained outcome is less than the standard, the individual feels a sense of moral outrage or dissatisfaction (Pettigrew, 1967). Parenthetically, worth mentioning is that the moral outrage or dissatisfaction was more intense for important outcomes and less intense for unimportant outcomes (Bernstein & Crosby, 1980). The key insight of RD researchers was that the value of an outcome was not defined objectively. Rather, value could be understood in reference to some point of comparison (Crosby, 1984; Kulik & Ambrose, 1992). For example, in RD research discussed by Martin (1981), when female managers compared themselves to their male counterparts in similar jobs they experienced a sense of pay inequity. However, when the same female managers compared themselves to other women in lower paying jobs, they felt more pay equity. For this reason similar pay rates engender more or less outrage, depending on the referent point.

Contemporary organizational justice research tends not to explicitly use RD theory. Nevertheless, the interviews provided substantial evidence of its influence. It is also noteworthy, that Joanne Martin (e.g., Martin, 1981), a prominent RD scholar was the chair of Robert Bies' doctoral committee. This provides a somewhat direct academic link between RD and current justice frameworks.

Other direct evidence exists as well. The earliest social-psychological application to workplace fairness, with which many justice researchers are now familiar, was an RD study by Stouffer, Suchman, DeVinney, Star, and Williams (1949). Stouffer and his colleagues examined promotion satisfaction among World War II soldiers. Specifically, they compared the satisfaction between those in the Military Police, in which promotions were few, to those in the Army Air Corps, in which promotions were many. Stouffer et al. (1994) found that promotion satisfaction was actually higher for the slow-rising military police. This readily lends itself to an RD interpretation: The Military Police compared themselves to others in their units and decided they were relatively advantaged and treated fairly, even when they did not obtain a promotion. Within the Army Air Corps, on the other hand, individuals compared themselves to others in their units. Thus, they were relatively disadvantaged when they did not receive a promotion.

Another example of RD's influence can be shown by examining Folger's (1986) Referent Cognitions Theory (RCT), as mentioned earlier. Modern justice researchers generally think of RCT as a theory emphasizing procedural justice, and this is so (Cropanzano & Folger, 1991; Folger & Cropanzano, 1998). However, during its initial formulation, RCT was treated as a theory of Relative Deprivation (Folger, Rosenfield, Rheaume, & Martin, 1983). In fact, it explicitly attempted to address some of the weaknesses in an earlier RD model tested by Bernstein and Crosby (1984; Folger, Rosenfield, & Rheaume, 1983).

For all of its historic importance, however, RD had its limitations. Perhaps the biggest problem was that RD was as much a general idea as it was a well-articulated theoretical position. It contributed the idea that justice was understood in reference to some focal standard, but the family of RD theories tended to be so broad that they did not lend themselves to precise predictions. One could potentially defend any outcome by changing the presumed referent. Stated at this level of generality, RD was difficult to falsify. Consider the case of Stouffer et al.'s (1949) Military Police. Suppose they had reported less satisfaction than the Air Corps. In this hypothetical example, it could have been argued that the Military Police saw themselves as disadvantaged in reference to soldiers in other units. In other words, RD could have been invoked as a causal explanation regardless of the pattern of data.

Indeed, the RD model was so broad that some might wonder if it was really a theory of justice. In his interview, Tyler suggested that "relative deprivation was not justice research, although it was an inspiration for justice researchers." This is an important point. As various scholars (e.g., Cropanzano & Greenberg, 1997; Tyler & Lind, 1992) noted a disadvantageous comparison may be unfortunate, but it is not necessarily unfair. An individual might be dissatisfied with his or her (relatively) low pay, but in and of itself this does not necessarily engender a sense of injustice (Van den Bos, Wilke, Lind, & Vermunt, 1998). Unfairness requires the violation of some moral or ethical standard, not simply giving one person less than another. As a result of these limitations, researchers began to revise their thinking about fairness.

Second Wave: Distributive Justice

According to Tyler, "Distributive justice was really the beginnings of organizational justice." Distributive justice evaluates the fairness of outcome distributions (Deutsch, 1985). Folger, Greenberg, Lind, and Tyler all concurred that distributive justice in organizations can be traced as far back as 1965 when Stacy Adams proposed a theory of inequity, most commonly referred to as equity theory. As it turns out, Webster's Thesaurus provides *injustice* and *unfairness* as synonyms for inequity, hence Adams was actually proposing a theory of injustice. "Stacy Adams' Equity Theory was a major breakthrough in organizational justice research," emphasized Lind during his interview. Adams was an extremely influential justice researcher. He was a direct influence on two of the justice researchers interviewed for this chapter. While on the faculty of the University of North Carolina at Chapel Hill, Adams chaired Folger's doctoral dissertation and served on the doctoral committee for Lind. Adams' equity theory was among the first justice theories explicitly cultivated in the context of work organizations. For example, in one early study Adams and Rosenbaum (1962) hired undergraduate students to conduct market research interviews.

In constructing equity theory, Adams (1965) elaborated on the justice theories of Homans (1961). In particular, Adams proposed that individuals make cognitive evaluations of the difference between their contributions and the resultant outcomes (i.e., economic or social compensation), as compared to the difference of others' input to outcomes ratio (Adams & Freedman, 1976). Folger explained, "Adams envisioned equity theory as an employer and employee exchange. Conceptually, the question is what am I getting in exchange for my labor. We use another coworker to judge the amount." Adams believed that individuals go beyond a simple ranking system in their assessment of inputs and outputs, to where they precisely quantify the equity or inequity of the comparison (Deutsch, 1985). The result of their evaluation or comparison is that the individual either feels inadequately compensated or overcompensated. Adams' theory suggested that if the comparison to others resulted in a balanced perspective (i.e., both parties receiving an appropriate amount for their respective contributions) then the parties involved would be satisfied. In the event the result of the mental comparison was unbalanced, the inadequately compensated individual would contribute less.

The ill-will created by under-reward inequity was neither surprising nor especially controversial. In fact according to Folger, "Adams ignored the underpay condition." This was, however, the very condition on which Folger extended Adams' theory. In his interview Folger explained that he examined why some people who were underpaid would not become angry, but instead would accept the situation. Folger said, "I found that some individuals would alter their cognitive evaluation and rationalize the situation such that they no longer framed it in the same manner. They enhanced the value of the task in which they were interested, as opposed to becoming angry and reducing their level of involvement."

Folger believed that this was a central dilemma in equity theory, and addressed it in his dissertation. Folger's contribution, however, came many years after Adams had already proposed equity theory. At the time of its introduction, the novel prediction of equity theory was the case of over-reward inequity. Adams (1965) argued that when an individual was relatively advantaged compared to a referent other, then he or she would experienced guilt or shame. To alleviate these bad feelings, the over-rewarded person would increase his or her inputs. For example, an overpaid person might work harder to earn the additional compensation. Although there were no shortage of critics, research generally supported Adams' model (see Greenberg, 1982, for a review). It is clear, however, that individuals are more tolerant of over-payment inequity than they are of underpayment. In addition, the greater effort engendered by over-reward dissipates over time (Greenberg, 1988).

Equity theory generated a tremendous interest causing a flood of research. It even seeped past the borders of social justice. For example, Berscheid and Walster (1978) used the framework as a general model for predicting interpersonal attraction. According to Berscheid and Walster, individuals were more attracted to one another if their relationship was equitable, rather than if one person contributed or received too many benefits. Until 1975, fairness researchers were preoccupied with extending Adams' equity theory. As Lind succinctly put it, "justice was synonymous with Adams' equity theory." Tyler, in his interview, offered a suggestion as to why equity theory become so popular. He explained that during the time that Adams introduced equity theory there was widespread societal concern over worker dissatisfaction. Equity theory was a solution for managing dissatisfaction with pay and promotions.

It is to equity theory's credit that it maintain RD's emphasis on the relative comparison of outcomes. In addition, equity theory embodied an implicit moral standard. An individual might have unfavorable outcomes, but they were only unfair if the ratio of ones input to outcomes differed from the ratio of a comparison other. In this important sense, equity theory was truly a theory of injustice. That said, the model was incomplete. Folger, in his interview, had previously noted that it was difficult to make precise predictions with equity theory. When would a wronged individual lower her inputs? When would he cognitively rationalize the current state of affairs? Equity theory was also silent concerning the interpersonal treatment that one might experience when outcomes were assigned. In his interview Tyler stated, "the inability of distributive justice to explain underlying work related issues led to the focus on procedural justice." Even with limitations, equity theory cast a long shadow over organizational justice research. For years, researchers continued to contend with equity theory. In fact, some early procedural justice research was explicitly presented as an extension of equity theory. For example, one influential paper by Leventhal (1980) was titled *What Should be Done with Equity Theory*. Likewise, the title of Cropanzano and Folger's (1989) procedural justice paper was *Referent Cognitions and Task Decision Autonomy: Beyond Equity Theory*.

It also should be emphasized that distributive justice research has never died, although the equity theory paradigm is less often utilized. As a research area, distributive justice remains alive and well (Deutsch, 1985). For example, researchers have examined distribution rules, other than equity, such as allocations based on equality or need (Kabanoff, 1991). Similarly, other distributive justice researchers have examined cross-cultural differences in outcome distributions (e.g., Chen, 1995; James, 1993). The focus on process has complemented, not supplanted, the focus on outcomes.

Third Wave: Procedural Justice

In describing procedural justice Lind, in his interview, emphasized, "You keep coming back to procedural justice. The justice effects are so substantial; almost surprisingly so. People say it's important." Additionally, Greenberg, in his interview, commented regarding his 1987a paper, "The paper was an unabashed effort to communicate that there is more than just equity theory. The more exposed we were to procedural justice, the more it revealed. We were onto something big." These quotations demonstrate the importance of the third wave—the focus on procedural justice. To fully appreciate the importance of this major shift from distributive to procedural justice, we need to take a closer look at the concept of procedural justice.

Procedural justice examines the perception of fairness about processes and procedures used to make decisions regarding outcomes (Lind & Tyler, 1988; Tyler & Lind, 1992). Although it may be difficult for modern researchers to understand, in the 1970s and 1980s procedural justice was a peculiar idea for an organizational scientist. A reasonable amount of scholarly thinking about organizations had been heavily influenced by a rational person perspective (Barley & Kunda, 1992). In the rational person model, people behave in such a way as to maximize their economic outcomes. Like many models of human motivation, this model is hedonistic (Sullivan, 1989), in the sense that individuals are seen as dutifully working to acquire as many goods for themselves as possible. In the popular culture this perspective is exemplified by the commonly seen bumper sticker, "He who dies with the most toys, wins."

Given the exclusive economic focus of the rational person perspective, relative deprivation and distributive justice seemed unusual enough. These frameworks defined the worth of outcomes in reference to some standard. Thus, value was socially constructed. The idea of procedural justice, on the other hand, came as almost a direct affront! In the third wave of research, justice scholars were beginning to maintain that individuals cared as much for *how* they were treated as they did for *what* they received. Outcome remained important, of course, but the interactions among individuals began to share the spotlight.

The five scholars interviewed did not mince words. As Lind put it, "Procedural fairness is inherent in the workplace and in how people relate to their social entities." Tyler echoed these sentiments, "Justice is the grease of social dynamics, the lubrication that makes interactions work," as did Greenberg, "Justice was inherent in a lot of organizational activities. It needed to be looked at more. We were constantly finding new large effects." Bies, as well, voiced the importance of the treatment of people with his comment, "It is the right thing to do, to treat people well." Tyler also added that, "We knew we were looking at something really important, something that mattered because of the magnitude of the effects." Emphasizing the importance of these procedures, Folger stated, "Research shows that over and over again—process matters. Justice is an eternal truth." During the interviews, and indeed in the published literature, words like "inherent" and "fundamental" were not uncommon.

Clearly, all five interviewees thought procedures were important, however they were making a more subtle point as well. The shift in emphasis from outcomes to processes was not the result of theoretical fancy. Rather, it was driven by pragmatic needs within work organizations and other social institutions. In other words, the observation of strong process fairness effects in real-world settings is what ignited the interested in procedural justice. In this way, theoretical developments within justice research were closely linked to practical considerations.

The Voice Tradition of Thibaut and Walker.   Although procedural justice now appears to be a fundamental aspect of the many social exchanges in the work place, research actually began in the legal arena, or more properly in social-psychological investigations of legal phenomena. Four pieces of work were especially influential. In 1974, Walker, LaTour, Lind, and Thibaut published an article in the *Journal of Applied Social Psychology*, followed shortly by Thibaut, Walker, La Tour, and Houlden's (1974) article in the *Stanford Law Review*. These articles documented their seminal research on procedural justice. Just one year later, in 1975, Thibaut and Walker published their now classic research monograph *Procedural Justice: A Psychological Analysis*. Finally, in 1978, Thibaut and Walker's *A Theory of Procedure* appeared in the *California Law Review*. All five interviewees agreed that these publications established the foundation for procedural justice research in psychology.

In both the 1974 and 1975 research, Thibaut and colleagues compared the Anglo-American adversarial legal system to the European Inquisitorial system. In order to make these comparisons they divided conflict resolution into two stages. First came the process stage. During this first stage, information was presented. Next came the decision stage, in which a judgment was rendered. A third-party decision maker, such as a judge, could exercise control at either, both, or neither of these two stages. According to Thibaut and Walker (1975), the Anglo-American adversarial system was seen as more fair than its inquisitorial counterpart. This, they determined, was because the adversarial system allowed the disputants process control or "voice" during the process stage. In a series of laboratory studies, it was further revealed that research participants reported the adversarial system as being reasonably fair, even when they lacked outcome control and when the outcome was not to their advantage. These findings were replicated in a field study of actual legal cases conducted by Lind, Kulik, Ambrose, and De vera Park (1993). Early applications of procedural justice research in organizations borrowed heavily from Thibaut and Walker (1975). For instance, in his model of organizational conflict management, Sheppard (1983; 1984) expanded the Thibaut and Walker model through the inclusion of additional stages and substages. Some research continues to use modified versions of the Thibaut and Walker legal–social psychological paradigm (e.g., Folger, Cropanzano, Timmerman, & Howes, 1995; Leung & Lind, 1986; Sheppard, 1985). What is most important for this chapter, however, is understanding how Thibaut and Walker's ideas were carried into the organizational sciences in the first place.

To answer this question, we can look closely at Lind's interview. As a graduate student at North Carolina Chapel Hill, Lind studied with Thibaut. In fact, Lind participated in the research that would later be documented in the 1975 monograph. During his interview, Lind explained that, "Our findings in this study, and later research, showed that it was having an opportunity to present one's views and evidence that was the key." Individuals' perceptions of fairness were influenced by their perceived control of the process and their input to the procedure. This is, of course, quite contrary to the rational person perspective in which positive reactions are engendered by advantageous outcomes.

Had Thibaut and Walker only raised their findings as an interesting conceptual issue, it would be assured that procedural justice research would never have gone as far as it has. As Lind emphasized, there were practical implications as well. According to Lind, "Thibaut found the results of Kelley and Stahelski's (1970) research bleak. Their research revealed that in the prisoners dilemma dispute, if one party was competitive, the other would be dragged in. This greatly disturbed Thibaut." It implied that the just resolution of conflicts would be exceedingly difficult to achieve. In confronting what appeared to be an intractable problem, Thibaut found his own research results promising. Procedural justice gave hope to dispute resolution because fair processes offered a check on both disputant competitiveness and third party abuse. Thus, Thibaut offered a way for people to resolve their disputes by designing proper procedures that everyone could follow during a dispute or negotiation.

Thibaut was not only an influential researcher, he too, like Adams, had a direct influence on two of the scholars interviewed for this chapter. Thibaut was Lind's advisor and a member of Folger's doctoral committee. Recall that earlier we mentioned that Adams chaired Folger's doctoral committee and served as a member of Lind's. Hence, Adams and Thibaut inevitably interacted. As a matter of fact, Folger added that "Adams took courses from Thibaut." In his interview, Folger credited Thibaut with being an important influence on his own research program. So much so that Folger's doctoral dissertation (Folger, 1977) examined *voice* or process control, in addition to extending equity theory.

The experience of Lind and Folger is uniquely interesting. Both credit Thibaut with having been an important, direct influence on their thinking, and both conducted early research that provided the foundation for organization justice. The work of these two researchers has some interesting implications for the history of organizational justice. Although it is true that they brought the social psychological literature to bear on organizational justice, it is intriguing to note that in their borrowing from this literature Lind and Folger were both selective. That is, they emphasized the work on process control or voice, at the expense of (what was at the time) more mainstream research on distributive justice. In no small part, the distinctive procedural flavor of early organizational justice research can be traced back to Thibaut and Walker and the graduate work of Lind and Folger.

Another interesting connection between the five organizational justice pioneers was between Tyler and Folger. Tyler completed his doctorate with social psychologist David Sears at UCLA. Although he only met Thibaut twice, Tyler reported feeling very influenced by Thibaut's work. At the same time that Tyler was an assistant professor at Northwestern University and a fellow at the American Bar Foundation, Folger was an assistant professor of social psychology at Southern Methodist University. Folger met Tyler while visiting Northwestern in 1978, on a year-long fellowship. During that time, Tyler was investigating the relation between procedures and outcomes in the context of police and citizen interactions. He invited Folger to work with him on this study. On its completion, Tyler and Folger determined that citizens' satisfaction with their exchange with the police officer was more influenced by whether the police officer closely adhered to procedures than with the actual outcome of the encounter (Tyler & Folger, 1980). This was another strong demonstration of procedural justice effects in real world situations.

The Leventhal Tradition.   After its publication, Thibaut and Walker's (1975) work continued to inspire social psychologists such as Morton Deutsch and Gerald S. Leventhal. These individuals, among others, began to note that the distributive justice paradigm required augmentation by investigations of processes. One of the first distributive justice researchers to begin systematically considering the role of procedures was Gerald S. Leventhal (for a sampling of Leventhal's work, see Leventhal 1976a, 1976b, 1980; Leventhal, Karuza, & Fry, 1980).

Interestingly, Folger mentioned in his interview that "Leventhal was a student of Thibaut and Adams." Leventhal was on the faculty at Wayne State University and chaired Greenberg's doctoral committee. As Greenberg told the story, Leventhal was an extremely talented justice researcher. He conducted air-tight experiments and achieved prominence working within the then standard distributive justice paradigm. During the mid-1970s, Leventhal began questioning the limitations of equity theory. Switching from data collection to a philosophical approach that Greenberg described as "arm chair theorizing," Leventhal and his colleagues (1980) outlined several rules for fair processes. These were consistency, bias-suppression, accuracy, correctability, representativeness, and ethicality. As a student Greenberg was exposed to these rules, although he had some concerns over the paucity of empirical data. Leventhal had a reasonably elaborate theory of procedural justice but relatively little data to support it. Thibaut and Walker (1975), on the other hand, had a good deal of data and a relatively simple theory. These researchers were all working on procedural justice but from different perspectives. The voice tradition of Thibaut and Walker, therefore, complemented the rule tradition of Leventhal. Interaction between the two was bound to be mutually beneficial.

In his interview, Greenberg clarified that prior to Thibaut and Walker he conducted research on distributive justice, as did most other justice researchers. When Greenberg joined the business school at Ohio State University in 1980, he sought to expand his research program in a way that would be more applicable to business settings and more palatable to his business colleagues. (Note again the connection between justice research and practical issues within organizations.) Toward this end, he began to closely examine the preliminary work on procedural justice conducted by his advisor, Leventhal. Looking to talk to someone about the potential of procedural justice in the context of organizations, Greenberg contacted Folger. Although they attended different universities, the two had met while they were graduate students. Folger was elected editor of the graduate student run journal, *Representative Research in Social Psychology*, and Greenberg served as a reviewer for the journal.

The Nag's Head Conference. Discussions between Folger and Greenberg were further nurtured in 1982. That year, Greenberg, Folger, Tyler, and Lind attended a week-long legal justice conference at Bibb Latane's Nag's Head Conference Center along the outer banks of North Carolina. As an afternoon getaway, the foursome took a short trip to the Cape Hatteras Lighthouse. If there was a climax to the history of organizational justice, it was at Nag's Head. Tyler, Lind, Folger, and Greenberg all explicitly recalled the impact of their discussions during the conference. For example, Greenberg mentioned the inspiration they derived from learning of one another's interests and ideas on procedural justice in organizations. Folger recalled discussing research and brainstorming ideas with the other three, throughout the week-long conference. In one sense, this conference marked the beginning of the fuel that started the fire of organizational justice. In another sense, Nag's Head triggered the ending of the early days. The rest of the organizational sciences were about to hear about procedural justice.

Folger and Greenberg (1985). Procedural justice appeared on the radar scope of the organizational sciences in 1985. In the annual volume of *Research in Personnel and Human Resources Management*, Folger and Greenberg published a chapter called "Procedural Justice: An Interpretive Analysis of Personnel Systems." Their chapter won the "New Concept Award" from the Organizational Behavior Division of the Academy of Management. On doing so, it generated tremendous interest in the topic of procedural justice. Greenberg, however, stressed during his interview, "We didn't make up the concept. It wasn't really new. We just reapplied it to organizations." What Greenberg said may be true, but in spite of that, this chapter was so influential that its 10-year anniversary was commemorated by a symposium at the 1995 meetings of the Academy of Management (Cropanzano, 1995).

In their chapter, Folger and Greenberg (1985) carefully explained how procedural justice was fundamental to personnel research and practice. They emphasized that insights into procedural justice research could be achieved by studying the concept within an organizational context. By making the connections between procedural justice and human resource practice so lucid, Folger and Greenberg permanently fused procedural justice into mainstream organizational science. In rapid succession, Greenberg followed the 1985 chapter with a 1987a review paper. In this review he presented a taxonomy that integrated research on procedural and distributive justice. This was also the paper in which he coined the term *organizational justice*.

The justice researchers interviewed for this chapter were uniform in their appreciation of the work of Folger and Greenberg (1985). Bies emphasized that "Folger and Greenberg (1985) opened the door for other justice researchers to follow." Lind also credited Greenberg and Folger for "playing a major role in making the study of social justice an accepted and important topic both in business schools and in industrial and organizational psychology." Lind added that "Greenberg and Folger were the 'jump start' that the field needed after Thibaut, Adams, and Leventhal, all contributed their works on procedural justice." Folger also said that "Greenberg became a spokesperson, a promoter, for organizational justice." As Greenberg recalled his efforts during the mid-1980s and early 1990s. He noted, "They were carefully designed to bring procedural justice into the forefront of the field of organizational behavior." Bies additionally commented that "Greenberg provided a service to organizational justice research by cutting a large path upon which other justice researchers, who were going beyond equity theory, could walk."

Whereas the interviewees concurred that the Folger and Greenberg (1985) and Greenberg (1987a) publications advanced procedural justice research in organizations, Tyler, in his interview, emphasized that it was the research efforts of Lind, Greenberg, Folger, Bies, Brockner, himself, and a few others combined, that stoked the fire. Without their aggregate contributions research in organizational justice could easily have dwindled away. An examination of the published literature of the time shows that Tyler's characterization of the situation was quite justified. Most importantly, the Folger and Greenberg (1985) and Greenberg (1987a) conceptual papers needed the support of empirical evidence. Fortunately, this work was forthcoming almost immediately. For example, Lind and his colleagues published two articles in the *Journal of Personality and Social Psychology* (Earley & Lind, 1987; Lind, Kanfer, & Earley, 1990) and one in the *Journal of Experimental Social Psychology* (Lind & Lissak, 1985). Greenberg (1986, 1987b) responded with two papers in the *Journal of Applied Psychology*. Two years later, Cropanzano and Folger (1989) published Cropanzano's masters thesis in that same outlet. Folger and Konovsky (1989) followed with their influential *Academy of Management Journal* paper demonstrating the importance of procedural justice perceptions in compensation decisions. At nearly the same time, Tyler and Lind (Lind & Tyler, 1988; Tyler, 1987, 1989; for a more recent review see Tyler & Lind, 1992) were publishing their initial work on the group-value (later the relational) model of procedural justice. The year 1987 also saw the publication of the first volume of *Social Justice Research*. There was a special issue of that volume, edited by Greenberg, that was dedicated to research on procedural justice. In additional to an important empirical paper by Alexander and Ruderman (1987), there were also manuscripts that involved the Nag's Head Participants (Folger, 1987; Greenberg, 1987c; and Kanfer, Sawyer, Earley, & Lind, 1987).

In 1988, Lind and Tyler summarized the existing procedural justice literature in an influential volume titled *The Social Psychology of Procedural Justice*. For justice researchers it is difficult to overstate the importance of this book. Among other things, it thoroughly reviewed the available literature and made it accessible to far more scholars than had ever been heretofore. In addition, Lind and Tyler did something more; they offered a well articulated account as to *why* process was so important. Lind and Tyler observed that fair procedures were most likely to guarantee beneficial outcomes over the long run. In effect, people liked procedural justice out of enlightened self-interest. Although sometimes outcomes are unfavorable, just processes were and are to one's eventual advantage. This self-interest or instrumental model traces back to the work of Thibaut and Walker (1975) and their colleagues (Thibaut et al., 1974). Lind and Tyler provided an additional unique contribution that was a second complementary perspective. They further argued that procedural justice provided individuals with information as to how much they are valued by some social group. According to their group-value or relational model, fair procedures supply one with dignity and respect, quite apart from their potential economic benefits. The relational model, as opposed to the instrumental perspective, directly challenged the rational–economic perspective of human behavior. Although not denying that outcomes were important, Lind and Tyler maintained that social considerations were valuable, as well. There is now considerable support for the relational model (e.g., Lind, 1995; Tyler & Lind, 1992).

Indeed, the late 1980s were heady times. In his interview, Greenberg expressed with excitement, "we never said 'No' to an opportunity to share our findings. We were fueled by everyone else. We were constantly finding new things to say about justice, and we were generating a lot of data . . . it was energizing." Greenberg also told an illustrative story about the clash that initially existed between the old and the new justice ideas. In the spring of 1986, Bies, Folger, and Greenberg participated on a panel at the Society for Industrial and Organizational Psychology (SIOP) Conference in Chicago. The panel was devoted to the then new research on procedural justice in organizations. The late Larry Cummings served as discussant. Cummings had mostly critical things to say about the existing procedural justice research. In his interview, Greenberg recalled, "at the time, we didn't know that Cummings would put us down. We waited to be blessed for our research and instead, he really criticized us." Greenberg added, "We were trying our best to defend ourselves, but we just couldn't argue at Cummings' level. There was a real hush over the room." Cropanzano can attest to the veracity of Greenberg's memory. As a graduate student, he was seated in the audience. Undaunted by this event, later that year, Bies (1986), organized another procedural justice symposium at the Academy of Management conference. Greenberg and Folger again participated, but with better results as Greenberg recalled.

Within a few years of the 1986 SIOP conference, Cummings had softened his criticism of justice research. In fact, he collaborated with Bies in justice research (Bies, Shapiro, & Cummings, 1988). Likewise, as Greenberg pointed out in his interview, the prestigious *Research in Organizational Behavior* series, jointly edited by Larry Cummings and Barry Staw, proved especially receptive to justice chapters. In fact the series published a sequence of papers on workplace fairness: Martin (1981), Crosby (1984), Bies (1987), Greenberg (1990b), and Folger, Konovsky, and Cropanzano (1992). Bies recalled, "Cummings and Staw gave a voice to justice issues."

The Coming of Interactional Justice. If the four Nag's Head participants were creating an earthquake, Bies was preparing to engineer an after shock. Although Bies did not attend Nag's Head, he was well acquainted with Tyler, Lind, Greenberg, and Folger as illustrated earlier. Bies was on the faculty at the business school of Northwestern University at the same time that Tyler held a position in the psychology department. The two met during their time at Northwestern. When Greenberg was introducing his taxonomy, Bies and Moag (1986) presented the idea of *interactional justice.* In their 1986 chapter, Bies and Moag defined interactional justice as the fairness of the interpersonal treatment that one receives at the hand of an authority figure. In this initial presentation of the idea, Bies and Moag focused on what would later be termed *interpersonal sensitivity* (see Greenberg, 1993)—the extent to which one is treated with respect and dignity. One year later Bies (1987) refined and extended the idea by adding the idea of social accounts to justice.

Bies developed the concept of interactional justice as a result of his earlier experiences. In his undergraduate studies designed to launch him into a law career, Bies was exposed to a human relations class in which the professor delivered passionate lectures on the issues of dignity and justice. Bies was intrigued by (in)justice in the workplace. His interest was further cultivated by the influence of Bill Scott at the University of Washington, where Bies obtained his Masters in business administration. Bies said that it was Scott who encouraged him "to take a broader perspective on justice and study how feelings of dignity and respect were influenced and shaped by socio-political and ideological forces." Later Bies attended Stanford University where he pursued his doctorate under the supervision of Joanne Martin. "Joanne Martin showed me how to frame research problems. She gave me a revolutionary and radical perspective," said Bies of his former advisor. It was at Stanford where Bies and his colleagues shared their experiences about the environment and culture. His peers shared stories of their feelings of being used, manipulated, and disrespected as students in the graduate program. Bies was aroused by this unfair treatment. He felt it was absolutely unnecessary and simply not right. In the basement of the School of Business at Stanford University Bies formulated his ideas about interactional justice. He felt that existing models of justice failed to capture the full experience shared by him and his fellow graduate students.

In his interview, Bies emphasized that, "Interactional justice research examines the quality of interpersonal treatment, the communication aspect of procedures, as separate from the procedures themselves." Although interactional justice was originally proposed as separate from distributive and procedural justice, researchers have since included interactional justice under the umbrella of procedural justice (Cropanzano & Greenberg, 1997; Tyler & Bies, 1990). However, the tide may be shifting back. Bies (in press) recently argued that interactional and procedural justice should be separated (see also Moye, Masterson, & Bartol, 1997). Taxonomic issues aside, all modern justice scholars agree that interactional fairness is a central topic in organizational justice. For example, Greenberg (1990a) drew inspiration directly from the Bies and Moag (1986) chapter to write his chapter on impression management and in many of his empirical studies that followed.

To summarize the progression through history, organizational justice research began with equity theory, proceeded through distributive justice, and moved to procedural justice within the legal arena. From the courtrooms, procedural justice advanced to the organizational context with the help of Folger, Greenberg, Lind, Tyler, and Bies. Organizational justice research today embodies the work of the past and current research trends in retributive (Folger & Baron, 1996; Greenberg & Scott, 1996; Tyler, 1996) and international justice (Leung, 1997). This historical review, however, seems incomplete without a glimpse into the crystal ball of the future.

COMING ATTRACTIONS AND NEW IDEAS

In his interview, Tyler summarized the current state of affairs as follows, "There is a steady diet of interest in organizational justice." If the volume of publications in organizational justice and a number of graduating students studying justice can attest to it, there is indeed a voracious appetite of interest. As one might expect, this bodes well for the future of justice research, and the five scholars we interviewed were optimistic.

Folger observed that "the core components of organizational justice are always relevant. Justice is an issue in everyday human social life. Organizational justice is not a fad. It is inherent in the way we interact, coordinate, and work together to resolve conflicts and come to mutual agreements." Organizational justice is especially relevant given today's business climate. In his interview, Lind emphasized "The next five years will continue to demonstrate the importance of the organizational justice phenomenon both inside and outside of the organization." Lind believed that changes and trends in organizations will necessitate further research in procedural justice. "Future researchers should also continue to forge acceptance of organizational justice research topics by the broader scientific community," emphasized Lind. He suggested this because one cannot be sure to get a reviewer who understands that a paper is about the reaction to a procedure and, for example, not the accuracy of the procedure, researchers must write so that it is clear what the paper is examining. The five interviewees shared their perspectives on the future needs of organizational justice research. We organized their comments into three broad categories: further theory development, attentiveness to real world concerns, and a sensitivity to the changing nature of work.

Further Theory Development

As seen in this historical overview, theories of fairness have always been in a state of dynamic flux, moving from relative deprivation to distributive justice to procedural justice. The scholars interviewed believed strongly that this process of growth and development would and should continue. Perhaps Greenberg put it best when he observed that the field is far from settled and needs some coherence and parsimonious theories. Greenberg likened organizational justice to "a precocious teenager that sometimes thinks it's an adult, only to realize, sometimes inelegantly, that it is only a child." He believed that future research should look at organizational justice as a whole, and not just the parts. The whole would include distributive, procedural, and interactional justice, integrated rather than as separate parts as was needed in the past. "It is time to pull them together and look at justice the way individuals do: as an omnibus concept not separate pieces," said Greenberg. He continued, "the field of organizational justice is still ripe for research. The phenomena of perceptions of fairness is a great 'breeding ground' in which social psychology can be brought to understand organizational phenomena." Folger also suggested that organizational justice researchers develop more parsimonious theories of justice.

The theories of the future may have a different flavor than those of the past. Bies felt that "although we now have a better understanding of justice rules than in the past, little detail is known about how injustice influences behavior. There is much room for research on the phenomenology of justice, how individuals experience injustice." Bies encouraged justice researchers to "discontinue engaging in their own emotional labor, and study what needs to be addressed and not just what the mainstream suggests. Push the agenda and research topics that might not show business in a good light." Bies also suggested that researchers tend too much to keeping the peace with business partners and hence fail to study the issues that create and support oppressive cultures in organizations. "Future research should also look toward giving a voice to the voiceless individuals and not get trapped in shaping theory only around management in business." Bies believed a significant group in the workforce is not represented in current organizational justice research, and that is the voiceless individual, the nonmanager.

One might see organizational justice research change its perspective in other ways as well. Folger further suggested, "future research needs to evaluate the governance of social relations, that is the rules for how individuals relate to others. The 'dark side of fairness' continues to fuel research ideas and will for some time to come." Folger mentioned that most justice researchers seem to take on the perspective that someone must be aggrieved before feeling that an injustice has occurred. "However, people feel outraged about events such as the Bosnia war, yet the war may not have had a direct impact on those people. Justice researchers need to look at the third person perspective," emphasized Folger during his interview. This view requires studying how one would react toward witnessing one person performing an injustice to another but with no direct impact on himself or herself. Folger indicated that he "would like to see organizational justice researchers look at perceptions of fairness from the angle of someone who is truly altruistic."

The Need to Link Justice to Real World Concerns

Organizational justice research is about organizations. Much of what has made this literature unique is its strong emphasis on real-world issues, such as family friendly work policies (Grandey, chap. 7, this volume) and affirmative action (Bobocel, Hing, Davey, & Zanna, chap. 6, this volume). In fact, theorizing about the justice has historically been driven by workplace and societal concerns. Greenberg urged that justice research continue developing new applications. Bies provided a cautionary note:

> There is a potential for stagnation in the organizational justice research, as it is a small community and everyone cites and references everyone else. Justice researchers must continue to look toward current business and political issues such as downsizing, outsourcing, changes in health benefits, violence, and a sagging economy where procedural justice can explain a great deal.

Bies added, "the degree to which we ground our research in real world life experiences makes it interesting and intellectually challenging."

Justice and the Changing Nature of Work

As organizations change, the way we think about them will likely change as well. All five interviewees were very attentive to upcoming changes in future organizations. "In the next 10 years, radical new theories in social justice must be developed to continue to address issues of perceptions of fairness in the changing workplace," Bies emphasized. He also added that "Current theories may not match or explain the practices of business over the next ten years, and hence modification or rediscovery may be necessary." Circumstances may force or lead us to raise the level of discussion to include broader more political issues. Within organizations, the governing structure, society, and culture will force researchers to ask different questions about how the organization as a political system influences perceptions of fairness.

With regard to future research, Tyler emphasized the need for evaluating the future organizational structures that are shaping the dynamics of justice. Tyler recognized that Blair Sheppard, for example, has suggested evaluating justice in the context of diminishing or vanishing hierarchies. Tyler also added, "Organizational justice research in the past has focused on the workplace of manager and subordinates, while the changing workforce sees more and more teams without hierarchy (self-managed, cross-functional, cross-geographical)." Tyler encouraged a new look at justice. "How does the changing nature of work change the nature of justice?" he asked. "Initially organizational justice focused on the consequences of injustice, then at the antecedents of justice, and now it should look at how the organizational structures are shaping the dynamics of justice." Additionally Tyler suggested focusing on diversity and multiculturalism. Tyler also added, "we must now look at the changing nature of work and the dynamics of work groups."

Lind also made similar comments regarding the changing nature of work and the future of justice research. He observed that contingent workers, self-managed teams, issues about trusting one part of a team and not another, and reward systems will all require further evaluation and scrutiny under the organizational justice lens.

CONCLUSIONS

In this chapter, we trace the development of organizational justice. What have we learned from this analysis? Loosely speaking, our conclusions can be divided into *who* and *how*. Let us begin with *who*. Most basical, the initial interest in organizational justice was largely the result of the efforts of five researchers: Bies, Folger, Greenberg, Lind, and Tyler. Throughout the interviews there was a distinct willingness to share credit, as each of the scholars referred back to the work of others. Moreover, each of the interviewees credited the others with influencing their own thinking. Our review shows considerable evidence of both formal collaboration (e.g., publications, conference symposia) and informal consultation (as when Folger, Greenberg, Lind, and Tyler took a short jaunt to Cape Hatteras). Although important, naming the principle players in organizational justice research does not address the more fundamental question: How did these scholars accomplish their task? We see several lessons for future researchers.

First, organizational justice researchers were well-versed in, and respectful of, the basic psychology literature. This allowed justice research to start from an eclectic base in which previously formulated ideas were applied to new problems. In essence, the basic literature provided justice scholars with a head start relative to other researchers who were trying to solve similar practical problems. They were inspired by the research of the past and the present.

Second, justice researchers were very attentive to what mattered in the real world. As we discussed previously, several of our interviewees realized the importance of procedural justice by observing the large-effect sizes in their own research findings. They listened to the voice of employees and managers, hearing them emphasize the value of fairness in the workplace. Likewise, as Greenberg mentioned in his interview, justice researchers did a good job of applying their findings to important human resource practices, such as international management (McFarlin & Sweeney, chap. 4, this volume) and workplace conflict (Bies & Tripp, chap. 9, this volume).

Third, the history of organizational justice attests to a dynamic interplay between theory, practice, and creativity. The leveraging of the basic literature was neither haphazard nor rigid. Justice researchers were willing to experiment. In so doing, they modified and extended original theories to fit into the organizational context. For example, Bies' (1987) theoretical discussion of social accounts was heavily influenced by the literature on communication. Bies reshaped existing theories and reinterpreted previous research in a social justice context. The interplay between theory and practice continues unabated. For example, Gilliland (1993) modified Leventhal's (1980) rules in order to apply them to workplace staffing.

In a way, the history of organizational justice can be seen as a series of steadily widening circles, like the rippling in a pond caused by a drop of water. Each circle runs from theory to practice and back to theory again. The next circle widens as justice theory broadens conceptual horizons to tackle new issues. The result is a healthy spiral of understanding, as we learn more and more about the social dynamics of the workplace.

REFERENCES

Adams, J. S. (1965). Inequity in social exchange. In L. Berkowitz (Ed.), *Advances in experimental social psychology* (Vol. 2, pp. 267–299). New York: Academic.

Adams, J. S., & Freedman, S. (1976). Equity theory revisited: Comments and annotated bibliography. In L. Berkowitz & E. Walster (Eds.), *Advances in experimental social psychology* (Vol. 9, pp. 43–90). New York: Academic.

Adams, J. S., & Rosenbaum, W. B. (1962). The relationship of worker productivity to cognitive dissonance about wage inequities. *Journal of Applied Psychology, 46*, 161–164.

Alexander, S., & Ruderman, M. (1987). The role of procedural and distributive justice in organizational behavior. *Social Justice Research, 1*, 177–198.

Alexander, S., & Sinclair, R. (1995). The role of organizational justice in defining and maintaining the employment relationship. *Organizational Behavior.* Washington, DC: APA.

Barley, S. R., & Kunda, G. (1992). Design and devotion: Surges of rational and normative ideologies of control in managerial discourse. *Administrative Science Quarterly, 37*, 363–399.

Bernstein, M., & Crosby, F. (1980). An empirical examination of relative deprivation theory. *Journal of Experimental Social Psychology, 16*, 442–456.

Berscheid, E., & Walster, E. A. (1978). *Interpersonal attraction* (2nd ed.). Reading, MA: Addison-Wesley.

Bies, R. J. (1986, August). *Moving beyond equity theory: New directions in research on justice in organizations.* Symposium conducted at the 1986 meeting of the Academy of Management, Chicago, IL.

Bies, R. J. (1987). The predicament of injustice: The management of moral outrage. In L. L. Cummings & B. M. Staw (Eds.), *Research in organizational behavior* (Vol. 9, pp. 289–319). Greenwich, CT: JAI.

Bies, R. J. (in press). Interactional (in)justice: The sacred and the profane. J. Greenberg & R. Cropanzano (Eds.). *Advance in organizational justice.* Lexington, MA: New Lexington.

Bies, R. J., & Moag, J. S. (1986). Interactional justice: Communication criteria of fairness. In R. J. Lewicki, B. H. Sheppard & M. H. Bazerman (Eds.), *Research on negotiation in organizations* (Vol. 1, pp. 43–55). Greenwich, CT: JAI.

Bies, R. J., Shapiro, D. L., & Cummings, L. L. (1988). Causal accounts and managing organizational conflict: Is it enough to say it's not my fault? *Communication Research, 15*, 381–399.

Brockner, J., & Wiesenfeld, B. M. (1996). An integrative framework for explaining reactions to decisions: The interactive effects of outcomes and procedures. *Psychological Bulletin, 120*, 189–208.

Chen, C. C. (1995). New trends in rewards allocation preferences: A Sino–U.S. comparison. *Academy of Management Journal, 38*, 408–428.

Cropanzano, R. (Ed.). (1993). *Justice in the workplace: Approaching fairness in human resource management.* Hillsdale, NJ: Lawrence Erlbaum Associates.

Cropanzano, R. (August, 1995). *Progress in procedural justice: Ten years after Folger and Greenberg (1985).* Symposium chair at the 1995 meeting of the Academy of Management. Vancouver, British Columbia.

Cropanzano, R., & Folger, R. (1989). Referent cognitions and task decision autonomy: Beyond equity theory. *Journal of Applied Psychology, 74*, 293–299.

Cropanzano, R., & Folger, R. (1991). Procedural justice and worker motivation. In R. M. Steers & L. W. Porter (Eds.), *Motivation and work behavior* (5th, pp. 131–143). New York: McGraw-Hill.

Cropanzano, R., & Greenberg, J. (1997). Progress in organizational justice: Tunneling through the maze. In C. L. Cooper & I. T. Robertson (Eds.), *International review of industrial and organizational psychology* (Vol. 12, pp. 317–372). Chichester, England.

Cropanzano, R., & Kacmar, M. K. (Eds.). (1995). *Organizational politics, justice, and support: Managing social climate at work.* Westport, CT: Greenwood Publishing Group.

Cropanzano, R., & Konovsky, M. A. (1995). Resolving the justice dilemma by improving the outcomes: The case of employee drug screening. *Journal of Business and Psychology, 10*, 221–243.

Crosby, F. (1976). A model of egotistical relative deprivation. *Psychological Review, 83*, 85–113.

Crosby, F. (1984). Relative deprivation in organizational settings. In B. M. Staw & L. L. Cummings (Eds.), *Research in organizational behavior* (Vol. 6, pp. 51–93). Greenwich, CT: JAI.

Deutsch, M. (1985). *Distributive Justice: A Social-Psychological Perspective.* New Haven: Yale University Press.

Earley, P. C., & Lind, E. A. (1987). Procedural justice and participation in task selection: The role of control in mediating justice judgments. *Journal of Personality and Social Psychology, 52*, 1148–1160.

Folger, R. (1977). Distributive and procedural justice: Combined impact of voice and improvement on experienced inequity. *Journal of Personality & Social Psychology, 35*, 108–119.

Folger, R. (1986). A referent cognitions theory of relative deprivation. In J. M. Olson, C. P. Herman & M. P. Zanna (Eds.), *Relative deprivation and social comparison: The Ontario symposium* (Vol. 4, pp. 33–54). Hillsdale, NJ: Lawrence Erlbaum Associates.

Folger, R. (1987). Distributive and procedural justice in the workplace. *Social Justice Research, 1*, 143–160.

Folger, R., & Baron, R. A. (1996). Violence and hostility at work: A model of reactions to perceived injustice. In G. R. Van den Bos & E. Q. Bulatao (Eds.), *Violence on the job: Identifying risks and developing solutions.* (pp. 51–85). Washington, DC: American Psychological Association.

Folger, R., & Cropanzano, R. (1998). *Organizational justice and human resource management.* Beverly Hills, CA: Sage.

Folger, R., & Cropanzano, R. (in press-b). Accountability. In J. Greenberg & R. Cropanzano (Eds.), *Advance in organizational justice.* Lexington, MA: New Lexington.

Folger, R., Cropanzano, R., Timmerman, T. A., Howes, J. C., & Mitchell, D. (1996). Elaborating procedural fairness: Justice becomes both simpler and more complex. *Personality and Social Psychology Bulletin, 22*, 435–441.

Folger, R., & Greenberg, J. (1985). Procedural justice: An interpretive analysis of personnel systems. In K. M. Rowland & G. R. Ferris (Eds.), *Research in personnel and human resources management* (Vol. 3, pp. 141–183). Greenwich, CT: JAI.

Folger, R., & Konovsky, M. A. (1989). Effects of procedural and distributive justice on reactions to pay raise decisions. *Academy of Management Journal, 32*, 115–130.

Folger, R., Konovsky, M. A., & Cropanzano, R. (1992). A due process metaphor for performance appraisal. In B. M. Staw & L. L. Cummings (Eds.), *Research in organizational behavior* (Vol. 14, pp. 129–177). Greenwich, CT: JAI.

Folger, R., Rosenfield, D., & Rheaume, K. (1983). Role playing effects of likelihood and referent outcomes on relative deprivation. *Representative Research in Social Psychology, 13*, 2–10.

Folger, R., Rosenfield, D., Rheaume, K., & Martin, C. (1983). Relative deprivation and referent cognitions. *Journal of Experimental Social Psychology, 19*, 172–184.

Gilliland, S. W. (1993). The perceived fairness of selection systems: An organizational justice perspective. *Academy of Management Review, 18*, 694–734.

Greenberg, J. (1982). Approaching equity and avoiding inequity in groups and organizations. In J. Greenberg & R. L. Cohen (Eds.), *Equity and justice in social behavior* (pp. 389–435). New York: Academic.

Greenberg, J. (1986). Determinants of perceived fairness of performance evaluations. *Journal of Applied Psychology, 71*, 340–342.

Greenberg, J. (1987a). A taxonomy of organizational justice theories. *Academy of Management Review, 12*, 9–22.

Greenberg, J. (1987b). Reactions to procedural injustice in payment distributions: Do the ends justify the means? *Journal of Applied Psychology, 72*, 55–61.

Greenberg, J. (1987c). Using diaries to promote procedural justice in performance evaluations. *Social Justice Research, 1*, 219–234.

Greenberg, J. (1988). Equity and workplace status: A field experiment. *Journal of Applied Psychology, 73*, 606–613.

Greenberg, J. (1990a). Organizational justice: Yesterday, today, and tomorrow. *Journal of Management, 16*, 399–432.

Greenberg, J. (1990b). Looking fair vs. being fair: Managing impression of organizational justice. In B. M. Staw & L. L. Cummings (Eds.), *Research in organizational behavior* (Vol. 12, pp. 111–157). Greenwich, CT: JAI.

Greenberg, J. (1993). The social side of fairness: Interpersonal and informational classes of organizational justice. In R. Cropanzano (Ed.), *Justice in the workplace: Approaching fairness in human resource management* (pp. 79–103). Hillsdale, NJ: Lawrence Erlbaum Associates.

Greenberg, J. (1996). *The quest for justice on the job: Essays and experiments.* Thousand Oaks, CA: Sage.

Greenberg, J., & Cropanzano, R. (Eds.). (In press). *Advance in organizational justice.* Lexington, MA: New Lexington.

Greenberg, J., & Scott K. S. (1996). Why do workers bite the hands that feed them? Employee theft as a social exchange process. In B. M. Staw & L. L. Cummings (Eds.), *Research in organizational behavior: An annual series of analytical essays and critical reviews* (Vol. 18, pp. 111–156). Greenwich, CT: JAI.

James, K. (1993). The social context of organizational justice: Cultural, intergroup, and structural effects on justice behaviors and perceptions. In R. Cropanzano (Ed.), *Justice in the workplace: Approaching fairness in human resource management* (pp. 21–50). Hillsdale, NJ: Lawrence Erlbaum Associates.

Homans, G. S. (1961). *Social behavior: Its elementary forms.* New York: Harcourt, Brace & World.

Homans, G. S. (1965). Effort, supervision, and productivity. In R. Dubin, G. C. Homans, F. C. Mann & D. C. Miller (Eds.), *Leadership and productivity: Some facts of industrial life* (pp. 51–67). San Francisco: Chandler.

Kabanoff, B. (1991). Equity, equality, power, and conflict. *Academy of Management Review, 16,* 416–441.

Kanfer, R., Sawyer, J., Earley, P. C., & Lind, E. A. (1987). Fairness and participation in evaluation procedures: Effects on task attitudes and performance. *Social Justice Research, 1,* 235–249.

Kelley, H. H., & Stahelski, A. J. (1970). The social interaction basis of cooperators' and competitors beliefs about others. *Journal of Personality and Social Psychology, 16,* 66–91.

Konovsky, M. A., & Brockner, J. (1993). Managing victim and survivor layoff reactions: A procedural justice perspective. In R. Cropanzano (Ed.), *Justice in the workplace: Approaching fairness in human resource management* (pp. 133–153). Hillsdale, NJ: Lawrence Erlbaum Associates.

Kulik, C. T., & Ambrose, M. L. (1992). Personal and situational determinants of referent choice. *Academy of Management Review, 17,* 212–237.

Leung, K. (1997). Relationships among satisfaction, commitment, and performance: A group-level analysis. *Applied psychology: An international review, 46,* 199–206.

Leung, K., & Lind, E. A. (1986). Procedural justice and culture: Effects of culture, gender and investigator status on procedural preferences. *Journal of Personality and Social Psychology, 50,* 1134–1140.

Leventhal, G. S. (1976a). The distribution of rewards and resources in groups and organizations. In L. Berkowitz & E. Walster (Eds.), *Advances in Experimental Social Psychology* (Vol. 9, pp. 91–131). New York: Academic.

Leventhal, G. S. (1976b). Fairness in social relationships. In J. W. Thibaut, J. T. Spence & R. C. Carson (Eds.), *Contemporary topics in social psychology* (pp. 211–240). Morristown, NJ: General Learning Press.

Leventhal, G. S. (1980). What should be done with equity theory? In K. J. Gergen, M. S. Greenberg & R. H. Willis (Eds.), *Social exchanges: Advances in theory and research* (pp. 27–55). New York: Plenum.

Leventhal, G. S., Karuza, J., & Fry, W. R. (1980). Beyond fairness: A theory of allocation preferences. In G. Milkula (Ed.), *Justice and social interaction* (pp. 167–218). New York: Springer-Verlag.

Lind, E. A. (1995). Justice and authority relations in organizations. In R. Cropanzano & M. K. Kacmar (Eds.), *Organizational politics, justice, and support: Managing the social climate of the workplace* (pp. 83–96). Westport, CT: Quorum.

Lind, E. A., Kanfer, R., & Earley, P. C. (1990). Voice, control, and procedural justice: Instrumental and noninstrumental concerns in fairness judgments. *Journal of Personality and Social Psychology, 59,* 952–959.

Lind, E. A., Kulik, C. A., Ambrose, M., & de Vera Park, M. V. (1993). Individual and corporate dispute resolution: Using procedural fairness as a decision heuristic. *Administrative Science Quarterly, 38,* 224–251.

Lind, E. A., & Lissak, R. I. (1985). Apparent impropriety and procedural fairness judgments. *Journal of Experimental Social Psychology, 21,* 19–29.

Lind, E. A., & Tyler, T. R. (1988). *The social psychology of procedural justice.* New York: Plenum.

Miner, J. B. (1992). *Industrial-Organizational Psychology.* New York: McGraw-Hill.

Martin, J. (1981). Relative deprivation: A theory of distributive justice for an era of shrinking resources. In L. L. Cummings & B. M. Staw (Eds.), *Research in organizational behavior* (Vol. 3, pp. 53–107). Greenwich, CT: JAI.

Miceli, M. P. (1993). Justice and pay system satisfaction. In R. Cropanzano (Ed.), *Justice in the workplace: Approaching fairness in human resource management* (pp. 257–283). Hillsdale, NJ: Lawrence Erlbaum Associates.

Moye, N. A., Masterson, S. S., & Bartol, K. M. (1997, August). *Differentiating antecedents and consequences of procedural and interactional justice: Empirical evidence in support of separate constructs.* Paper presented at the annual meeting of the Academy of Management. Boston, MA.

Pettigrew, T. F. (1967). Social evaluation theory: Convergence and applications. In D. Levine (Ed.), *Nebraska symposium on motivation* (Vol. 15, pp. 241–315). Lincoln: University of Nebraska Press.

Sheppard, B. H. (1983). Managers as inquisitors: Some lessons from the law. In M. H. Bazerman & R. J. Lewicki (Eds.), *Negotiation in organizations* (pp. 193–213). Beverly Hills, CA: Sage.

Sheppard, B. H. (1984). Third party conflict intervention: A procedural framework. In B. M. Staw & L. L. Cummings (Eds.), *Research in organizational behavior* (Vol. 6, pp. 141–191). Greenwich, CT: JAI.

Sheppard, B. H. (1985). Justice is no simple matter: Case for elaborating our model of procedural fairness. *Journal of Personality and Social Psychology, 49,* 953–962.

Sheppard, B. H., Lewicki, R. J., & Minton, J. W. (1992). *Organizational justice: The search for fairness in the workplace.* Lexington, MA: Lexington.

Stouffer, S. A., Suchman, E. A., DeVinney, L. C., Star, S. A., & Williams, R. M. (1949). *The American solider: Adjustment during army life* (Vol. 1). Princeton, NJ: Princeton University Press.

Sullivan, J. J. (1989). Self theories and employee motivation. *Journal of Management, 15,* 345–363.

Thibaut, J., & Walker, L. (1975). *Procedural justice: A psychological analysis.* Hillsdale, NJ: Lawrence Erlbaum Associates.

Thibaut, J., & Walker, L. (1978). A theory of procedure. *California Law Review, 66,* 541–566.

Thibaut, J., Walker, L., LaTour, S., & Houlden, P. (1974). Procedural justice as fairness. *Stanford Law Review, 26,* 1271–1289.

Tyler, T. R. (1984). The role of perceived injustice in defendants' evaluations of their courtroom experience. *Law and Society Review, 18,* 51–74.

Tyler, T. R. (1987). Conditions leading to value expressive effect in judgments of procedural justice: A test of four models. *Journal of Personality and Social Psychology, 52,* 333–344.

Tyler, T. R. (1989). The psychology of procedural justice: A test of the group-value model. *Journal of Personality and Social Psychology, 57,* 830–838.

Tyler, T. R. (1990). Intrinsic versus community-based justice models: When does group membership matter? *Journal of Social Issues, 46,* 83–94.

Tyler, T. R. (1994). Psychological models of the justice motive: Antecedents of distributive and procedural justice. *Journal of Personality and Social Psychology, 67,* 850–863.

Tyler, T. R., & Bies, R. J. (1990). Beyond formal procedures: The interpersonal context of procedural justice. In J. S. Carroll (Ed.), *Applied social psychology and organizational settings* (pp. 77–98). Hillsdale, NJ: Lawrence Erlbaum Associates.

Tyler, T. R., Boekmann, R., Smith, H., & Huo, Y. (1997). *Social justice in a diverse society.* Boulder, CO: Westview.

Tyler, T. R., & Folger, R. (1980). Distributional and procedural aspects of satisfaction with citizen-police encounters. *Basic and Applied Social Psychology, 1, 281*–292.

Tyler, T. R., & Lind, E. A. (1992). A relational model of authority in groups. In M. P. Zanna (Ed.), *Advances in experimental social psychology* (Vol. 25, pp. 115–191). San Diego, CA: Academic.

Van den Bos, K., Wilke, H. A. M., Lind, E. A., & Vermunt, R. (1998). Evaluating outcomes by means of the fair process effect: Evidence for different processes in satisfaction and fairness judgments. *Journal of Personality and Social Psychology, 74,* 1493–1503.

2

▼▼▼▼▼▼▼▼

Stress and Justice in Organizations: An Exploration Into Justice Processes With the Aim to Find Mechanisms to Reduce Stress

Riël Vermunt
Herman Steensma
Leiden University

A literature scan with stress as the topic reveals numerous articles and books on this subject matter. Hundreds of titles including concepts as job stress, role stress, organizational stress, stress and coping, and the like can be obtained from the library overview list. It is surprising to find relatively few titles of articles that include the concepts of stress and justice, whereas a global view of the theoretical background of stress and justice shows remarkable similarities. In this chapter we investigate the relation between the concepts of stress and justice. In doing so, we focus on the important role injustice may play in the development of stress.

One of the characteristics of stress that mostly is mentioned in the literature is that stress is mainly caused when individuals sense a difference between their own capacities and possibilities and the demands of the social and physical environment (Lazarus & Folkman, 1984). For example, workers having to do too many tasks in a time period that is too short or is felt as too short, may feel stressed. Emphasizing the misfit between one's response capacity and demands from the environment is the long-since accepted interpretation of stress. In addition, another interpretation is possible as well. The other interpretation emphasizes the active role of the superior as allocator of resources in the development of stress. Looking from the perspective of allocation decision processes and the related feelings of justice and injustice, one might argue that workers are subordinates that have been allocated too little resources from their supervisors to perform their tasks properly. For example, supervisor's allocated time (or control) is insufficient to carry out the task adequately. Conceived in this way, stress reflects an important aspect of the relationship between supervisor and subordinate exemplified by the endstate (the insufficient amount of time) and the procedure (supervisors inaccurate estimation of the capacities of the subordinates) of an allocation decision process.

Having said that, it must be added immediately that not all antecedent of feelings of stress can be explained by referring to resource allocation processes. For example, an interpersonal conflict between supervisor and subordinate may not have to do with the allocation of scarce resources (see Foa & Foa, 1974) but with incompatibility of personality characteristics. In this case the conflict may cause stress, but the antecedent condition is not a felt injustice. However, an experienced injustice can play a role in stress development in such a conflict. For example, the stress may be felt as less severe when the subordinate sees the supervisor as legitimate (Tyler, 1994) as compared to a supervisor that is seen as illegitimate. In other words, feelings of justice and injustice may moderate feelings of stress.

In this present chapter we explore the relation between stress and justice–injustice in order to gain insight into the process that doing justice or being just may decrease feelings of stress. Section 2 goes into the concept of stress and focuses on the sources of stress (the stressors), and the effects of stress (the strains). It ends with a description of the relation between stress and satisfaction. The argument for emphasizing the relation between stress and satisfaction is that one of the effects of stress is dissatisfaction, and satisfaction models may give us insight into the processes of stress and gives us the opportunity to relate stress and justice phenomenon. Section 3 focuses on justice. The main point is that a person's overall evaluation of the justice of an allocation situation is a combination of justices and injustices experienced in the situation. Some characteristics of processing justice information are described. In Section 4, it is argued that supervisors' just behavior (Vermunt & Steensma, 1996) is important to reduce stress of subordinates. In that sense, a supervisor's just behavior is a crucial antistress factor next to subordinates' coping behavior to overcome the negative consequences of stress and next to social support. Four types of justice repair strategies are discussed.

STRESS

Stress is one of the most widely used concepts in the social sciences (see Buunk & de Wolff, 1992; Fried, 1993). At the same time, it is a rather fuzzy concept that is notorious for the imprecision with which it is used by researchers. Stress is defined in different ways by different authors, but all of those definitions incorporate the idea that stress is experienced when people try to meet demands from the environment that " either approach or exceed their capacities to respond" (Carver, 1995, p. 635). A rather similar definition and one that suits our purposes as well is the definition by Cropanzano, Howes, Grandey & Toth (1997), "stress is the subjective feeling that work demands exceed the individual's belief in his or her capacity to cope" (p. 164). There is no need to enter further into the highly complicated definitional arguments here, for although authors differ in several respects, they also share a lot of common ground. Almost all authors share the idea of stress as a stimulus-organism-response model and emphasize the existence of a stress cycle (Beehr & Newman, 1978; Edwards, 1992; French, Caplan, & Harrison, 1982; Kahn, Wolfe, Quinn, Snoeck, & Rosenthal, 1964; Lazarus, 1966; Lazarus & Folkman, 1984; Winnubst, 1995). This stress cycle functions as follows: People are sensing their environment. The perceived environment is compared with a criterion. (In reality, several environmental characteristics are compared with several reference criteria.) If a discrepancy between the perceived environment and the criterion value exists, the sensing person feels stress, and will try to reduce this discrepancy—but only if this discrepancy is seen as important and as damaging to the well-being of the person. The attempt to change the discrepancy has consequences for the person (although not necessarily the consequences that were intended). The new situation is sensed again, and a new chain of events follows.

This is the basic framework of the stress cycle. Most authors elaborate on this basic framework. Complex theories have been built, containing large collections of theoretical (or empirically found) constructs, connected with each other in an impressive structure with multiple links. Still, the basic elements of the stress cycle always can be recognized easily (Edwards, 1992). Theories of stress in organizations can be clustered into a few categories. Especially important is the classification into *reactive models* and *coping models* (Winnubst, 1995). This division is based on different assumptions about human nature. Reactive models look on people as rather passive. Although it is sometimes recognized that individual differences exist, stress is seen as something that happens to people. This is true, both for models that focus on stress as a response (Selye, 1978) and models that consider stress as mainly caused by a stimulus. However, stress may also be regarded as resulting from the interaction between person and environment (Lazarus, 1966). In these kind of models, persons have coping abilities, for instance, are willing and often able to cope with stressful situations. So, people are not seen as helpless, although, again, individual differences in coping ability may be very large. Hardiness and competence may be innate or they may be seen as characteristics that can be developed. Both views imply that persons are not at the mercy of the situation.

Coping can take several forms. *Problem-focused* or *control coping* involves attempting to alter the relationship between the person and the environment. *Emotion-focused* or *avoidance coping* is the name given to attempts to regulate the emotional problems that have been caused by the stressing environment. Frequently, this latter form amounts to avoidance of problems (Lazarus, 1966; Lazarus & Folkman, 1984). Coping ceases when the problems have been solved, or the emotions have been regulated satisfactorily. In such cases, a sense of well-being may result; otherwise, negative consequences are to be expected. Research has shown that avoidance coping has hardly any beneficial effects, whereas the findings with regard to problem coping are inconsistent (Koeske, Kirk, & Koeske, 1993). It seems that the most beneficial effects of coping are realized if problem coping strategies as well as avoidance-coping strategies were used in combination.

SOURCES OF STRESS

Stress theories distinguish between sources of stress (often called *stressors*) and reactions to these sources. Again, sources may be categorized. In organizations, stress may be produced by sources belonging to one or more of the following common categories (see also Allegro, Kruidenier, & Steensma, 1991; Beehr & Newman, 1978; McGrath, 1976):

- *Job content:* Employees may experience job stress because of work overload, lack of autonomy, a monotonous job; ambiguity.
- *Material working conditions* (quality of the work environment): dirt, noise, temperature, toxic materials, and so forth.
- *Industrial and organizational relations* (see Kelloway, Barling, & Shah, 1993): Stress may be caused by the conflict over domains of work control between management and subordinates (Fried, 1993). A distinction can be made between formal and informal relations, although it must be admitted that relations often have a mixed character. The Works' Council (a committee of employer and employees that advises on several matters regarding the company) and job consultation are examples of formal organizational relations. Low-quality relations (conflict about control) of these two organizational structures may be stressful to employees. However, social relations with colleagues, supervisors, and counselors are, although informal, in general are seen as more important by workers. They may cause more stress if their quality is low. But if their quality is good, these relations may support the workers in such a way that far more stress can be tolerated.
- *Working conditions and personnel policy:* the allocation of rewards and the system of promotion; the working hours and the spread of holidays. These and other aspects of personnel policy are potential sources of stress (see also Cropanzano et al., 1997).

Unfortunately, sources of organizational stress often covary with each other. This leads to some social inequality in the quality of working life for different professional groups. For example, blue-collar workers work under considerably worse conditions than do white-collar workers. This is an example of macroinjustice (Brickmann, Folger, Goode, & Schul, 1981). It may give rise to social tensions between groups in organizations (and also between groups and social categories in society). And it implies that, in general, most blue-collar workers have to spend or consume more of their coping capacities in organizations than their white-collar colleagues have to.

So far this chapter has discussed the organizational sources of stress. It should not be forgotten that persons may experience stress in their private lives as well (Jones & Fletcher, 1993). Persons may bring stress with them to the organizations and from the organization to their private lives. It can be assumed that people do not have an infinite amount of coping capacities. So, persons who have problems at home cannot bear the same amount of stress as those lucky persons who do not experience life changes like, for example, the death of a spouse or close family member, divorce, major illness etcetera (Holmes & Rahe, 1967).

NEGATIVE EFFECTS OF STRESS

In the long run, stress may have several negative effects or *strains* as these effects generally are called (French, Caplan, & Harrison, 1982; Katz & Kahn, 1966; Winnubst, 1995). Stress is damaging to physical or somatic health. For example, blood pressure, headaches, and respiratory and cardiovascular illnesses may result from long-term exposure to stress. Mental health is also at risk: feelings of depression, boredom, mental fatigue, and dissatisfaction are related to the presence of stressors. At the behavioral level, persons suffering from stress often demonstrate escapist behaviors like drinking or smoking too much. And often job stresses are related to absenteeism and turnover intentions and turnover behaviors of employees (see, e.g., Cooper & Marshall, 1976; Fried, Rowland, & Ferries, 1984; Shirom, 1989; for reviews). An important reason for this withdrawal behavior is, of course, the fact that stress is extremely aversive to most workers. A second explanation is that an indirect relation exists between stress and withdrawal with job dissatisfaction as an intervening variable (Gupta & Beehr, 1979).

Physiological responses (e.g., blood pressure), mental responses (e.g., boredom), and behavioral responses (e.g., absenteeism) are indicators of a misfit between organizational and work aspects and the worker. The stimulus–response relation is not a simple one, however. Some workers are prone to react with headaches, others develop high blood pressure or begin to drink. There are large individual differences in the final reactions of workers to a stressful, organizational situation. In addition, large individual differences exist in the coping abilities of workers (and people in general).

Stress and Personality Differences

Individuals differ in their tolerance for stress, although individual tolerance for stress cannot be generalized across all stressors. Tolerance for physical work load, for example, largely depends on the physical health of workers, whereas tolerance for information overload covaries with cognitive abilities of the persons involved.

By and large, however, it is true that persons who are in good shape (both the physical and mental condition is meant here), can tolerate more stress than other persons. Research has demonstrated convincingly that particular personality dimensions are indicators that the person who owns these characteristics is at risk of getting health problems, caused by stress that is not managed well. Perhaps the best known of these characteristics is the *Type A* personality dimension. Type A persons are highly committed to their work. However, they are impatient, competitive, hostile, and always feel the pressure of deadlines (Friedman & Rosenman, 1974; Marcelissen, 1987). Although some of these characteristics are highly valued in most organizations, such type A persons incur more mental and physical health risks than the so-called *type B* persons (who can be characterized more or less as the opposites of type A persons).

In this chapter findings are connected from stress research with theories of social justice, with particular attention to procedures and outcome distributions. Therefore, we will not focus on personality differences. Suffice it to say, that two personality characteristics that are studied primarily in the domain of social justice seem to be important factors in the explanation of individual differences in tolerance for stress in organizations: The *Just World Belief* that the fate of persons corresponds to what they deserve (Lerner, 1980) and the input–outcome orientation (i.e., the inclination to perceive job elements as inputs or outcomes; Tornow, 1971). This module of our new stress model has been presented elsewhere (Steensma, Vermunt, & Allegro, 1997).

Perceived Gaps as Causes of Stress

As Lazarus and Folkman (1984) stated, the negative appraisal of the difference between demands of the environment and own response capacity is an important factor for causing stress. Now some demands and some response capacities are seen as more important than other demands and other capacities. A misfit between important demands and capacities is far more stressing than a misfit between demands and capacities that are deemed to be of low importance by the person. Moreover, there is the problem that people attribute causes to a misfit, especially when the misfit is perceived as important. It is known, of course, that there is the risk of several attribution errors.

In organizations, it is tempting for workers to attribute a misfit to failure behaviors of their supervisor. Such a self-serving bias allows workers to maintain high self-esteem. However, often this creates another nuisance. Why does the supervisor fail? People try to attach meaning to what is happening to them. The subordinate's appraisal of the misfit can be stated in terms of the supervisors' inability or unwillingness to allocate sufficient resources to the subordinate; but, unfortunately, this perception of inability or unwillingnes may also be experienced as a threat. In particular, the subordinate might attribute the inability or unwillingness to a negative relationship between himself or herself and the superior. Interpersonal treatment can be interpreted as an indicator for the attitudes each person has toward the other. So, if a supervisor applies procedures that are seen as unjust, or the supervisor does not allocate the resources that are needed, the subordinate often will draw the conclusion that the supervisor has a negative attitude toward him or her. It is argued, therefore, that stress can be caused by the subordinate's perception of an unjust allocation of a scarce resource by the superior, which is seen as the consequence of a negative relationship between both parties.

A cause of stress is, therefore, the perceived discrepancy between one's response capacity and the resources one gets from the superior. We assume that this discrepancy is an important cause of stress because it regards the relationship between worker and supervisor. The question, then, becomes important as to how these discrepancies or gaps can best be conceptualized. One way to look at the discrepancies is by referring to the theoretical framework developed by Campbell, Converse, and Rogers (1976) and Michalos (1985) and what is called *multiple discrepancies theory*. The theory was developed to explain happiness and satisfaction with different domains of life, such as work and family (Vermunt, Spaans, & Zorge, 1989).

In his review of work on job satisfaction, satisfaction and happiness with life as a whole, and the quality of life Michalos (1985) noted that the large majority of gap-theoretical explanations are successful in predicting associations between satisfaction and a (perceived) gap. For example, ones satisfaction with housing can be well predicted with the discrepancy between the housing one has and what comparable others have. So, it certainly seems useful to put resources in the further development of gap theories. Michalos did so in his own research in which he followed an approach developed by Campbell, Converse, and Rogers (1976). These three authors described a model of satisfaction with a particular domain (housing, finances, etc.) as a function of several comparisons (e.g., comparisons with most-liked previous experiences, comparisons with relatives, comparisons with typical Americans or average folks, etc.). Thus, this Campbell et al. model is called a multiple discrepancies theory by Michalos (1985) because of its appeal to multiple gaps.

Referring to this chapter's introduction, note the similarity with the stress cycle that has been described: the discrepancy between perceptions and criteria and the importance of these discrepancies as core concepts. It may pay to take a closer look at such discrepancies. In particular, interest lies in the criterion values with which the perceptions are compared. Michalos (1985) published an interesting review of gap-theoretical explanatory theories in which he described six different accounts of satisfaction and happiness:

1. The *goal-achievement gap theory:* Satisfaction (or happiness, for that matter) is regarded as a function of the perceived gap between what one actually has (achievement) and what one wants to have (goal).

2. *Ideal–real gap theory:* Satisfaction and happiness are regarded as a function of the perceived gap between what one actually has, or expects to have, and what one considers to be ideal, preferable or desirable.

3. *Expectation–reality gap theory:* in which the perceived gap between what is the case now and what one expects (or expected) to be the case, is used to explain satisfaction. So, subjective probabilities are matched against what is happening (or happened) in reality.

4. *Previous–best comparison theory:* where satisfaction (happiness) is a function of the perceived gap between what one has now and the best one has ever had in the past.

5. *Social comparison theory:* satisfaction (happiness) is strongly influenced by the perception of a gap between what one has, and what some relevant other person or group has.

6. *Person–environment fit:* or "congruence" theories involve the gap between some personal attribute of a subject and some attribute of that subject's environment. This kind of theory can be regarded as a residual category: members of this category do not fit into one of the other classes.

The explanatory power of this theory has been convincingly demonstrated in several surveys conducted by Michalos; particularly the variance in satisfaction and happiness with life as a whole could be explained remarkably well by only three perceived gaps (namely, a goal-achievement gap; a comparison with previous best, and the social comparison with average folks). It must be added, however, that the relation of (dis)satisfaction with the discrepancy between perception and reference criterion can have different forms.

Locke (1976) developed some interesting ideas about these forms. He saw satisfaction as resulting from the perception that one's job fulfills one's important job values, providing and to the degree that these values are congruent with one's needs. *Needs* are the objective requirements of the survival and well-being of an organism, whereas values are subjective standards that are acquired during socialization. People do not differ in their basic needs, but they do differ in what they value. Locke pointed out that the perceived job situation, in relation to the individual's values, directly determines (job) satisfaction. An individual's values can be ranked as to their importance. Values of low importance are hardly able to influence the range of affect that a person feels: One is not very satisfied, nor very dissatisfied with the amount of what one gets. However, important values will lead to a greater range of feelings, from very dissatisfied to very satisfied, depending on the difference between the perceived amount of the value provided by the job, and the amount of the value content that is wanted by the person. Locke noted that the shape of the function that relates value-perception discrepancy and importance to satisfaction sometimes is monotonic, but for other values the shape may be nonmonotonic. For example, for a philatelist the stamp function is monotonically rising: The more stamps he or she has collected, the more satisfied he or she is. Discrepancies from the most preferred temperature, however, are related to a bell-shaped function to the felt satisfaction with the temperature. Temperatures may be too hot or too cold, and in both situations people are dissatisfied.

According to equity researchers like Adams (1965), the distributive justice function has such a bell-shape: getting less than is equitable as well as getting more than is equitable results in lower justice evaluations (not satisfaction) than an equitable pay. As can be inferred from Carver's (1995) definition of stress, the stress function may also have a bell-shape. Environmental demands that approach and exceed one's response capacity are both experienced and stressful, whereas a fit between demands and capacity is not experienced as stressful.

JUSTICE

The work situation can best be characterized as an exchange relationship in which an employer hires a person (the employee) with more or less specific abilities to perform a group of tasks that are structured according to a more or less explicit plan. The employee is rewarded for his or her contribution according to a payment scheme. One could say that an employer allocates jobs, tasks, salaries, and other things to employees. The employer applies certain procedures to allocate jobs and salaries. For instance, in many companies and institutions, employers use a set of procedures to hire personnel: The employer starts a campaign to attract people for a vacant job; the employer installs a committee, sets up criteria for selection, and so on. In other words, many facets of the work situation can be conceived as intricate resource allocation processes, in which an authority allocates resources (Foa & Foa, 1974) by applying a procedure.

Employees evaluate the end result of the resource allocation process, the procedure that is applied to arrive at the end result as well as the total allocation process. Foa and Foa (1974) distinguished six types of resources: money, goods, information, status, services, and love. Although in an exchange relationship between employer and employee all six resources may be present, in practice some resources are more salient than others. We assume that in the work situation, money and especially status are very prominent. Money may take the form of salary and financial bonuses. Status is a resource in which the relationship between employer and employee is most relevant in the daily routine. Most employees are very sensitive to status and possible changes in their status. Status has to do with allocation of: (a) positions (Bruins & Wilke, 1996), for instance, whether one will be promoted or not, (b) tasks, for instance, whether one is allocated new and challenging tasks or not, and (c) quality of the relationship, for instance, the relationship with the employer may be good or may be bad (Bales, 1980). Because of the salience of status (Tyler & Lind, 1992), employees will feel strongly affected by changes in their work situation that regard their status position.

People evaluate allocation of resources predominantly in terms of fairness. Fairness is an important orientation in people's life (Lerner, 1980, 1991). According to Lerner, justice or fairness is such an important orientation that people do everything to maintain the belief that the world in which they live is a just place. People blame innocent victims of crime in order to maintain their belief in a just world (Lerner, 1980). People vary in the strength of their belief in a just world. The just world belief affects people's attitudes, cognitions, and behavior. More-over, Lind and Tyler (1988) stated that people who cede power to an authority feel uncertain and uneasy about their relationship with the authority. Subordinates will look for signs indicating whether the authority can be trusted, shows respect, and is neutral. According to Lind and Tyler, a shortcut way to become certain about the trustworthiness, the neutrality, and perceived respect for the subordi-nate, is to look at the fairness of the authority's allocation decisions (see Van den Bos & Lind, chap. 3, this volume). Thus, from a normative point of view (Lerner, 1980), as well as from a social relationship point of view (Lind & Tyler, 1988; Tyler & Lind, 1992; Vermunt, Blaauw, & Lind, 1998) one may infer that employ-ees will look sharply at the fairness of the superior's allocation behavior.

Evaluation Standards

How do employees determine the fairness of the allocation decision of the supe-rior? One of the most important techniques of the subordinates evaluative capac-ity is social comparison (Crosby, 1976; Folger, 1987; Vermunt, Wit, Van den Bos & Lind, 1996; Van den Bos, Vermunt, & Wilke, 1997). Employees compare the allocated resources they have received: (a) with the resource others have received (social comparison), (b) with resources they have received in the past (temporal comparison), and/or (c) with an internalized norm. Employees may conclude from the outcome of the comparison process that the received resource is in agreement or is not in agreement with the comparison standard. According to most justice researchers, when the received resource is not in agreement with what one expected, people will evaluate the resource as unfair, and the more un-fair the more the received outcome deviates from the comparison standard.

Authors do not agree about the impact of each of the comparison standards on fairness evaluations. Adams (1965) developed the concept of own equity (com-paring the actual input–outcome ratio with one experienced before) and compar-ison equity (comparing own input–outcome ratio with that of a comparison other). Lerner (1980) would emphasize the importance of the internalized norm, as this norm is the result of a personal contract of the growing child with itself. The personal contract holds that people will get what they deserve. This internal-ized norm is a strong motivational force for the evaluation of ones own behavior as well as for the evaluation of others. It can explain, for instance, why people blame innocent victims (Lerner, 1980). Folger (1987) applied the simulation heuristic (Kahneman & Tversky, 1982) to social justice phenomenon. According to Folger, people confronted with an outcome and motivated to evaluate the fair-ness of the outcome simulate outcomes that could have been achieved when certain conditions had been met. Folger labeled the simulated outcomes referent outcomes: the referent outcomes may be inferred from comparing with others, by comparing with a standard, or with comparing with ones own situation earlier in time. Lind and Tyler (1988) seemed to emphasize an absolute norm that people apply when they evaluate the fairness of procedures. Lind and Tyler argued that procedures can be interpreted more easily than outcomes because experiencing that an authority behaves unfairly can be determined directly and no simulation or comparison process is needed. Vermunt (Van den Bos, Vermunt, & Wilke, 1997; Vermunt & Shulman, 1996; Vermunt, Wit, Van den Bos, & Lind, 1996) stated that procedures—just as outcomes—are evaluated by comparing the actual procedure with a simulated procedure. Empirical evidence is found in favor of all theoretical positions, and it is at this moment not clear which of the standards is most effective in affecting fairness evaluations.

Discrepancy Approach of Justice

Where most authors agree with each other is that a discrepancy between actual endstate or procedure may cause feelings of unfairness, and the larger the discrepancy the more unfair the evaluation of the endstate or procedure will be. For Adams (1965), Folger (1987), and Vermunt, Wit, Van den Bos, & Lind (1996), it is quite evident that discrepancies affect fairness evaluations. In the case of Lerner's (1980) theory of justice it is more difficult to understand whether discrepancies play a role in the fairness evaluation of behaviors and events. By taking blaming the victim as an example, it may become clear that discrepancies are important in affecting fairness evaluations. According to Lerner, people believe that the world is a just place where everyone gets what he or she deserves: good things to good people, and bad things to bad people. However, when people perceive an innocent person becomes harmed this is an experience that is discrepant with their general idea of a just world. Experiencing a discrepancy is unpleasant and may cause people to restore consistency, for instance, by blaming the victim. Tyler and Lind's (1992) theory of procedural fairness is based on the idea that people have developed a standard of fair treatment. An authority's behavior that deviates from the standard may be judged as unfair.

Vermunt, Wit, Van den Bos, and Lind (1996) tested the assumption that the more inaccurate the procedure was, the more unfair the procedure was judged. In their study Vermunt et al. first offered subjects an accurate procedure (Leventhal, 1980) in which 10 of the 10 subtasks were examined. Participants received 3 groups of 10 subtasks in order to set a standard for an accurate procedure. After the three groups of tasks (each with 10 subtasks) a fourth group of tasks was planned in which the experimenter announced that he would examine only 1 (very inaccurate) or only 9 (slightly inaccurate) of the 10 subtasks. Participants experienced a clear discrepancy between the first three evaluation procedures and the fourth one (as was shown in the answers to control questions), and indicated a greater discrepancy the more the amount of examined subtasks deviated from the total amount of (10) subtasks. It was also found that the greater the discrepancy the more unfair the procedure was evaluated. The study showed that participants indicated negative emotions as reaction to the unfair procedure, with more negative emotions in the very inaccurate procedure condition (very unfair) than in the slightly inaccurate (less unfair) procedure condition.

Vermunt and Shulman (1996) found, using a similar experimental set-up, a relation between unfairness of the procedure and self-esteem: Participants who evaluated the procedure as more unfair, showed lower state self-esteem scores (Heatherton & Polivy, 1991). It is worthy to note that, in both studies, participants did not relate the inaccurateness of the procedure to the perceived chance of getting an unfavorable outcome. In other words, differences in fairness evaluations could not be attributed to differences in outcome expectations, but only to differences in the inaccurateness of the procedure: the pure procedural effect.

The Vermunt et al. (1996) studies showed it is possible to investigate the unfairness of procedures by inducing a discrepancy between an actual procedure and a procedure received in the (near) past. The studies also showed that the magnitude of the discrepancy affected the magnitude of the feelings of unfairness as well as the magnitude of negative emotion and that of lowered self-esteem. One may conclude from these findings that unfairness of procedures can be determined by inducing a discrepancy between an actual procedure and a procedure that has been experienced in the past (the referent procedure). In this way, feelings of unfairness can be realized by inducing high-referent outcomes (see Folger & Konovsky, 1986) as well as by inducing high-referent procedures. This discussion shows the similarities of the processes that cause stress and the ones leading to feelings of unfairness—the gap theoretical notion.

Justice Contra Injustice

The preceding paragraph describes the situation of a discrepancy in only one end state (outcome) or one procedure. Daily working life is not that simple, unfortunately. In most cases, a resource allocation decision contains other information about the endstate as well as information about the procedure. For instance, the superior who communicates the allocation decision can refuse subordinates the opportunity to comment on the decision; or the superior gives subordinates an opportunity to voice their opinion but communicates the information very rudely. Communications about resource allocation decisions always contain information about many aspects of the resource allocation process. It will, therefore, not surprise anyone that in many cases the pieces of information are inconsistent with each other. One aspect of the resource allocation process may be judged as fair, whereas another aspect may be judged as unfair. Aspects of a resource allocation process can match with each other in which case the different aspects are all judged as fair or all as unfair, or there can be a mismatch in which aspects of an allocation process contradict each other in terms of fairness (Foa & Foa, 1974; Törnblom & Vermunt, 1999), one aspect is judged as fair, and another aspect as unfair. Realizing that different aspects of the resource allocation process may be judged as fair, while other aspects may be evaluated as unfair opens opportunities to study the impact of fairness on unfairness.

In some resource allocation decision processes, information about the different aspects of the process will reach the people who concern the decision practically at the same time (e.g., when a superior communicates his or her decision to give voice, but does so in a disrespectful way). This type of information may give rise to online processing of the information (Hastie & Park, 1986). (Interestingly, the voice may be conceived in this specific situation as an endstate of the resource allocation decision process instead of viewing it as part of the procedure.)

In other resource allocation situations information about one aspect of the process may reach the people whom it concerns earlier in time than other aspects. Sometimes, information about the procedure is known before the information about the endstate is known. For instance, job evaluations start mostly with a meeting between the parties as part of the resource allocation decision process (the procedure) after which a decision is taken. However, a reverse order is possible as well, that is, that information about the endstate is known before the information about the procedure is known. For instance, the bonus for the best and cheapest production innovation idea is communicated first, after which the committee explains how he or she arrived at the final decision. The time lapse that often exists between receiving both pieces of information may give rise to memory based processing of information (Hastie & Park, 1986). The effects of both types of information processing on judgments of fairness are not well-known. We also do not know how these processes effect the impression one forms of the resource allocation authority about his or her trustworthiness, and so forth. It is likely that experiencing inconsistencies between information about aspects of the resource allocation process will be processed differently when information is received practically at the same time or when the information is received serially.

The distinction between the two types of receiving information may be of interest if the distinction between different types of justices is taken into account. Folger (1996) differentiated between distributive justice, procedural justice, and interactional justice. Interactional justice is viewed as the way decision makers communicate with subordinates. One can distinguish between the content of the communication as well as the way the information is communicated (Bies & Moag, 1986). But information about content and way of communicating are strongly related to each other and are received at the same time, practically. One may assume, therefore, that information about the endstate of the resource allocation decision and information about the interpersonal communication (how the information is communicated) are processed online. For the more formal properties of the procedure, as exemplified by Leventhal's (1980) procedural rules, information about the endstate and about the procedure may be received at different times, depending on the specific situation. Information about the endstate and information about the procedure may be received at different points in time; sometimes the time lapse may be as long as 14 days as in the example of job application situations, or even longer as in the case of a court trial. The strong effects of interpersonal aspects of the resource allocation process on justice judgments may be attributed to the type of information processing that is applied. We do not know much about these processes. Research on these cognitive processes of justice judgments is needed.

MANAGING STRESS BY RESTORING JUSTICE

There are several ways to reduce stress or even to prevent stress in an organizational context by choosing and applying individual coping strategies, and by asking for *social support* (see Thoits, 1995, for an overview). Social support is defined as a resource that people call on when they cope with stress (Heaney et al., 1993). In other words, coping as well as social support are initiated by the worker.

Another way to reduce and to prevent stress is one in which the superior, unlike in the case of social support, is involved directly. The superior can take the initiative. As discussed, a superior is an authority who allocates resources (tasks, time, bonuses) to subordinates by applying rules and procedures. Resources, as well as the application of the rules and procedures to arrive at the endstate, can be allocated unjustly. We assume that the unjust allocation of a resource, and even more so the inappropriate application of a procedure, is seen by subordinates as a threat to their relationship with the superior. The threat may increase the already existing stress due to negative appraisal of the difference between environmental demands and capacities of the person. A subordinate may judge the allotted time for performing the task as unjust and as a severe demand to which he or she can not respond properly. But the main factor that causes stress is the subordinate's threat that the injustice is an indication of a negative relationship with the superior. This threat may be increased by the subordinate's insight that the superior evidently did not do justice to the ability and capacity of the subordinate, as well as by showing little consideration for the subordinate. We are convinced that by doing justice and by compensating for eventual injustices, superiors may reduce or even prevent stress of their subordinates.

There are two basic ways that injustice may influence stress reactions. One way is that an injustice is a factor that may cause stress. In testing this assumption, Zohar (1995) asked hospital nurses to indicate how fairly or unfairly role senders reacted to possible sources of stress (role justice). Next, Zohar measured other potential stressors as well: role conflict, role ambiguity, role overload, and decision latitude (control). Role strain was measured by the *General Health Questionnaire* and by the *Intentions to Leave* index and formed the dependent variables. It was found that role justice acts as an independent and additional factor for experiencing stress.

Reactions to a stressful situation may also be moderated by justice concerns. After a stressful task, participants who strongly believe that the world is a just place where everyone gets what he or she deserves reported less strains, had better performance, and experienced the task as more challenging than subjects low in just-world beliefs (Tomaka & Blascovich, 1994). It must be added, however, that Zohar (1995), in his study with nurses, could not find any moderating effects of justice concerns on stress reactions.

Injustice may be conceived as a stress factor, as well as a factor in which the discrepancy between the actual situation and a comparison standard is emphasized. The main difference between injustice as a stress factor and other stress factors is that the discrepancy is attributed to the allocators decision toward the subordinate, and as such, reflects the relationship between supervisor and subordinate. Injustice as a stress factor can be overcome. One of the ways to overcome an initial unfairness is to behave fairly. It is in this respect that Folger (Folger et al., 1979) introduced the term *fair process effect*: the beneficial effects of a fair procedure on an unfair outcome. The fair process effect, however, is just one way to overcome the unfairness of a previous decision. In the pages that follow, four tactics for overcoming initial injustices are described. The four ways are the results of a combination of the fairness of the endstate of a resource allocation process with the fairness of the procedure of that process. An endstate as well as a procedure may be judged as fair or unfair. An unfair endstate may be followed by a fair endstate as well as by a fair procedure. An unfair procedure may be followed by a fair endstate or by a fair procedure. In Table 2.1 the four combinations are shown.

Compensation

An unfair endstate may be judged as less unfair if it is followed by another but fair endstate. We have labeled this instance of fairness contra unfairness *Compensation*. An employee whose demotion is judged as unfair may be compensated for the unfairness by a raise in salary. The raise in salary will probably not fully compensate the unfair endstate but will be viewed by the employee as an indication that the superior has an eye for the interests of the subordinate. The respect

TABLE 2.1
The Four Modes of Acting Fairly After an Unfairness

		Acting fairly via	
		endstate	procedure
Prior unfairness	endstate	COMPENSATION	JUSTIFICATION
	procedure	APPRECIATION	MITIGATION

shown in this way, as well as the financial bonus, may compensate to a great extent the rejected opportunity for promotion.

It should be emphasized that unfair outcomes may cause negative effects. Direct tests to investigate the negative effects of an inequitable reward on fairness are carried out by Adams (1965) and many others (see Messick & Cook, 1983). Results of most studies support predictions derived from equity theory: Underpaid subjects perform worse than equitable paid subjects; overpaid subjects perform better than equitable paid subjects (Cropanzano & Greenberg, 1997). Moreover, in their review of the literature, Cropanzano and Greenberg conclude that unfair endstates result in high rates of turnover and absenteeism. But it is not quite clear what the described effects of inequity can be attributed to.

In the first place, in many studies investigators have not controlled for the fairness feelings that may have accompanied the inequitable reward. Too many studies have asked not for the fairness of the reward, but for participants to indicate their satisfaction with the reward. Many social scientists view satisfaction and fairness as almost identical concepts, but the scarce research investigating differences between the two concepts is quite explicit that satisfaction and fairness are not interchangeable. In the second place, in many studies it is quite obvious that the manipulation of payment is not done by only varying the outcome but also by manipulating the procedure. For instance in a study by Steensma, Roes, Wippler, and Zoete (1981) the outcome was manipulated by referring to three companies who payed differently for the same work. It seems to us that not only payment is varied but also the procedural criterion consistency. Participants might have been upset by the fact that companies differ in their payment policy. Studies focusing on the beneficial effects of a fair endstate on an unfair endstate are scarce. What is known is that an unfair reward will be followed by some form of restoration of the unfairness by decreasing the input (Adams, 1965). There are as far as we know no studies investigating compensation of unfair endstates by introducing another but fair endstate.

Justification

Folger's (e.g., Folger, 1987) Referent Cognitions Theory is a theoretical framework that may be thought of as a special design to study the impact of fair procedures on unfair endstates. According to Folger, by using justifications in allocating a resource, the negative effects of an unfair endstate may be overcome. In their classical study Folger, Rosenfield, Grove, and Corkran (1979) induced in subjects a high- or a low-referent outcome: if the procedure to evaluate the performance had not been changed participants would have had a high versus a low chance to get the desired outcome. None of the participants received the outcome. The high-referent participants' unfairness was softened by the justification the experimenter gave for the applied procedure: a lengthy account or a short communication. High-referent participants who received a thorough justification, felt less unfairness about not getting the outcome than high-referent participants who received a less thorough justification. Folger labeled the softening effect of a fair procedure on an unfair endstate the *fair process effect*. To be in line with the former process of compensation, we label the fair process effect *Justification* (see also Folger, 1987).

Appreciation

Unfair procedures have probably more severe negative consequences than unfair endstates. Although some authors are convinced that outcomes are more important than procedures (e.g., Lerner & Whitehead, 1980; Rutte & Messick, 1996), it is now generally accepted that procedures have a strong impact on subsequent attitudes and behaviors. The two models that explain the impact of procedures on attitudes and behaviors are the instrumental model and the relational model. Excellent accounts of both models are found in Tyler and Lind (1992) and Cropanzano and Greenberg (1997). According to the instrumental model, the effects of fair procedures are attributed to the positive impact procedural measures will have on reaching the final endstate; according to the relational model the impact of fair procedures can be attributed to the positive effects of fair procedures on the relationship between the authority who is responsible for the allocation and the subordinate. Research has shown that fair procedures lead to higher levels of organizational commitment (Tyler, 1991), greater trust in management (Konovsky & Pugh, 1994), lower turnover intentions (Dailey & Kirk, 1992), more positive organizational citizenship behavior (Organ & Moorman, 1993), softer influence tactics (Van Knippenberg, Blaauw, Vermunt, & Van Knippenberg, 1997), and to some extent, higher job performance (Konovsky & Cropanzano, 1991). Moreover, unfair procedures create lower levels of self-esteem (Koper, Van Knippenberg, Bouhuijs, Vermunt, & Wilke, 1993; Vermunt & Shulman, 1996), stronger negative emotions (Vermunt, Wit, Van den Bos, & Lind, 1996), harder influence tactics (Van Knippenberg et al., 1997), and higher levels of norm-violating behavior (Modde, Vermunt, & Wiegman, 1996).

To overcome the negative effects of unfair procedures authorities may try to do justice by inducing fair endstates or by inducing other but fair procedures. It is sometimes difficult for a decision maker to apply fair procedures. A recent example is the announcement of the downsizing of the Renault automobile manufacturing site at Vilvoorde, Belgium. The financial losses of the French automobile company were tremendous. To prevent the whole company from suffering, a part of the company was sacrificed. The president of the Renault company planned to prepare the personnel for the shock and to inform them as well as possible. The Flemish government judged the downsizing as a blow in the face of Belgium and demanded that Renault announced the negative news immediately. So, Renault did. Unfair procedures may be applied because external pressures are exerted.

Anyway, to overcome the negative effects of an unfair procedure an authority may try to reach a fair endstate. The negative effects of an unfair procedure may be improved by a fair endstate. We label this process *Appreciation*. The one study that has investigated the beneficial effects of a fair endstate on an unfair procedure has been carried out by Van den Bos, Vermunt, and Wilke (1997; see chap. 3, this volume, for an extensive description of the experiment). The authors labeled this phenomenon the *fair outcome effect*.

Mitigation

The fourth way an injustice can be overcome by doing justice is when an unjust procedure is followed by a just procedure. We have labeled this process *Mitigation*: In mitigation, the negative effects of an unfair procedure may be softened by another but fair procedure. It is often found in daily working life that procedures are not applied in a proper way. For instance, the authority has not used all relevant information (Leventhal, 1980) to base the decision of hiring–not hiring an applicant. An excuse may mitigate the unfair treatment by the authority. In this case, the endstate of the resource allocation process is the hiring–not hiring of the applicant; the procedure is the accuracy of the information used to base the decision on, whereas the mitigating procedure is the justification given for not using all the relevant information. Moreover, information to justify the use of a procedure may be inadequate and viewed as unfair, but the way the information is communicated—face-to-face—may mitigate the unfair justification (Shapiro, Buttner, & Barry, 1994).

Not all combinations of an unfair procedure followed by a fair procedure will lead to a desirable total procedure. The combination of a fair procedure to mitigate the effects of unfair procedure may sometimes result, however, in a more unfair overall judgment of the procedure. In a study by Vermunt and Shulman (1996) subjects who received an inaccurate evaluation procedure (Leventhal, 1980) and were offered predecisional voice judged the total procedure as less fair than subjects with an inaccurate procedure and postdecisional voice. Earlier research has demonstrated that predecisional voice is judged as more fair than postdecisional voice (Lind, Kanfer, & Earley, 1991). Clearly, knowing before that one has voice in an inaccurate procedure will not increase the trust in the authority. In other words, one should be careful in how to combine procedures to arrive at a fair endstate or a fair procedure.

CONCLUSION

In sum, we have sketched the outlines of a new model of stress in organizations. Both procedures to allocate outcomes and the outcomes that are received may be experienced as unjust. Injustice is created by the gap between procedures or outcomes and the norm of procedural and distributive justice respectively. It has also been discussed how a prior unfairness can be redressed by four ways of acting fairly: compensation, justification, mitigation, and appreciation. In general, one may conclude that doing just will have beneficial effects on people's attitudes and behavior and will reduce stress.

ACKNOWLEDGMENT

We thank Russell Cropanzano for his valuable comments on earlier versions of the chapter.

REFERENCES

Adams, J. S. (1965). Inequity in social exchange. In L. Berkowitz (Ed.), *Advances in experimental social psychology* (Vol. 2, pp. 267–299). New York: Academic.

Allegro, J., Kruidenier, H., & Steensma, H. (1991). Aspects of distributive and procedural justice in quality of working life. In H. Steensma & R. Vermunt (Eds.), *Social justice in human relations, Part 2* (pp. 99–116). New York: Plenum.

Bales, R. (1980). *SYMLOG*. New York: Free Press.

Beehr, T. A., & Newman, J. E. (1978). Job stress, employee health and organizational effectiveness: A facet analysis, model and literature review. *Personnel Psychology, 31*, 665–699.

Bies, R. J., & Moag, J. S. (1986). Interactional justice: Communication criteria of fairness. In R. Lewicki, B. Sheppard, & M. Bazerman (Eds.), *Research on negotiations in organizations* (pp. 43–55). Greenwich, CT: JAI.

Brickman, P., Folger, R., Schul, Y., & Goode, E. (1981). Microjustice and macrojustice. In M. J. Lerner & S. C. Lerner (Eds.), *The justice motive in social behavior: Adapting to times of scarcity and change* (pp. 173–202). New York: Plenum.

Bruins, J., & Wilke, H. (1996). Feelings of injustice after violation of succession rules in simulated organizations. *European Journal of Social Psychology, 26*, 149–155.

Buunk, A. P., & de Wolff, C. (1992). Social psychological aspects of stress at work. In P. Drenth, H. Thierry, & C. de Wolff (Eds.), *New handbook work and organization psychology* (pp. 447–496). Houten: Bohn, Stafleu, Van Logham.

Campbell, A., Converse, P. E., & Rogers, W. L. (1976). *The quality of American life*. New York: Sage.

Carver, C. S. (1995). Stress and coping. In A. S. Manstead & M. Hewstone (Eds.), *The Blackwell encyclopedia of social psychology* (pp. 635–639). Oxford: Blackwell.

Cooper, C. L., & Marshall, J. (1976). Occupational sources of stress: A review of the literature relating to coronary heart disease and mental ill health. *Journal of Occupational Psychology, 49*, 11–28.

Cropanzano, R., & Greenberg, J. (1997). Progress in organizational justice: Tunneling through the maze. In C. Cooper & I. Robertson (Eds.), *International review of industrial and organizational psychology* (pp. 317–372). New York: Wiley.

Cropanzano, R., Howes, J. C., Grandey, A. A., & Toth, P. (1997). The relationship of organizational politics and support to work behaviors, attitudes and stress. *Journal of Organizational Behavior, Vol. 18*, 159–189.

Crosby, F. (1976). A model of egoistical relative deprivation. *Psychological Review, 83*, 112.

Dailey, R. C., & Kirk, D. J. (1992). Distributive and procedural justice as antecedents of job dissatisfaction and intent to turnover. *Human Relations, 45*, 305–317.

Edwards, J. R. (1992). A cybernatic theory of stress, coping, and well-being in organizations. *Academy of Management Review, 17*, 238–274.

Foa, U. G., & Foa, E. B. (1974). *Societal structures of the mind.* Springfield, IL: Charles C. Thomas Publishers.

Folger, R. (1996). Distributive and procedural justice: Multi-faceted meanings and interrelations. *Social Justice Research, Vol. 9,* 395–416.

Folger, R. (1987). Reformulating the preconditions of resentment: A referent cognitions model. In J. Masters & W. Smith (Eds.), *Social comparison, social justice, and relative deprivation: Theoretical, empirical, and policy perspectives* (pp. 183–215). Hillsdale, NJ: Lawrence Erlbaum Associates.

Folger, R., & Konovsky, M. (1986). Effects of procedural and distributive justice on reactions to pay raise decisions. *Academy of Management Journal, 32,* 115–130.

Folger, R., Rosenfield, D., Grove, J., & Corkran, L. (1979). Effects of "voice" and peer opinions on responses to inequity. *Journal of Personality and Social Psychology, 37,* 2253–2261.

French, J. R. Jr., Caplan, R. D., & Harrison, R. V. (1982). *The mechanism of job stress and strain.* New York: Wiley.

Fried, Y. (1993). Integrating domains of work stress and industrial relations: Introduction and overview. *Journal of Organizational Behavior, Vol. 14,* 397–399.

Fried, F., Rowland, M. K., & Ferris, G. R. (1984). The physiological measurement of work stress: A critique. *Personnel Psychology, 37,* 583–615.

Friedman, M., & Rosenman, R. H. (1974). *Type-A behavior and your heart.* New York: Knopf.

Gupta, N., & Beehr, P. A. (1979). Job stress and employee behaviors. *Organizational Behavior and Human Performance, 23,* 373–387.

Hastie, R., & Park, B. (1986). The relationship between memory and judgment depends on whether the judgment task is memory based or online. *Psychological Review, 93,* 258–268.

Heaney, C. A., Israel, B. A., Schurman, S. J., Baker, E. A., House, J. S., & Hugentobler, M. (1993). Industrial relations, work-site stress reduction, and employee well-being: A participatory action research investigation. *Journal of Organizational behavior, Vol. 14,* 495–510.

Heatherton, T. F., & Polivy, J. (1991). Development and validation of a scale measuring state self-esteem. *Journal of Personality and Social Psychology, 60,* 895–910.

Holmes, T. H., & Rahe, R. H. (1967). The social readjustment rating scale. *Journal of Psychomatic Research, 11,* 213–218.

Jones, F., & Fletcher, B. (1996). Taking work home: A study of daily fluctuations in work stressors, effects on mood and impacts on marital partners. *Journal of Occupational and Organizational Psychology, 69,* 89–106.

Kahn, R. L., Wolfe, D. M., Quinn, R. P., Snoeck, J. D., & Rosenthal, R. A. (1964). *Organizational stress: Studies in role conflict and ambiguity.* Chichester: Wiley.

Kahneman, D., & Tversky, A. (1982). Availability and the simulation heuristic. In D. Kahneman, P. Slovic, & A. Tversky (Eds.), *Judgment under uncertainty: Heuristics and biases* (pp. 201–208). New York: Cambridge University Press.

Katz, D., & Kahn, R. L. (1966). *The social psychology of organizations.* New York: Wiley.

Kelloway, E. K., Barling, J., & Shah, A. (1993). Industrial relations stress and job satisfaction: Concurrent effects and mediation. *Journal of Organizational Behavior, Vol. 14,* 447–457.

Koeske, G. F., Kirk, S. A., & Koeske, R. D. (1993). Coping with job stress: Which strategies work best? *Journal of Occupational and Organizational Psychology, 66,* 319–335.

Konovsky, M. A., & Pugh, S. D. (1994). Citizenship behavior and social exchange. *Academy of Management Journal, 37,* 656–669.

Koper, G., Van Knippenberg, D., Bouhuys, F., Vermunt, R., & Wilke, H. (1993). Procedural Fairness and Self-esteem. *European Journal of Social Psychology, 26,* 313–325.

Lazarus, R. S. (1966). *Psychological stress and the coping process.* New York: McGraw-Hill.

Lazarus, R. S., & Folkman, S. (1984). *Stress, appraisal and coping.* New York: Springer.

Lerner, M. J. (1980). *The belief in a just world: A fundamental delusion.* New York: Plenum.

Lerner, M. J. (1991). Integrating societal and psychological rules. The basic task of each social actor and a fundamental problem for the social sciences. In R. Vermunt & H. Steensma (Eds.), *Social justice in human relations, Part 1* (pp. 13–32). New York: Plenum.

Lerner, M. J., & Whitehead, L. A. (1980). Procedural justice viewed in the context of justice motive theory. In G. Mikula (Ed.), *Justice and social interaction: Experimental and theoretical contributions from psychological research* (pp. 219–256). Bern: Huber.

Leventhal, G. S. (1980). What should be done with equity theory? New approaches to the fairness in social relationships. In K. Gergen, M. Greenberg & R. Willis (Eds.), *Social exchange theory* (pp. 27–55). New York: Plenum.

Lind, E. A., & Tyler, T. R. (1988). *The social psychology of procedural justice*. New York: Plenum.

Lind, E. A., Kanfer, R., & Earley, P. C. (1990). Voice, control, and procedural justice: Instrumental and non-instrumental concerns in fairness judgments. *Journal of Personality and Social Psychology, 59*, 952–959.

Locke, E. A. (1976). The nature and causes of job satisfaction. In M. D. Dunnette (Ed.), *Handbook of industrial and organizational psychology* (pp. 1297–1349). Chicago: Rand.

Marcelissen, F. H. G. (1987). *Initiators in the stress process*. Leiden: NIPG/TNO

McGrath, J. E. (1976). Stress and behavior in organizations. In M. Dunnette (Ed.), *Handbook of industrial and organizational psychology*. Chicago: Rand McNally.

Messick, D., & Cook, K. (Eds.). (1983). *Equity theory: Psychological and sociological perspectives*. New York: Preager.

Michalos, A. C. (1985). Multiple discrepancies theory (MDT). *Social Indicators Research, 16*, 347–413.

Modde, J., Vermunt, R., & Wiegman, O. (1995). Procedural justice and norm-violating behavior. In N. Ellemers, N. de Vries, R. Vonk (Red.). *Fundamentele Sociale Psychologie, 9*, 107–117.

Organ, D. W., & Moorman, R. H. (1993). Fairness and organizational citizenship behavior: What are the connections? *Social Justice Research, 6*, 5–18.

Rutte, C. G., & Messick, D. M. (1995). An integrated model of perceived unfairness in organizations. *Social Justice Research, 8*, 239–262.

Shapiro, D. L., Buttner, E. H., & Barry, B. (1994). Explanations for rejection of decisions: What factors enhance their perceived adequacy and moderate interventions of justice perceptions? *Organizational Behavior and Human Decision Processes, 58*, 346–368.

Shirom, A. (1989). Burnout in work organizations. In C. L. Cooper & I. Robertson (Eds.), *International Review of Industrial and Organizational Psychology* (pp. 26–48). Chicester: Wiley.

Selye, H. (1978). *Stress*. Utrecht: Het Spectrum.

Steensma, H., Roes, F., Wippler, R., & Zoete, F. (1981). Equity repair by male and female subjects after induction of inequity by contribution and outcome manipulation. *Gedrag, 9*, 143–159.

Steensma, H., Vermunt, R., & Allegro, J. (1997). *Toward a new model of social justice to explain reactions to organizational restructuring*. Paper, VIth Biennial Meeting International Network for Social Justice Research, Potsdam, Germany.

Thoits, P. A. (1995). Stress, coping and social support: Where are we? What next? *Journal of Health and Social Behavior*, 53–79.

Tomaka, J., & Blascovich, J. (1994). Effects of justice beliefs on cognitive appraisal of and subjective, physiological and behavioral responses to potential stress. *Journal of Personality and Social Psychology, 67*, 732–740.

Törnblom, K .Y., & Vermunt, R. (1999). An integrative perspective on social justice: Distributive and procedural fairness evaluations of positive and negative outcome allocations. *Social Justice Research, 12*, 39–64.

Tornow, W. W. (1971). The development and application of an input–outcome moderator test on the perception and reduction of inequality. *Organizational Behavior and Human Performance, 6*, 614–638.

Tyler, T. R. (1991). Using procedures to justify outcomes: Testing the viability of a procedural strategy for managing conflict and allocating resources in work organizations. *Basic and Applied Social Psychology, 12*, 259–279.

Tyler, T. R. (1994). Psychological models of the justice motive: Antecedents of distributive and procedural justice. *Journal of Personality and Social Psychology, 67*, 850–863.

Tyler, T. R., & Lind, E. A. (1992). A relational model of authority in groups. In M. Zanna (Ed.), *Advances in experimental social psychology* (Vol. 25, pp. 115–191). San Diego, CA: Academic.

Van den Bos, K., Vermunt, R., & Wilke, H. A. M. (1997). The relationship between procedural and distributive justice: What is fair depends more on what comes first than on what comes next. *Journal of Personality and Social Psychology, 72,* 95–104.

Van Knippenberg, B., Blaauw, E., Vermunt, R., & Van Knippenberg, D. (1997). Influence tactics and procedural justice. *Toegepaste Social Psychologie, 10* (pp. 65–74). Tilburg: University Press.

Vermunt, R., Blaauw, E., & Lind, E. A. (1998). Fairness evaluations of encounters with police officers and correctional officers. *Journal of Applied Social Psychology, 29*(12), 1107–1124.

Vermunt, R., & Shulman, S. (1996). Responding to an unfair procedure. *Nederlands Tijdschrift voor de Psychologie, 51,* 35–46.

Vermunt, R., Spaans, E., & Zorge, F. (1989). Satisfaction, happiness and well-being of Dutch students. *Social Indicators Research, 21,* 1–33.

Vermunt, R., & Steensma, H. (1996). Leadership and Justice. In R. Van der Vlist & H. Steensma (Eds.). *Leadership in organizations* (pp. 157–174). Heerlen: Open Universiteit.

Vermunt, R., Wit, A., Van den Bos, K., & Lind, E. A. (1996). The effects of unfair procedure on negative affect and protest. *Social Justice Research, 9,* 109–120.

Winnubst, J. A. M. (Ed.) (1995). *Work, life cycle, and health.* Heerlen: Open Universiteit

Zohar, D. (1995). The justice perspective of job stress. *Journal of Organizational Behavior, 16,* 487–495.

The Psychology of Procedural and Distributive Justice Viewed From the Perspective of Fairness Heuristic Theory

Kees van den Bos
Leiden University

E. Allan Lind
Duke University

Henk A. M. Wilke
Leiden University

Justice is a key issue for understanding organizational behavior (Cropanzano & Folger, 1989, 1991; Cropanzano & Greenberg, 1997; Folger & Konovsky, 1989). The study of organizational justice has focused on at least two major issues: How people respond to the fairness of the outcomes they receive (e.g., whether someone gets a pay raise, whether a person is laid off), and how people react to the fairness of the ways in which these outcomes are obtained (e.g., whether people are allowed an opportunity to voice their opinion about important decisions, whether someone is treated politely and with respect). Although concerns about distributive justice are crucial in organizations and were the first to draw the attention of organizational scientists they constitute only a part of the complete issue of organizational justice. People's perceptions of procedural fairness are also very important in organizations.

In fact, survey studies conducted with respondents involved in organizations (e.g., Folger & Konovsky, 1989) and other situations (e.g., Lind, Kulik, Ambrose, & De Vera Park, 1993; Tyler & Caine, 1981, Studies 2 and 4; Tyler & Folger, 1980; Tyler, Rasinski, & McGraw, 1985) have shown that variables related to procedural justice explain more variance in fairness judgments (and other judgments) than variables related to distributive justice. These findings led some *procedural* justice researchers to conclude that the cognitive process leading to the formation of judgments may be more strongly affected by procedures than by outcomes (see, e.g., Lind & Tyler, 1988, Tyler & Lind, 1992). As a result, procedural justice research nowadays tends to neglect the importance of outcome fairness and to focus only on one aspect of the psychological process leading to fairness and other judgments: procedures. *Distributive* justice researchers, on the other hand, also tend to focus on one aspect of the fairness judgment process: outcomes. Some researchers have suggested that outcomes may be more important for people's fairness judgments than procedures (e.g., Lerner & Whitehead, 1980; Rutte & Messick, 1995). Thus, both procedural and distributive justice research tends to focus on one aspect of the fairness judgment process, at the expense of other important concepts. As several authors have pointed out, it is now time to integrate the procedural and distributive justice domains (Brockner & Wiesenfeld, 1996; Cropanzano & Folger, 1991; Greenberg, 1990; Sweeney & McFarlin, 1993; Van den Bos, Lind, Vermunt, & Wilke, 1997; Van den Bos, Vermunt, & Wilke, 1997).

The primary aim of this chapter is to try to integrate the procedural and distributive justice domains by providing a new perspective on the psychology of procedural and distributive justice. To achieve this purpose we present, for the first time, an overview of fairness heuristic theory (Lind, 1992, 1995a, 1995b, 1998; Lind et al., 1993; Van den Bos, 1996; Van den Bos, Lind, et al., 1997; Van den Bos, Vermunt, & Wilke, 1997). Fairness heuristic theory has been explicitly designed to provide a deeper understanding of procedural and distributive justice issues, and we hope that—together with other important developments (e.g., Brockner & Wiesenfeld, 1996; Cropanzano & Ambrose, 1997; Cropanzano & Folger, 1991; Folger, 1986, 1996; Greenberg, 1990; Lind & Tyler, 1988; Sweeney & McFarlin, 1993; Tyler & Lind, 1992)—the theory might provide a point of departure for integrating the two research domains. This analysis of the psychology of procedural and distributive justice yields previously unidentified and unexplored explanations of established research findings.

In this chapter, it is argued that one of the most important contributions of fairness heuristic theory is that it makes clear that in order to explain how people form fairness judgments, it must be known what information is (vs. is not) available to people. It is shown that this rather simple point can have far-reaching implications for the understanding of important issues in the procedural and distributive justice domain. For illustration purposes, two issues are highlighted in this chapter. The first issue deals with one of the most striking discoveries in research on social justice: the finding that perceived procedural fairness positively affects how people react to outcomes. On the basis of fairness heuristic theory an explanation is provided of this fair process effect. The second issue is related but somewhat different from the first issue and focuses on the question whether people rely more on procedures or outcomes to arrive at overall impressions of fairness. First, however, we will present an overview of fairness heuristic theory because this theory is central in our psychology of procedural and distributive justice.

FAIRNESS HEURISTIC THEORY

Fairness heuristic theory is based on the group-value model (Lind & Tyler, 1988) and relational model (Tyler & Lind, 1992) accounts of procedural justice. The theory specifies three cognitive phases in which the fairness concept may play an important role. It is hypothesized that in each phase one issue serves as the main focus of attention. The *first phase* we distinguish pertains to the situation before a person has started forming fairness judgments, and is labeled the *preformation phase*. The question that is pertinent in this phase is whether or not a person starts forming fairness judgments. More generally, the first issue deals with why and when a person cares about fairness. In the *second phase*, fairness judgments are formed. This phase is labeled the *formation phase* and becomes relevant after the first question (whether a person starts forming fairness judgments) has been answered in the affirmative. The question that is important in the second phase is how fairness judgments are formed. The *third phase* may be denoted as the *postformation phase*. The question that is posed in this phase is relevant once the person has constructed fairness judgments (i.e., after the second phase has been finished) and asks how the person uses fairness judgments in his or her reactions to subsequent events and subsequent fairness information (i.e., events that happen after the person has finished the fairness judgment process and information that becomes available after the person has formed [initial] fairness judgments). In fairness heuristic theory's three-phase, three-issue model, it is assumed that information received in the third phase may trigger another round of forming fairness judgments (depending on the person's motivation and capability of doing so).

Thus, fairness heuristic theory asks three questions: Why and when are fairness judgments formed?; how are fairness judgments formed?; how are fairness judgments used? Although it should be noted from the start that the processes involved in our three-phase, three-issue approach are interrelated, we believe that they are distinct enough to justify our claim that they can be separated for clarity of presentation and for theoretical development. For illustration purposes, we discuss some recent findings that, more or less, are relevant to each of the three phases. Most of the studies discussed in this chapter apply to more than one of the stages and one of the issues, but the studies are presented where we think they are most relevant. The studies are reviewed in a short, condensed way; for details of a particular study, refer to the write-up of that study.

PHASE 1: WHY AND WHEN DO PEOPLE FORM FAIRNESS JUDGMENTS?

With regard to the question why and when fairness is important, the theory recognizes that in several situations fairness is a salient issue. More specifically, fairness heuristic theory proposes that people especially need fairness judgments when they are concerned about potential problems associated with social interdependence and socially based identity processes—problems that are related to what Lind (1995a) referred to as the fundamental social dilemma. Basically, the fundamental social dilemma is concerned with the question of whether one can trust others not to exploit or exclude one from important relationships and groups (cf. Huo, Smith, Tyler, & Lind, 1996; Lind & Tyler, 1988; Smith, Tyler, Huo, Ortiz, & Lind, 1998; Tyler & Lind, 1992). Fairness heuristic theory argues that people frequently start looking for fairness information to answer this question.

An important subgroup of social relations addressed by this first element are authority processes. That is, an important condition in which fairness becomes important is suggested by fairness heuristic theory's assumption that, because ceding authority to another person raises the possibility of exploitation and exclusion, people frequently feel uneasy about their relationship with authorities. Therefore, the theory argues, people look to the fairness of authorities to help them assess the security of their position in a group, organization, or society. In other words, the theory proposes that the most common approach to the resolution of the uncertainty that is caused by having to cede authority, is to refer to impressions of fairness, and therefore this is one reason why people start forming fairness judgments. This suggests one way in which fairness may act as a heuristic: Fairness information is used as a heuristic substitute to decide whether or not an authority can be trusted.

Recently, we collected some data that corroborates this line of reasoning (Van den Bos, Wilke, & Lind, 1998): The aforementioned line of thought suggests that fairness information should become more important for people when they are not sure about whether they can trust an authority. To investigate this issue we varied whether participants knew that they could trust an authority (Trust Explicit Positive condition), whether they knew that they could not trust the authority (Trust Explicit Negative condition), or—as a control condition—whether they had not received any information about whether or not they could trust the authority (Trust Information Absent condition). This was followed, as an example of a fair versus unfair procedure manipulation, by varying whether or not participants were allowed an opportunity to voice their opinion (Voice vs. No Voice conditions). Main dependent variables in the two studies—one scenario study and one real, traditional experiment—that we conducted were: how satisfied participants were with their outcome and how fair participants judged their outcome. In addition, dependent variables in the experimental study included how respectful participants felt they were treated by the supervisor, and whether participants felt the supervisor judged them to be a valued group member. As predicted by fairness heuristic theory, results showed that people's reactions were strongly affected by procedural fairness information when they did not know whether the authority could be trusted, but that they did not use procedural fairness information when they had been explicitly informed that the authority could or could not been trusted.

The results of Van den Bos, Wilke, and Lind (1998) suggest that people may resolve the question how one can trust others not to exploit them or not to exclude them from important relationships by starting to form fairness judgments—as heuristic substitutes—when direct information about authority's trustworthiness is missing. More generally, these findings suggest that one answer to the question *why* people care about justice is that people do so because they want to find out whether they can trust others not to exploit or exclude them from important relationships and groups. The findings imply that an answer to the question *when* people care about justice may be that people are especially in need of fairness information when they do not have direct, explicit information regarding whether they can trust others.

PHASE 2: HOW DO PEOPLE FORM FAIRNESS JUDGMENTS?

When people start forming fairness judgments, the question becomes how do they do this? More specifically, fairness heuristic theory tries to answer what information do people use in this cognitive process? Fairness heuristic theory proposes that the central issue is whether the person in question believes he or she has received generally fair treatment by the authority or authorities, with little distinction being made between fairness in terms of procedures and fairness in terms of outcomes. Nonetheless—in accordance with the aforementioned survey findings on the relative importance of procedural and distributive justice—the theory predicts that some aspects of procedural justice judgments tend to make procedures more powerful than outcomes in determining where one believes oneself to be on the fairness continuum (Van den Bos, 1996; Van den Bos, Lind et al., 1997).

One factor giving procedural information an advantage in determining fairness judgments has to do with the special capacity of procedures to carry easily interpretable information about inclusion. Following the group-value model of procedural justice (Lind & Tyler, 1988), fairness heuristic theory argues that much of what people mean when they say they are being treated fairly involves feelings of inclusion and standing in the group, organization, or society in question. Procedures can enhance feelings of inclusion by guaranteeing voice or access to decision makers, and they can enhance feelings of inclusion by carrying messages of value, through obviously dignified process or expressions of respect. In both instances it is easy to interpret the procedure as indicating that one is a valued member of the group. Fairness heuristic theory recognizes that outcomes and distributions can carry information about inclusion or exclusion, but the theory suggests that this information is usually not as easily interpreted as is the information contained in procedures (an issue that is illustrated in the studies that are discussed in later sections of this chapter).

According to fairness heuristic theory, information about inclusion or exclusion in turn predisposes the person in question to be more accepting or rejecting, respectively, of the outcomes received from the social unit. This prediction has not been directly tested, but it is supported indirectly by a recent study reported by Huo et al. (1996): A survey was conducted among respondents from four ethnically based work unions at a public-sector organization who had a conflict with their work supervisor. Results indicated that process-linked perceptions have a greater impact on distributive fairness judgments in intragroup settings, where inclusion is presumably a more potent consideration, than in intergroup settings.

Another recent study, conducted by Smith et al. (1998), also provides supportive evidence for this element of the theory: On the basis of the group-value model (Lind & Tyler, 1988), Smith et al. reason that people use their treatment by authorities to infer whether they are valued members of their group. Furthermore, these authors argued that because authorities of one's own group represent an important reference group, these ingroup authorities will have a stronger impact on group members than outgroup authorities. Two experiments and two correlational studies provide supportive evidence for this line of reasoning: The results suggest that people judge the fairness of authority's procedures to be more important when the authority is from an ingroup than from an outgroup. These findings support fairness heuristic theory's claim that fairness—and especially, procedural fairness—is important because it communicates to people that they are valued and respected members of their group.

PHASE 3: HOW DO PEOPLE USE FAIRNESS JUDGMENTS?

The third and final question fairness heuristic theory poses predominantly pertains to the situation in which fairness judgments have been formed. This question asks how people use fairness. Fairness heuristic theory argues that once fairness judgments have been formed, people use these judgments to guide them as they evaluate and decide how to react to the outcomes and procedures they encounter and the policies, requests, and demands they receive from authorities. The theory also argues that people use fairness judgments to assess how to respond to other people, including for instance equal power others. If other persons' behavior seems to be fair, then people react favorably and acquiesce to demands or requests of those persons with little consideration of material outcomes. However, if a person is judged to be unfair, then people react largely in terms of the immediate material costs and benefits associated with various courses of action. This is another way in which fairness may act as a heuristic substitute: Once an individual has established a fairness judgment—whether it is based on procedure or outcome fairness—perceived fairness serves as a heuristic that guides the interpretation of subsequent events.

A study by Lind et al. (1993) is relevant for this element of fairness heuristic theory. Respondents in the Lind et al. studies were corporate and individual litigants in federal tort and contract actions that were subjected to court-ordered arbitration. Lind et al. examined the link between disputants' judgments of the fairness of a mediation procedure in U.S. federal courts and the disputants' acceptance of proposed case resolutions produced by the resolution procedure. The results across nine different federal courts indicated that people tended to accept the proposed resolution if they felt that their case had been fairly heard and that they themselves had been fairly treated in the course of the mediation. Remarkably, justice judgments were three to six times more powerful than were economic considerations in determining whether a proposed resolution was accepted. Furthermore, this effect was found whether the case involved corporate or individual litigants, and it was seen across a variety of case types. Moreover, the effect occurred whether the amount in dispute was relatively modest or even involved thousands of U.S. dollars (the amounts of money in the Lind et al. studies ranged up to $800,000).

THE FAIR PROCESS EFFECT

The fairness heuristic's line of reasoning is illustrated here by discussing a recent empirical paper by Van den Bos, Lind, et al. (1997). This study predominantly pertains to the second cognitive phase, in which people are forming fairness judgments, and asks what information is available to people in this phase. The paper focuses on the fair process effect (i.e., the finding that perceived procedural fairness positively affects how people react to their outcome). To try to explain this effect, Van den Bos, Lind, et al. argued that we have to carefully assess what information is (vs. is not) available to people when they try to judge whether their outcome is fair. A starting point for classifying information conditions was the idea that distributive justice theories (e.g., equity theory and relative deprivation theory) all emphasize the importance of social comparison information in the process of evaluating the fairness of outcomes (Messick & Sentis, 1983).

This suggested that, in order to judge whether an outcome is fair, people have to know what outcomes comparison others have received. However, do people always know the outcomes of others? Van den Bos, Lind, et al. (1997) argued that they frequently do not. For example, in everyday life we often do not know the salaries of the people with whom we work, and even if we do, we may well not have a good idea of their contributions. Thus, we argued that social comparison information about outcomes often is not available to people. We therefore proposed that in everyday life the issue of how people form outcome judgments is more complicated than is suggested by distributive justice theories.

Furthermore, we reasoned that when information about outcomes of others is not available, people will start using information that is available. But what information is available? We proposed that procedure information frequently is present. This suggested that in many situations people may turn to the fairness of the procedure to assess how to react to their outcome. In other words, people may use procedural fairness as a heuristic substitute to determine how fair they judge their outcome. Therefore, in situations where a person only knows his or her own outcome (and is not informed about the outcome of another person), we predicted a fair process effect: The person will react more positively toward his or her outcome following a fair procedure than following an unfair procedure.

However, we also proposed that when a person does have information about the outcome of a comparable other person, he or she will use this social comparison information to assess how to react to his or her outcome. Therefore, we expected less strong fair process effects in situations where a person does know what the referent other receives. In other words, when people do have social comparison information about outcomes, we predicted that there would be less need for procedural fairness to serve as a heuristic substitute in the outcome judgment process.

The results of two studies, one scenario study and one traditional experimental study, corroborated our line of reasoning. In this chapter, only the last experiment is discussed. In this study, participants were invited to the laboratory to participate in a study on how people perform tasks. In the first part of the instructions, participants were informed that they participated in the experiment with another person, referred to as Other. Participants were informed that, after all participants were run, a lottery would be held among all participants. The winner of this lottery would receive 100 Dutch guilders (approximately 60 U.S. dollars). Participants were told that a total of 200 lottery tickets would be divided among all participants. It was also communicated to the participants that after the work round the experimenter would divide some lottery tickets between them and Other. The task was then explained to the participants. After this, participants practiced the tasks for 2 minutes, after which they worked on the tasks for 10 minutes. After the work round had ended, participants were told how many tasks they had completed in the work round, and—to ensure that participants compared themselves to Other—it was communicated to the participant that Other had completed an equivalent number of tasks.

This was followed by our experimental manipulations. First, the Procedure that participants received was manipulated. In the Voice condition, the experimenter allegedly asked participants to type in their opinion about the percentage tickets that they should receive relative to Other. Participants in the No Voice condition were informed that they would not be asked to type their opinion about the percentage tickets that they should receive relative to Other. It was then communicated to the participants that they received 3 lottery tickets. This was followed by the manipulation of Outcome Other Participant. In the Other Better condition, the participant was informed that Other received 5 tickets. In the Other Worse condition, participants were informed that Other received 1 ticket. In the Other Equal condition, participants were told that Other received 3 tickets. In the Other Unknown condition, participants were not told anything about the number of tickets Other received. After this, participants were asked how fair they considered the 3 lottery tickets that they received, how satisfied they were with the 3 lottery tickets that they received, how fair they considered the procedure used to assess the number of tickets that they received, and how satisfied they were with the procedure used to assess the number of tickets that they received.

As expected, participants' *procedural* judgments (procedural fairness and satisfaction) were not affected by the manipulation of Outcome (Outcome Other Better, Worse, Equal, or Unknown), and only showed a main effect of Procedure: Participants judged the procedure as more fair and were more satisfied with the procedure following an opportunity to voice their opinion than not following a voice opportunity.

The results of participants' *outcome* judgments (outcome fairness and satisfaction) are presented in Table 3.1. As hypothesized, the results show that participants who did not know the outcome of the other participant judged their outcome as more fair and as more satisfying when they had received an opportunity to voice their opinion than when they had not received such an opportunity (the former procedure having been identified as more fair). Furthermore, the results revealed that in the conditions in which participants knew the outcome of the other participant, outcome judgments did not differ as a function of whether participants were or were not allowed a voice.

These findings strongly support fairness heuristic theory's line of reasoning: When people do not have information about outcomes of others they indeed use procedural fairness as heuristic substitutes to assess how to react to their outcome (yielding fair process effects on people's outcome judgments), but that people rely less on procedure information when they are informed about the outcome of another person (resulting in absent fair process effects). More generally, the findings point out that it makes sense to carefully assess what information is available to people when they are trying to form fairness and other judgments. The results of Van den Bos, Lind, et al. (1997; cf. Van den Bos, Wilke, Lind, & Vermunt, 1998) suggest that classifying information conditions is an important precondition before we can understand the psychology of the fair process effect.

PROCEDURAL AND DISTRIBUTIVE JUSTICE

Another study discussed in this chapter was conducted by Van den Bos, Vermunt, and Wilke (1997). This study pertains to the cognitive phase in which people form fairness judgments but also—although to a lesser extent—to the phase in which (initial) fairness judgments have been formed and people react to subsequent information. The starting point for the Van den Bos, Vermunt, and Wilke study was the aforementioned survey findings that showed that procedural justice factors explain more variance in fairness judgments than distributive justice factors. In order to explain these survey findings, Van den Bos, Vermunt, and Wilke set out to explore under what information conditions people form judgments about procedural and distributive justice. Two conditions in this study were established.

TABLE 3.1

Fairness Heuristic Theory: Mean Outcome Judgments in Van den Bos, Lind, Vermunt, and Wilke (1997, Experiment 2)

Dependent Variable	Procedure	Outcome of Other Participant			
		Unknown	Better	Worse	Equal
Outcome fairness	Voice	4.7_b	2.1_d	1.8_d	6.2_a
	No Voice	3.4_b	2.4_d	2.0_d	6.1_a
Outcome satisfaction	Voice	$5.1_{b,c}$	2.3_e	$4.4_{c,d}$	6.1_a
	No Voice	3.5_d	2.8_e	5.0_c	$6.0_{a,b}$

Note.   From "How do I judge my outcome when I do not know the outcome of others?: The psychology of the fair process effect" by K. van den Bos, E. A. Lind, R. Vermunt, and H. A. M. Wilke, 1997, *Journal of Personality and Social Psychology, 72*, p. 1041. Copyright 1997 by the American Psychological Association.

Entries are means on 7-point Likert-type scales; higher values indicate more positive ratings of the dependent variable in question. For each dependent variable, means with no subscripts in common differ significantly, as indicated by a Least-Significant Difference test for multiple comparisons between means ($p < .05$).

An important and typical condition under which procedural and distributive fairness judgments are formed is that in which people receive procedure information before they receive outcome information. For instance, the manner in which a court trial is conducted is typically known before the verdict becomes apparent. A second type of situation, however, is also possible: People may become informed about the outcome before they receive information about the procedure that was followed. For example, a student can take a multiple choice test. Two weeks later he or she is informed that he or she has failed to pass the test, and only 2 months after this he or she receives information that the professor graded only 10 of the 40 multiple choice items of his or her test.

On the basis of a rather elaborate literature overview, Van den Bos, Vermunt, and Wilke (1997) argued that in the condition in which procedure information is available before outcome information becomes available, procedure information will affect people's judgments more strongly than in the condition in which people receive procedure information after having received outcome information. Furthermore, we reasoned that outcome information would affect people's judgments more strongly in the last than in the first condition. In short, the information that comes first exerts a stronger influence on judgments than information that comes second. To test these predictions, two studies were conducted; one scenario study and one traditional experiment. Again, in this chapter only the last experiment is discussed. In this experiment, participants were invited to the laboratory to participate in a study on how people make estimations. Participants were instructed that they would perform an estimation test consisting of 10 estimation items. Furthermore, participants were informed that at the end of the experiment they would receive a bonus of 5 Dutch guilders if they succeeded in passing the estimation test. After participants had completed the estimation test, the manipulations were induced.

In the condition where participants were informed about the procedure before they received information about the outcome, participants first received information about the procedure that was used to assess the outcome of the estimation test: In the Accurate Procedure condition, the participants were told that the experimenter had graded all 10 estimation items to assess the outcome of the estimation test, and in the Inaccurate Procedure condition, participants were informed that the experimenter had graded 1 of the 10 estimation items. After this, these participants were informed about the outcome of the estimation test: In the Favorable Outcome condition, the experimenter informed the participants that they had succeeded in passing the estimation test. In the Unfavorable Outcome condition, participants were informed that they had not succeeded in passing the estimation test.

In the condition where participants were informed about the outcome before they received information about the procedure, participants first received information about the outcome of the estimation test: In the Favorable Outcome condition, the experimenter informed the participants that they had succeeded in passing the estimation test. In the Unfavorable Outcome condition, participants were informed that they had not succeeded in passing the estimation test. After this, these participants were informed about the procedure used to assess the outcome of the estimation test: In the Accurate Procedure condition, participants were informed that the experimenter had graded all 10 estimation items. In the Inaccurate Procedure condition, participants were informed that the experimenter had graded 1 of the 10 estimation items.

After this, participants were asked how fair they considered the procedure used to assess the outcome of the estimation test, how fair they considered the outcome of the estimation test, and how satisfied they were. Furthermore, to measure intention to protest, participants were asked to what extent they were willing to criticize the situation, to what extent they were willing to protest against the situation, and to what extent they would be willing to participate in the study for a second time (reverse coded). These three items were averaged to form a reliable index of protest intention.

The main results of the experiment are presented in Table 3.2. The findings of Van den Bos, Vermunt, and Wilke (1997) strongly supported our predictions: Participants' judgments were more strongly affected by the procedure manipulation when procedure was available first than when it was available second, and the outcome manipulation exerted stronger effects on participants' judgments when outcome was presented first than when it was presented second. These results suggest that an important factor giving procedural information an advantage in determining fairness judgments has to do with the timing of exposure to procedure versus outcome information. Fairness heuristic theory notes that people generally encounter process information prior to outcome information. According to the theory, people generate fairness judgments very quickly—because they need the fairness judgments to guide their behavior—and for this reason early information has greater impact than later information. The quickly formed fairness judgments can be changed by later information, but not as easily as is the case for early information. The theory argues that because information about procedures is usually available early and outcome information is often not available until later, people usually form their first fairness judgments largely on the basis of the procedural information. These early fairness judgments provide anchors that are at most only adjusted by later information, including later outcome information.

The Van den Bos, Vermunt, and Wilke (1997) findings suggest, as predicted by fairness heuristic theory, that the first information, whether procedural or distributive, set the stage for the interpretation of later fairness information. Furthermore, these results even may have revealed some new insights about the relative importance of procedural and distributive justice. It should be noted that it is always difficult, of course, to calibrate two or more experimental manipulations (e.g., variations in procedures and outcomes) in some way to make them comparable. Furthermore, it should be emphasized explicitly that, before conducting the Van den Bos, Vermunt, and Wilke experiments, we took great care and went

TABLE 3.2

Fairness Heuristic Theory: Mean Judgments in Van den Bos, Vermunt, and Wilke (1997, Experiment 2)

		Order			
		Procedure Before Outcome		Outcome Before Procedure	
Dependent Variable	Outcome	Accurate	Inaccurate	Accurate	Inaccurate
Procedural fairness	Favorable	6.5_a	2.5_c	6.5_a	6.4_a
	Unfavorable	6.5_a	1.5_d	3.8_b	$2.1_{c,d}$
Outcome fairness	Favorable	5.1_a	3.5_b	5.2_a	5.2_a
	Unfavorable	5.2_a	1.6_d	3.8_b	2.6_c
Satisfaction	Favorable	5.9_a	3.5_b	5.8_a	5.7_a
	Unfavorable	5.7_a	1.9_c	3.4_b	2.0_c
Protest intention	Favorable	2.0_a	3.2_b	3.0_b	3.1_b
	Unfavorable	2.0_a	4.4_c	4.3_c	5.8_d

Note. From "Procedural and distributive justice: What is fair depends more on what comes first than on what comes next" by K. van den Bos, R. Vermunt, and H. A. M. Wilke, 1997, *Journal of Personality and Social Psychology, 72*, p. 101. Copyright 1997 by the American Psychological Association.

Entries are means on 7-point Likert-type scales; higher values indicate more positive ratings of the dependent variable in question. For each dependent variable, means with no subscript in common differ significantly, as indicated by a Least-Significant Difference test for multiple comparisons between means ($p < .05$).

through considerable pilot testing in order to ensure that the procedure and out-come manipulations would be comparable to each other.

This said, however, the findings of Van den Bos, Vermunt, and Wilke (1997) suggest that procedural fairness may be more important than distributive fairness when people are informed about procedures before they are informed about out-comes, whereas distributive fairness may exert stronger effects on people's judg-ments when they are informed about outcomes before they are informed about procedures. Moreover, this suggests (Van den Bos, 1996; Van den Bos, Vermunt, & Wilke, 1997) that frames of reference that are available at an early moment in time will affect the fairness judgment process more strongly than frames that be-come available at a later moment in time (see also Van den Bos, Vermunt, & Wilke, 1996).

GENERAL DISCUSSION

Presented here is a general overview of fairness heuristic theory and some recent studies that we have conducted to test elements of fairness heuristic theory's line of reasoning. We are still developing and revising our framework, but we have tried to describe and discuss our current thoughts as clearly as possible in the hope that this will stimulate future research to integrate the domains of procedural and distributive justice. An important aspect of fairness heuristic theory's per-spective on the psychology of procedural and distributive justice is that it de-mands that researchers specify what information is known to people and what in-formation is not (yet) available or is difficult to interpret. For instance, equity theory has developed an intriguing and stimulating model of how people assess outcome fairness in organizations and other social situations (for overviews, see, e.g., Adams, 1965; Greenberg, 1982; Walster, Walster, & Berscheid, 1978). How-ever, fairness heuristic theory points out that frequently everyday life does not provide us with enough information to act according to equity's model of the out-come judgment process (Van den Bos, Lind, et al., 1997). Furthermore, fairness heuristic theory argues that under incomplete or insufficient information condi-tions, people process information heuristically; for example, they use other infor-mation (e.g., procedural fairness) to substitute for information that would be most directly relevant but that actually is missing. This suggests that fairness heuristic theory offers a more contextual account of the justice judgment process than do previous theories. Taking such a descriptive stand may greatly enhance our un-derstanding of the exciting issues of the procedural and distributive justice do-mains.

The fairness heuristic theory studies may also be interesting because some findings reveal that procedural and outcome information can be used inter-changeably: The results of Van den Bos, Vermunt, and Wilke (1997) suggest that procedure information will substitute for outcome information and outcome information will substitute for procedure information, depending on whatever information is available first (see Table 3.2). However, in other fairness heuristic theory studies we have found that people clearly distinguish procedure from outcome issues: In Van den Bos, Lind, et al. (1997, Experiment 2) and Van den Bos, Wilke, et al. (1998, Experiment 2) we have found that people's outcome judgments clearly were affected by our manipulations of outcome information (although in these studies the outcome manipulations took place after the procedure manipulations had been induced; see Table 3.1, for mean outcome judgments in Van den Bos, Lind, et al., 1997, Experiment 2) but that participants' procedure judgments were not affected by variations in outcome information: In both studies, independent of the outcome manipulations, participants' procedural fairness and satisfaction judgments were more positive following an opportunity to voice their opinion than not following such an opportunity. These differential effects on participants' procedure and outcome judgments suggest that participants made a distinction between procedural and distributive justice issues.

A similar conclusion can be drawn on the basis of research by Greenberg (1986) and by Sheppard and Lewicki (1987). These authors asked respondents to describe fair and unfair events that had occurred in their lives. The findings of their studies revealed that—even when assessed with such an unconstrained measurement technique as writing down events—people make a distinction between issues related to procedural and distributive justice.

Although perhaps somewhat speculative, these are important findings in light of recent critiques of procedural and distributive justice research: Folger (1996) pointed at some conceptual and practical confusions and difficulties about the distinction between procedural and distributive justice. Moreover, in a thought-provoking paper, Cropanzano and Ambrose (1997), argued that there is no such thing as procedural justice and proposed that the distinction between procedural and distributive justice should be abolished. The findings by Van den Bos, Lind, et al. (1997), Van den Bos, Wilke, et al. (1998), Greenberg (1986), and Sheppard and Lewicki (1987), however, indicate that people themselves make a distinction between issues related to procedural justice and issues related to distributive justice. Future research should elaborate on conceptual and practical problems with the distinction between procedural and distributive justice (cf. Folger, 1996), and should explore the conditions under which these two concepts are perceived as different concepts and when they are not (cf. Cropanzano & Ambrose, 1997). Our current position in this scientific debate, however, is that the distinction between procedural and distributive justice is not merely a conceptual one, invented by theorists, but frequently—or maybe even typically—arises naturally in people's cognitions about justice.

We hasten to say, however, that according to fairness heuristic theory (Van den Bos, Lind, et al., 1997) the difference between procedure and outcome may be ecological rather than fundamental. That is, people's differential reactions to procedures and outcomes may not result from any unalterable, fundamental feature of the two types of information but from circumstances that usually exist in everyday life and that make people react differently toward procedures than toward outcomes. For example, people usually receive procedure information before they receive outcome information (cf. Van den Bos, Vermunt, & Wilke, 1997), and they frequently do not have information about outcomes of others that give procedure information an opportunity to affect people's judgments (cf. Van den Bos, Lind, et al., 1997). It is our true hope that the aforementioned papers may stimulate future research investigating the intriguing issues related to this and other scientific discussions.

The findings discussed in this chapter may reveal important insights for understanding justice issues in the workplace. We hope to have shown that it is important that when we want to understand why people behave in organizations in the way they do, we may want to find out what information is available to them. Furthermore, following this availability of information analysis, we may ask ourselves whether we can supply people with additional information that would make them react differently and hopefully more positively for themselves as well as the organization. More generally, the "takeaway message" from this chapter is not unlike that of much recent work on social cognition (e.g., Fiske & Taylor, 1991), decision making (e.g., Kahneman & Miller, 1986), and social justice (e.g., Baron, 1993; Messick, 1993): People use a variety of cognitive shortcuts in developing and using justice judgments, not the full-blown analyses suggested by previous justice theories. By understanding how these shortcuts are affected by the context in which the judgments are made and, especially, by understanding the information available when justice judgments are made, we will better understand how people actually behave in organizations in general and how they react to procedural and distributive justice in the workplace in particular.

ACKNOWLEDGMENTS

The research reported in this chapter was supported by the American Bar Foundation, National Science Foundation Grant SBR-96-96244, and a fellowship of the Royal Netherlands Academy of Arts and Sciences awarded to Kees van den Bos. We thank Russell Cropanzano for his comments on an earlier version of this chapter.

REFERENCES

Adams, J. S. (1965). Inequity in social exchange. In L. Berkowitz (Ed.), *Advances in experimental social psychology* (Vol. 2, pp. 267–299). New York: Academic Press.

Baron, J. (1993). Heuristics and biases in equity judgments: A utilitarian approach. In B. A. Mellers & J. Baron (Eds.), *Psychological perspectives on justice: Theory and applications*. Cambridge, NY: Cambridge University Press.

Brockner, J., & Wiesenfeld, B. M. (1996). An integrative framework for explaining reactions to decisions: Interactive effects of outcomes and procedures. *Psychological Bulletin, 120,* 189–208.

Cropanzano, R., & Ambrose, M. L. (1997). *There is no such thing as procedural justice.* Manuscript submitted for publication.

Cropanzano, R., & Folger, R. (1989). Referent cognitions and task decision autonomy: Beyond equity theory. *Journal of Applied Psychology, 74,* 293–299.

Cropanzano, R., & Folger, R. (1991). Procedural justice and worker motivation. In R. M. Steers & L. W. Porter (Eds.), *Motivation and work behavior* (Vol. 5, pp. 131–143). New York: McGraw-Hill.

Cropanzano, R., & Greenberg, J. (1997). Progress in organizational justice: Tunneling through the maze. In C. L. Cooper & I. T. Robertson (Eds.), *International review of industrial and organizational psychology* (pp. 317–372). New York: Wiley.

Fiske, S. T., & Taylor, S. E. (1991). *Social cognition* (2nd ed.). New York: McGraw-Hill.

Folger, R. (1986). Rethinking equity theory: A referent cognitions model. In H. M. Bierhoff, R. L. Cohen & J. Greenberg (Eds.), *Justice in social relations* (pp. 145–162). New York: Plenum.

Folger, R. (1996). Distributive and procedural justice: Multi-faceted meanings and interrelations. *Social Justice Research, 9,* 395–416.

Folger, R., & Konovsky, M. (1989). Effects of procedural and distributive justice on reactions to pay raise decisions. *Academy of Management Journal, 32,* 115–130.

Greenberg, J. (1982). Approaching equity and avoiding inequity in groups and organizations. In J. Greenberg & R. L. Cohen (Eds.), *Equity and justice in social behavior* (pp. 389–435). New York: Academic Press.

Greenberg, J. (1986). Determinants of perceived fairness of performance evaluations. *Journal of Applied Psychology, 71,* 340–342.

Greenberg, J. (1990). Organizational justice: Yesterday, today, and tomorrow. *Journal of Management, 16,* 399–432.

Greenberg, J. (1993). Stealing in the name of justice: Informational and interpersonal moderators of theft reactions to underpayment inequity. *Organizational Behavior and Human Decision Processes, 54,* 81–103.

Huo, Y. J., Smith, H. J., Tyler, T. R., & Lind, E. A. (1996). Superordinate identification, subgroup identification, and justice concerns: Is separatism the problem; is assimilation the answer? *Psychological Science, 7,* 40–45.

Kahneman, D., & Miller, D. T. (1986). Norm theory: Comparing reality to its alternatives. *Psychological Review, 93,* 136–153.

Lerner, M. J., & Whitehead, L. A. (1980). Procedural justice viewed in the context of justice motive theory. In G. Mikula (Ed.), *Justice and social interaction: Experimental and theoretical contributions from psychological research* (pp. 219–256). Bern, Austria: Huber.

Lind, E. A. (1992, March). *The fairness heuristic: Rationality and "relationality" in procedural evaluations.* Paper presented at the Fourth International Conference of the Society for the Advancement of Socio-Economics, Irvine, CA.

Lind, E. A. (1995a). *Social conflict and social justice: Lessons from the social psychology of justice judgments.* Inaugural oration, Leiden University, Leiden, The Netherlands.

Lind, E. A. (1995b). Justice and authority relations in organizations. In R. Cropanzano & K. M. Kacmar (Eds.), *Organizational politics, justice, and support: Managing the social climate of the workplace.* Westport, CT: Quorum.

Lind, E. A. (1998). Procedural justice, disputing, and reactions to legal authorities. In A. Sarat, M. Constable, D. Engel, V. Hans & S. Lawrence (Eds.), *Everyday practices and problem cases* (pp. 177–198). Evanston, IL: Northwestern University Press.

Lind, E. A., Kulik, C. T., Ambrose, M., & De Vera Park, M. V. (1993). Individual and corporate dispute resolution: Using procedural fairness as a decision heuristic. *Administrative Science Quarterly, 38,* 224–251.

Lind, E. A., & Tyler, T. R. (1988). *The social psychology of procedural justice.* New York: Plenum.

Messick, D. M. (1993). Equality as a decision heuristic. In B. A. Mellers & J. Baron (Eds.), *Psychological perspectives on justice: Theory and applications* (pp. 11–31). Cambridge, NY: Cambridge University Press.

Messick, D. M., & Sentis, K. (1983). Fairness, preference, and fairness biases. In D. M. Messick & K. S. Cook (Eds.), *Equity theory: Psychological and sociological perspectives* (pp. 61–94). New York: Praeger.

Rutte, C. G., & Messick, D. M. (1995). An integrated model of perceived unfairness in organizations. *Social Justice Research, 8*, 239–261.

Sheppard, B. H., & Lewicki, R. J. (1987). Toward general principles of managerial fairness. *Social Justice Research, 1*, 161–176.

Smith, H. J., Tyler, T. R., Huo, Y. J., Ortiz, D. J., & Lind, E. A. (1998). The self-relevant implications of the group-value model: Group-membership, self-worth and procedural justice. *Journal of Experimental Social Psychology, 34*, 470–493.

Sweeney, P. D., & McFarlin, D. B. (1993). Workers' evaluations of the "ends" and the "means": An examination of four models of distributive and procedural justice. *Organizational Behavior and Human Decision Processes, 54*, 23–40.

Tyler, T. R., & Caine, A. (1981). The influence of outcomes and procedures on satisfaction with formal leaders. *Journal of Personality and Social Psychology, 41*, 642–655.

Tyler, T. R., & Folger, R. (1980). Distributional and procedural aspects of satisfaction with citizen–police encounters. *Basic and Applied Social Psychology, 1*, 281–292.

Tyler, T. R., & Lind, E. A. (1992). A relational model of authority in groups. In M. Zanna (Ed.), *Advances in experimental social psychology* (Vol. 25, pp. 115–191). San Diego, CA: Academic Press.

Tyler, T. R., Rasinski, K. A., & McGraw, K. M. (1985). The influence of perceived injustice on the endorsement of political leaders. *Journal of Applied Social Psychology, 15*, 700–725.

Van den Bos, K. (1996). *Procedural justice and conflict*. Unpublished doctoral dissertation, Leiden University, Leiden, The Netherlands.

Van den Bos, K., Lind, E. A., Vermunt, R., & Wilke, H. A. M. (1997). How do I judge my outcome when I do not know the outcome of others?: The psychology of the fair process effect. *Journal of Personality and Social Psychology, 72*, 1034–1046.

Van den Bos, K., Vermunt, R., & Wilke, H. A. M. (1996). The consistency rule and the voice effect: The influence of expectations on procedural fairness judgements and performance. *European Journal of Social Psychology, 26*, 411–428.

Van den Bos, K., Vermunt, R., & Wilke, H. A. M. (1997). Procedural and distributive justice: What is fair depends more on what comes first than on what comes next. *Journal of Personality and Social Psychology, 72*, 95–104.

Van den Bos, K., Wilke, H. A. M., & Lind, E. A. (1998). When do we need procedural fairness? The role of trust in authority. *Journal of Personality and Social Psychology, 75*, 1449–1458.

Van den Bos, K., Wilke, H. A. M., Lind, E. A., & Vermunt, R. (1998). Evaluating outcomes by means of the fair process effect: Evidence for different processes in fairness and satisfaction judgments. *Journal of Personality and Social Psychology, 74*, 1493–1503.

Walster, E., Walster, G. W., & Berscheid, E. (1978). *Equity: Theory and research*. Boston: Allyn & Bacon.

4

▼▼▼▼▼▼▼▼

Cross-Cultural Applications of Organizational Justice

Dean B. McFarlin
University of Dayton

Paul D. Sweeney
University of Central Florida

Our knowledge of how fairness issues affect corporate life has grown tremendously since the beginning of the 1990s. Distributive, procedural, and interactional justice can help us understand much of what happens to employees—from the time they join the firm until they leave. Clearly, fairness issues are often the source of trust (or lack thereof) that employees feel toward their companies. In essence, justice concerns are the basis of the psychological contract that exists between employees and the firm (Morrison & Robinson, 1997).

For example, the perceived fairness of selection practices can have many effects both during and after the hiring process (Gilliland, 1993). Likewise, the fairness of decisions about grievances, performance appraisals, promotions, and reward allocations—as well as the procedures used in the process—can impact employee morale, commitment, job performance, and even retaliatory behaviors, such as theft from the company (Cowherd & Levine, 1992; Fryxell, 1992; Greenberg, 1990; Konovsky & Cropanzano, 1991; Leung, Chiu, & Au, 1993; McFarlin & Sweeney, 1992; Skarlicki & Folger, 1997). Justice concerns can also affect employee relationships with supervisors (Folger & Bies, 1989; Sashkin & Williams, 1990), behavior in work groups (Tyler, Degoey, & Smith, 1996), and level of organizational citizenship (Eskew, 1993; Konovsky & Pugh, 1994; Moorman, 1991). Finally, the way that employees react to layoffs may reflect how fairly they feel that those layoffs were carried out. This is true for both layoff "victims" and "survivors" (Brockner et al., 1994).

THE INTERSECTION OF CULTURAL VALUES AND JUSTICE

It is also true that multinational corporations need to be concerned with justice issues when implementing their international strategies. At the same time, however, the increasingly global economy raises questions about the robustness of the justice effects mentioned previously. The fact is that most justice research has relied on U.S. subjects—with all of the cultural baggage that goes with it. There is plenty of evidence that U.S. management and motivation theories often do not translate well abroad (Hofstede, 1993). The same may be true for justice theories. As a result, more researchers are examining the impact of cultural values on justice perceptions and outcomes. This work has important implications for international management.

CHAPTER GOALS

The main goal of this chapter is to examine the relation between culture and justice perceptions and outcomes. We pay special attention to the applications of this emerging area of research. As a result, our review is organized around the effects of interest to firms. For instance, this chapter examines the role of culture in producing fair selection practices, performance appraisals, and reward allocations. Also considered is how culture affects the relation between justice perceptions and various *group-level outcomes,* such as group productivity and organizational citizenship. Before beginning the review process, however, it is important to explain how culture weaves its way into organizational life.

LINKING CULTURES, COUNTRIES, AND WORK VALUES

Explaining exactly what culture is continues to be a worthy research goal in itself (Boyacigiller, Kleinberg, Phillips, & Sackmann, 1996). Although several definitions exist, we agree with Hofstede (1993) who defined culture as "the collective programming of the mind which distinguishes one group or category of people from another" (p. 89). It is unlikely that employees are fully aware of the pervasive impact of culture on their own attitudes and behaviors (Triandis, 1996). Nevertheless, culture can account for the divergent perceptions that employees in different countries have about their performance, what they value in work, and what they expect from management (Dorfman, 1996; Farh, Dobbins, & Cheng, 1991; Frese, Kring, Soose, & Zempel, 1996; Ralston, Gustafson, Cheung, & Terpstra, 1993). These findings have prompted researchers to identify basic cultural dimensions and then use them to categorize countries. Such efforts to cluster countries by cultural values can help international managers determine the best ways to lead and motivate employees in various cultures.

Hofstede's (1980, 1984) survey of more than 100,000 workers in 40 countries represents the most influential effort to cluster countries by cultural values. Based on these data, Hofstede suggested that four major cultural dimensions exist: Individualism–Collectivism, Masculinity–Femininity, Power Distance, and Uncertainty Avoidance. *Individualism–Collectivism* describes whether people view themselves primarily as individuals or as members of a group. In individualistic cultures (e.g., the United States, United Kingdom), people are expected to take care of themselves, and a high value is placed on autonomy, individual achievement, and privacy. In collectivist cultures (e.g., Mexico, Japan), however, people are viewed as being embedded in a group that protects and takes care of them in exchange for loyalty and devotion. *Masculinity–Femininity* describes whether the assertive acquisition of money and power is highly valued (e.g., Venezuela), or whether people, the quality of life, and good relationships with co-workers should take precedence (e.g., Sweden). *Power Distance* reflects the extent to which people can accept large differences in status between individuals or groups in an organization. People in low-power distance cultures are more likely to fear the concentration of power (e.g., the United States). As a result, the use of power in such cultures is often subject to certain laws, procedures, and standards, which, if violated, can create problems for managers. On the other hand, people in high-power distance cultures are more likely to feel that some individuals are destined to be in command and others are not (e.g., India). Finally, *Uncertainty Avoidance* refers to how people react to uncertain or ambiguous events. People in weak uncertainty avoidance cultures (e.g., Denmark) embrace the idea that life is unpredictable by definition. On the other hand, people in strong uncertainty avoidance cultures tend to feel threatened by ambiguity and will go to great lengths to create stable and predictable work environments (e.g., France). As a result, rules and procedures designed to reduce uncertainty may proliferate in such cultures.

Hofstede (1980, 1984) also created cultural maps by crossing pairs of cultural dimensions and plotting the corresponding scores for various countries. For example, Hofstede found that large power distance and collectivism often go together for many Asian- and Latin-American countries. Similarly, many northern European and Anglo countries (e.g., the United States, Netherlands) tend toward small-power distance and individualism.

Of course, Hofstede's (1980, 1984) work has some limitations. For one, many countries in eastern Europe, Asia, and Africa were not included. More recent efforts to cluster countries by cultural values have included emerging countries such as China and Russia (Bond, 1991; Smith, Dugan, & Trompenaars, 1996; Trompenaars, 1993). These efforts have been useful for supporting and extending Hofstede's results. Hofstede's work also ignores differences between countries within a specific cluster. For instance, research suggests that cultural differences exist between the United States and Australia despite their similar scores on Hofstede's cultural dimensions (Dowling & Nagel, 1986). Finally, within-country differences are also an issue. New immigrant populations coming to the United States have put managers in the position of having to motivate employees from various cultural backgrounds (Adler, 1997; Cox & Blake, 1991). Despite these limitations, Hofstede's work continues to have a tremendous impact on international management.

CONNECTING CULTURE, JUSTICE, ATTITUDES, AND BEHAVIOR

In fact, cultural values may be especially useful for understanding justice concerns in an international context. For example, research on U.S. employees has found that distributive justice may be a stronger predictor of personal attitudes—like pay satisfaction—than procedural justice, whereas the opposite tends to be true for organizational attitudes—like commitment to the firm (McFarlin & Sweeney, 1992; Sweeney & McFarlin, 1993). It may be that when Americans evaluate their company's capacity to treat people fairly, they focus on the procedures that the firm or its managers use. Over time, these procedures may determine whether Americans feel they can get a fair shake from their employer. Therefore, if procedures are generally fair, but outcomes are low (e.g., low pay raises), American employees may stay positive about the firm because they believe that outcomes will be distributed fairly in the future.

But these results may, at least in part, be due to American cultural values. Of course, possible cultural limitations have not stopped American researchers from suggesting that companies should try to improve procedural justice as a way to enhance organizational commitment (cf. McFarlin & Sweeney, 1992, 1996). For instance, researchers have suggested that companies do more to involve employees in the design of procedures that will affect them. However, American-style efforts to increase involvement in decision making have failed in some European cultures (McFarlin, Sweeney, & Cotton, 1992). One possible reason for this is that cultural values may affect how employees view justice issues. For example, employees from a collectivist culture that values group harmony may see procedures that treat everyone equally—regardless of performance—as fair. In contrast, employees from an individualistic culture may see procedures that stress equity— you get what you deserve—as fair.

Our review of research on culture and justice will consider selection practices, performance appraisal, reward allocation, and conflict resolution. Next, we consider how cultural values and justice perceptions may impact employee behaviors such as organizational citizenship. Finally, we examine how justice and culture may affect human-resource management issues in international mergers and acquisitions. In all cases, managerial implications are highlighted.

THE IMPACT OF CULTURE AND JUSTICE IN SPECIFIC WORK DOMAINS

Hiring and Selection of Employees

There is, of course, a long research tradition in employee selection. Most of this research is based on American employees. Justice concerns have also been a recent focus. For instance, the perceived fairness of various selection techniques (e.g., ability tests, assessment centers, interviews, and drug screening) can have a bottom-line impact on companies. Applicants who feel unfairly treated may be more likely to sue, refuse a job offer to begin with, or, once on the job, perform poorly (Arvey, 1992, 1993; Folger & Cropanzano, 1998).

In fact, Gilliland (1993) developed a comprehensive, justice-based model of employee's reactions to various types of selection methods. Consistent with the model, Gilliland (1994) found that face validity (job relatedness) of the selection method was a major predictor of the perceived fairness of the hiring process. Likewise, employees who have input into the process, or better yet can demonstrate their abilities, tend to view the process as fair (Lind & Tyler, 1988). Finally, the nature of the interactions during the selection process also affect perceptions of justice. Selection methods that are definitive, not invasive of personal privacy, but perhaps more empirically based seemed to be preferred (Smither, Reilly, Millsap, Pearlman, & Stoffey, 1993).

However, these effects may be specific to the United States and related cultures. For instance, Steiner and Gilliland (1996) examined the criteria used by American and French college students to judge the fairness of several selection methods. They replicated the typical finding that Americans use face validity as a way to establish the procedural fairness of a method but also found that French were more likely to use it as an element of procedural fairness. This suggests that employees from a low-power distance culture (e.g., the United States) may feel competent and confident enough to challenge a selection procedure used by a firm. But, in relatively high-power distance cultures (e.g., France), more respect may be offered to the expertise of the test provider.

Steiner and Gilliland (1996) also found that the scientific quality of a selection method was more useful in building procedural justice in Americans than in the French. For example, the French were much more favorable about graphology as a useful selection method than were Americans. Steiner and Gilliland noted that it is common in France for job ads to request a handwritten job-application letter for this purpose. In fact, at least one study has showed that over 90% of French organizations use graphological evaluations (see Steiner & Gilliland, 1996). Conversely, Americans were more likely to endorse a biodata technique that relies on specific information about work experiences, education, and so on.

What do these few studies suggest about the inherent fairness of cross-cultural selection methods? Employees in low-power distance cultures apparently feel free to criticize selection methods, especially ones with little or no scientific support. This criticism may accelerate to more formal action (e.g., a lawsuit) if the violation is egregious and the culture is very low in power distance. We can also speculate about the criteria used to screen employees. In collective cultures, the willingness to sacrifice personal initiative for group goals may be a very important criterion. Plus, the use of explicit, individual comparisons for selection will likely be avoided (Love, Bishop, Heinisch, & Cooper, 1994). In individualistic cultures, a more fair way to proceed is to expect applicants to make an effort to sell themselves by establishing their personal credentials. This may be further exacerbated in masculine cultures where individual achievement and challenge are valued. Clearly, the role of culture and justice in employee selection needs further study.

Performance Appraisal

Once employees are hired and trained, their performance often needs to be evaluated. This, however, may be among the only thing universal about performance appraisal. Once again, Hofstede's (1980, 1984) work can help identify the most culturally fair way to approach and deliver performance feedback. One important dimension about appraising performance is the issue of exactly how feedback should be delivered. In individualistic cultures, feedback is typically provided on a one-to-one basis with an eye toward clearly differentiating employees (Love et al., 1994). Collective cultures like those in Japan, South Korea, and Taiwan, however, try to minimize differences among their employees in an evaluation (Love et al., 1994; Shaw, Tang, Fischer, & Kirkbride, 1993). This minimization tendency is further promoted by an Asian (and often collectivistic) concern with maintaining face and harmony (Milliman, Nason, Lowe, Kim, & Huo, 1995). As a result, performance appraisals in collective cultures are often based on group performance rather than individual output (Davis, Kerr, & Von Glinow, 1987). The procedural fairness of a performance evaluation, therefore, is likely to be strongly affected by this cultural orientation. In practice, this is probably a frequently encountered problem. For example, Americans managing in Japan may take their individualized, differentiating style into a group-oriented culture, a setting in which "the nail that sticks out must get hammered down." Clearly, there is great opportunity here to offend.

Another important way that evaluations differ across cultures is in their degree of formality. In the United States, for example, many employees feel that fair performance appraisals require appropriate performance criteria, clear forms, and careful scheduling. The fact that complaints about performance appraisals are pervasive and that many U.S. firms do a lousy job of conducting appraisals underscores employee attitudes about what should constitute a fair appraisal process (Folger & Cropanzano, 1998). Partly, these attitudes are based on the belief that individuals, and not groups or teams, are the main source of performance. They may also be based on the masculine tendencies of U.S. business practices. U.S. culture stresses recognition and achievement—something that a formal, systematic, and well-documented analysis of performance can help deliver.

In feminine cultures, however, the opposite has been found. Ali (1988), for example, studied appraisal systems in five Arab countries and found that they were basically informal. For instance, in Saudi Arabia there was little if any use of forms or documents that are common in countries such as the United States. As a result, feedback in these countries was largely subjective, with an emphasis on the interpersonal aspects of performance. It was unlikely to see papers change hands during an appraisal and even less likely to see documents filed for future reference.

Another important aspect about evaluations is the degree of employee input in the process—both formal and informal. Here there are also dramatic differences across cultures. A common component of fair performance evaluation systems in the United States seems to be the opportunity, if not obligation, for employees to express their views about their performance. Research clearly shows that such procedures can increase the perceived fairness of a performance evaluation, even when that appraisal is negative (Folger & Konovsky, 1989). This may be due to the generally low degree of power distance inherent in U.S. In cultures that emphasize high-power distance, the reverse could be predicted. For example, McEvoy and Cascio (1990) found that compared to their U.S. counterparts, Taiwanese employees (relatively high-power distance) were more comfortable with an autocratic evaluation and were less likely to make suggestions to their managers about their appraisals.

But what about the nature of that feedback? What form of feedback is likely to be perceived as fair? As it turns out, at least some cultures are uncomfortable with receiving explicit feedback, especially if it is negative. For example, among collectivist cultures, direct feedback is rarely given (Cascio & Bailey, 1995). Instead, criticism is likely to be very subtle, possibly nonverbal, and often given through third parties. However, in individualistic cultures a strengths-and-weaknesses component is often built into evaluations. In many cases this praise and criticism is delivered in two modes—verbally and in written form (Cascio & Bailey, 1995). Such feedback would be difficult to miss.

Even when direct praise and criticism is provided, this does not automatically mean that it will be properly weighted and accepted. In fact, there is some reason to believe that power distance may play a role in the perceived fairness of positive or negative feedback. For example, Earley (1984, 1986) found that English workers placed more credence in praise than they did in critical feedback they received. No such difference was observed for American workers. Post-feedback performance also showed that the English responded better to praise than criticism. This was not true for Americans; performance was just as likely to increase after praise as it was after criticism. The United Kingdom tends to be higher in power distance than the United States, and this is negatively related to the degree of trust workers place in management. Earley (1984, 1986) suggested that this lack of trust promotes a perception of lack of fairness in negative evaluations. In at least one other study, high-power distance also seemed to produce skepticism about negative feedback among Germans (Trompenaars, 1993).

The implications for practicing managers are many. First, what is considered a procedurally just performance appraisal varies across cultures. Managers need to be aware of these variations. It would be inappropriate, for example, for American expatriate managers to assume that what is natural in the United States—the individual performance interview—would also be typical in China, South Korea, or Mexico. In fact, such methods may be among the least likely to produce a sense of procedural justice in collective cultures. Likewise, American managers should not expect an employee from a collective culture that is also high in power distance to participate equally—or at all—in the performance appraisal process. Employees from low-power distance and masculine cultures may feel that contributing their opinion promotes fairness. But the use of such techniques in a high-power distance culture may leave employees wondering why their manager failed to prepare and control the appraisal interview. Finally, managers must be aware of when to be subtle and when to be explicit in presenting feedback. Even if the situation requires them to be explicit, prior cultural standards may undercut the value of constructive and appropriate criticism. International managers clearly have their work cut out for them in performing this important organizational function (McFarlin & Sweeney, 1998).

Reward Allocations

Of course, in many organizations rewards are distributed after performance appraisals are conducted. The distribution of these rewards has long been a focus in justice research. Equity theory, for example, equates fairness with outcomes that are distributed according to deservingness (Adams, 1965). Research conducted in the United States has been generally supportive of equity theory ideas. In fact, when rewards are not distributed based on performance or other deserving criteria—as is often the case with CEO pay and two-tier wage systems—U.S. managers often end up dealing with a host of negative attitudinal and behavioral consequences (McFarlin & Frone, 1990; Wilhelm, 1993). Even product quality has been related to interclass pay equity for American and British employees. In other words, as the size of the pay gap between top management and lower level employees in a particular unit increased, product quality dropped (Cowherd & Levine, 1992). However, procedures (e.g., careful explanations, apologies from top management) can mitigate against what many Americans might see as unfair reward allocations. For instance, Greenberg (1990) found that after a pay cut, employee theft rates were lower when management apologized and made a sincere effort to explain why the cut was necessary.

But relatively few studies have looked at how equity theory applies across cultures (Bhagat & McQuaid, 1982; James, 1993; Miles & Greenberg, 1993). Hofstede (1984) argued that countries that tend toward femininity, are collectivistic, high in power distance, and strong in uncertainty avoidance are least likely to embrace equity concepts. Employees from countries that fit many of these criteria (e.g., China, Saudi Arabia) often feel that external factors (e.g., fate) control their lives to a great extent (Adler, 1997; Shenkar & Von Glinow, 1994).

These observations dovetail with a number of studies that compare American reward allocation preferences against those in other countries. Americans tend to see the individual pursuit of higher achievement (also a masculine orientation) as a worthy goal, even if there will be ups and downs along the way (reflecting weak uncertainty avoidance). As a result, individual performance is seen as important (inputs) and should be rewarded accordingly (outcomes). On the other hand, in collectivist cultures rewards are more likely to be distributed equally—regardless of performance—to preserve group harmony and cohesiveness. Similarly, more feminine cultures tend to place a higher value on relationships and quality of life concerns than the pursuit of individual achievement.

A study by Pennings (1993) on American, French, and Dutch managers underscores this point. Pennings found that American managers valued money highly and felt that bonuses should be strongly linked to performance—even if bonus levels would fluctuate wildly as a result. This perspective is consistent not only with weak uncertainty avoidance, but the idea that equity—"one gets what one deserves"—should be the guiding principle in reward allocations. In contrast, French and Dutch managers were less interested in money than the Americans. They were also more skeptical about their firms' ability to link pay and performance. The actual bonuses earned by French and Dutch managers were smaller and varied less than those earned by the Americans. Few French and Dutch executives had well-developed compensation contracts, but all the American executives did. According to Hofstede, these reactions were predictable. The Dutch tend to have a more feminine orientation and score somewhat lower on individualism than Americans. As a result, Dutch managers may be less likely to view pay as a way to keep score for individual achievement. Similarly, countries with strong uncertainty avoidance (e.g., France) are less likely to use highly variable performance bonuses because they create more ambiguity than executives are willing to accept (Pennings, 1993).

A similar situation exists in Germany, a country that tends to be less individualistic, but stronger in uncertainty avoidance than the United States. Many German executives are reluctant to use bonuses as a way to publicize their individual achievements. In general, German firms tend to have lower bonus levels than U.S. firms for comparable positions. For example, currency traders in a U.S. bank might earn bonuses equal to 700% of their base salaries in a good year compared to perhaps 50% in Germany. German managers often feel that tempting employees with huge bonuses prompts unnecessary risk taking. Another concern is the destructive competition that may accompany performance bonuses that are tied only to individual targets. As a consequence, some German firms encourage co-operation by making part of the bonus contingent on an employee's ability to work well with colleagues (Steinmetz, 1995).

Other research on reward allocations also tends to support the idea that cultural values affect the importance of distributive justice and reward allocation preferences. For example, McFarlin and Sweeney (1996) found that Americans rated distributive justice as higher in importance than a comparable group of South African employees. *Distributive justice* in this case was defined as the fairness of the individual rewards given by the company. Furthermore, as perceived reward fairness increased, so too did Americans' organizational commitment. There was no connection, however, between levels of distributive justice and organizational commitment for South African employees. This pattern is consistent with the idea that relative to the United States, many African cultures embrace more collec-tivistic and feminine values. In other words, individual reward distribution would be less likely to affect employees' attitudes toward the company. Instead, the dis-tribution of rewards on a work group, unit, or even community-wide basis may have more impact on employee attitudes in many sub-Saharan African cultures.

For example, under Apartheid in South Africa the White minority basically de-termined where Blacks could live, go to school, and work. Now that Apartheid is gone, Black employees' feelings of distributive justice often depends on whether they feel their employers are funding efforts to remove the inequalities left over from Apartheid (e.g., inferior housing and primary schools). This linkage be-tween work and life outside of work also reflects African cultural values that em-phasize the importance of community and family. Such values are not part of most Western approaches to management (Mbigi, 1994; McFarlin, Coster, & Mo-gale-Pretorius, 1999).

In fact, for many Africans, "just management" is captured by concepts like *ubun-tu*. This cultural perspective views organizations much like an African village where an informal communal orientation holds sway. As such, ubuntu stresses supportiveness, cooperation, and people working for the common good as op-posed to the individual pursuit of achievement (Khoza, 1994). Large South African corporations, which usually have been run using American or Northern European management philosophies, have had considerable success motivating Black employees by embracing Ubuntu concepts. South African Airways is one such example (McFarlin et al., 1999).

Along the same lines, Berman, Murphy-Berman, & Singh (1985) found that compared to Americans, Indian subjects were more likely to distribute monetary rewards in ways that supported a financially strapped employee, regardless of the employee's performance. This was consistent with other studies showing that Americans tend to rely on merit or deservingness in making reward allocations, whereas Indians are more likely to emphasize need (Murphy-Berman, Berman, Singh, Pachauri, & Kumar, 1984). However, the link between culture and equity-based rewards is more complex than it appears. For instance, in India, caste may also affect reward allocation preferences. Pandey & Singh (1997) found that members of India's upper caste were less likely to use need as a reward allocation criterion than members of middle and lower castes.

Researchers have also looked at the types of job inputs considered when rewards are distributed. Task inputs directly contribute to group performance and goal attainment. Working in a group also requires maintenance inputs, such as efforts to maintain good interpersonal relations. Both types of inputs need to be considered in the distribution of rewards to individual group members. In one study, for example, Americans and Chinese were asked to evaluate hypothetical members of a work group. Although both Americans and Chinese tended to distribute rewards based on an equity norm for task and maintenance inputs, the Chinese used a weaker equity standard to avoid creating conflict in the group. These results seem to confirm that collectivist cultures are less likely to apply equity concepts when distributing rewards than individualistic cultures, at least to other in-group members (Bond, Leung, & Wan, 1982).

In a related study, Leung and Bond (1984) found that Chinese subjects were more likely to use whatever reward distribution rule would best preserve group harmony. When their own performance was high relative to a friend's, Chinese subjects tended to divide a monetary reward equally. However, when their performance was low, Chinese subjects tended to rely on an equitable distribution of the money available (thus favoring the friend). In contrast, Chinese subjects were actually more likely to use equity norms to distribute pay when they were working with a stranger (an out-group member) than were their American counterparts. Hui, Triandis, and Yee (1991) found similar reward allocation patterns when comparing Chinese and American subjects. Once again, relative to their American counterparts, Chinese subjects were more generous with their work partners, especially when the partner was a friend. This egalitarian pattern diminished when collectivism was statistically controlled.

Kim, Park, and Suzuki (1990) suggested, however, that collectivist cultures may use equity norms most when rewarding maintenance inputs because they value group cohesiveness so highly. To test this idea, they had Americans, Japanese, and South Koreans evaluate the hypothetical contributions of a group member with either high- or low-task inputs (e.g., work quality) and high- or low-maintenance inputs (e.g., friendliness shown other group members). For task inputs, the group member was rewarded with an overall evaluation and recognized with a grade. These rewards were called *primary rewards*. For maintenance inputs, *social rewards* were allocated (e.g., whether one would want to work with the group member again). The prediction was that task inputs would have the greatest impact on the reward distributions made by the more individualistic Americans. In contrast, it was expected that Japanese and South Koreans would be more likely to reward group members with a high level of maintenance inputs. The actual results were quite complex and highlight the need for more research.

In all three countries, rewards increased as task and maintenance inputs increased. However, Americans were the most generous and Japanese the least generous with primary rewards. South Koreans were the most generous in rewarding low levels of maintenance inputs. It may be that social acceptance and harmony are so critical in highly collectivistic, feminine cultures such as South Korea that even when members contribute little in the way of maintenance inputs they are still supported and rewarded (Kim, Park, & Suzuki, 1990).

So far, the research we have reviewed implicitly suggests that cultural values are relatively static. But another interesting set of studies addresses the tantalizing possibility that economic and social changes can affect cultural values and in so doing impact reward allocation preferences. For instance, Pearce, Branyiczki, and Bakacsi (1994) compared employees in Hungarian companies that relied on personal criteria to distribute rewards (e.g., whether the supervisor liked a particular employee) with employees in Hungarian firms that used performance-based criteria to distribute rewards. Consistent with research done on Americans, Pearce et al. found that person-based reward systems were more likely to lead to negative consequences than performance-based systems (e.g., employees who felt that the reward system was unfair). This suggests that the economic and political changes that have occurred in Hungary since the 1980s have encouraged Hungarian employees to think more in terms of a meritocracy than was previously the case under the old state-dominated economy. Likewise, among Russian managers there seems to be an increasing emphasis on equity since the Soviet Union dissolved—such as giving monetary or other tangible rewards to subordinates for good performance (e.g., Puffer, 1993). It may be working. Research shows that Russian workers respond better to equity-based extrinsic rewards than other motivation techniques (Welsh, Luthans, & Sommer, 1993).

However, other studies suggest that although rapid social, political, and economic changes have occurred in Eastern Europe, the cultural values linked to workplace justice perceptions may change more slowly. For example, Frese, Kring, Soose, and Zempel (1996) found that Germans raised in the formerly communist eastern part of the country still have less personal initiative and are less likely to view distributive justice in terms of achievement and deservingness than Germans raised in the western half of the country. Although this difference may shrink over time, it underscores the power of organizational and social institutions to affect individual motivation and justice perceptions over a long period. In East Germany and other former Soviet-Bloc countries, subservience to the state was taught in schools and organizations. The effects of those teachings linger although many of the institutions responsible for them have vanished.

Nevertheless, there is some evidence that emerging changes in cultural values do affect what employees see as fair reward allocations. For example, over the past few decades, Americans have become more concerned with humanistic values like cooperation and less concerned with wealth. The opposite trend is happening in China as it focuses more on economic gain and less on the egalitarian practices of the past. Both trends may put pressure on traditional cultural values in each country. Chen (1995) had Chinese and American managers read a scenario in which they had to make decisions about the allocation rules that would be used to distribute rewards among employees. Two types of rewards were examined—*material rewards* (e.g., a pay raise) and *socioemotional rewards* (e.g., more supportive managers). Overall, Chinese managers preferred to use equity based rules (e.g., performance) to distribute both types of rewards. Americans, however, based material rewards like pay raises on performance but preferred to distribute socioemotional rewards equally. These results are consistent with the idea that America is becoming less individualistic and less masculine whereas China moves in the opposite direction (Chen, 1995). Currently, many Chinese companies seem to be obsessed with productivity and are eager to overcome cultural traditions that prevented reforms in the past. Although rewarding performance is still critical for U.S. firms, the relatively new emphasis on teamwork requires more harmonious interpersonal relationships. This is something that the equal distribution of socioemotional rewards may help promote.

Overall, the failure to recognize the cultural distinctions that remain can still get American managers in big trouble overseas. For instance, a few years ago we visited a Shanghai plant run by an American manufacturing company. To encourage employee initiative, the company tried to reward a small group of employees who came up with new ways to improve manufacturing operations. These individuals had been coached to make suggestions for improvement to management. The company decided to give each group member a leather jacket as a reward and to set an example for the rest of the plant. The company hoped that rewarding initiative would help break down Chinese workers' passivity and tendency to defer decision making to managers. Instead, the leather jackets sparked a near revolt in the plant. Once other Chinese employees discovered jackets were being "given away," they demanded to know why they had not received theirs. The American management tried to explain that the jackets were a reward for performance. It did not work. Soon the company was fielding questions from local Chinese officials. Eventually, the American managers gave in and presented all 1,500 Chinese employees with a leather jacket.

Traditionally, rewards in China were not based on performance. Instead, Chinese workers expected their managers to take care of them in exchange for loyalty and obedience. In addition, Chinese companies historically had a social contract with workers that included a variety of benefits (including housing allowances and subsidized food) as well as job security. Firing workers for poor performance was rare because it caused social problems. As we have suggested, justice perceptions in China are changing as the country continues to evolve. However, it would be a mistake to conclude that the old "iron rice bowl" perspective has completely disappeared. American companies need to consider this when trying to motivate their Chinese employees (Bond, 1991; Shenkar & Von Glinow, 1994).

Overall, what do the complex findings on culture and reward allocation mean for managers? Our advice is that managers should pay attention to how their own cultural values might affect their willingness to use equity rules in reward allocations, and how their subordinates' cultural values might affect reactions to the use of equity rules. Plus, managers need to keep in mind that the world is not a static place. As countries evolve, their business practices and traditional cultural values may change in ways that affect reward allocation rules (see Ralston, Holt, Terpstra, & Kai-Cheng, 1997).

Work Group Behavior

Of course, regardless of whether a culture is collectivist or individualist, masculine or feminine, a good deal of work is accomplished in groups. The manner in which group activity is handled can also have direct and indirect consequences for feelings of fairness. How might cultural dimensions affect the group process–justice relationship?

Perhaps the strongest effect might be noted for individualism–collectivism. It might be expected that collectivists would much prefer a group orientation to work and that individualists would prefer to go it alone. As just discussed in the reward allocation section, however, the type of group that is studied will have a major effect. Evidence shows that in-group members are more likely to be rewarded in an equal manner by collectivists than by individualists.

These effects also spill over to group processes. For example, the quality and quantity of work done in groups has been studied cross-culturally. In the individualistic United States, people tend to be more productive working alone than when they work with others (i.e., a social loafing effect). Furthermore, individualists sometimes complain about the unfairness of a group-based production and reward system. They feel that individual performance and reward is the best way to proceed and thus tend to "loaf" when performing in groups. However, we might expect collectivists to show the opposite effects, especially when they interact with other in-group members. To look at this question, Earley (1993) studied the performance of managers from China, Israel, and the United States. Some of these managers were asked to work alone, whereas others were placed in one of two different group situations. An in-group condition was created by leading some managers to believe that they shared a number of similar characteristics that usually lead to close friendships. An out-group condition was created by telling another set of managers that other members had very different characteristics and that they came from very different backgrounds. In all cases, the managers worked on simulated management tasks. When they did work in groups, the managers always worked with their fellow nationals. Chinese and Israelis were chosen to participate because they are relatively collectivistic and Americans because they are often individualists.

The results were interesting. First, Earley (1993) showed that there was a reduction in group performance (social loafing) for Americans but not for the Israeli or Chinese managers when they worked in groups. The Chinese and Israelis also showed social loafing when they performed with an out-group. These collectivists reduced their input when the work group held few ties of any importance to them. When the collectivists worked with an in-group, however, their performance was not reduced. Similar results have also been found in several other studies (Earley, 1989; Espinoza & Garza, 1985; Gabrenya, Latane, & Wang, 1985; Matsui, Kakuyama, & Onglatco, 1987).

These results have some important management implications. First, work strategies that are based on individual performance may not be effective in a collectivistic culture; indeed, they may backfire and be seen as unfair as we showed earlier with our leather jacket example. Individual strategies fail to recognize the importance of groups in cultures such as Israel and China. At the same time, however, simply adopting any group-based system could also be shortsighted. Group-based systems are likely to be seen as fairer and more effective in collective cultures when applied to a natural collection of individuals (an in-group).

The results also suggest that individualistic Americans may have a hard time in group-based work schemes. This is especially interesting given that teamwork in the United States appears to be increasing; current estimates are that about 10% of American employees are organized into some type of team (Dumaine, 1990; Work Team Trivia, 1992). Overall, group-based approaches may be seen as a less fair way to operate and as an unfair basis for compensation in individualistic cultures.

The implications we have drawn are again based on a static view of culture. These implications may be mitigated by recent changes in some individualistic and collectivistic cultures. In the United States, for example, the workforce is becoming increasingly diverse. By all accounts, managers will have to be especially attuned to the changing group dynamics and the effects this diversity may have for distributive, procedural, and interactional justice. The same is true for prototypic collective cultures like China. In that rapidly developing economy, primarily in-group work structures will likely give way to more diverse forms. Although many groups in China are likely to be composed of in-group members, the booming economy has led to dramatic shifts in travel and work patterns. Despite laws requiring a work permit to move from a rural location to a city like Shanghai or Guangzhou, there is still remarkable (albeit illegal) movement of the labor force. Therefore, it is reasonable to expect increasing diversity in Chinese work groups. This means that managers, including American expatriates, will have to be especially clever and insightful when seeking to introduce new group techniques in such settings.

Of course, there is already a good bit of cultural diversity in work groups that may bring justice issues to a head. One interesting study was conducted by Merritt and Helmreich (1996). These researchers studied the behavior of flight crews of commercial aircraft, groups that can exceed 20 people. Data show that flight crew behavior, rather than technical failures, have caused 70% of all commercial aviation accidents from 1959 through 1995. Merritt and Helmreich studied the culturally appropriate behaviors of flight crews from different countries (the United States and several Asian countries) and the effects these may have in preventing accidents. Interview data with the crews showed that Americans preferred a captain who encouraged questions (low-power distance) but who also took charge in an emergency (individualistic). Asian crews thought that the most appropriate interaction style for the pilot was autocratic (high-power distance) but also communicative to others in the crew (collectivist).

These researchers concluded that the cultural propensity to interact in these ways provides both assets and liabilities in terms of accident prevention. Whereas the U.S. pilots were relatively open to critical information provided by others in the flight crew, they also had a tendency to take on an individualist "fly-boy" approach to cockpit management. Asians, as collectivists, appear to be more attuned to the group goals, but are also high in power distance and thus less likely to receive critical feedback from other crew members. These interaction styles are extremely difficult to alter without significant retraining. Perhaps the best approach is to train flight crews to recognize the strengths and weaknesses associated with their interaction styles (Merritt & Helmreich, 1996).

What sorts of effects might be observed in a multicultural work setting? This is a question raised by Bochner and Hesketh (1994) in their study of over 260 workers in an Australian bank. These workers were from 28 different countries, but were divided into groups by power distance and level of individualism. They found that collectivists were more comfortable with an informal contact style with other group members. Collectivists were also more likely to know other group members well than were individualists. Likewise, collectivists were more likely to work in a team rather than alone. Bochner and Hesketh also found that out-group members (high-power distance–collectivist) were more likely to believe that ethnic groups are discriminated against by managers than were in-group members (low-power distance–collectivists). These out-group members were also more likely to believe that ethnic diversity impeded group productivity and that multicultural workforces were generally more difficult and disadvantageous. This underscores our earlier point that when people with different work values interact with one another, even on a roughly equal basis, problems can arise (see also Leung, Chiu, & Au, 1993). Interestingly, one common recommendation for creating greater mutual understanding and respect is cross-cultural contact among equal status group members. This study is therefore generally supportive of Hofstede's (1993, 1996) pessimism that training will mitigate expected processes and styles of interaction, primarily because these styles are so deeply rooted in culture.

Conflict Management

As just shown, allocating rewards and working in groups, even if conducted in a culturally appropriate way, can sometimes be a source of conflict. Of course, there are many other causes of conflict as well and perhaps this accounts for why American managers spend 20% or more of their time dealing with conflict situations

(Thomas & Schmidt, 1976). But what are the effects of conflict management on justice perceptions, and how might these vary across culture? Very few studies have addressed this question directly (Folger & Cropanzano, 1998).

Clearly, the very presence of conflict in some cultures is viewed as inappropriate and hence less than fair. Collective cultures devise many social mechanisms to avoid getting involved in conflict in the first place. The Japanese, for example, avoid directly saying no in order to smooth interpersonal relationships and to avoid direct conflict (Ueda, 1978). If a Japanese negotiator finds a request impossible to satisfy, he or she might say "I shall give it careful consideration." Other collectivists might be able to interpret this phrase as a no and thereby avoid any subsequent conflict. Americans, however, might interpret this to mean that even more attention will be given to the matter. Later, when it becomes clearer that the phrase really meant no, the Americans may feel that the other party proceeded unfairly. So, the tendency to avoid conflict in the first place is viewed as fair in some cultures, whereas others prefer direct attention to differences.

Of course, a good deal of conflict does occur—even in collective cultures. How do people in different cultures resolve conflicts, and what type of resolution is the most just or fair? Several methods of settling conflict have been studied across cultures. Most commonly, adjudication procedures (trial–court methods) which are formal and binding have been compared to less formal and nonbinding methods, such as bargaining and mediation. An important study by Leung (1987) compared the conflict resolution preferences of American and Chinese subjects. Each person was asked to choose their preferred resolution method in a dispute situation. Leung reasoned that because methods such as mediation and bargaining involve compromise and exchange of concessions, the parties to the conflict would be more likely to maintain a harmonious relationship after the dispute is settled. Accordingly, collectivists like the Chinese should prefer these procedures and see outcomes resulting from them as more likely to lead to reduction of animosity (and thus as more just). Conversely, individualists like the Americans should be more likely to see adjudication, with its "all or none" approach to outcomes as more likely to reduce animosity or conflict. Accordingly, Leung found that collectivists were more likely to endorse a bargaining-type settlement, whereas individualists were more likely to view adjudication as a useful and fair method. Several other studies found similar results. For example, mediation seems to be preferred in Japan (Sullivan, Peterson, Kameda, & Shimada, 1981).

The cultural dimension of masculinity–femininity may also moderate the conflict–justice relation. Indeed, this dimension may be central to cross-cultural differences. Recall that feminine cultures value interpersonal cooperation and friendly atmospheres, whereas masculine cultures stress achievement and challenge. Leung, Bond, Carment, Krishnan, and Liebrand (1990) studied preferred methods of resolving conflict among Canadian and Dutch subjects. The Dutch score highly on femininity, whereas Canadians are a relatively masculine culture. Leung et al.'s results showed that the Dutch preferred approaches that allow compromise to come about (negotiation/mediation). In contrast, Canadians saw methods that heightened confrontation and competitiveness as the most fair way to resolve conflicts. As in the earlier study by Leung (1987), both groups thought that their approach was the most likely to reduce animosity and conflict between parties.

So what do these few cross-cultural studies on conflict and justice suggest for practicing managers? Clearly, Leung's (1987) research suggests that some cultures may be more willing to cede process and decision control to a third party than others. As a result, union-management relations in collectivist–high-power distance cultures will likely be low in conflict, relatively smooth over the long term, and based on nonbinding negotiation methods. Likewise, in such cultures, a supervisor's position regarding the conflict situation will be seen as more just and carry more weight than that of an employee. Finally, formal procedures that produce a definitive solution to the conflict are likely to be admired in individualistic and masculine cultures, and probably in high power distance cultures as well. Informal and indirect methods should be more effective in collective and feminine cultures. Nevertheless, more research is needed before we can fully embrace this advice. In fact, some studies have found that employees in countries as diverse as the United States, Turkey, Mexico, and Argentina all reacted positively to procedures that allowed them to participate in the conflict resolution process (see Folger & Cropanzano, 1998).

Organizational Citizenship

Of course, most managers would rather encourage organizational citizenship than have to resolve conflicts. Organizational citizenship behaviors (OCBs) are discretionary, extra-role activities that help the company, but that are not formally or explicitly recognized and rewarded (Eskew, 1993; Organ, 1990). The willingness of employees to perform such behaviors may help companies succeed in the face of international competition (McFarlin & Sweeney, 1998; Morrison, 1996; Organ, 1990). Of course, this raises the obvious question: What are the determinants of OCBs? Although the answer is complex, justice perceptions have been linked to employees' willingness to engage in OCBs, at least in the U.S. (Konovsky & Pugh, 1994; Moorman, 1991; Morrison, 1996; Organ, 1990). Perceptions that the firm uses unfair procedures has been found to predict whether employees consider suing their employers—certainly the antithesis of OCBs (Bies & Tyler, 1993).

Currently, research on justice and OCBs is moving into the international arena. For instance, studies have shown that the presence or absence of procedural justice affected the relationships that British subsidiaries had with their foreign parent companies in a variety of ways (Taggart, 1997). In fact, Kim and Mauborgne (1991, 1993) showed that management in multinational corporations need to pay attention to how their international strategies are created if they expect managers in foreign subsidiaries to enthusiastically carry them out. Specifically, if the processes used to create international strategy were perceived to be fair, then sub-sidiary managers were more likely to implement them. Fair procedures in this case included: (a) the home office familiarized itself with foreign operations; (b) two-way communication occurred when international strategy was being devel-oped; (c) the home office was consistent across foreign subsidiaries in making de-cisions; (d) foreign subsidiaries were able to challenge headquarters' opinions and perspectives; and (e) foreign subsidiaries were given a full explanation for the strategic decisions that were ultimately made.

In a more recent study, Kim and Mauborgne (1996) took things one step fur-ther by arguing that managers in foreign subsidiaries really must engage in OCBs to do an outstanding job of implementing the corporation's international strategy. They were able to show that by creating procedural fairness in the way global re-source allocation decisions were made, commitment among foreign subsidiary managers to the decisions themselves was increased. This increased commitment was directed related to a willingness by managers to perform OCBs. These in-cluded various innovative, spontaneous, and creative behaviors designed to im-plement international resource allocation decisions that went beyond normal role expectations.

Of course, the research by Kim and Mauborgne (1996), although fascinating, does not directly address the relation between cultural values, justice, and OCBs. Because OCBs ultimately support the collective (the company) as opposed to di-rectly benefitting an individual, a question has been raised as to whether cultural distinctions—especially individualism versus collectivism—are related to the performance of OCBs. For instance, it has been suggested that employees from collectivistic cultures will be more likely to engage in OCBs than employees who embrace individualism (Earley, 1989). Interestingly, the link between procedural justice and OCBs may operate much like collectivistic values. In other words, to the extent that fair procedures in a company encourage employees to think of the corporation as a collective and to embrace group values, then the performance of OCBs becomes more likely (Lind & Tyler, 1988; Moorman, Niehoff, & Organ, 1993).

Moorman and Blakely (1995) found that employees who embraced collec-tivistic values were more likely to engage in various OCBs (e.g., individual ini-tiative, loyal boosterism, and interpersonal helping), even after controlling for the effects of procedural justice on OCBs. American employees were the subjects and individualism–collectivism was assessed as an individual difference variable. Moorman and Blakely argued, as we did earlier in this chapter, that within-culture diversity in values should not be ignored. They went on to suggest that American companies ought to continue to explore ways to encourage collective thinking, both through the use of procedural justice and reward systems that emphasize group performance. These steps may help promote OCB performance, even in the United States where individual achievement is often highly prized.

Other research has examined justice-OCB relationships outside of the United States and found some intriguing results. Konovsky, Elliott, and Pugh (1996) found that for Mexican employees, distributive justice tended to be a stronger predictor of OCBs than procedural justice. Earlier research found that the reverse tended to be true for American employees (Konovsky & Pugh, 1994). This suggests that enhancing distributive fairness would help prompt OCBs in Mexico but that focusing on procedural fairness might be a better option in the United States. Of course, these are generalities not supported by specific data linking justice and cultural differences to OCBs.

Nevertheless, it is tempting to speculate about the role of culture here, especially given some of the problems American companies have had managing plants in Mexico. Compared to the United States, Mexico is much less individualistic but higher in power distance and uncertainty avoidance. As a result, many Mexicans feel that conformity, respect, and personal loyalty to supervisors are important and should be rewarded. Not surprisingly, American managers' efforts to encourage participative decision making and problem solving—usually seen as key components of procedural justice—are often confusing to Mexican workers. At the same time, American managers are sometimes confused by the fact that policies and procedures are often loosely followed in Mexico. The problem is that Americans and Mexicans seem to view procedural justice differently. To many American managers, procedural fairness results when policies and standards are applied consistently across workers. To Mexicans, however, procedural fairness may be something more informal and interactional in nature, embodied in the form of loyalty to an authority figure rather than a policy manual (de Forest, 1994; Gowan, Ibarreche, & Lackey, 1996). These anecdotal findings, although speculative, may help explain why procedural justice seems to have less impact on Mexican employees' OCBs.

A study by McFarlin and Sweeney (1996) addressed this issue more directly. In a survey of American and South African employees, McFarlin and Sweeney found that as a group, the South Africans were stronger in uncertainty avoidance, higher in power distance, more collectivistic, and more feminine in their orientation than the Americans. Several justice–outcome relationships were examined across the two groups. Among them was organizational loyalty, the willingness of employees to defend and promote the interests of the firm to others (Van Dyne, Graham, & Dienesch, 1994). An interaction was found such that the relation between procedural justice and organizational loyalty stronger for Americans than for South Africans. Procedural justice was measured in terms of the formal procedures used to appraise performance, distribute rewards, make promotions, and solve problems. This result is consistent with the idea that formal procedures may be less important for employees in collectivist, high-power distance cultures. In such cultures, obeying a paternalistic leader may be more crucial than following specific procedures. In contrast, in individualistic, low-power distance cultures, written policies may define a firm's capacity to treat people fairly and lead more directly to a willingness to engage in OCBs.

However, Agarwal (1993) suggested that if American companies go too far and create a rule-bound and overly bureaucratic environment, then worker alienation—rather than a propensity to engage in OCBs—may be the result. Agarwal also argued that this may be an effect limited to individualistic, low-power distance countries like the United States. He found that for Indian employees, closely following rules and procedures was associated with higher organizational commitment. Indian employees tend toward dependency and paternalism; India is another high-power distance society that has a more collective orientation overall than the United States.

How can these apparently inconsistent results about the value and impact of formal procedures across cultures be reconciled? One possibility is that following formal procedures closely is one way to show respect for a paternalistic leader in high-power distance, collectivistic societies—especially when procedural justice is whatever the leader says the rules should be. Therefore, the rules per se are not what is valued but rather the relationship with the leader. This may explain why some studies have shown that the fairness of formal policies and rules has less of an impact on OCBs in high-power distance, collectivistic societies. It also highlights the need to treat formal procedures and relational or interactional procedures separately (Masterson & Taylor, 1996), especially in a cross-cultural context.

Other studies examining high-power distance, collectivistic societies have found results that appear to be consistent with this explanation. For instance, a recent study by Smith, Peterson, and Wang (1996) found that Chinese managers relied more on rules and procedures than their British and American counterparts when dealing with day-to-day events (e.g., subordinate problems, choosing new subordinates, etc.). Smith et al. suggested that in high-power distance cultures, managers are loathe to bother their superiors about such routine issues. In fact, although Chinese managers reported relying on rules to a great extent, this usage did not correlate with whether Chinese managers thought that they had handled various events well. So, although procedures and rules were heavily used, their perceived impact was minimal. Instead, Chinese managers often develop elaborate networks of personal contacts based on the exchange of favors and gifts as a way to get things done. Americans trying to do business in China have been advised to develop these connections (*guanxi*) if they want to succeed (Xin & Pearce, 1996).

Farh, Lin, and Earley (1995) complemented these results in their investigation of the link between justice perceptions and OCBs in Chinese employees. They found that Chinese employees produced the same positive relationships between distributive and procedural justice and OCBs generally found with samples of Americans. However, Farh et al. also found that for Chinese who endorsed traditional values (e.g., paternalism, fatalism), the link between justice (both distributive and procedural) and OCBs was much weaker than for Chinese who had a less traditional or more modern outlook. In fact, many Chinese businesses operate as traditional extended families, with deep but narrow loyalties. Employees often have strong loyalties to immediate superiors, but little interest in the company as a whole. The leader is seen as the wise, moral father whose decisions are to be obeyed without question, but who also is concerned for the personal needs of his subordinates. Wisdom is defined in terms of the leader's judgement. This view of leadership has its roots in centuries-old Confucian values (Bond, 1991). Overall, Farh et al.'s results imply that for Chinese who embrace traditional values, rules and procedures reflect a personal commitment to a leader rather than a means to an end in and of themselves (i.e., to create a fair work environment). Clearly, however, many unanswered questions remain about the intersection of cultural values, justice perceptions, and OCBs.

International Mergers and Acquisitions

International mergers and acquisitions represent yet another area where culture and justice can have important effects. In 1996, the total value of international mergers and acquisitions hit nearly $300 billion, a new record (Koretz, 1997). Buying or merging with foreign companies gives firms quick access to technology, products, and markets worldwide. Unfortunately, however, firms often fumble the human-resource management issues that accompany international acquisitions (Briscoe, 1995; Calori, Lubatkin, & Very, 1994; McFarlin & Sweeney, 1998; Napier, Schweiger, & Kosglow, 1993). In fact, underestimating the differences between the cultures of the firms (and countries) involved in the acquisition is a common problem.

Especially interesting for our purposes are the justice-related culture clashes that may be involved in international acquisitions. For example, the 1996 merger between Sweden's Pharmacia AB and U.S.-based Upjohn Company was plagued by a variety of unexpected management differences. Swedish managers resented the more aggressive and top-down management style of their American counterparts. They found it especially unfair—and a waste of time—to have to write detailed monthly reports for their American counterparts. These American procedures were inconsistent with the Swedish tendency to let employees operate on their own in small groups and to give such groups a voice in decisions made by top executives. Sweden is one of the few countries to be lower in power distance and weaker in uncertainty orientation than the United States. In short, the Americans were not informal enough for the Swedes. Eventually, Upjohn decided not to insist that Swedish employees comply with certain policies used in the United States (Frank & Burton, 1997).

Studies also show that national culture affects the ways firms handle cross-border acquisitions to begin with (Napier et al., 1993). Calori et al. (1994), for example, compared the human-resource strategies used by French and American firms that had purchased British companies. French firms relied more on procedures designed to ensure tight control over their British acquisitions (like more centralized decision making at headquarters) than did American firms. In contrast, American firms tended to rely more on informal procedures aimed at breaking down barriers (e.g., teamwork and informal communications from managers of the acquiring firm) than did their French counterparts. Like the Pharmacia versus Upjohn clash mentioned previously, differences in power distance and uncertainty avoidance may help explain these patterns. In this case, however, France is higher on power distance and stronger in uncertainty avoidance than the United States. Interestingly, Calori et al. found that an informal and open approach seemed to work best overall in cross-border acquisitions—performance was better and so were employee attitudes (e.g., perceptions of fairness, etc.).

However, more research needs to be done to find out whether these results would generalize to other cross-national contexts. For example, if the *target company* was in a high-power distance, strong uncertainty avoidance country (unlike the United Kingdom), then informal procedures designed to solicit input may backfire and actually raise resistance levels. In fact, a few years ago we interviewed French executives at one of General Electric's newly acquired subsidiaries outside of Paris. Several French managers said that they resisted the informal efforts their American counterparts made to solicit their input and participatively decide on how best to run the subsidiary. In general, they found this "American process" confusing and unclear.

SOME CONCLUDING ADVICE
FOR INTERNATIONAL MANAGERS

In many ways, the current state of research linking cultural values, justice perceptions, and various employee attitudes and behaviors is still in its infancy. There are many unanswered questions and inconsistent results. Therefore, it seems best to conclude with some general suggestions. First, we would advise international managers to explicitly take cultural values into account when designing fair systems to hire, reward, and motivate employees (Gomez-Mejia & Welbourne, 1991). This task is complicated by the fact that international managers may not recognize their own cultural values and how they can affect justice perceptions. As a result, it may be very useful to start with the idea that whatever strategy is adopted, it should be *culturally synergistic*. In other words, it should complement rather than conflict with the various cultures involved. The process of actually developing a culturally synergistic strategy involves four basic steps (Adler, 1997):

1. *Describe the situation.* How does the manager view the justice issues in a particular organizational context (e.g., designing a reward strategy, etc.)? What perspectives do subordinates take on these issues? The purpose of this first step is to discover whether different perspectives exist and whether these differences create problems.

2. *Identify cultural assumptions about justice issues.* The next step is to un-cover the cultural values that help explain why different perspectives on jus-tice exist. The goal is to be able to reverse perspectives and see things from another culture's point of view.

3. *Generate culturally synergistic alternatives.* Once cultural assumptions have been identified, the next challenge is to develop an approach to or-ganizational justice that blends elements of the cultures involved or even goes beyond them.

4. *Select and implement a synergistic approach to justice.* The final step in-volves picking what appears to be the best justice approach and imple-menting it. A critical issue here is to have all parties involved observe the strategy from their own cultural perspective. The chosen strategy may need to be fine-tuned based on any feedback received.

To help international managers develop culturally synergistic strategies, multi-national firms may want to include culture and justice issues in their leadership training programs. Ideally, international managers should have a justice perspec-tive that goes beyond a particular culture or country. As firms continue to inter-nationalize, the variety of cross-cultural justice issues that managers must deal with is likely to increase (McFarlin & Sweeney, 1998).

AUTHORS' NOTE

The authors contributed equally to this work. Order of authorship was determined randomly.

REFERENCES

Adler, N. J. (1997). *International dimensions of organizational behavior* (3rd ed.). Cincinnati, OH: South-Western Publishing.

Adams, J. S. (1965). Inequity in social exchange. In L. Berkowitz (Ed.), *Advances in Experimental Social Psychology*, Vol. 2 (pp. 267–299). New York: Academic.

Agarwal, S. (1993). Influence of formalization on role stress, organizational commitment, and work alienation of salespersons: A cross-national comparative study. *Journal of International Business Studies, 23*, 715–739.

Ali, A. (1988). A cross-national perspective of managerial work value systems. In R. N. Farmer & E. G. McGowen (Eds.), *Advances in international comparative management* (pp. 212–265). Greenwich, CT: JAI.

Arvey, R. D. (1992). Fairness and ethical considerations in employee selection. In D. M. Saunders (Ed.), *New approaches in employee selection* (Vol. 1, pp. 1–19). Greenwich, CT: JAI.

Arvey, R. D., & Sackett, P. R. (1993). Fairness in selection: Current developments and perspectives. In N. Schmitt & W. Borman (Eds.), *Personnel selection* (pp. 171–202). San Francisco: Jossey-Bass.

Berman, J. J., Murphy-Berman, V., & Singh, P. (1985). Cross-cultural similarities and differences in perceptions of fairness. *Journal of Cross-Cultural Psychology, 16*, 55–67.

Bies, R. J. & Tyler, T. R. (1993). The "litigation mentality in organizations: A test of alternative psychological explanations. *Organization Science, 4*, 352–366.

Bhagat, R. S., & McQuaid, S. J. (1982). Role of subjective culture in organizations: A review and directions for future research. *Journal of Applied Psychology, 67*, 653–685.

Bochner, S., & Hesketh, B. (1994). Power distance, individualism/collectivism, and job-related attitudes in a culturally diverse work group. *Journal of Cross-Cultural Psychology, 25*, 233–257.

Bond, M. H. (1991). *Beyond the Chinese face*. Hong Kong: Oxford University Press.

Bond, M. H., Leung, K., & Wan, K. C. (1982). How does cultural collectivism operate? The impact of task and maintenance contribution on reward distribution. *Journal of Cross-Cultural Psychology, 13*, 186–200.

Boyacigiller, N. A., Kleinberg, M. J., Phillips, M. E., & Sackmann, S. A. (1996). Conceptualizing culture. In B. Punnett & O. Shenkar (Eds.), *Handbook for international management research* (pp. 157–208). Cambridge, MA: Blackwell.

Briscoe, D. R. (1995). *International human resource management*. Englewood Cliffs, NJ: Prentice-Hall.

Brockner, J., Konovsky, M., Cooper-Schneider, R., Folger, R., Martin, C. L., & Bies, R. J. (1994). The interactive effects of procedural justice and outcome negativity on the victims and survivors of job loss. *Academy of Management Journal, 37*, 397–409.

Calori, R., Lubatkin, M., & Very, P. (1994). Control mechanisms in cross-border acquisitions: An international comparison. *Organization Studies, 15*, 361–379.

Cascio, W., & Bailey, E. (1995). International human resource management: The state of research and practice. In O. Shenkar (Ed.), *Global perspectives of human resource management* (pp. 15–36). Englewood Cliffs, NJ: Prentice-Hall.

Chen, C. C. (1995). New trends in reward allocation preferences: A sino-U.S. comparison. *Academy of Management Journal, 38*, 408–428.

Cowherd, D. M., & Levine, D. I. (1992). Product quality and pay equity between lower-level employees and top management: An investigation of distributive justice theory. *Administrative Science Quarterly, 37*, 302–320.

Cox, T., & Blake, S. (1991). Managing cultural diversity: Implications for organizational competitiveness. *Academy of Management Executive, 5*, 45–56.

Davis, J., Kerr, S., & Von Glinow, M. A. (1987). Is the Japanese management craze over? *International Journal of Management, 4*, 486–495.

de Forest, M. E. (1994). Thinking of a plant in Mexico? *Academy of Management Executive, 8*, 33–40.

Dorfman, P. (1996). International and cross-cultural leadership. In B. Punnett & O. Shenkar (Eds.), *Handbook for international management research* (pp. 267–349). Cambridge, MA: Blackwell.

Dowling, P. J., & Nagel, T. W. (1986). Nationality and work attitudes: A study of Australian and American business majors. *Journal of Management, 12*, 121–128.

Dumaine, B. (1990, May 7). Who needs a boss? *Fortune*, 52–60.

Earley, P. C. (1984). Social interaction: The frequency of use and valuation in US, England, and Ghana. *Journal of Cross-Cultural Psychology, 15*, 477–485.

Earley, P. C. (1986). Trust, perceived importance of praise and criticism, and work performance: An examination of feedback in the United States and England. *Journal of Management, 12*, 457–473.

Earley, P. C. (1989). Social loafing and collectivism. *Administrative Science Quarterly, 34*, 565–581.

Earley, P. C. (1993). East meets West meets Mideast: Further explorations of collectivistic and individualistic work groups. *Academy of Management Journal, 36*, 319–348.

Eskew, D. E. (1993). The role of organizational justice in organizational citizenship behaviors. *Employee Responsibilities and Rights Journal, 6*, 185–194.

Espinoza, J. A., & Garza, R. T. (1985). Social group salience and inter-ethnic cooperation. *Journal of Experimental Social Psychology, 23*, 380–392.

Farh, J. L., Dobbins, G. H., & Cheng, B. S. (1991). Cultural relativity in action: A comparison of self-ratings made by Chinese and U.S. workers. *Personnel Psychology, 44*, 129–147.

Farh, L., Lin, S., & Earley, P. C. (1995). Impetus for extraordinary action: A cultural analysis of justice and extra-role behavior in Chinese society. Unpublished manuscript.

Folger, R., & Bies, R. J. (1989). Managerial responsibilities and procedural justice. *Employee Responsibilities and Rights Journal, 2,* 79–90.

Folger, R., & Cropanzano, R. (1998). *Organizational justice and human resource management.* Beverly Hills, CA: Sage.

Folger, R., & Konovsky, M. A. (1989). Effects of procedural and distributive justice on reactions to pay raise decisions. *Academy of Management Journal, 32,* 115–130.

Frank, R., & Burton, T. M. (1997, February 4). Cross-border merger results in headaches for a drug company. *The Wall Street Journal,* pp. A1, A12.

Frese, M., Kring, W., Soose, A., & Zempel, J. (1996). Personal initiative at work: Differences between East and West Germany. *Academy of Management Journal, 39,* 37–63.

Fryxell, G. E. (1992). Perceptions of justice afforded by formal grievance systems as predictors of a belief in a just workplace. *Journal of Business Ethics, 11,* 635–647.

Gabrenya, W. K., Latane, B., & Wang, Y. (1981). Social loafing in cross-cultural perspective. *Journal of Cross-Cultural Psychology, 14,* 368–384.

Gilliland, S. W. (1993). The perceived fairness of selection systems: An organizational justice perspective. *Academy of Management Review, 18,* 694–734.

Gilliland, S. W. (1994). Effects of procedural and distributive justice on reactions to a selection system. *Journal of Applied Psychology, 79,* 691–701.

Gomez-Mejia, L. & Welbourne, T. (1991). Compensation strategies in a global context. *Human Resource Planning, 14,* 29–41.

Gowan, M., Ibarreche, S., & Lackey, C. (1996). Doing the right things in Mexico. *Academy of Management Executive, 10,* 74–81.

Greenberg, J. (1990). Employee theft as a reaction to underpayment inequity: The hidden costs of cuts. *Journal of Applied Psychology, 75,* 561–568.

Hofstede, G. (1980, Summer). Motivation, leadership, and organization: Do American theories apply abroad? *Organizational Dynamics,* 42–63.

Hofstede, G. (1984). *Culture's consequences.* Newbury Park, CA: Sage.

Hofstede, G. (1993). Cultural constraints in management theories. *Academy of Management Executive, 7,* 81–94.

Hofstede, G. (1996). An American in Paris: The influence of nationality on organization theories. *Organizational Studies, 17,* 525–537.

Hui, C. H., Triandis, H. C., & Yee, C. (1991). Cultural differences in reward allocation: Is collectivism the explanation? *British Journal of Social Psychology, 30,* 145–157.

James, K. (1993). The social context of organizational justice: Cultural, intergroup, and structural effects on justice behaviors and perceptions. In R. Cropanzano (Ed.), *Justice in the workplace: Approaching fairness in human resource management* (pp. 21–50). Hillsdale, NJ: Lawrence Erlbaum Associates.

Khoza, R. (1994). The need for an Afrocentric management approach. In P. Christie, R. Lessem & L. Mbigi (Eds.), *African management: Philosophies, concepts, and applications* (pp. 117–124). Johannesburg: Knowledge Resources.

Kim, W. C., & Mauborgne, R. A. (1991). Implementing global strategies: The role of procedural justice. *Strategic Management Journal, 12,* 125–143.

Kim, W. C., & Mauborgne, R. A. (1993, Spring). Making global strategies work. *Sloan Management Review,* 11–25.

Kim, W. C., & Mauborgne, R. A. (1996). Procedural justice and managers' in-role and extra-role behavior: The case of the multinational. *Management Science, 42,* 499–515.

Kim, K. I., Park, H. J., & Suzuki, N. (1990). Reward allocations in the U.S., Japan, and Korea: A comparison of individualistic and collectivistic cultures. *Academy of Management Journal, 33,* 188–198.

Konovsky, M. A., & Cropanzano, R. (1991). Perceived fairness of employee drug testing as a predictor of employee attitudes and job performance. *Journal of Applied Psychology, 76,* 698–707.

Konovsky, M. A., Elliott, J., & Pugh, S. D. (1996). The dispositional and contextual predictors of citizenship behaviors in Mexico. Paper presented at the meetings of the *Academy of Management,* Cincinnati, OH.

Konovsky, M. A., & Pugh, S. D. (1994). Citizenship behavior and social exchange. *Academy of Management Journal, 37*, 656–699.

Koretz, G. (1997, February 17). Dealmakers go on a global tear. *Business Week, 25.*

Leung, K. (1987). Some determinants of reactions to procedural models for conflict resolution: A cross-national study. *Journal of Personality and Social Psychology, 53*, 898–908.

Leung, K., & Bond, M. H. (1984). The impact of cultural collectivism on reward allocation. *Journal of Personality and Social Psychology, 47*, 793–804.

Leung, K., Bond, M. H., Carment, D. W., Krishnan, L., & Liebrand, W. B. G. (1990). Effects of cultural femininity on preference for methods of conflict processing: A cross-cultural study. *Journal of Experimental Social Psychology, 26*, 373–388.

Leung, K., Chiu, W. H., & Au, Y. F. (1993). Sympathy and support for industrial actions: A justice analysis. *Journal of Applied Psychology, 78*, 781–787.

Lind, E. A., & Tyler, T. R. (1988). *The social psychology of procedural justice.* New York: Plenum.

Love, K. G., Bishop, R. C., Heinisch, D. A., & Montei, M. S. (1994). Selection across two cultures: Adapting the selection of American assemblers to meet Japanese job performance demands. *Personnel Psychology, 47*, 837–846.

Masterson, S. S., & Taylor, M. S. (1996). The broadening of procedural justice: Should interactional and procedural components be separate theories? Paper presented at the meetings of the *Academy of Management,* Cincinnati, OH.

Matsui, T., Kakuyama, T., & Onglatco, M. L. U. (1987). Effects of goals and feedback on performance in groups. *Journal of Applied Psychology, 72*, 407–415.

Mbigi, L. (1994). The spirit of African management. In P. Christie, R. Lessem & L. Mbigi (Eds.), *African management: Philosophies, concepts, and applications* (pp. 77–92). Johannesburg: Knowledge Resources.

McEvoy, G. M., & Cascio, W. R. (1990). The U.S. and Taiwan: Two different cultures look at performance appraisal. In G. R. Ferris & K. M. Rowland (Eds.), *Research in personnel and human resources management* (Vol. 6, pp. 201–19). Greenwich, CT: JAI.

McFarlin, D. B., Coster, E. A., & Mogale-Pretorius, C. M. (1999). Management development in South Africa: Moving toward an Africanized framework. *Journal of Management Development, 18*, 63–78.

McFarlin, D. B., & Frone, M. R. (1990). Examining a two-tier wage structure in a non-union firm. *Industrial Relations, 29*, 145–157.

McFarlin, D. B., & Sweeney, P. D. (1992). Distributive and procedural justice as predictors of satisfaction with personal and organizational outcomes. *Academy of Management Journal, 35*, 626–637.

McFarlin, D. B., & Sweeney, P. D. (1996). The impact of culture on organizational justice. Paper presented at the annual meeting of the *Society for Industrial and Organizational Psychology,* San Diego, CA.

McFarlin, D. B., & Sweeney, P. D. (1998). *International Management: Trends, Challenges, and Opportunities.* Cincinnati, OH: South-Western College Publishing.

McFarlin, D. B., Sweeney, P. D., & Cotton, J. C. (1992). Attitudes toward employee participation in decision-making: A comparison of European and American managers in a U.S. Multinational. *Human Resource Management Journal, 31*, 363–383.

Merritt, A. C., & Helmreich, R. L. (1996). Human factors on the flight deck: The influence of national culture. *Journal of Cross-Cultural Psychology, 27*, 5–24.

Miles, J. A., & Greenberg, J. (1993). Cross-national differences in preferences for distributive justice norms: The challenge of establishing fair resource allocations for the European Community. In J. Shaw, P. Kirkbride, K. Rowland & G. Ferris (Eds.), *Research in personnel and human resources management* (Suppl. 3, pp. 133–156). Greenwich, CT: JAI.

Milliman, J. F., Nason, S., Lowe, K., Kim, N., & Huo, P. (1995). An empirical study of performance appraisal practices in Japan, Korea, Taiwan and the U.S. Paper presented at the meetings of the *Academy of Management,* Vancouver, Canada.

Moorman, R. H. (1991). Relationship between organizational justice and organizational citizenship behaviors: Do fairness perceptions influence employee citizenship? *Journal of Applied Psychology, 76,* 845–855.

Moorman, R. H., & Blakely, G. L. (1995). Individualism–collectivism as an individual difference predictor of organizational citizenship behavior. *Journal of Organizational Behavior, 16,* 127–142.

Moorman, R. H., Niehoff, B. P., & Organ, D. W. (1993). Treating employees fairly and organizational citizenship behaviors: Sorting the effects of job satisfaction, organizational commitment, and procedural justice. *Employee Responsibilities and Rights Journal, 6,* 209–225.

Morrison, E. W. (1996). Organizational citizenship behavior as a critical link between HRM practices and service quality. *Human Resource Management, 35,* 493–512.

Morrison, E. W., & Robinson, S. L. (1997). When employees feel betrayed: A model of how psychological contract violation develops. *Academy of Management Review, 22,* 226–256.

Murphy-Berman, V., Berman, J., Singh, P., Pachauri, A., & Kumar, P. (1984). Factors affecting allocation to needy and meritorious recipients: A cross-cultural comparison. *Journal of Personality and Social Psychology, 46,* 1267–1272.

Napier, N. K., Schweiger, D. M., & Kosglow, J. J. (1993). Managing organizational diversity: Observations from cross-border acquisitions. *Human Resource Management, 32,* 505–523.

Organ, D. W. (1990). The motivational basis of organizational citizenship behavior. In B. Staw (Ed.), *Research in Organizational Behavior* (Vol. 12, pp. 43–72). Greenwich, CT: JAI.

Pandey, J., & Singh, P. (1997). Allocation criterion as a function of situational factors and caste. *Basic and Applied Social Psychology, 19,* 121–132.

Pearce, J. L., Branyiczki, I., & Bakacsi, G. (1994). Person-based reward systems: A theory of organizational reward practices in reform-communist organizations. *Journal of Organizational Behavior, 15,* 261–282.

Pennings, J. M. (1993). Executive reward systems: A cross-national comparison. *Journal of Management Studies, 30,* 261–279.

Puffer, S. M. (1993). Three factors affecting reward allocation in the former USSR: An empirical study. In J. Shaw, P. Kirkbride, K. Rowland & G. Ferris (Eds.), *Research in Personnel and Human Resources Management* (Suppl. 3; pp. 279–298). Greenwich, CT: JAI.

Ralston, D. A., Gustafson, D. J., Cheung, F. M., & Terpstra, R. H. (1993). Differences in managerial values: A study of U.S., Hong Kong, and PRC managers. *Journal of International Business Studies, 23,* 249–275.

Ralston, D. A., Holt, D. H., Terpstra, R. H., & Kai-Cheng (1997). The impact of national culture and economic ideology on managerial work values: A study of the United States, Russia, Japan, and China. *Journal of International Business Studies, 28,* 177–207.

Sashkin, M., & Williams, R. L. (1990). Does fairness make a difference? *Organizational Dynamics, 75,* 56–71.

Shaw, J. B., Tang, S. F. Y., Fisher, C. D., & Kirkbride, P. S. (1993). Organizational and environmental factors related to human resource management practices in Hong Kong: A cross-cultural expanded replication. *International Journal of Human Resource Management, 4,* 785–816.

Shenkar, O., & Von Glinow, M. A. (1994). Paradoxes of organizational theory and research: Using the case of China to illustrate national contingency. *Management Science, 40,* 56–71.

Skarlicki, D. P. & Folger, R. (1997). Retaliation in the workplace: The roles of distributive, procedural, and interactional justice. *Journal of Applied Psychology, 82,* 434–443.

Smith, P. B., Dugan, & Trompenaars, F. (1996). National culture and the values of organizational employees: A dimensional analysis across 43 nations. *Journal of Cross-Cultural Psychology, 27,* 231–264.

Smith, P. B., Peterson, M. F., & Wang, Z. M. (1996). The manager as mediator of alternative meanings: A pilot study from China, the USA and U.K. *Journal of International Business Studies, 27,* 115–137.

Smither, J. W., Reilly, R. R., Millsap, R. E., Pearlman, K., & Stoffey, R. W. (1993). Applicant reactions to selection procedures. *Personnel Psychology, 46,* 49–76.

Steiner, D. D., & Gilliland, S. W. (1996). Fairness reactions to personnel selection techniques in France and the United States. *Journal of Applied Psychology, 81*, 134–141.

Steinmetz, G. (1995, May 9). German banks note the value of bonuses. *The Wall Street Journal*, p. A18.

Sullivan, J. Peterson, R. B., Kameda, N., & Shimada, J. (1981). The relationship between conflict resolution approaches and trust: A cross-cultural study. *Academy of Management Journal, 24*, 803–815.

Sweeney, P. D., & McFarlin, D. B. (1993). Workers' evaluations of the "ends and the "means": An examination of four models of distributive and procedural justice. *Organizational Behavior and Human Decision Processes, 55*, 23–40.

Taggart, J. H. (1997). Autonomy and procedural justice: A framework for evaluating subsidiary strategy. *Journal of International Business Studies, 28*, 51–76.

Thomas, K. W., & Schmidt, W. N. (1976). A survey of managerial interests with respect to conflict. *Academy of Management Journal, 10*, 315–318.

Triandis, H. C. (1996). The psychological measurement of cultural syndromes. *American Psychologist, 51*, 407–415.

Trompenaars, F. (1993). *Riding the waves of culture*. London: Brealey.

Tyler, T., Degoey, P., & Smith, H. (1996). Understanding why the justice of group procedures matters: A test of the psychological dynamics of the group-value model. *Journal of Personality and Social Psychology, 70*, 913–930.

Ueda, K. (1978). Sixteen ways to avoid saying 'no' in Japan. In. J. C. Condon & M. Saito (Eds.), *Intercultural encounters with Japan. Communication—contact and conflict* (pp. 185–195). New York: Simul Press.

Van Dyne, L., Graham, J. W., & Dienesch, R. M. (1994). Organizational citizenship behavior: Construct redefinition, measurement, and validation. *Academy of Management Journal, 37*, 765–802.

Welsh, D. H. B., Luthans, F., & Sommer, S. M. (1993). Managing Russian factory workers: The impact of US-based behavioral and participative techniques. *Academy of Management Journal, 36*, 58–79.

Wilhelm, P. G. (1993). Application of distributive justice theory to the CEO pay problem: Recommendations for reform. *Journal of Business Ethics, 12*, 469–482.

Work Team Trivia. (1992). The competitive edge. March–April, p. 12.

Xin, K. R., & Pearce, J. L. (1996). Guanxi: Connections as substitutes for formal institutional support. *Academy of Management Journal, 39*, 1641–1658.

5

▼▼▼▼▼▼▼▼▼

Fairness as a Dependent Variable: Why Tough Times Can Lead to Bad Management

Robert Folger
Tulane University

Daniel P. Skarlicki
The University of Calgary

Without warning, 17 workers at Middlebury College learned one morning that they had lost their jobs. College officials drove them to a building on the edge of campus and delivered them to members of an outplacement firm. Employees could not finish their work, call their offices, or even say good-bye to co-workers. A form letter from the college's president stated that they would continue to receive benefits but only if they cooperated with the outplacement firm (Greenberg & Baron, 1993). As the result of this incident, the college president later resigned.

Sutton, Eisenhardt, and Jucker (1986) described how Atari workers were laid off without notice. They were given directions to a local high school where they could pick up their final checks, their badges were collected, and they were escorted off the premises. Some managers later derogated the former employees (e.g., "now we've gotten rid of all the rummies and the company's strong and all the good people are left"; p. 23). Such statements lowered morale among survivors, who saw the process as "humiliating," "demeaning," and conducted in a "haphazard and unkind" manner (p. 22).

Anecdotes such as these suggest that managers do not always do the right thing when administering layoffs (Brockner, 1992; Folger, 1993a; Folger & Pugh, 1997; Folger & Skarlicki, 1998). Precisely when employees most need managers to treat them fairly—by providing personal attention, treating them with sensitivity, giving them an adequate explanation—managers often distance themselves from layoff victims, failing to treat them with respect and dignity. Inhumane managerial treatment of employees during layoffs is not an isolated phenomenon. Rather, it illustrates an unsettling trend that can cut across many areas of managerial practice, a tendency captured by the phrase in this chapter's subtitle about tough times leading to bad management.

This chapter extends the examination of that tendency in three ways. First, we use insights from the literature on organizational justice but apply them differently than how they have been applied in the past. Most research to date has examined organizational justice as an independent variable and has investigated its effects on individuals' attitudes and behavior. Instead, this chapter conceptualizes fair treatment as a dependent variable and attempts to explain why managers do not always practice fairness principles. Behaviors are focused on, such as interpersonal distancing, that are perceived by employees as violations of interactional justice. Distancing behaviors tend to seem rude and demeaning; they are deemed unfair because they imply undue disregard for other people and their rights. In interactional justice terms, distancing behaviors are deemed unfair because in doing so managers fail to provide employees with explanatory information and fail to display interpersonal sensitivity that respects dignity and human worth (Folger, 1993b; Folger, 1998; Greenberg, 1993).

Second, research has studied the effects of perceived unfair treatment on the attitudes and behaviors of the layoff victims and survivors. There is a dearth of research, however, that considers determinants of the perspective adopted by managers. Managers are not necessarily villains when they act in ways perceived by others as being unfair; they can be good people making bad decisions in response to threat, adversity, and unrecognized sources of biased perceptions on their part. This chapter examines both emotional and cognitive explanations relevant to explaining managers' behavior. In particular, we look for sources of impact on emotions and cognitions that derive from situational variations rather than dispositional variations.

Third, interpersonal distancing during layoffs is the initial focus for research on unfair managerial behavior as a dependent variable, but then we try to generalize our explanations and their applicability. Related processes are responsible for similar effects—those we label generically as "Churchill Effects" for reasons to be revealed shortly—in a variety of situations.

CHURCHILL EFFECTS AS SURPRISINGLY DYSFUNCTIONAL BEHAVIOR BY MANAGERS

Downsizing and restructuring has had a significant impact on organizations throughout North America. From a human-resource perspective, however, these stand out because of the oddly dysfunctional behavior they reveal: Despite considerable evidence that fair treatment positively impacts employees' performance, motivation, and job attitudes, managers often choose not to do the right thing when implementing layoffs. Simple practices that display sensitivity—expressing dignity and respect for laid off employees—are ignored or underutilized, although they would take some of the pain out of hard times and put management in a better position to manage. As a result, some of these management practices make bad times even worse.

Although curt, impersonal layoffs, such as those described previously, have been justified as necessary security measures (e.g., Dubose, 1994), these behaviors have other potential implications. For instance, they can be part of a vicious cycle in which the victim is blamed for the layoff—even to rationalizations that condone abusive treatment, such as layoffs conducted in callous and demeaning ways (cf. Brockner, 1994).

Unfair layoffs could have repercussions worth noting. For example, laid-off employees who resent such treatment might generate ill will in their communities against former employers (Feldman & Leana, 1989). Studies of workplace violence suggest that homicide can be largely a response to feelings of unfair treatment (Fox & Levin, 1994). Research by Folger and his colleagues (Cropanzano & Folger, 1989; Folger & Martin, 1986; Folger, Robinson, Dietz, McLean-Parks, & Baron, 1998; Folger, Rosenfield, Rheaume, & Martin, 1983; Folger, Rosenfield, & Robinson; Skarlicki & Folger, 1997) found that retaliation and resentment are highest among individuals when unfavorable outcomes are combined with unfair procedures or poor interpersonal treatment (for a review of support for this prediction from Folger's, 1987, referent cognitions theory, see Brockner & Wiesenfeld, 1996). Similarly, survivors of layoffs learn vicariously about the treatment that they might expect. Fear and anger regarding layoffs can impact adversely their level of performance, motivation, and job attitudes, with potentially negative implications for the organization (Brockner, 1994).

Of course, the sheer size of some layoffs might make it difficult to personalize treatment. Labeling organizationally mass-produced responses like severance pay and the hiring of outplacement services as impersonal might underestimate the genuine concern for employees that employers and managers feel. It is also true that not all examples of handling hardship show disregard for employee dignity. Moreover, it would be erroneous to assume that management automatically adopts a callous attitude to harmed employees and always displays insensitive, depersonalizing treatment. Faced with the potential consequences of abusive layoffs and with only the small cost of displaying sensitivity as a potentially effective deterrent of retaliation, why would an otherwise intelligent manager neglect to show minimal civility toward victims?

Understanding the answer to this question is important for several reasons. First, we contend that managers are not villains; good people all too often do foolishly insensitive things by mistake. An unfortunate tendency occurs when they compound an initial misjudgment by taking subsequent actions that lead to worse problems. Colloquially, they shoot themselves in the foot. Second, observers of managers' behavior often engage in the fundamental attribution error—the tendency to overemphasize disposition rather than situational explanations (Ross, 1977). Thus, as a result of distancing themselves from the victims of adversity, managers might be labeled as people who are hard-nosed and uncaring. Third, managers personify the organization for employees (Levinson, 1965); the behavior of a manager is often seen as representative of the entire organization. Managers and leaders implicate the organization as the result of the way they behave, and individuals who feel unfairly treated conclude that the entire organization as unfair. Finally, organizational change increases people's sensitivity to fairness issues (Neuman & Baron, 1996). During pervasive organizational change, doing the right thing from a fairness perspective becomes the next challenge for human-resources managers. Understanding why managers behave in the way they do becomes increasingly important for both academics and practitioners.

The Churchill Effect

Folger (1993a) referred to the tendency for managers to distance themselves from victims of adversity as the Churchill effect (see also Folger & Pugh, 1997; Folger & Skarlicki, 1998), based on events following the bombing of Pearl Harbor. British Prime Minister Winston Churchill wrote to inform the Japanese ambassador that Great Britain had formally declared war on Japan. Churchill communicated this message in a very proper British letter, closing as follows: "I have the honor to be with high consideration, Sir, Your obedient servant, Winston S. Churchill" (Churchill, 1950, p. 610). The British press published the text, which provoked a public outcry criticizing the politely deferential manner in which Churchill addressed the enemy. Churchill's memoirs contain the following comment in response to that criticism: "When you have to kill a man, it costs nothing to be polite" (p. 611).

Churchill's reference to cost-free politeness (i.e., considerate treatment of a person whom one is about to harm) is instructive in several respects. First, raising the issue of cost suggests why considerate treatment might not always be forthcoming. Although the direct, material costs of civility might ordinarily seem minimal, devoting extra time and special effort to showing interpersonal sensitivity to layoff victims does entail some emotional and even physical cost. Managers might under some conditions see such time and effort as aversive and burdensome. If so, it could constitute a form of cost deemed to be as real as incurring economic costs.

Second, an ironic aspect of Churchill's comment is highlighted by research showing the considerable benefits and low cost of demonstrating interpersonal sensitivity when laying off employees. Brockner (1992; Brockner, DeWitt, Grover, & Reed, 1990; Brockner & Greenberg, 1990) suggested that displaying sensitivity (e.g., taking sufficient time to meet with those who suffer losses) enhances the perceived fairness of managerial conduct. That fair conduct thereby mitigates negative reactions during times such as downsizing, when scarce resources dictate inevitable outcome losses or reductions for at least some employees (see also Konovsky & Folger, 1991). These studies show that employee reactions to layoffs vary considerably based on how employees felt about management conduct. Management sensitivity (i.e., providing adequate explanations, expressing remorse, showing consideration) substantially reduced negative reactions of both layoff victims and survivors. Thus, fair and interpersonally sensitive conduct (concern for employees' well-being and dignity) reduces hostility and fosters tolerance for negative outcomes. Yet, those very managerial behaviors that can positively impact how employees feel and react seem almost inexplicably avoided by some downsizing companies.

In the following two sections on emotional and cognitive–perceptual sources of Churchill effects, we try to make the seemingly inexplicable a little more explicable. Once we have laid out some possible explanatory mechanisms, we then broaden the focus by identifying related effects possibly subject to the same types of explanations.

Emotional Sources of Churchill Effects

Increased emotional distress might provide one plausible reason for avoiding contact with another person. Churchill, as noted previously, claimed that being polite was cost-free. Moreover, he implicitly chided the public's lack of willingness to condone his politeness to an enemy. The person who must actually behave with emotional empathy toward a harmed victim, however, might often pay a price in increased stress. For example, one condition under which a manager might demonstrate distancing behavior involves when he or she is to blame for the adversity. The theoretical relevance of blame as emotional stress traces in part to studies of shame (e.g., Tangney, 1992) that have examined the avoidance or minimization of interpersonal contact (i.e., distancing) as a function of blameworthiness—a person's having been identified as a cause of another person's plight. Research has shown that the potential loss of face associated with blameworthiness, such as based on the threat of being criticized, can be aversive and hence costly. People thus seek to avoid encounters that might focus on embarrassing aspects of conduct or raise questions regarding whether their prior actions had been prudent (Tangney, 1992).

Blameworthiness is associated with feelings of personal discomfort and embarrassment. Moreover, with blame comes a desire to hide or escape from the situation (Lewis, 1971; Tangney, 1992). Distancing, therefore, might sometimes occur as a way to avoid the costs associated with blameworthiness. Managers and leaders have learned the importance of not talking too much lest they reveal potentially incriminating information to employees. Moreover, managers may be reluctant to "open a can of worms" and reveal that their mistaken strategic judgments might have had a negative impact on others.

Empirical research has found support for this proposal. Folger and Skarlicki (1998) conducted an experiment in which respondents participated in an in-basket exercise. As part of the study, participants were asked to allocate a fixed amount of time to a number of competing tasks, including announcing a layoff to staff, budgeting, conducting performance appraisals, and meeting with customers. A letter from the CEO that was contained in the exercise manipulated blameworthiness for the layoff. For one half of the participants, the letter stated that their own mismanagement was responsible for the failure of the project leading to the layoff. For the other participants, the letter described the layoff as a result of the external environment (i.e., the economy). The results showed that participants in the blame condition allocated significantly less time with each of the layoff victims than did the participants in the no-blame condition. An unexpected finding, however, was that the feelings-of-discomfort measure did not seem very related to the distancing measure.

If managers' emotions were not a factor when anticipating actual contact with employees to be terminated, what else could account for the distancing effect? One candidate seems plausible: Respondents' cognitive awareness of situations that might be aversive. Consider as an analogy, that a person does not need to experience actual or vicarious variations in the type or intensity of emotions in order to recognize that someone about to leap over a deep chasm would be more afraid (and more likely to want to avoid the experience) than someone about to hop over a small pothole. Similarly, distancing behavior could be caused by differences in anticipated consequences. Thus, differences in response to adversity may be caused by the perceptions of aversive-feature cues rather than by differences in an actual emotional experience per se.

Cognitive–Perceptual Sources of Churchill Effects: A "Dysfunctional Vision" Metaphor

The theme of perceived costs plays a central role in Churchill-effect dynamics. Good people do bad things when they fail to see as they should. And when they fail to see as they should, a major "sight deficiency" (cf. occlusion, myopia, tunnel vision, etc.) involves the way in which costs are mistakenly identified, misperceived, distorted, or given excessive salience. Recall one of the key features of Churchill's remarks concerning how it costs nothing—namely, that his statement came as a reminder to the public. The public saw the cost of being nice as too high, whereas Churchill emphasized its costless nature. Churchill might have said that the public misperceived the costs of being polite and had exaggerated the expensiveness of civility.

Similarly, leaders with a vulnerable status might have an exaggerated view of the cost of having problems revealed to particular audiences (e.g., employees, stockholders, governance boards, the public). A related problem has to do with paying attention only to certain types of costs, ignoring others, and overlooking certain types of compensating benefits that might help to offset the costs that are perceived. This is a lack of visual acuity (metaphorically), a focus-of-attention problem. The excessive attention to certain types of costs (rather than other, alternative types, or to various benefits) causes people's judgments—and, hence, their action proclivities—to go awry. Leaders who anticipate the worst, who are preoccupied with certain dangerous possibilities, might fail to notice other prospects that are not only better but also more likely.

Managers more often recognize the potential benefits of forthright disclosure if they learned from the lessons of history. In 1982, Johnson & Johnson faced a crisis when seven people in Illinois died from poisoned Tylenol. Rather than keep the public at bay, CEO James Burke went public almost immediately. He appeared on both the Donahue show and 60 Minutes to explain the extent of the accident and how the company was reacting to the crisis. In the aftermath there has been an even higher regard for Johnson & Johnson because of the company's performance during the tragedy. A current axiom about how to conduct oneself in similar crises contends that "if you want to be believed when the news is good, you have to be forthcoming when it's bad" (Guzzadi, 1985; p. 66).

This general theme of "vision" problems can be expanded to distinguish among various types of difficulties. At present, our extensions are still at the metaphorical level. In other words, the following descriptions refer to images of eyesight and the impediments to seeing. For example, managers can be myopic; they may focus only on the immediate environment and have difficulty seeing things beyond a certain range. In our metaphor we describe this limited visual focus as volitional rather than pertaining to one's ability. That is, managers and leaders choose not to look at the broader negative consequences associated with adversity and how others are affected by managers' dysfunctional response to the adversity.

Theory and research suggest that distancing oneself from people who suffer adversity is a way not to look beyond one's own condition. Milgram's (1974) studies on obedience to authority show that participants were more likely to inflict physical pain on innocent victims when they were psychologically or physically distant from the victims. He argued that psychological closeness and the discomfort of empathy reduced harmdoing, whereas increased psychological remoteness made harmdoing easier because the victim's suffering took on an "abstract, remote quality" (p. 34)—just as a "bombardier can reasonably suppose that his weapons will inflict suffering and death—yet this knowledge is divested of affect and does not arouse in him an emotional response to the suffering he causes" (p. 35). Related advice suggests that surgeons should not become emotionally attached to patients; farmers should not make pets out of animals to be slaughtered. During layoffs, perhaps managers want to avoid getting too close to employees for similar reasons. Milgram also noted an out-of-sight, out-of-mind tendency: Seeing a victim can make psychological defenses such as denial harder to employ.

Economist George Stigler (1984), in his "First Law of Sympathy," said that "my sympathy for a person fell off the more distant he was" and that "he could be far off not only in a geographical sense but also socially" (p. 35). In contrast, a proximate victim can observe the harm-doer, adding to the latter's discomfort because "it is easier to harm a person when he is unable to observe our actions than when he can see what we are doing (Milgram, 1974, p. 35).

Bandura (1990) gave a related example of gas chamber operators in Nazi prison camps, who found it necessary to derogate and dehumanize their victims rather than become overwhelmed by distress. In discussing how harm-doers selectively disengage self-sanctions for inhumane conduct, he noted that perceiving a victim as another human activates empathetic and vicarious emotional reactions. To disengage moral control, harm-doers divest the victim of human qualities, blunting empathetic responses. Similarly, Kelman and Hamilton (1989) noted that once victims are stripped of human status, the usual principles of morality no longer apply.

Consistent with the theme of myopia is the managers' choice to see things in such a way as to reinforce their general view of the world. For example, Lerner (1980) proposed that people consider a "just world" to be one in which individuals get what they deserve and that people expect an appropriate fit between what a person does (effort) and his or her outcomes. One aspect of this perspective is that people will arrange their cognitions so as to maintain the belief that people get what they deserve or, conversely, deserve what they get, so as not to jeopardize their belief in a just world (Lerner & Simmons, 1966). Lerner (1980) found that people derogate an innocent victim as a way to maintain the notion of deservingness. Thus, managerial distancing might go hand-in-hand with victim derogation.

Alternatively, leaders and managers can be metaphorically hyper-visual (i.e., they can become far-sighted and focus only the potential for the undesirable consequences associated with adversity). For example, in layoff situations, managers may distance themselves from the victims because they anticipate and are reluctant to face employee reactions. Interestingly, the very act of delivering bad news seems to have some aversive consequences in and of itself, as indicated by research on what Tesser and Rosen (1975) called the MUM effect (the reluctance to transmit bad news). Often, people would rather "keep mum" than convey bad news that might provoke negative reactions on the part of the receiver.

Note, however, that key differences exist between Churchill effects (e.g., distancing, depersonalizing, and being abusively insensitive) and the MUM effect as conceptualized and investigated by Tesser and Rosen (1975). A MUM effect occurs when communicators suppress the information that a message involves bad news. For example, a typical MUM finding involves a person who tells someone that "a message came for you." The communicator who knows that the message contains good news will also tell the recipient, whereas the communicator who knows that the message contains bad news will not. Churchill effects, in contrast, always involve bad news that does get transmitted. Rather than the MUM effect of revealing or not revealing an indication about a message's valence, the presence versus absence of a Churchill effect involves differences in the style of revealing the content and the valence of the bad-news message. The same bad news is disclosed whether the Churchill effect is present or absent; the difference lies in whether that disclosure occurs in an insensitive manner (e.g., presence of interpersonal distancing) or in a sensitive manner (absence of distancing). The absence of a Churchill effect occurs when bad news is delivered with aspects of interactional justice. Those might include various ways in which the communicator heeds Churchill's reminder to be polite, such as by a thorough explanation delivered in a caring and sensitive manner that politely conveys respect for the recipient's dignity.

Evidence that anticipated consequences lead managers to engage in distancing behavior comes from Folger and Skarlicki (1998; Study 2). Forty managers were asked to allocate their time among competing demands during an in-basket exercise (see Folger & Skarlicki, 1998, described previously). They also noted their perceptions of aversive conditions that might accompany a layoff announcement. We assessed whether they expected to be accused of mismanagement by the employees who were being laid off. We hypothesized that the respondents would recognize the greater likelihood for such accusatory comments when the scenario had described the layoff as having resulted from the manager's past mistakes (i.e., the mismanagement condition) than if the layoff occurred due to external forces (no mismanagement condition).

Second, we also conceptualized the possible aversiveness of an encounter with laid-off employee in terms of the potential danger or harm that might be expected from a layoff victim (e.g., spreading ill-will, theft, embezzlement). We similarly hypothesized that anticipated harm to be greater in the mismanagement condition than in the no-mismanagement condition.

Results showed that the potential for criticism of mismanagement is related to the time that a manager takes to dismiss layoff victims. Mismanagement respondents, compared to those in the no-mismanagement condition, also reported significantly greater expectations that the layoff victims would blame them for the layoff, and the victims would potentially harm the organization because of the layoff. However, neither the accusation or harm measure nor the discomfort measure yielded correlations sufficient for evidence of mediation.

Summarizing Before Generalizing: The Picture Thus Far

To this point we have looked at reasons why managers might act in ways deemed unfair by employees during only one type of disclosure dilemma, namely downsizing or restructuring accompanied by layoffs. The remainder of this chapter seeks to extend that analysis in new directions. Specifically, the chapter argues for the presence of Churchill effects in settings as diverse as recruiting, performance appraisal, disciplinary sanctioning, and "stonewalling" to hide potentially blameworthy activity, all as a function of conditions made more understandable by the preceding analysis of dysfunctional distancing during disclosures about layoffs.

We argue that other disclosures about negative forms of information can often elicit the same types of dynamics (the Churchill effects of distancing) as frequently occur when layoffs are conducted.

BEYOND LAYOFFS: GENERALITY OF DYSFUNCTIONAL RESPONSES TO DISCLOSURE DILEMMAS

By definition, someone laid-off no longer works for the company that has terminated the employment relationship. Perhaps, then, the circumstances of blameworthiness that can produce distancing during layoffs do not act with the same force in other contexts. After all, the audience faced during layoffs are those who will soon be gone. Without a long-term relationship at stake, the benefits of acting kind might seem minimal to nonexistent. The prospect of only minute or virtually nonexistent benefits does not easily compensate for enduring costly effort, even if the cost of being polite is itself as minimal as Churchill suggested. We believe, however, that the Churchill effects of distancing during layoffs are far from being an isolated phenomenon or one that occurs only very unusual circumstances. The following sections explore the generality of Churchill effects and show that they extend across a wide range of situations.

Expanding the Dependent Variable: Stonewalling as Distancing

Although company actions during the past decade of downsizing illustrate the Churchill effect as interpersonal distancing by managers from layoff victims, managers and leaders have historically demonstrated another form of distancing: *stonewalling*. The practice of taking drastic steps to cover up alleged wrongdoing became known as stonewalling after that term achieved popular usage during the Watergate era (cf. plausible deniability as a related phenomenon discussed by Browning & Folger, 1994). A memorable example from that era is the 18-minute gap on one tape recording of an otherwise clandestine conversation in the Oval Office of the White House. President Nixon apparently tried to cover up his involvement in the Watergate break-in. The stonewalling efforts ultimately failed, as shown by the famous "smoking gun" of eventual revelations that led to Nixon's resignation from office.

Numerous recent U.S. presidents seem to have had problems from unsuccessful attempts to stonewall. They tried to cover up, failed, and received harsh criticism as a result. Notably, the public reaction seems to have produced much harsher criticism than if only these leaders had confessed immediately. Common sense tells us that quick confession often has tremendous advantages. Sure, there is humiliation to endure in admitting one's errors and faults. When we see someone who did not confess quickly, however, we often think it foolish. The short flash of bad publicity (embarrassment, etc.) burns bright only for a limited period of time; soon, all is forgotten. Newspapers might give a public figure's problems much play for awhile, for instance, but a myriad of other happenings also clamor for attention. Bad news has limited shock value. After a few days or weeks it is old news, replaced by current headlines of other disasters.

Moreover, politicians are not alone in such shortsightedness. News items show that many business leaders make the same judgment error. Often, it seems, their automatic first response is denial. Pollute that stream with industrial chemicals— "no, not us!" Encourage people to become addicted to nicotine in cigarettes? Why, how could you think such a thing?

Cover-up can follow denial as night follows day. As the lies get more elaborate, the CEO and top management team become hip deep in obfuscation. More and more effort is expended to shore up yet another line of defense before it crumbles from the onslaught of investigation. Oh what a tangled web we weave, when first we practice to deceive! If this scenario rings true, then some inappropriate actions are performed regularly by otherwise very smart people.

Granted, gathering proof of a cover-up is difficult, a fact that made the exposure of Nixon by two Washington reporters, Woodward and Burnstein, so notable. We know of no empirical literature in the organizational sciences on stonewalling as a cover-up practice, and relevant data might be hard to acquire. The result is that illustrations come in the form of anecdotal evidence, and the suggestion that stonewalling might have actually occurred is only by way of indirect inference. Still, popular accounts seem to reveal a number of cases that fit the basic pattern. For example, an executive vice president of a large firm noted the following sources of displeasure with Intel's handling of initial questions about a flaw in new Pentium chips: "I watched amazed as Intel attempted to handle this controversy with bluster, stonewalling, and weasel words until they finally appeared to surrender under the weight of public outrage" (Morgan, 1995, p. 18). Indeed, the same article called the incident Pentiumgate, and the author wrote that "I don't trust Intel anymore" (p. 18).

In some ways the phenomenon of stonewalling seems related to research on threat-rigidity effects (e.g., Ocasio, 1995; Staw, Sandelands, & Dutton, 1981) (i.e., examples of dysfunctional ways that organizations cope with adversity). The anxiety and stress brought on by a crisis elicits individual behavioral responses of withdrawal (Glass, 1955), reductions in critical information processing (Menninger, 1952), and constriction in behavioral responses (Whithey, 1962). Moreover, adversity leads to increased reliance on readily available hypotheses about the identity of stimulus objects, less flexibility in the choice of solutions methods, decreased tolerance for ambiguity, and an increased tendency toward emitting well-learned dominant responses (Staw et al., 1981). The manager's search for solutions concentrates less on generating new schemas, and more on well-learned schemas or scripts. The reduced quality of decision making under adversity may lead to a subjective underestimation of the risks involved in the selection of previously experienced responses (Ocasio, 1995). Thus managers may choose solutions that are not appropriate for the adversity, and prove deficient when the environment changes. Evidence suggests that both the organization and the environment have experienced significant changes associated with the restructuring. As noted previously, organizational change increases people's sensitivity to fairness issues (Cobb, Folger, & Wooten, 1995; Cobb, Wooten, & Folger, 1995; Neuman & Baron, 1996). Taken together, during current economic trends, managers may tend underestimate employees' sensitivity concerning fairness.

In response to a crisis, managers can either approach or avoid those affected by the adversity. At the level of individual decision making, response to adversity is enacted and attention is allocated through the application of schemas in the construction of *mental models*. Mental models are working integrated representations of goals, data, inferences, and plans that serve to interpret and attend to environmental stimuli, permit inferences, make decisions, and guide behavior (Holyoak & Gordon, 1984). Mental models utilize schemas to interpret environmental stimuli, and permit mental simulations of the outcomes of alternative plans or scenarios. The choice by managers to approach or avoid, therefore, depends on what information is attended to. An important function of mental models is to focus attention on data or environmental stimuli that are included in the model, and to restrict attention to all others.

A theoretical approach to understand distancing and stonewalling is the degree to which managers frame the adversity as a loss versus an opportunity for change (Dutton & Jackson, 1987). Prospect theory (Kahneman & Tversky, 1979) says that individuals are risk-seeking in response to perceived loss. For example, in situations where the manager perceived that there is a risk that he or she may be exposed as an incompetent, prospect theory predicts that a manager may stonewall others and risk a cover-up instead of facing a problem. Cover-up is deemed the risky response because there always exists a potential for being caught. Conversely, if the manager frames the adversity as a potential gain, it is less likely that stonewalling will be selected as an alternative. In fact, it was by building on prospect theory that we proposed a metaphor of seeing to portray the broader confines of the approach–avoid phenomenon.

Summarizing, it can be said that the analyses of stonewalling and layoff distancing have focused on a key way in which one type of cost gets exaggerated. Specifically, both situations seem threatening to face (valued social identity) based on the prospects of being blamed for misfortune. Our empirical findings even indicate that distancing from layoff victims occurs when the manager who delivers the bad news is not personally to blame, but merely would anticipate hostility because of possible mismanagement by others

Both situations raise the specter of communicating not only bad news but also news about illegitimacy. Laid-off employees often might suspect mismanagement as a cause of the financial conditions leading to the layoff. Members of the public often might suspect mismanagement as a cause of product damages or other types of harmful externalities (effects whose costs are not born by the producer, e.g., pollution). In both cases, perception is everything. Objective facts not withstanding, the manager in a position to communicate with an audience of those who might feel harmed must contend with prospects of their also feeling wrongfully, unfairly harmed.

The essence of our analysis of these two situations as Churchill effects, therefore, is that they represent a case where unfairness leads to unfairness. Now the analysis of Churchill effects is extended even more broadly by specifically focusing on other types of instances in which perceived unfairness might arise as a source of anticipated blame. First, we examine one of the original contexts in which the concept of interactional justice was invoked: recruiting. After that, we consider the broader context of conveying negative news possibly accompanied by illegitimacy or impropriety indicators. Specifically, this section looks at such occasions for rejection, refusal, and negative feedback as those occurring when performance evaluations are delivered, employees fail to receive promotions, or budget requests are denied.

Recruiting Nightmares: Bad News Delivered Badly

The topic of recruiting allows us to extend our analysis further beyond layoffs and corporate cover-ups. In addressing unfair interpersonal conduct by recruiters toward job candidates, Churchill effects can be related directly to interactional justice. Indeed, distancing-like behavior during recruiting episodes constituted one of the earliest sources (Bies, 1986) of unfair treatment classified as interactional justice (Bies, 1987). Another early reference to interactional justice referred to the criteria for fairness of communications (Bies & Moag, 1986), and certainly recruiting activities are heavily laden with communications (e.g., interviews).

In the research cited above, some of the data came from MBA students recruited for jobs after graduation. For example, Bies (1986) asked MBA job candidates to describe their reactions to corporate recruiting practices. Some students responded, in an open-ended fashion, to a question asking them to describe fairness criteria that they thought recruiters should follow during interviews and callbacks. Other MBA job candidates described positive and negative experiences they had already experienced. A content analysis of episodes from the latter group produced the same types of communication criteria for fairness as the former group had generated. Notably pertinent to Churchill's comments on politeness, "the job candidates felt unfairly treated when recruiters were rude" (Bies, 1987, p. 292).

The interpersonal treatment expected from recruiters involved norms of interactional justice now familiarly applied to a host of settings in the literature on organizational fairness. The fairness criterion of truthfulness identified by candidates, for example, shows that they valued candidness and deplored deception. Other responses indicated a concern about the impropriety of questions that seemed prejudicial or discriminatory (along with those that violated norms of privacy concerning personal matters, such as marital status). Moreover, students evaluated recruiting communications by also using two other criteria that we find especially germane to the Churchill effect of interpersonal distancing. First, they mentioned frequently the importance of being treated with respect and dignity. Second, they called for justifications in the case of negative decisions. In an incident illustrating unfair treatment on both dimensions, one student described being deposited in the reception area of a second interviewer who never appeared. The student expressed anger because neither an explanation nor an apology was provided.

In a follow-up investigation, Bies and Shapiro (1988, Study 1) manipulated justification by varying the content of a rejection letter in a recruitment role-playing study. Half of the respondents read that the company was not extending an offer for another round of interviews to this candidate, but the letter provided no explanation for the candidate's rejection (a no-justification condition). The rejection letter in the justification condition, on the other hand, explained that the company had instituted a hiring freeze due to a sudden economic downturn. Respondent gave higher ratings concerning the procedural fairness of company recruiting practices in the justification condition than in the no-justification condition.

Note how our analysis of Churchill effects would revise that research paradigm to turn its independent variable into a dependent variable. The research described above has shown that with interactional justice as an independent variable (differences in interpersonal conduct by recruiters), the responses of candidates become more negative as a function of such conditions as the lack of explanations. The company's reputation for fairness suffers as a result. Our analysis turns the situation around, making recruiters' conduct the dependent variable. Why would recruiters simply fail to meet with some candidates, rather than give the bad news that the candidate has not "made the cut" to another round of interviews? Why would companies mail perfunctory rejection announcements that lacked explanatory justification?

Personal encounters impose interpersonal cost when bad news has to be delivered, and a large number of rejected candidates can make writing separate, personalized explanations a chore. Some distancing might be expected as a natural consequence. Our analysis leads us to speculate, however, that the costs of disclosing negative information also vary as a function of situational factors. In particular, both the distancing-during-downsizing and the cover-up of controversy examples suggest an avoidance of censure for wrongdoing. It is bad enough to be the bearer of bad tidings. It is worse to bear bad tidings of a potentially unfair nature.

Personnel decisions contain a great deal of ambiguity and hence are highly subject to distorted impressions and biased perceptions. Those who make such decisions are, no doubt, aware of this inherent subjectivity. We suggest that recruiters for companies whose practices they consider to be fair, therefore, will be more forthcoming in disclosures to rejected candidates (providing more adequate explanations and treating these candidates with greater politeness and less distancing). Recruiters who use more objective techniques such as behaviorally structured questions or whose selection tests have gone through a validation program, for example, should show less distancing than those who use less valid interviewing techniques or whose selection methods are applied inconsistently. Ironically, the potential for perceived unfairness at the prior stage of the procedures and practices themselves (procedural injustice) would, in this case, increase the likelihood of additional unfairness at the subsequent stage when it is time for decisions about the results of those procedures to be announced.

When Low Performance Leads to Getting Hit Below the Belt

The notorious phenomenon of vanishing performance reviews (Folger & Cropanzano, 1998) also illustrates dysfunctional distancing when the legitimacy of negative evaluations can be questioned. Superiors will swear that they have put someone on notice about subpar performance or actions that might eventually call for disciplinary action, but the employees themselves often claim not to have heard the message. Allegedly formal performance review sessions sometimes take place in such a rushed, distancing fashion that the garbling of intended communication should really be no surprise. Criticism offered abruptly and in an aloof, impersonal fashion does not actually convey its substantive content effectively. The implicit message about a lack of respect for the subordinate, however, is heard loud and clear.

Research by Taylor and her colleagues (Taylor, Tracy, Renard, Harrison, & Carroll, 1995; Taylor, Masterson, Renard, & Tracy, 1998) has begun to offer evidence germane to Churchill effects in this context. Moreover, some of their analyses demonstrate the paradigm shift we have recommended, which turns managerial fairness as an independent variable into managerial fairness as a dependent variable. Taylor et al. (1995) designed a procedurally fair system for evaluating performance based on the "due-process model" developed by Folger, Konovsky, and Cropanzano (1992). In their study they measured not only subordinates' but also supervisors' reactions to either the new system or its replacement, which was still being used by employees randomly assigned to a control condition. They proposed that if supervisors do not trust an appraisal system, they are less likely to feel comfortable being candid in providing negative feedback based on its use. Their measures also included an item that asked managers to rate the fairness of their own recent performance appraisal.

Results showed that the due-process experimental group provided greater negative feedback in comparison with the inflated ratings of the control group that embodied relatively less procedural fairness. Second, supervisors did not differ in their satisfaction with performance-appraisal systems. Although the experimental implementation of a due-process system constituted a marked improvement over the relatively inadequate features of the existing system overall, the new approach also made greater demands on managers. These basic findings set the stage for further interpretation drawn on the basis of results from the moderator analysis.

The moderator analysis approximates how investigators can move backstream. Their analyses revealed effects on two variables of particular interest from the standpoint of the Churchill effect, the cordiality of the working relationship with the subordinate (cf. politeness and interpersonal sensitivity) and the tendency to distort the appraisal results (cf. distancing by truncated communications that distort the news). Within the control group, the moderator effects of the manager's own prior appraisal fairness show what might often occur under many typical appraisal systems. The greater the extent to which control-group managers perceived that they themselves had been unfairly evaluated in the past, the more they reported a tendency to distort the appraisal results of their subordinates. In other words, unfairness at an earlier point in the causal chain of events led to unfairness at a later point. Similarly, control-group managers who felt more unfairly treated in the past also reported having a less favorable working relationship with their employees. If interpretable as a sign that interpersonal distancing would be more common as the result of managers who themselves felt that the appraisal system was unfair, this effect is again consistent with evidence of Churchill effects. Note that both effects were significantly attenuated among managers who used the new appraisal system that implemented due-process components of fair treatment.

Communicating Bad News:
Fear of Being the Messenger Who Is Killed

We speculate that the underlying dynamics of Churchill effects may apply widely to situations in which bad news might also raise questions about the legitimacy of managerial conduct. History teachers tell students about ancient eras in which messengers who reported battle losses to kings were summarily killed. Perhaps the fear of symbolic, if not actual, death makes managers want to keep their distance—physically as well as psychologically and interpersonally—because they remember hearing about such events (or have themselves been the victim of a boss's temperamental tirade when giving bad news). We argue, however, that the fear of bad news being received badly, with hostility toward the messenger, is moderated by specific features concerning the nature of the bad news.

In particular, our analysis of anticipated blameworthiness at the heart of Churchill effects suggests that the taint of illegitimacy serves as a moderator variable. The Taylor et al. (1995) results discussed previously suggest that as a possibility. Furthermore, the context of their results seems generalizable. After all, receiving bad news of a negative-performance rating is not so different from many other contexts in which feedback reflects negatively on the recipient of bad news. Employees not receiving promotions might also be treated in a distancing manner by managers who doubt the legitimacy of the promotion system, for example, just as disciplinary action might be delivered in a less interpersonally sensitive manner the more that the disciplinary agent questions the applicable guidelines.

To provide an example of another potential source wherein the prospect of illegitimacy might arise and to illustrate again how this focus reverses the normal order of independent and dependent variables, we use a study by Bies and Shapiro (1988) as a brief illustration. In their Study 2, Bies and Shapiro focused attention on the context of budget turn-downs. Their study involved managers who made budget requests or proposals that needed approval by their superiors. In describing specific instances of such events by recounting a recent episode, the managers were under instructions to recall occasions characterized by a single feature held constant: When allocations had been made subsequent to the request or proposal, the boss had decided not to provide the resources in question. The recall of those rejected request–proposal incidents, in turn, provided the context in which the managers responded to a set of survey items.

Among those items, questions assessing how the turn-down had been communicated are especially relevant to the study of Churchill effects. Attention focused specifically on whether the boss tried to provide justification and claimed that mitigating circumstances beyond managerial control dictated the necessity of the rejection. Similar to the findings in Folger and Skarlicki (1998), we would expect that managers who turn down budget requests due to external circumstances (uncontrollable market forces) distance themselves less from the people making those requests than managers who had full discretion over the decision.

Because the Bies and Shapiro (1988, Study 2) investigation was not designed in the new paradigm format of reversed independent and dependent variables, their results bear only indirectly on our speculation about possible Churchill effects in that context. Nevertheless, the type of evidence they obtained seems reasonably consistent with such speculation. They assessed the extent to which respondents reported their bosses' having attempted to justify the turn-down. Two items constituted this index of justification as a measured independent variable or predictor. Two other questions asked about the procedural fairness of the boss's decision-making approach. The results showed a positive predictor–criterion relationship: The more that a justifying claim of mitigating circumstances was absent, the lower the ratings of procedural fairness.

The use of justification was a measured variable, however, and so we can conceptualize it as a dependent variable subject to an unknown degree of determination by unmeasured causes. The data show that more than 47% of the respondents had experienced little or no justification provided. In our terms, the distancing that characterizes Churchill effects seems to have been evident. What cannot be known from these data, of course, is why superiors failed to explain themselves to subordinates, just as it cannot be known from the Taylor et al. (1998) study why some managers felt that their own previous appraisal had been unfair. Both contexts, therefore, are ripe with potential for investigating from the perspective of Churchill-effect determinants.

SOME FINAL WORDS ABOUT BAD NEWS:
SHOULD THE MESSENGER FEAR BEING KILLED?

We conclude not so much with a summary as with a rhetorical question and a brief amount of further discussion in the vein of a hypothetical, speculative response. The message, as indicated at the outset, has consisted of three strands. First, we have turned the traditional independent–dependent ordering of variables on its head. Rather than asking how employees respond when managers act fairly or unfairly, we argue for asking the prior question that traces a step backward along a temporal sequence of cause and effect: What factors determine whether managers practice fair or unfair treatment? Second, we suggested that although dispositional factors might well be determinative, the role of situational factors also needs investigation. This attempt to avoid the fundamental attribution error led to a second question, closely related to the first: What leads good people to do bad things? We suggested that being placed in potentially blameworthy circumstances was one prominent answer to that question. Third, we explored the generalizability of our answers to those two thematic questions by extending our discussion of Churchill effects beyond layoffs to such domains as stonewalling, recruiting, performance appraisals, and turn-downs experienced during the budgeting or proposal-consideration process.

The rhetorical question that heads this final section refers again to historical epochs in which messengers with bad news literally had reason to fear for their lives. We leave the reader with this same question to ponder as it might apply to the present era. No definitive answer will be forthcoming without considerable research in what we have suggested is a new arena begging for investigation. Until such time as more data are available, however, we close with but two types of comments as our own speculative replies to issues implied by that question.

First, consider one respect in which the present era does not differ so radically from earlier historical epochs. Although overall crime rates including violent crimes seem to be in decline at present, an alarming number of instances have been reported in which disgruntled employees or former employees sought to kill someone else in the workplace. Indeed, the number of homicides in that category appears to be going up. Popular accounts often quote the perpetrator of workplace violence, or summarize interviews with surviving colleagues, and those narratives reveal quite a few examples of statements directly relevant to the Churchill effects we have examined in this chapter. That is, violently disgruntled employees frequently seem to have been led to take hostile action in response to negative events such as turndowns (e.g., tenure denials or failures to receive an anticipated promotion), layoffs, and disciplinary actions. Moreover, they recount or are characterized as having indicated that their rage stemmed not so much from the negative outcome itself or even its undeserved (i.e., perceived as unfair quality). Rather, the source of greatest venom many times turned out to be the manner in which news about the unpleasant event was conveyed. Examples that we would label as distancing behavior abound in this anecdotal evidence that Churchill effects are not only real but also deadly earnest.

Second, we ask and give our own brief answer to an additional question implicit in this section title's reference to killing the messenger. The subtitle asks whether the messenger should fear being killed. The immediately preceding discussion of homicides at work might be taken as an emphatic affirmative as the answer to that question, taken quite literally. Instead, however, we suggest some ironic twists in this most serious of all dilemmas facing managers when it comes time to give bad news. Succinctly put, the irony is that those who most fear being killed might be the most susceptible. Moreover, the ultimate irony is that their very fear itself might contribute to dysfunctionally unfair conduct that actually increases the danger for them precisely as a result of their attempts to decrease it.

To explain the nature of these ironic twists, we reaffirm a message perhaps slighted if our presentation has underemphasized it. Recall the role of blame and illegitimacy as precursors to Churchill effects (e.g., Folger & Skarlicki, 1998). Some managers delivering bad news feel that they are in a more vulnerable position than others do. Those who feel most vulnerable, we hypothesize, are managers who think of themselves as having become associated with the taint of unfairness or the possibility of censure accompanying perceived blameworthiness. Note that neither actual illegitimacy nor blame need be the determinant of the extent to which the manager delivering bad news feels vulnerable and anticipates potentially hostile responses. Rather, the manager's own assumptions about how the hearer might respond color the orientation adopted by that manager and hence the distancing tendencies that he or she becomes inclined to put into practice. A manager who feels innocent but believes that the hearer of bad news will presume guilt, in other words, feels more vulnerable than does the manager who feels guilty but believes that the hearer will presume innocence.

What, then, prompts our reference to a tragic irony of dysfunctional distancing that leads to death in the workplace? Suppose you fear that when you give bad news, it will seem unfair to the hearer. In particular, you expect the hearer to hold you at fault because of assumptions and interpretations that even you might find reasonable, if you were in the other person's shoes. You know such views to be false, but can you be sure of convincing the other person? What if you fail? Perhaps the best course of action is simply to minimize all contact with that person. Such conduct on your part would result, of course, in a reduced display of sympathy and other indications of interpersonal sensitivity to the victim. The victim now feels not only unfairly treated from some distributive sense of relative deprivation or an undeservedly low level of outcomes. Insult has been added to injury because you have heaped interactional injustice on top of whatever unfairness perceptions might have existed initially. The desire for vengeance grows with each successive rumination about the indignity of it all.

How can managers navigate their way through the course of this chilling scenario? That topic is far too broad for us to attempt to answer at this late point, and any replies we might give would be highly speculative anyway. Perhaps all we can do for now, besides pointing to this potentially self-defeating behavior and calling for research to investigate its causes and cures, is to offer a single type of comment. If the message of this chapter has had any validity, we believe a return to the thrust of Churchill's original commentary is in order. Being polite can, indeed, cost far less than some managers seem to realize. Imagining the worst from trying to explain or even remotely considering the possibility of an apology (or at least recognizing the appropriateness of expressing remorse in sympathy with a victim's pain), managers instead frequently can concentrate only on their own vulnerability under such circumstances. In our opinion, they can too easily be led to overestimate the emotional (or even physical) costliness of such behavior. Besides, if there is some validity in the specter of the vengeful employee as killer prompted by insult on top of injury, then the costliness of not being polite could be far greater. Work on theory, research, and practice might all be usefully stimulated by considering how to convey this one simple truth: Politeness costs less than you think, and it stands to reap greater benefits than you might have realized. Paraphrased and shortened, fairness pays. Thus, put consistently with our dependent-for-independent switch between variables of interest, the paramount issue for future study becomes how to teach that lesson and have it be applied more often.

REFERENCES

Bandura, A. (1990). Selective activation and disengagement of moral control. *Journal of Social Issues, 46*, 27–46.

Bies, R. J. (1986). *Individual reactions to corporate recruiting: The importance of fairness*. Unpublished manuscript.

Bies, R. J. (1987). The predicament of injustice: The management of moral outrage. In L. L. Cummings & B. M. Staw (Eds.), *Research in organizational behavior* (Vol. 9, pp. 289–319). Greenwich, CT: JAI.

Bies, R. J., & Moag, J. S. (1986). Interactional justice: Communication criteria of fairness. In R. J. Lewicki, B. H. Sheppard & M. H. Bazerman (Eds.), *Research on negotiations in organizations* (Vol. 1, pp. 43–55). Greenwich, CT: JAI.

Bies, R. J., & Shapiro, D. (1988). Voice and justification: Their influence on procedural fairness judgments. *Academy of Management Journal, 31*, 676–685.

Brockner, J. (1992). Managing the effects of layoffs on survivors. *California Management Review, 34*, 9–28.

Brockner, J. (1994). Perceived fairness and survivors' reactions to layoffs, or how downsizing organizations can do well by doing good. *Social Justice Research, 7*, 345–363.

Brockner, J., DeWitt, R. L., Grover, S., & Reed, T. (1990). When it is especially important to explain why: Factors affecting the relationship between managers' expectations of a layoff and survivors' reaction to the layoff. *Journal of Experimental Social Psychology, 26*, 389–407.

Brockner, J., & Greenberg, J. (1990). The impact of layoffs on survivors: An organizational justice perspective. In J. S. Carroll (Ed.), *Applied social psychology and organizational settings*. Hillsdale, NJ: Lawrence Erlbaum Associates.

Brockner, J., & Wiesenfeld, B. (1996). An integrative framework for explaining reactions to decisions: The interactive effects of outcomes and procedures. *Psychological Bulletin, 120*, 184–208.

Browning, L. D., & Folger, R. (1994). Communication under conditions of litigation risk: A grounded theory of plausible deniability in the Iran Contra affair. In S. B. Sitkin & R. J. Bies (Eds.), *The legalistic organization* (pp. 251–280). Newbury Park, CA: Sage.

Churchill, W. S. 1950. *The grand alliance.* Boston: Houghton-Mifflin.

Cobb, A. T., Folger, R., & Wooten, K. C. (1995). The role justice plays in organizational change. *Public Administration Quarterly, 19,* 135–151.

Cobb, A. T., Wooten, K. C., & Folger, R. (1995). Justice in the making: Toward understanding the theory and practice of justice in organizational change and development. In W. A. Pasmore & R. W. Woodman (Eds.), *Research in organizational change and development* (pp. 243–295). Greenwich, CT: JAI.

Cropanzano, R., & Folger, R. (1989). Referent cognitions and task decision autonomy: Beyond equity theory. *Journal of Applied Psychology, 74,* 293–299.

Dubose, C. (1994). Breaking the bad news. *Human Resource Management, 39,* 62–64.

Dutton, J. E., & Jackson, S. E. (1987). Categorizing strategic issues: Links to organizational action, *Academy of Management Review 12,* 760–790.

Feldman, D. C., & Leana, C. R. 1989. Managing layoffs: Experiences at the Challenger disaster site and the Pittsburgh steel mills. *Organizational Dynamics, 18,* 52–64.

Folger, R. (1987). Reformulating the preconditions of resentment: A referent cognitions model. In J. C. Masters & W. P. Smith (Eds.), *Social comparison, justice, and relative deprivation: Theoretical, empirical, and policy perspectives* (pp. 183–215). Hillsdale, NJ: Lawrence Erlbaum Associates.

Folger, R. (1993a, August 8–11). *The "Churchill Paradox" in managing hard times.* Presentation at the national meeting of the Academy of Management, Atlanta, GA.

Folger, R. (1993b). Reactions to mistreatment at work. In K. Murnighan (Ed.), *Social psychology in organizations: Advances in theory and research* (pp. 161–183) Englewood Cliffs, NJ: Prentice-Hall.

Folger, R. (1998). Fairness as a moral virtue. In M. Schminke (Ed.), *Managerial ethics: Morally managing people and processes.* Mahwah, NJ: Lawrence Erlbaum Associates.

Folger, R., & Cropanzano, R. (1998). *Organizational justice and human resource management.* Thousand Oaks, CA: Sage.

Folger, R., Davison, K., Dietz, J., & Robinson, S. (1997). *Workplace violence and aggression as reactions to perceived injustice: They shoot bosses, don't they?* Unpublished manuscript.

Folger, R., Konovsky, M. A., & Cropanzano, R. (1992). A due process metaphor for performance appraisal. In B. M. Staw & L. L. Cummings (Eds.), *Research in organizational behavior* (Vol. 14, pp. 129–177). Greenwich, CT: JAI.

Folger, R., & Martin, C. (1986). Relative deprivation and referent cognitions: Distributive and procedural justice effects. *Journal of Experimental Social Psychology, 22,* 531–546.

Folger, R., & Pugh, D. (1997). *The Churchill effect in managing hard times: Kicking employees when they're down and out.* Unpublished manuscript.

Folger, R., Robinson, S. L., Dietz, J., McLean-Parks, J., & Baron, R. (1998). *Predicting threats and assaults among employees: The role of societal violence and organizational injustice.* Unpublished manuscript.

Folger, R., Rosenfield, D., Rheaume, K., & Martin, C. (1983). Relative deprivation and referent cognitions. *Journal of Experimental Social Psychology, 19,* 172–184.

Folger, R., Rosenfield, D., & Robinson, T. (1983). Relative deprivation and procedural justifications. *Journal of Personality and Social Psychology, 45,* 268–273.

Folger, R., & Skarlicki, D. P. (1998). When tough times make tough bosses: Managerial distancing as a function of layoff blame. *Academy of Management Journal, 41,* 79–87.

Fox, J. A., & Levin, J. (1994). *Overkill.* New York: Plenum.

Glass, A. J. (1955). *Psychological considerations in atomic warfare.* Washington, DC: Walter Reed Army Medical Center.

Greenberg, J. (1993). The social side of fairness: Interpersonal and informational classes of organizational justice. In R. Cropanzano (Ed.), *Justice in the workplace: Approaching fairness in human resource management* (pp. 79–103). Hillsdale, NJ: Lawrence Erlbaum Associates.

Greenberg, J., & Baron, R. A. (1993). *Behavior in organizations*, 4th ed. Boston: Allyn & Bacon.

Guzzardi, W., Jr. (1985, March 4). How much should companies talk? *Fortune*, 64–65.

Holyoak, K, J., & Gordon, P. C. (1984). Information processing and social cognition. In R. S. Wyer & T. K. Srull (Eds.), *Handbook of social cognition* (pp. 39–70). Hillsdale, NJ: Lawrence Erlbaum Associates.

Kahneman, D., & Tversky, A. (1979). Prospect theory: An analysis of decisions under risk. *Econometrika, 47*, 263–291.

Kelman, H. C., & Hamilton, V. L. 1989. *Crimes of obedience*. New Haven: Yale University Press.

Konovsky, M. A., & Folger, R. (1991). The effects of procedures, social accounts, and benefit level on victims' layoff reactions. *Journal of Applied Social Psychology, 21*, 630–650.

Lerner, M. J. (1966). Observers' reactions to the "innocent victim": Compassion or rejection? *Journal of Personality and Social Psychology, 4*, 203–210.

Lerner, M. J. (1980). *The belief in a just world: A fundamental delusion*. New York: Plenum.

Levinson, H. (1965). Reciprocation: The relationship between man and organization. *Administrative Science Quarterly, 9*, 370–390.

Lewis, H. B. (1971). *Shame and guilt in neurosis*. New York: International Universities Press.

Menninger, W. C. (1952). Psychological reactions in an emergency (flood). *American Journal of Psychiatry, 109*, 128–130.

Milgram, S. (1974). *Obedience to authority*. New York: Harper & Row.

Morgan, B. (1995). A tale of two crises, or lessons of brand management vs. engineering. *Brandweek*, March 13, p. 18.

Neuman, J. H., & Baron, R. A. (1996). Aggression in the workplace. In R. Giacalone & J. Greenberg (Eds.), *Antisocial behavior in organizations* (pp. 37–67). Thousand Oaks, CA: Sage.

Ocasio, W. (1995). The enactment of economic adversity: A reconciliation of theories of failure-induced change and threat-rigidity. In L. L. Cummings & B. M. Staw (Eds.), *Research in organizational behavior* (Vol. 17, pp. 287–331). Greenwich, CT: JAI.

Ross, L. (1977). The intuitive psychologist and his shortcomings. *Advances in experimental social psychology, 10*, 174–221.

Skarlicki, D., & Folger, R. (1997). Retaliation for perceived unfair treatment: Examining the roles of procedural and interactional justice. *Journal of Applied Psychology, 82*, 434–443.

Staw, B. M., Sandelands, L. E., & Dutton, J. E. (1981). Threat-rigidity effects in organizational behavior: A multilevel analysis. *Administrative Science Quarterly, 26*, 501–524.

Stigler, G. J. (1984). *The intellectual and the marketplace*. Cambridge, MA: Harvard University Press.

Sutton, R., Eisenhardt, K. M., & Jucker, J. V. (1986). Managing organizational decline: Lessons from Atari. *Organizational Dynamics, 14*, 17–29.

Tangney, J. P. (1992). Situational determinants of shame and guilt in young adulthood. *Personality and Social Psychology Bulletin, 18*, 199–206.

Taylor, M. S., Tracy, K. B., Renard, M. K., Harrison, J. K., & Carroll, S. J. (1995). Due process in performance appraisal: A quasi-experiment in procedural justice. *Administrative Science Quarterly, 40*, 495–523.

Taylor, M. S., Masterson, S. S., Renard, M. K., & Tracy, K. B. (1998). Managers' reactions to procedurally just performance management systems. *Academy of Management Journal*.

Tesser, A., & Rosen, S. (1975). The reluctance to transmit bad news. *Advances in experimental social psychology, 8*, 193–232.

Withey, S. B. (1962). Reactions in uncertain threat. In G. W. Baker & D. W. Chapman (Eds.), *Man and society in disaster* (pp. 93–123). New York: Basic Books.

II
▼▼▼▼▼▼▼▼

APPLICATIONS OF ORGANIZATIONAL JUSTICE

6

▼▼▼▼▼▼▼▼

The Concern for Justice and Reactions to Affirmative Action: Cause or Rationalization?

D. Ramona Bobocel
Liane M. Davey
Leanne S. Son Hing
Mark P. Zanna
University of Waterloo

There is now a sizable literature demonstrating links between employee reactions to various organizational policies and their judgments of the fairness of those policies (e.g., distributive, procedural, and interactional fairness). On the basis of these findings, it is often recommended that enhancing employee fairness perceptions might mitigate certain negative reactions. Although there is sufficient experimental research to warrant confidence in the idea that justice concerns can underlie employee reactions to a variety of organizational policies, it is also possible that what purportedly is a concern for justice might instead be a rationalization for other motivations, in at least some instances. In other words, the concern for justice might not always be a true cause of employee reactions; rather, it may be masking less socially desirable attitudes.

Whether justice concerns serve as a cause or as a rationalization is particularly relevant in the context of employee reactions to affirmative action (AA) policies or other initiatives to increase diversity in the workplace. This is because the debate about AA often centers on the issues of prejudice and justice. Thus, it is common to read allegations by proponents that people who oppose AA are prejudiced (i.e., racist or sexist); in contrast, opponents of AA often claim that their disdain derives from another source: They claim, for example, that AA is unfair because it considers group membership, in addition to merit, when allocating valued outcomes (e.g., jobs, promotions, training opportunities).

But does our concern for justice determine our attitudes toward AA, or does it merely rationalize them, perhaps covering our prejudices? Note that the process of rationalization to which we are referring might occur in one or more of several related ways: For example, in an effort to justify existing attitudes, prejudiced individuals might claim post hoc that AA is unfair; alternatively, prejudiced individuals might be primed to perceive AA policies as unfair in a more on-line fashion. Given that these processes are inextricably linked, there is no attempt to disentangle them here.

Although we believe that prejudice is likely one important predictor of opposition to AA, we also believe that justice-based opposition can be genuine. The general goal in this chapter is to provide an overview of our program of research aimed at directly testing this idea (for more details, see Bobocel, Son Hing, Davey, Stanley, & Zanna, 1998). In the following sections, AA is defined, past research that laid the foundation for our work is reviewed, and our program is discussed. Finally, we highlight some implications for future research on, and the practical management of, AA in the workplace, as well as for research and theory on justice more broadly.

DEFINITION OF AFFIRMATIVE ACTION

As defined elsewhere, AA refers broadly to a "body of policies and procedures designed to eliminate employment discrimination against women and ethnic minorities, and to redress the effects of past discrimination" (Kravitz et al., 1997, p. vii). The term *affirmative action* is thus a general concept that can be operationalized in a variety of ways.

Most researchers agree that a primary distinguishing feature of AA policies is the extent to which group status is used as a criterion in decision making. At one extreme of a simple classification scheme are workplace policies that can be labeled *equal treatment programs*—these are programs designed to remove systemic barriers, and they involve such initiatives as providing mentorship policies, maternity–paternity leaves, flexible work schedules, and so forth. Although such programs might be of greater benefit to target-group members in view of their special needs, they are in principle available to all employees, and therefore also of potential benefit to all.

At the other extreme are *preferential treatment programs*, which use group status as a criterion in allocating desired organizational outcomes. In what have been labeled weak forms of preferential treatment, group status affects decisions only if traditional indices of deservingness (i.e., factors contributing to one's ability to perform the job) are equal across those in competition. In strong forms of preferential treatment, group status might outweigh the role of the traditional indicators of merit, such that an outcome could be awarded to a target-group member who is relatively less qualified than a competitor (although a minimum performance standard would have to be met). In the most extreme form of preferential treatment—often labeled quotas—group status would be used in decision making with little regard to qualifications or merit. It is noteworthy that quotas are rare in organizational practice (see Kravitz et al., 1997, for details on the distinction between AA legislation and related laws).

A large body of research demonstrates that, in general, both nontarget and target-group members react less favorably to AA programs that involve preferential treatment than to programs that do not (Clayton & Tangri, 1989; Kravitz & Platania, 1993; Kravitz, Stinson, & Mello, 1994; Nacoste, 1985; Nacoste & Hummels, 1994; Nosworthy, Lea, & Lindsay, 1995). Unfortunately, in much of the past research investigating the roles of prejudice and justice as determinants of opposition, the characteristics of the program being evaluated have not been clearly specified (i.e., participants have typically evaluated the global concept of AA). Consequently, it is difficult to summarize the results on past research on predictors, in view of the general finding that policy characteristics influence attitudes.

JUSTICE AS A CAUSE OF OPPOSITION?
PAST RESEARCH FINDINGS

Numerous scholars have discussed the importance of the concept of justice in relation to understanding attitudes toward AA (for some examples, see Barnes-Nacoste, 1994; Clayton & Tangri, 1989; Crosby, 1994; Heilman, 1994; Kravitz, 1995; Nacoste, 1985; Nosworthy et al., 1995; Tougas, Joly, Beaton, & St. Pierre, 1996; Turner & Pratkanis, 1994). Two empirical findings are particularly robust. First, many studies have demonstrated that, as people's perceptions of the fairness of AA decreases, their opposition increases (e.g., Kravitz, 1995; Nosworthy et al., 1995; Tougas & Veilleux, 1988). Second, other studies have shown that, in general, people perceive AA to be more unfair the more that preferential treatment is involved (e.g., Chacko, 1982; Clayton & Tangri, 1989; Kravitz & Platania, 1993; Nacoste, 1985, 1987). Although such findings are consistent with the idea that justice-based objections are likely to be genuine, there are several methodological or conceptual problems that limit one's ability to make firm conclusions regarding the role of justice as a cause versus as a rationalization.

One problem that limits the ability to draw firm conclusions is that typically researchers have studied either the relation between perceptions of fairness and opposition or the relation between policy characteristics and fairness perceptions. Yet, it has often been inferred that fairness perceptions mediate the effect of policy characteristics on opposition; consequently, it is assumed that fairness perceptions are a determinant. Although recently some researchers (e.g., Kravitz, 1995) have tested and provided support for the mediation hypothesis, the correlational nature of the fairness and attitudes data in these studies still does not permit a clear causal inference regarding fairness perceptions as the determinant of attitudes per se.

Critically, researchers have typically not ruled out the possibility that opposition purportedly deriving from fairness concerns is actually rationalized prejudice. This possibility is pertinent, given evidence of a positive relation between people's prejudice level and their opposition to AA. Research using both classical (i.e., a belief in innate interracial differences and the superiority of one's own race) and symbolic (i.e., a more subtle mixture of anti-Black affect and an adherence to traditional values, such as individualism and hard work; Kinder & Sears, 1981; McConahay, 1986) forms of racism suggests that prejudice relates to negative attitudes toward the general concept of AA (e.g., Jacobson, 1985; Kluegel & Smith, 1983; Sidanius, Pratto, & Bobo, 1996). Moreover, in line with research on racism, Tougas, Brown, Beaton, and Joly (1995) found that *neo-sexism*—a more subtle form of sexism—predicts opposition toward the general concept of AA.

Recognizing the possibility that prejudice (i.e., racism or sexism) might account, at least in part, for the hypothesized fairness-to-opposition relation, some researchers have statistically controlled respondents' prejudice levels in recent research on AA attitudes (for a review, see Kravitz et al., 1997). The evidence suggests that perceptions of program fairness predict unique variance in opposition even when controlling prejudice (e.g., Kravitz, 1995). On the basis of such findings, it has been claimed that fairness perceptions might actually be a stronger predictor of opposition to AA than is prejudice.

We believe, however, that it might be questionable to expect either predictor—prejudice or the concern for justice—to be the stronger predictor across all forms of AA. Rather, to the extent that there are meaningful psychological differences among various AA programs (an assumption that guided our research, as seen later), we expected program characteristics to moderate the relative importance of prejudice and the concern for justice as determinants of opposition.

A recent study by Nosworthy et al. (1995) aimed at assessing the unique roles of prejudice and justice beliefs in predicting attitudes toward AA provides some initial evidence that is consistent with the idea that program characteristics might moderate the role of these variables. More specifically, they examined the roles of justice beliefs and prejudice in predicting students' attitudes toward four AA programs designed to increase representation of Black students at their university: targeted advertising, increased funding, a change in grade requirements, and enrollment quotas.

In brief, the authors found that, first, respondents' perceptions of program fairness were a significant unique (negative) predictor of endorsement, with the smallest contribution in the ads program and the greatest contribution in the quota program. Second, consistent with this finding, in a regression analysis to examine the unique roles of prejudice and individual differences in justice beliefs as predictors of endorsement, respondents' justice beliefs—when indexed by the Just World Scale (Rubin & Peplau, 1975)—negatively predicted endorsement most strongly in the quota program as compared with the ads program.[1] Finally,

---

[1]Inexplicably, respondents' scores on the Just World Scale (Rubin & Peplau, 1975) but not the Proportionality Scale (Rasinsky, 1986) correlated significantly with how fair the quota program was perceived to be.

in an analysis regressing participants' racial affect, self or group interest, and perceptions of program fairness on endorsement of four AA programs, Nosworthy et al. found that racism contributed most strongly and, indeed, accounted for unique variance over and above fairness perceptions, only within the mildest AA program (i.e., targeted ads).

Although these findings were not predicted by the researchers a priori, the general pattern makes sense conceptually. Specifically, given that perceptions of program fairness predicted attitudes most strongly in the quota program, it follows that individual differences in justice beliefs should also predict most strongly in that program. Furthermore, although it might be less obvious on the surface, it is possible that prejudice is a particularly strong determinant of opposition to mild versus strong AA programs—this is because the difference in attitudes between people high and low in prejudice might be smaller in the context of a strong preferential treatment policy in which concerns other than prejudice, namely justice concerns, presumably come into play. Some additional evidence exists to corroborate the idea that prejudice might relate to AA attitudes differentially, as a function of program type, although few studies have directly examined this question. Specifically, in a large survey aimed at validating a unidimensional conceptualization of forms of racism, Kleinpenning and Hagendoorn (1993) found that Dutch secondary school students' scores on racism were correlated more highly with their opposition to a question about equal opportunity in society than to a question about preferential treatment in job hiring.

The Nosworthy et al. (1995) and Kleinpenning and Hagendoorn (1993) studies highlight another characteristic of the AA literature that limits one's ability to make firm conclusions regarding the role of justice concerns as a determinant of opposition: Specifically, the psychological dimensions underlying the policies being evaluated in past research are rarely specified a priori. As noted by others (e.g., Nosworthy et al., 1995), to assess more clearly the role of justice concerns in predicting opposition to AA, researchers must vary systematically the degree to which policies objectively violate specific justice principles.

With the preceding work as a foundation, the next section briefly outlines how procedural and distributive justice theory can apply to the study of opposition to AA. This framework has served as the basis for our research aimed at directly assessing the role of justice concerns as a cause of opposition.

Distributive and Procedural Justice: An Application to AA

Although there is some debate over the number of justice dimensions (for reviews, see Bobocel & Holmvall, in press; Cropanzano & Greenberg, 1997; Greenberg, 1993), the traditional distinction between distributive and procedural justice continues to have both theoretical and applied utility (cf. Cropanzano & Ambrose, in press). In brief, whereas the concept of distributive justice is concerned with people's perceptions of the fairness of the distribution of resources or outcomes (e.g., Adams, 1965; Homans, 1961; for a review, see Greenberg & Cohen, 1982), the concept of procedural justice is concerned with the fairness of the procedures by which a distributive allocation norm is implemented (e.g., Leventhal, 1980; Leventhal, Karuza, & Fry, 1980; Lind & Tyler, 1988; Thibaut & Walker, 1975).

As noted by others (e.g., Cohen, 1994; Dovidio, 1996; Esses & Seligman, 1996; Nacoste, 1987; Smith Winkelman & Crosby, 1994), AA can be conceptualized from a distributive or procedural justice perspective. That is, given that AA involves the distribution of resources (e.g., jobs, pay, promotions) among groups, distributive justice principles are relevant. More specifically, affirmative action could be perceived as unfair at the distributive level because people perceive that equity, or merit (e.g., Deutsch, 1975, 1985; Lerner, 1977, 1981)—the allocation norm generally agreed to be appropriate in the workplace in Western culture—is being violated.

Affirmative action could also be considered unfair at the procedural level because people perceive that it violates specific procedural justice criteria, such as consistency across people (e.g., Leventhal, 1980; Leventhal et al., 1980). That is, it could be argued that AA treats target-group and nontarget-group members inconsistently in that group status is an advantage for some and a disadvantage for others. Indeed, sensitivity to procedural inconsistency might help to explain why people generally dislike AA programs that give preferential treatment even in instances of "tied" merit (e.g., Kravitz & Platania, 1993). Given that such programs do not allow a less qualified target-group candidate to be favored over a more qualified nontarget-group candidate, merit is not violated. Thus, it is plausible that participants react negatively because such programs violate the consistency rule of procedural justice.

In summary, concerns about the violation of distributive justice, procedural justice, or both could underlie justice-based objections to AA. To directly test whether justice concerns can uniquely cause opposition to AA, we used the distributive–procedural justice framework as an a priori basis to distinguish among AA programs.

OUR RESEARCH PROGRAM

Put plainly, our general logic was this: If it were true that justice concerns can be a cause of opposition to AA, then at least three effects should hold: (a) when an AA program violates certain principles of distributive or procedural justice, individual differences in the belief in those justice principles should predict opposition; (b) these effects should be independent of respondents' prejudice level; and (c) when an AA program is nonjustice-violating, individual differences in justice beliefs should not predict opposition. In addition, we expected that prejudice could predict opposition more strongly when an AA program in nonjustice-violating than when it is justice violating. This is because, as noted earlier, the difference between people high and low in prejudice might be reduced (i.e., both types of people may be equally opposed) in programs that violate justice principles. Consequently, justice beliefs, rather than people's prejudice level, might be what distinguishes those who oppose a justice-violating AA program and those who do not.

If justice concerns are not a true cause of opposition—rather, they are merely a rationalization of prejudice—prejudice should predict opposition regardless of whether or not the AA program violates justice principles (i.e., there should be a main effect of prejudice across program type). Moreover, individual differences in specific justice beliefs should not predict opposition differentially as a function of program characteristics. The goal of our research program has been to test these differential predictions.

Overview of the Initial Research (Studies 1 & 2)

We began our research with two studies in which we asked people to evaluate one of two AA programs—one that either did or did not violate the distributive justice principle of equity, or merit. Thus, we created a description of an equal treatment program (ET) and a strong preferential treatment program (PT), which modeled the definitions presented earlier. More specifically, in the ET program, participants evaluated an AA policy that was designed to remove systemic barriers for all employees by offering maternity–paternity leaves, flexible work hours, affordable daycare, mentorship opportunities, and more training and development. Strictly speaking, this program does not violate justice principles in that the benefits were said to be available to all employees. In contrast, in the PT program, participants evaluated a program in which target-group members could be hired or promoted for jobs over nontarget-group members, even if the former were relatively less qualified. Thus, our PT program was explicitly designed to violate the distributive justice principle of merit. To the extent that opposition to AA is genuinely determined by justice concerns, we expected that individual differences in the endorsement of the merit principle would predict opposition but only when that principle was violated—namely, in our PT but not our ET program.

To test our hypothesis, we pretested a large sample of University of Waterloo undergraduate students on both prejudice (sexism in Study 1; sexism & modern racism in Study 2) and justice beliefs. In some of our earlier research (Davey, 1995; Davey, Bobocel, Son Hing, & Zanna, 1999), we developed the Belief-in-Merit (BIM) Scale, which assesses individuals' preference for allocations that are based on the distributive justice norm of equity, or the merit principle.[2] To provide a more rigorous test of the role of justice concerns as a cause of opposition

---

[2]Two sample items from the BIM are "In almost any business or profession, people who do their job well should rise to the top" (positively keyed) and "Sometimes it is appropriate to give a raise to the worker who most needs it, even if he or she is not the most hard working" (negatively keyed). Note that, in our subsequent research, the BIM Scale has been relabeled the Preference for the Merit Principle Scale (PMP; see Davey et al., 1999).

to AA, our index of justice beliefs was developed to be relatively free of prejudice content (as well as of related constructs, e.g., conservativism, and social dominance orientation). In an experimental session, conducted approximately 1 month after pretesting, we assessed students' attitudes by asking them to evaluate an ET or a PT program.

Our findings in Studies 1 and 2 were identical. First, as expected on the basis of past research, we found that, overall, people reported greater opposition to the PT program as compared with the ET program. Second, we found the predicted BIM x program interaction: The stronger people's belief-in-merit, the more they were opposed to the PT program but not the ET program. Unexpectedly, prejudice failed to predict opposition.

On the basis of our early studies, then, we had some evidence for the idea of justice concerns as a cause of opposition to AA: Individual differences in the belief in the merit principle predicted opposition but only when the program violated the merit principle. Encouraged by these data, we conducted a third study, as follows, to extend our initial findings. We focus on Study 3 in this chapter, given that it replicated and extended our earlier data (for a more detailed version of the research, see Bobocel et al., 1998).

Study 3

It could be argued that the PT program in our initial research not only violated the merit principle but also the consistency principle of procedural justice (i.e., people are treated differently). Thus, in Study 3, we added an AA program that violated the consistency principle of procedural justice but not the merit principle. In this program, which we labeled a *Tie* program, target-group members could be hired or promoted over nontarget-group members only in instances in which the candidates were equally qualified. Thus, this program involves inconsistent treatment of candidates (i.e., group membership is an advantage for some); nevertheless, strictly speaking, the merit principle is not violated because in no case would a less qualified target-group member be hired or promoted over a more qualified nontarget-group member.

Extending the logic of our initial studies, we expected that, in Study 3, individual differences in the endorsement of the consistency principle of procedural justice would predict opposition but only when this principle was violated—namely, in our Tie program. In contrast to the Tie program, we expected that the difference between people scoring high and low in belief-in-consistency should be smaller in the ET program, in which consistency is not violated. Moreover, although the PT program does violate consistency, we expected that the difference in attitudes between people scoring high and low in belief-in-consistency would be reduced in the PT program, given that the program also violates merit; in other words, we thought that once an AA program violates merit, this would become the most salient justice-based objection. (This might be particularly true in Western society where beliefs about merit violation are generally quite strong). Finally, consistent with the findings of our initial studies, we expected that individual differences in belief-in-merit would predict opposition to the PT but not the ET or Tie programs.

Similar to the initial research, we pretested University of Waterloo students on both prejudice (sexism and modern racism) and BIM. In addition, we included the Belief-in-Consistency Scale (BIC; Son Hing, 1997), which assesses people's beliefs that it is most fair to treat people the same (vs. differently) procedurally. Finally, although it is not a primary focus of this chapter, it is noteworthy that we also assessed participants' perceptions of workplace discrimination (Son Hing, 1997).[3,4] Several justice researchers (e.g., Leventhal, 1980) have recognized that inconsistent treatment might not always be objectionable. Indeed, Crosby and her colleagues (Crosby, 1994; Smith Winkelman & Crosby, 1994) suggested that, in the context of AA, inconsistent treatment might be judged as fair by people who believe that target-group members continue to face discrimination. Thus, when making decisions concerning people who we believe face discrimination, we might object less to inconsistent treatment. On the basis of this reasoning, we thought that perceived discrimination might be negatively related to opposition toward our Tie program, given that it involves inconsistent treatment. In contrast, perceived discrimination might not be sufficient to influence attitudes to the PT program (in which both those scoring high and low in perceived discrimination would tend to be opposed because merit is violated) or to the ET program (in which both those scoring high and low in perceived discrimination would tend to be supportive).

As in Studies 1 and 2, a randomly selected subset of students participated in a second phase, which occurred about 1 month following pretesting. Specifically, participants were telephoned by a (male) experimenter who claimed to be a work-study student employed for the term in a nearby city at a company called Cochrane Industries. The experimenter told participants that Cochrane Industries (in fact, a fictitious organization) was planning to implement an AA program and that they were attempting to gauge reactions to different types of programs. To enhance experimental realism, participants were told that their opinions regarding the AA programs would be used to aid Cochrane Industries in making their decision about which program to implement. In other words, we attempted to create

---

[3]Two items from the BIC are "To treat everyone the same, students for whom English is a second language ought not to be given extra time to write exams, even though mental translation could take extra time" (positively keyed) and "To equalize affordability, many places (e.g., movie theaters) ought to offer cheaper admission prices for groups with low fixed incomes like seniors and students" (negatively keyed).

[4]The scale assesses beliefs that women and visible minorities have faced discrimination both currently and historically, as well as at the systemic and individual levels. Two example items are: "Currently, women are disadvantaged by negative stereotypes regarding their ability to perform work" (positively keyed) and "Historically, visible minorities were not disadvantaged in their chances of being hired or promoted because of inherent barriers in the workplace" (negatively keyed).

a situation akin to a focus group, where, ostensibly, people were providing a vote. Moreover, to bolster our cover story that this was a real corporate survey, and hence to reduce suspicion that it was a psychology experiment, the second phase of the data collection took place in building unrelated to the psychology department. As well, the experimenter was dressed in a business suit.

Participants were asked to read a four-page article, designed to resemble a corporate survey. We made both gender and race salient by placing a picture that included a Black woman, an Asian woman, and an Hispanic man in the top right-hand corner of the first page. The article stated that Cochrane wished to implement an AA program to remove employment barriers faced by visible minorities, women, and disabled people. Furthermore, it stated that Cochrane was investigating the types of AA programs already being used by other companies (simply labeled Corporations A, B, & C), as potential programs that Cochrane might adopt. Following this information, which appeared on the first page of the survey, was the experimental manipulation: type of program (ET, Tie, PT). Specifically, on each of the next three pages was a description of one of the AA programs, as well as the dependent measures pertaining to the specific program. The order in which the three programs were presented was counterbalanced, with participants receiving one of six possible combinations.

Table 6.1 presents the means on the attitude dependent variable, as well as on manipulation-check questions—to assess merit and consistency violation— across the three programs. First, as expected, we found a program main effect on attitudes, such that participants were most opposed to the PT, least opposed to the ET, and moderately opposed to the Tie program. (Further analyses showed that attitudes toward the three programs were not statistically intercorrelated, indicating their independence). Second, also shown in Table 6.1, analyses of the justice-violation questions revealed that our manipulations were successful. Specifically, as expected, participants reported more merit violation in the PT program as compared with both the Tie and the ET programs (which did not differ statistically).

TABLE 6.1
Mean Ratings on Dependent Variables as a Function of AA Program

Dependent Variable	AA Program		
	ET	Tie	PT
Opposition	2.08_a (0.81)	3.36_b (1.42)	5.48_c (1.05)
Merit violation	2.99_a (1.49)	3.04_a (1.89)	5.80_b (1.73)
Consistency violation	3.14_a (1.65)	3.94_b (1.71)	5.77_c (1.28)

Note. AA = affirmative action; ET = equal treatment program; Tie = tie program; PT = preferential treatment program. Standard deviations are in parentheses. Higher scores (1–7) reflect more of the construct. Groups not sharing a subscript differ significantly at $p < .05$ (Kirk, 1982). $N = 86$. Copyright © 1998 by the American Psychological Association. Adapted with permission.

Moreover, they reported more consistency violation in the Tie program as compared with the ET program. It is interesting that participants also reported more consistency violation in the PT as compared with the Tie program. Although we had not anticipated this last finding, it suggests that perceptions of merit violation were influencing perceptions of consistency violation, a possibility that is consistent with other evidence demonstrating that distributive justice perceptions can sometimes influence procedural justice perceptions.

Finally, it is noteworthy that our justice and prejudice predictors were relatively independent: Scores on BIM were not significantly correlated with any other predictor, including BIC. Scores on BIC were weakly positively related (0.30) to prejudice and weakly negatively related (−0.21) to perceptions of discrimination (i.e., the more prejudiced the respondent, the more strongly he or she endorsed the consistency principle, and the more workplace discrimination respondents perceived, the less strongly they endorsed the consistency principle). Prejudice and perceptions of discrimination were moderately negatively correlated (−0.54); higher scores on prejudice were associated with lower scores on perceived workplace discrimination.

Table 6.2 presents the primary results.[5] As indicated by the standardized regression coefficients (betas), prejudice predicted opposition but only in the ET program. That is, the more prejudiced the respondent, the more he or she disliked this relatively more popular program. BIM and BIC each predicted opposition uniquely (i.e., with prejudice controlled), in the PT and Tie programs, respectively. Thus, as expected, the stronger people's belief-in-merit, the more they opposed the PT. Similarly, the stronger people's belief-in-consistency, the more they tended to oppose the Tie program.[6]

As shown in Table 6.2, we also found that perceptions of workplace discrimination were inversely related to opposition to the Tie program. Thus, the more people perceived target-group members to be discriminated against, the less they opposed the Tie program. In contrast, perceived discrimination was not sufficient to influence attitudes to the relatively less popular PT program nor to the relatively more popular ET program.

---

[5]Two more preliminary points are noteworthy. First, there were no significant differences in opposition among the six orders within the ET (where mean attitudes ranged from 1.74 to 2.56) nor the PT program (where mean attitudes ranged from 4.97 to 5.75); in the Tie program, attitudes did differ significantly according to order, but an examination of the means showed that there was only one significant difference among the six orders. Specifically, participants reported more opposition to the Tie when they received the following order: ET, Tie, PT ($M = 4.44$), as compared with when the order was: Tie, PT, ET ($M = 2.42$); the mean attitudes for the remaining orders fell in between these two values. Second, no sex differences in opposition as a function of program were found.

[6]Although it is speculation, we believe that the failure of prejudice to predict opposition in our earlier studies might have been due, at least in part, to the inadequate priming of prejudice in our stimulus materials. Specifically, in our initial research, we used a picture of a White woman in the materials; in contrast, in Study 3, we made race and gender salient by using a picture of a Black woman, an Asian women, and an Hispanic man, as noted in the text.

TABLE 6.2
Standardized Regression Coefficients (Betas)
for the Within-Cell Regressions of Opposition on the Predictors

	AA Program		
Predictor	ET	Tie	PT
Prejudice	0.34*	0.16	0.12
BIM	−0.01	0.05	0.35**
BIC	−0.06	0.18†	−0.03
Discrim	0.12	−0.20†	0.06

Note. AA = affirmative action; ET = equal treatment program; Tie = tie program; PT = preferential treatment program; BIM = belief-in-merit; BIC = belief-in-consistency; Discrim = perceived workplace discrimination. $N = 86$. Copyright © 1998 by the American Psychological Association. Adapted with permission.

**$p < .01$. *$p < .05$. †$p < .09$.

Follow-Up Analyses.   We conducted a follow-up analysis in the Tie program for two reasons: First, we were interested in controlling an effect of order found in the Tie program (see Footnote 5); second, we included the BIC x perceived discrimination interaction term in the Tie program to test whether the first-order effect of BIC was moderated by perceptions of workplace discrimination. Whereas, in general, the higher people's scores on BIC, the more they should oppose inconsistent treatment, we wondered whether this effect could be overridden by perceptions of workplace discrimination.

The analysis revealed that, first, the positive beta for BIC remained marginally significant when order was controlled, consistent with the idea that our original justice finding was not accounted for by order. Second, the beta for the BIC x perceived discrimination interaction attained marginal statistical significance (and the original first-order effect for discrimination was no longer marginally significant). A plot of the regression lines to examine the pattern of the BIC x discrimination interaction, revealed that the effect of BIC on opposition to the Tie was indeed stronger among those who perceived low (vs. high) discrimination. Thus, although these results are preliminary, they are consistent with the idea that perceptions of workplace discrimination might excuse, or mitigate, adverse reactions to violation of the consistency principle among individuals who generally endorse this justice principle (see Nacoste & Hummels, 1991, for results that are conceptually similar to those found here).

Given that there was a trend such that perceptions of workplace discrimination moderated the more general effect of justice beliefs—namely, BIC—in the Tie program, we wondered whether perceptions of discrimination might similarly mitigate the effect of justice beliefs—namely, BIM—in the PT program. Thus, we conducted a second follow-up analysis, in which we entered the BIM x perceived discrimination interaction in the regression predicting opposition to the PT program. In this case, the interaction was not significant. In sum, then, in our data, perceptions of workplace discrimination served to mitigate opposition to the violation of certain justice principles but not others. Hence, it is possible that the perception of workplace discrimination might justify inconsistent treatment (i.e., a Tie AA program) among people who generally value consistent treatment, but it might not be sufficient to justify preferential treatment (i.e., a PT program) by people who generally value meritocracy. Given, however, that it is generally difficult to detect moderation effects, more research is necessary before we can draw firm conclusions about the mitigation of justice-based opposition.

Justice as a Cause?　Overall, the results of Study 3 provide strong support for the idea that justice-based opposition to AA can be genuine. It is unlikely that our justice findings can be interpreted as the mere rationalization of prejudiced individuals, for at least two reasons: First, the effects of justice beliefs (assessed 1 month earlier) on opposition were evident when prejudice was controlled statistically. Even more compelling, however, are the findings that individual differences in specific justice beliefs (BIM and BIC) each predicted opposition uniquely to the AA program as theoretically expected: When the program violated the merit principle, BIM predicted opposition; when the program violated the procedural justice rule of consistency, BIC predicted opposition.

Justice as a Rationalization?　Whereas our justice findings supported our original thinking about the role of justice as a cause of opposition (vs. a rationalization of prejudice), we were interested in attempting to understand why prejudice predicted opposition to the ET program. In particular, we wondered whether, consistent with the rationalization hypothesis, prejudiced people opposed the ET program because they construed it as violating justice principles, although the majority of participants did not. To explore this possibility, we conducted a mediation analysis (e.g., Baron & Kenny, 1986; Cohen & Cohen, 1983) to assess whether the effect of prejudice on opposition to the ET program (presented in Table 6.2) was mediated by participants' construal of the program as merit or consistency violating.

In brief, as shown in the path analysis in Fig. 6.1, the data are consistent with the notion that the effect of prejudice on opposition to the ET program was mediated by participants' construal of the program as justice violating. Specifically, when perceptions of merit and consistency violation were controlled, the significant path (beta = 0.22, $p < .05$) between prejudice and opposition no longer attained statistical significance (beta = 0.07; the drop in beta was statistically significant, $z = 2.27$). The nonsignificant path (beta = 0.10) between perceptions of merit violation and opposition, tentatively implicates consistency violation as the mediator. But given that perceptions of merit and consistency violation were highly intercorrelated in the ET program (as well as having been indexed with single items), it is difficult to draw firm conclusions about the precise nature of

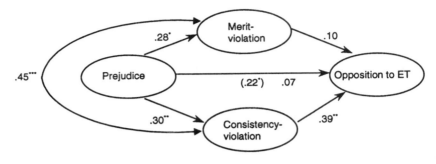

FIG. 6.1.   Path analysis depicting the mediating role of justice construal in the link between prejudice and opposition to the equal treatment (ET) program. Numbers on paths are betas: The relation between prejudice and opposition before controlling construal is given inside of parentheses; the relation after controlling construal is given outside of parentheses. The drop in beta before and after controlling construal was statistically significant, $z = 2.27$; $N = 84$. Copyright © 1998 by the American Psychological Association. Adapted with permission.

the justice construal from these data (see Baron & Kenny, 1986). Moreover, we cannot ascertain with certainty from our mediation analysis whether prejudiced individuals' construal comes before (i.e., is a perceptual filter) or after their attitude, given that the construal and attitude data were assessed concurrently.

Although the mediation analyses are somewhat preliminary, we nonetheless find them intriguing because, as noted earlier, they could help to explain why prejudiced people oppose certain AA programs. Indeed, at a general level, our prejudice findings are consistent with an argument made elsewhere (Dovidio, 1996; Gaertner & Dovidio, 1986; Murrell, Dietz-Uhler, Dovidio, Gaertner, & Drout, 1994) that prejudiced people might rationalize, or justify, (either pre- or postopinion) their opposition to AA in the name of justice.[7]

To shed more light on the process by which prejudice might operate on opposition, one could conceptualize our mediation results in terms of Fishbein and Ajzen's (1975) model of attitudes. According to Fishbein and Ajzen, attitudes are

---

[7]In Study 2, we also had some reason to believe that high- and low-prejudiced individuals construed the ET program differently. That is, although, overall, participants reported that the PT program was more merit violating than the ET program, there was also a prejudice x program interaction: High-prejudiced individuals perceived more merit violation than did low-prejudiced individuals, but only when evaluating the ET program. Thus, the more prejudiced the respondent, the more he or she construed the ET as violating distributive justice.

a function of the evaluative implications of the beliefs we hold about the attitude object. If we assume that our construal measures (i.e., perceptions of merit and consistency violation) represent participants' beliefs about the attitude object— the ET program—then our mediation analysis could conceivably indicate whether the link between prejudice and opposition is influenced by different beliefs that people scoring high versus low in prejudice have about the attitude object or by different evaluations that people scoring high and low in prejudice have of the beliefs. Put differently, to the extent that the relation between prejudice and opposition to the ET program is fully mediated by construal, this would be consistent with the idea that the differing attitudes of those high and low in prejudice are due to their differing beliefs about the ET program. In contrast, no mediation would be consistent with the idea that the differing attitudes of participants scoring high versus low in prejudice are due to their differing evaluations of the characteristics attributed to the ET program. Restating this conceptualization in Asch's (1948) classic terms, no mediation would be consistent with the interpretation that people high versus low in prejudice have "different judgments of object," whereas complete mediation would be consistent with the interpretation that people who score high versus low in prejudice have "different objects of judgment."

Thus, the fact that the prejudice effect on opposition to the ET was completely mediated by construal of the program as consistency violating is consistent with the idea that people scoring high versus low on prejudice have different beliefs about the ET program (i.e., their differing attitudes could stem from the fact that people high in prejudice systematically construe the ET as more consistency violating than do people low in prejudice).

Study 4

Given that prejudice enhanced construal of the ET program as justice violating— when by design it was not—we wondered whether prejudice might have a similar effect on people's interpretation of an unspecified AA program, the dependent variable used in much of the past prejudice research. Thus, we conduced a fourth study, of correlational design, in which students completed the individual difference measures (prejudice, BIM, BIC), as well as a short questionnaire comprising items to assess their opinion of a typical AA program in the workplace, and their beliefs about how much the typical program violates merit and consistency.

Interestingly, we found, first, of all the individual difference predictors, only prejudice was significantly correlated with opposition, $r(242) = 0.30$, $p < .001$. (The relations between opposition to the unspecified program and justice beliefs—BIM, BIC—were not statistically significant: 0.10 and 0.01, respectively.) Second, a path analysis like that presented in Fig. 6.1 indicated that the relation between prejudice and opposition was again mediated—although this time only in part—by construal of the program as violating the consistency principle.

Summary of the Research Program

Our research program supports our initial view that justice concerns can be a genuine determinant of opposition to AA rather than merely a device to mask prejudice. Contrary to much popular opinion, then, our data indicate that, although people who oppose AA programs might be prejudiced, opposition to certain forms of AA is not necessarily rooted in prejudice. We found that people can oppose AA programs that violate certain distributive and procedural justice norms as a result of genuine beliefs in the principles of fairness that the programs violate (and this is independent of respondents' prejudice level). It is interesting, however, that we also found evidence consistent with the idea that certain people, namely prejudiced individuals, might oppose nonjustice violating AA programs through their tendency to construe them as violating justice principles, although in the eyes of most people the programs do not do so. Thus, in the case of an ET or an undefined program—in which justice principles are not violated—prejudiced people might use the claim of injustice as a rationalization for their opposition.

THE PRACTICAL MANAGEMENT
OF AFFIRMATIVE ACTION

What implications does our research have for organizations that wish to reduce opposition to AA initiatives? Although we recognize that there are limits in our ability to generalize our results to working employees, our data have several potential implications for the practical management of AA. First, our results suggest that, if an AA program truly violates the merit principle in distributing scarce resources, such as jobs or promotions (i.e., it is a strong PT program) then it will likely be both difficult to justify and strongly opposed. Opposition will be particularly strong among those who believe firmly in the merit principle, the norm that is generally judged as most appropriate in the workplace. Thus, if organizations wish to avoid opposition to AA or other diversity initiatives, we would recommend not instituting a strong preferential treatment program.

Second, our data suggest strategies to reduce opposition to AA programs that do not violate the merit principle. For example, to make it difficult for individuals—especially prejudiced individuals—to rationalize their opposition on the basis of misconstruals or unwarranted assumptions about programs like our Tie program, organizations should clearly communicate that the program does not, in fact, violate merit (i.e., it is not a strong PT program). Similarly, if the program is like our ET program, then organizations should be clear that the policy violates neither merit nor consistency principles, again, to make it difficult for prejudiced individuals to rationalize their opposition on the basis of justice violation. Finally, there was preliminary evidence to suggest that opposition to programs like our Tie might be lessened among those who most strongly endorse the principle of consistent treatment, if organization were to increase awareness of discrimination in the workplace. Clearly, these recommendations require that organizational leaders are first aware of the various components of their AA policy, so as to communicate to employees what is and is not involved.

DIRECTIONS FOR FUTURE RESEARCH

Future Research on AA

Our research demonstrates that both prejudice and justice beliefs are important predictors of opposition to AA, but their relative influence depends on the characteristics of the AA program. Put differently, our research suggests that there are multiple psychologies of opposition to AA, contingent on the characteristics of the policy. Some implications for future research on AA are discussed next.

First, our data demonstrate why, from a theoretical perspective, it is essential for researchers to clearly specify the nature of the AA program under investigation: Depending on how participants perceive the specifics, results could differ substantially between investigations. The idea that there are multiple psychologies of opposition to AA could help to both explain inconsistencies in past research and guide future investigations on AA or other workplace diversity initiatives. Given that, at present, the AA literature is somewhat fragmented (see Kravitz et al., 1997), efforts to integrate past findings and to guide future research would be highly valuable, both from a theoretical and an applied perspective.

Second, whereas we focussed primarily on prejudice and justice beliefs as predictors, it is possible that other constructs might account for additional variance in opposition to specific AA programs. For example, it might be useful to extend the psychology we have implicated in our research by examining the unique contribution of conservative versus liberal political ideology (e.g., Sidanius et al., 1996; Sniderman & Piazza, 1993), self- and group interest (e.g., Kravitz, Stinson, & Mello, 1994; Sears & Funk, 1991; Tougas et al., 1995), or social dominance orientation (e.g., Sidanius et al., 1996) in predicting opposition. Although it is unlikely that these variables can account for our findings (i.e., our program x individual difference interactions), it is reasonable to assume that they might aid in explaining additional variance in opposition to specific programs.

In keeping with other justice theorists, we drew broadly on the concepts of distributive and procedural justice to differentiate the programs under investigation. It would be useful to elaborate on the approach taken here and conduct research (e.g., using multidimensional-scaling techniques) to identify additional underlying psychological dimensions, such as effectiveness in remedying discrimination, on which AA programs might differ. If it were possible to categorize specific initiatives on a broader set of more fundamental dimensions, this would clearly benefit future research: In particular, it would encourage theoretically deduced predictions regarding the antecedents of opposition to AA or other diversity initiatives, as well as the variables that might moderate or mediate effects.

A fourth useful direction for future research on AA would be to systematically investigate the effect of justifications, or social accounts, in mitigating negative reactions to specific AA or diversity initiatives (e.g., Bobocel & Farrell, 1996; Bobocel, McCline, & Folger, 1997; Heilman, 1994; Murrell et al., 1994). Whereas some of our findings would support the recommendation made elsewhere (e.g., Heilman, 1994) that justifications should emphasize the qualifications of target-group members (thereby minimizing suspicions that merit has been violated), our data indicate that it might also be important to directly address procedural justice concerns.

Moreover, in keeping with the idea of multiple psychologies of opposition to AA, we expect that different justifications should be most effective, depending on characteristics of the policy or of the respondent. For example, the follow-up analyses indicated a trend such that perceptions of workplace discrimination moderated objections to the violation of the consistency principle among those who strongly endorse this justice principle; this suggests that justifications aimed at increasing awareness of workplace discrimination could be effective in reducing opposition to certain types of AA programs. Interestingly, perceptions of workplace discrimination were not sufficient to mitigate objections to violation of the merit principle among those who strongly endorse this justice principle. Thus, the variables that mitigate, or excuse, the effect of people's more general justice beliefs on opposition might differ depending on the justice norm that, in the eyes of most people, is violated by the AA program.

Future Research on Organizational Justice

On the one hand, our data reassure us that justice-based opposition to controversial organizational policies can be genuine. On the other hand, the data also suggest that, in some instances, people who object to an organizational policy or decision in the name of fairness might, in truth, be motivated by less socially desirable attitudes. In such cases, the claim of injustice might be a more socially acceptable way for individuals to object.

Thus, we believe that there would be utility in research to examine, in domains other than AA and for attitudes other than prejudice, whether justice-based opposition is genuine or, rather, is acting in the service of alternative constructs (e.g., social dominance orientation, right-wing authoritarianism, or organizational cynicism). For example, among individuals with power or status in an organization, those with a high (vs. low) social dominance orientation might claim that organizational interventions aimed at empowering low-status employees are unfair, not because the interventions truly violate principles of fairness but because such changes could alter what those high in social dominance see as a natural ordering of social groups. Research in this vein could provide useful conceptual linkages between the literatures on justice and related topics, such as power (e.g., see James, 1993; Kabonoff, 1991). It would also be of significant interest to determine empirically whether respondents' claim of injustice, when operating in the service of less desirable attitudes, is mindful–controlled or mindless–automatic (Langer, 1978; Schneider & Shiffrin, 1977).

Another general line of justice research that we believe would be of benefit is to examine systematically the conditions that moderate the criteria by which we judge both distributive and procedural justice. For example, under what conditions does consistency in procedures become more or less influential as a determinant of fairness perceptions? Put differently, under what conditions do individuals perceive inconsistent treatment to be procedurally fair? In addition to our finding that some individuals might have general preferences for consistent versus differential treatment, we also found (as noted previously) that respondents' beliefs about the level of discrimination faced by target-group members lessened their opposition to an organizational policy that violated consistency in treatment. Given that the workplace is becoming more diverse, it seems particularly timely to further examine situational or intrapersonal variables that might serve to moderate the role of consistency in treatment as an antecedent of procedural justice.

CONCLUSIONS

In this chapter, we raised the question of whether justice concerns can be a genuine cause of opposition to AA or whether they serve merely to rationalize less desirable social motivation, such as prejudice. We reported our research program aimed at testing this question directly. Our data support the view that the concern for justice can be a genuine determinant of opposition to, at least some forms of, AA: Specifically, we found that people oppose AA programs that violate certain distributive and procedural justice norms as a result of genuine beliefs in the principles of fairness that the programs violate. Interestingly, we also found evidence consistent with the idea that prejudiced people might oppose nonjustice violating AA programs through the tendency to construe them as violating justice principles, even though, in the eyes of most people, they do not. In summary, although prejudiced individuals might rationalize their opposition to some forms of AA in the name of justice, it is not true that all justice effects are the mere rationalization of prejudiced individuals.

ACKNOWLEDGMENTS

This project was funded by research grants from the Social Sciences and Humanities Research Council of Canada awarded to D. Ramona Bobocel and Mark P. Zanna. The contributions to this research of Liane Davey and Leanne Son Hing were equal. A version of this chapter was presented by the first author at the International Conference for Social Justice Research, 5th Biennial Meeting, July 1–4, 1997, Potsdam, Germany. We are grateful to Russell Cropanzano for helpful comments on an earlier version of this chapter. Correspondence concerning this chapter should be addressed to Ramona Bobocel, Department of Psychology, University of Waterloo, Ontario, Canada, N2L 3G1. E-mail: rbobocel@watarts. uwaterloo.ca.

REFERENCES

Adams, J. S. (1965). Inequity in social exchange. In L. Berkowitz (Ed.), *Advances in experimental social psychology* (Vol. 2, pp. 267–299). New York: Academic.

Asch, S. E. (1948). The doctrine of suggestion, prestige, and imitation in social psychology, *Psychological Review, 55,* 256–277.

Barnes Nacoste, R. (1994). If empowerment is the goal . . . : Affirmative action and social interaction. *Basic and Applied Social Psychology, 15,* 87–112.

Baron, R. M., & Kenny, D. A. (1986). The moderator–mediator variable distinction in social psychological research: Conceptual, strategic, and statistical consideration. *Journal of Personality and Social Psychology, 51,* 1173–1182.

Bobocel, D. R., & Farrell, A. C. (1996). Sex-based promotion decisions and interactional fairness: Investigating the influence of managerial accounts. *Journal of Applied Psychology, 81,* 22–35.

Bobocel, D. R., & Holmvall, C. M. (in press). Are interactional justice and procedural justice different?: Framing the debate. To appear in S. Gilliland, D. Steiner, & D. Skarlicki (Eds.), *Research in Social Issues in Management* (Vol. 1). Greenwich, CT: Information Age Publishing, Inc.

Bobocel, D. R., & McCline, R. L., & Folger, R. (1997). Letting them down gently: Conceptual advances in explaining controversial organizational policies. In C. L. Cooper & D. M. Rousseau, *Trends in Organizational Behavior, Vol. 4,* 73–88. Wiley.

Bobocel, D. R., & Son Hing, L. S., Davey, L. M., Stanley, D. J., & Zanna, M. P. (1998). Justice-based opposition to social policies: Is it genuine? *Journal of Personality and Social Psychology, 75,* 653–669.

Chacko, T. L. (1982). Women and equal employment opportunity: Some unintended effects. *Journal of Applied Psychology, 67,* 119–123.

Clayton, S. D., & Tangri, S. S. (1989). The justice of affirmative action. In F. A. Blanchard & F. J. Crosby (Eds.), *Affirmative action in perspective* (pp. 177–192). New York: Springer-Verlag.

Cohen, R. L. (1994). Some reflections on Smith and Crosby's "Affirmative action: Setting the record straight." *Social Justice Research, 7,* 329–344.

Cohen, J., & Cohen, P. (1983). *Applied multiple regression/correlation analysis for the behavioral sciences* (2nd ed.). Hillsdale, NJ: Lawrence Erlbaum Associates.

Cropanzano, R., & Ambrose, M. L. (in press). Procedural and distributive justice are more similar than you think: A monistic perspective and a research agenda. In J. Greenberg & R. Cropanzano (Eds.), *Advances in Organizational Justice.* Lexington, MA: The New Lexington Press.

Cropanzano, R., & Greenberg, J. (1997). Progress in organizational justice: Tunneling through the maze. In I. T. Robertson & C. L. Cooper (Eds.), *International Review of Industrial and Organizational Psychology,* 317–372.

Crosby, F. J. (1994). Understanding affirmative action. *Basic and Applied Social Psychology, 15,* 13–41.

Davey, L. M. (1995). *Development and validation of two resource allocation surveys.* Unpublished masters thesis, University of Waterloo, Waterloo, Ontario, Canada.

Davey, L. M., Bobocel, D. R., Son Hing, L. S., & Zanna, M. P. (1999). Preference for the Merit Principle Scale: An individual difference measure of distributive justice preferences. *Social Justice Research, 12,* 223–240.

Deutsch, M. (1975). Equity, equality, and need: What determines which value will be used as the basis of distributive justice? *Journal of Social Issues, 31,* 137–149.

Deutsch, M. (1985). *Distributive justice: A social psychological perspective.* New Haven: CT: Yale University Press.

Dovidio, J. F. (1996, August). *Affirmative action and contemporary racial bias: Need and resistance.* Paper presented at the annual meeting of the American Psychological Association, Toronto, Canada.

Esses, V. M., & Seligman, C. (1996). The individual-group distinction in assessments of strategies to reduce prejudice and discrimination: The case of affirmative action. In R. M. Sorrentino & E. T. Higgins (Eds.), *Handbook of motivation and cognition: The interpersonal context* (Vol. 3, pp. 570–590). New York: Guilford.

Fishbein, M., & Ajzen, I. (1975). *Belief, attitude, intention, and behavior: An introduction to theory and research.* Reading, MA: Addison-Wesley.

Folger, R. (1994). Workplace justice and employee worth. *Social Justice Research, 7,* 225–241.

Gaertner, S. L., & Dovidio, J. F. (1986). The aversive form of racism. In J. F. Dovidio & S. L. Gaertner (Eds.), *Prejudice, discrimination, and racism* (pp. 61–89). Orlando, FL: Academic.

Greenberg, J. (1993). The social side of fairness: Interpersonal and informational classes of organizational justice. In R. Cropanzano (Ed.), *Justice in the workplace: Approaching fairness in human resource management* (pp. 79–103). Hillsdale, NJ: Lawrence Erlbaum Associates.

Greenberg, J., & Cohen, R. L. (Eds.). (1982). *Equity and justice in social behavior.* New York: Academic.

Heilman, M. E. (1994). Affirmative action: Some unintended consequences for working women. In B. M. Staw & L. L. Cummings (Eds.), *Research in organizational behavior* (Vol. 16, pp. 125–169). Greenwich, CT: JAI.

Homans, G. C. (1961). *Social behavior: Its elementary forms.* New York: Harcourt, Brace, and World.

Jacobson, C. K. (1985). Resistance to affirmative action. *Journal of Conflict Resolution, 29,* 306–329.

James, K. (1993). The social context of organizational justice: Cultural, intergroup, and structural effects on justice behaviors and perceptions. In R. Cropanzano (Ed.), *Justice in the workplace: Approaching fairness in human resource management* (pp. 133–154). Hillsdale, NJ: Lawrence Erlbaum Associates.

Kabanoff, B. (1991). Equity, equality, power, and conflict. *Academy of Management Review, 16,* 416–441.

Kinder, D. R., & Sears, D. O. (1981). Prejudice and politics: Symbolic racism versus racial threats to the good life. *Journal of Personality and Social Psychology, 40,* 414–431.

Kirk, R. E. (1982). *Experimental design: Procedures for the behavioral sciences* (2nd ed.). Belmont, CA: Brooks/Cole.

Kleinpenning, G., & Hagendoorn, L. (1993). Forms of racism and the cumulative dimension of ethnic attitudes. *Social Psychology Quarterly, 56,* 21–36.

Kluegel, J. R., & Smith, E. R. (1983). Affirmative action attitudes: Effects of self-interest, racial affect, and stratification beliefs on Whites' views. *Social Forces, 61,* 797–824.

Kravitz, D. A. (1995). Attitudes toward affirmative action plans directed at Blacks: Effects of plan and individual differences. *Journal of Applied Social Psychology, 25,* 2192–2220.

Kravitz, D. A., Harrison, D. A., Turner, M. E., Levine, E. L., Chaves, W., Brannick, M. T., Denning, D. L., Russell, C. J., & Conrad, M. A. (1997). *Affirmative action: A review of psychological and behavioral research.* Bowling Green, OH: Society for Industrial and Organizational Psychology.

Kravitz, D. A., & Platania, J. (1993). Attitudes and beliefs about affirmative action: Effects of target and of respondent sex and ethnicity. *Journal of Applied Psychology, 78,* 928–938.

Kravitz, D. A, Stinson, V., & Mello, E. W. (1994, August). Public reactions to affirmative action. In M. E. Turner (Chair), *Affirmative action at work: Towards reducing barriers to the integrated workplace.* Symposium conducted at the Fifth International Conference on Social Justice Research, Reno, NV.

Langer, E. J. (1978). Rethinking the role of thought in social interaction. In J. H. Harvey, W. J. Ickes & R. F. Kidd (Eds.), *New directions in attribution research* (Vol. 2, pp. 35–58). Hillsdale, NJ: Lawrence Erlbaum Associates.

Lerner, M. J. (1977). The justice motive: Some hypotheses as to its origins and its forms. *Journal of Personality, 45,* 1–51.

Lerner, M. J. (1981). The justice motive in human relations: Some thoughts on what we know and need to know about justice. In M. J. Lerner & S. C. Lerner (Eds.), *The justice motive in social behavior: Adapting to times of scarcity and change* (pp. 11–35). New York: Plenum.

Leventhal, G. S. (1980). What should be done with equity theory? New approaches to the study of fairness in social relationships. In K. Gergen, M. Greenberg & R. Wills (Eds.), *Social exchange: Advances in theory and research* (pp. 27–55). New York: Plenum.

Leventhal, G. S., Karuza, J., & Fry, W. R. (1980). Beyond fairness: A theory of allocation preferences. In G. Mikula (Ed.), *Justice and social interaction* (pp. 167–218). New York: Springer-Verlag.

Lind, E. A., & Tyler, T. (1988). *The social psychology of procedural justice.* New York: Plenum.

McConahay, J. B. (1986). Modern racism, ambivalence, and the modern racism scale. In S. F. Dovidio & S. L. Gaertner (Eds.), *Prejudice, discrimination and racism: Theory and research.* New York: Academic.

Murrell, A. J., Dietz-Uhler, B. L., Dovidio, J. F., Gaertner, S. L., & Drout, C. (1994). Aversive racism and resistance to affirmative action: Perceptions of justice are not necessarily color blind. *Basic and Applied Social Psychology, 15,* 71–86.

Nacoste, R. W. (1985). Selection procedure and responses to affirmative action: The case of favorable treatment. *Law and Human Behavior, 9,* 225–242.

Nacoste, R. W. (1987). Social psychology and affirmative: The importance of process in policy analysis. *Journal of Social Issues, 43,* 127–132.

Nacoste, R. W., & Hummels, B. (1994). Affirmative action and the behavior of decision makers. *Journal of Applied Social Psychology, 24,* 595–613.

Nosworthy, G. J., Lea, J. A., & Lindsay, R. C. L. (1995). Opposition to affirmative action: Racial affect and traditional value predictors across four programs. *Journal of Applied Social Psychology, 25,* 314–337.

Pedhauzar, E. J. (1982). *Multiple regression in behavioral research: Explanation and prediction* (2nd ed.). Orlando, FL: Harcourt Brace.

Price, J. L., & Mueller, C. W. (1986). *Handbook of organizational measurement.* Marshfield, MA: Pitman.

Rasinski, K. A. (1987). What's fair is fair—or is it? Value differences underlying public views about social justice. *Journal of Personality and Social Psychology, 53,* 201–211.

Rubin, Z., & Peplau, L. A. (1975). Who believes in a just world? *Journal of Social Issues, 31,* 65–89.

Schneider, W., & Shriffin, R. M. (1977). Controlled and automatic information processing: I. Detection, search, and attention. *Psychological Review, 84,* 1–66.

Sears, D. O., & Funk, C. L. (1991). The role of self-interest in social and political attitudes. *Advances in Experimental Social Psychology, 24,* 1–31.

Sidanius, J., Pratto, F., & Bobo, L. (1996). Racism, conservatism, affirmative action, and intellectual sophistication: A matter of principled conservatism or group dominance? *Journal of Personality and Social Psychology, 70,* 476–490.

Son Hing, L. S. (1997). *Opposition to affirmative action based on type of program, prior attitudes and construals.* Unpublished master's thesis, University of Waterloo, Waterloo, Ontario, Canada.

Stanley, D., Davey, L. M., Zanna, M. P., & Bobocel, D. R. (1996, May). *Prejudicial and merit-based opposition to affirmative action.* Poster presented at the Annual Meeting of the Society for the Psychological Study of Social Issues (Div. 9, APA), Ann Arbor, MI.

Smith Winkelman, C., & Crosby, F. J. (1994). Affirmative action: Setting the record straight. *Social Justice Research, 7,* 309–328.

Sniderman, P. M., & Piazza, T. (1993). *The scar of race.* Cambridge, MA: Harvard University Press.

Thibaut, J., & Walker, L. (1975). *Procedural justice: A psychological analysis.* Hillsdale, NJ: Lawrence Erlbaum Associates.

Tougas, F., Brown, R., Beaton, A. M., & Joly, S. (1995). Neo-sexism: Plus ça change, plus c'est pareil. *Personality and Social Psychology Bulletin, 21,* 842–849.

Tougas, F., Joly, S., Beaton, A. M., & St. Pierre, L. (1996). Reactions of beneficiaries to preferential treatment: A reality check. *Human Relations, 49*, 453–464.

Tougas, F., & Veilleux, F. (1988). The influence of identification, collective relative deprivation, and procedure of implementation on women's response to affirmative action: A causal modelling approach. *Canadian Journal of Behavioural Science, 20,* 15–28.

Turner, M. E., & Pratkanis, A. R. (1994). Affirmative action: Insights from social psychology and organizational research. *Basic and Applied Psychology, 15*, 1–11.

Family Friendly Policies: Organizational Justice Perceptions of Need-Based Allocations

Alicia A. Grandey
Pennsylvania State University

Any human-resource policy has certain functions: creating or modifying procedures, distributing resources, and regulating behavior (Zimmerman, 1995). Family friendly policies are no exception. Policies are adopted that create new procedures, distribute resources such as flextime and paid leave, and establish norms about how the organization feels about family needs. The organizational justice literature has much theory and research on how fairness is involved in processes, distribution, and norms. As such, the justice literature is particularly relevant to our understanding of how well family friendly policies work.

This chapter explores a new issue in organizations: How to fairly adopt and implement policies that are, by nature, not given to everyone and not based on performance. First, the issue of work–family conflict is introduced, to present the rationale for the policies in the first place. Then, family friendly policies are discussed in terms of their different manifestations and organizational and individual outcomes. Next, justice theory and research is briefly reviewed and applied to family friendly policies. This chapter concludes with recommendations about family friendly policies that consider the justice literature.

WORK–FAMILY CONFLICT: THE PRESENTING PROBLEM

Workers with families are torn by competing forces because their family responsibilities are also demanding. Company culture frequently tells them to leave their family troubles at home. This is frequently impossible today because there is seldom anyone at home.—James J. Renier, Chairman and CEO of Honeywell, Inc. (Peters, Peters, & Caropreso, 1990, p. 45)

The changing demographics of our workforce is by now a familiar topic to those interested in organizations. In 1992, 58% of U.S. women populated the workforce (U.S. Bureau of the Census, 1993), and by 2000 almost 80% of women (between 25 and 54 years) will be paid U.S. employees (National Commission on Working Women, 1989). What this means is that more couples are juggling both work and family responsibilities (Gupta & Jenkins, 1985). In scientific and popular journals, this balancing act is referred to as work–family conflict.

One study reported that over 75% of the married women surveyed experienced conflict between work and family every day (Wortman, Biernat, & Lang, 1991). Although having multiple roles, such as employee and mother, has been associated with positive outcomes like higher self-esteem and life satisfaction (Barnett & Baruch, 1985; Barnett & Marshall, 1992; Roskies & Carrier, 1994), the lack of time and energy to perform both roles successfully is associated with detrimental outcomes. These outcomes include the individuals' health and psychological state, as well as organizational outcomes such as job satisfaction, work tension, burnout, absenteeism, and turnover intentions (e.g., Adams et al, 1996; Burke, 1989; Frone, Russell, & Cooper, 1991; Goff, Mount, & Jamison, 1990; Grandey & Cropanzano, 1997; Kopelman, Greenhaus, & Connolly, 1983). For example, having to pick up a sick child at day care can result in absenteeism from work. Also, child-care needs are a reason cited for distraction from work productivity (Mize & Freeman, 1989). Because economic demands may require both spouses to work, it is unlikely that this interrole conflict will just go away. Thus, employees are looking to corporations to provide means of coping with these multiple demands.

FAMILY FRIENDLY POLICIES:
THE PROPOSED SOLUTION

One proposed method of coping with the prevalent issue of work–family conflict is the adoption of family friendly policies. These are policies or programs designed to meet the family needs of employees, sponsored by the organization. Examples of these policies include paid and job-secure parental leave, flexible scheduling by the employee to work around family needs, and on-site child-care centers. Most employees desire family friendly policies in their organizations (Friedman, 1987). The extent of interest in this issue is apparent when one reads the popular press, with a column devoted to work and family issues in *The Wall Street Journal*, cover articles in *Business Week* (Hammonds, 1996) and *Ms.* (Carter & Peters, 1996), and lists of family friendly corporations in magazines like *Working Mother* and *Working Woman*. There are also professional groups newly formed to address this issue, such as the Families and Work Institute and The Alliance of Work/Life Professionals. The federal government also has begun to respond to this issue with mandates: In 1993, the Clinton administration passed the Family and Medical Leave Act, which states that businesses with 50 or more employees must provide 12-week (unpaid) leave for those with child- and elder-care needs. Offering affordable child care to working parents is the newest cause that the current administration is addressing.

These popular and governmental responses to the issue of balancing work and family roles speak to the changing nature of the roles' relation to one another. Although in the past organizations have been hesitant to cross over to the family domain (Zedeck & Mosier, 1990), it is now more common to find organizations embracing a holistic view of their employees' lives. The existence of the policies demonstrate the organization's willingness to respond to nonwork demands on employees' time and energy. This willingness is not only for the sake of societal responsibility. Because work–family conflict is associated with a variety of detrimental outcomes for organizations (see aforementioned), the desire to decrease this conflict is economically sound. It is believed that the use of family friendly policies will decrease work–family conflict, which will lead to a healthier and happier workers (Auerbach, 1990; Christensen & Staines, 1990; Galinsky & Stein, 1990). Likewise, because child- or elder-care demands are suspected to distract employees from work tasks and physically require them to be with their families, it seems reasonable to expect that work performance, absenteeism, and turnover will be affected by the policies as well.

Thus, high expectations surround family friendly policies when they are adopted. Unfortunately, many companies do not evaluate how changing their policies affects individual and organizational outcomes. Evaluating the outcomes within each organization is important; if the programs are not having the desired effect, the reason should be assessed. Some researchers have attempted to fill this gap, but few have performed controlled studies. In fact, the limited research that has assessed the effect of family friendly policies on work–family conflict has not been overly positive (Goff et al., 1990; Solomon, 1994), although there is more support for the beneficial effect on other organizational outcomes. The next section introduces the general outcomes attributed to the adoption of family friendly policies, describes specific types of family friendly policies, and outlines the limited research relevant to assessing their outcomes.

Family Friendly Policies and Their Outcomes

Business needs specific, targeted work–family programs because they will help alleviate immediate problems faced by our employees and their families . . . we are all more productive when we can give work and home their due time.—James L. Renier, Chairman and CEO of Honeywell, Inc. (Peters et al., 1990, p. 45)

In general, simply offering family friendly policies seem to have positive results for organizations. For instance, those who offer these nonmandated fringe benefits are often considered progressive companies and may appear on a list of family friendly corporations in magazines and newspapers (Hammonds, 1996; Leib, 1996; Starrett, 1987; Trost, 1987). This may be good public relations in terms of recruitment and retention. A controlled study by Honeycutt and Rosen (1997) demonstrated that offering family friendly leave policies made an organization more attractive to prospective applicants. These policies also seem related to retention; offering a family friendly program had a positive relationship with organizational commitment and a negative relation to turnover intentions (Grover & Crooker, 1995).

To look more specifically at the outcomes of family friendly benefits, one needs to consider how various types of policies may influence outcomes differently. Although the argument has been made that policies as a whole affect employees (Grover & Crooker, 1995), for the purposes of this section policies are categorized in two types: segmentative policies, which provide the employee with the means to deal with family demands but continue to focus on work, and integrative policies, which allow employees to restructure their work in order to more clearly focus on both work and family demands. In addition to a brief description of these categories of policies, the following section presents some of the research that has examined the relation of policies with attraction to the organization, absenteeism, turnover, and performance.

Segmentative Policies. These types of policies are work focused, in that they encourage the employee to cope with their family demands as efficiently as possible and focus on their work demands. They attempt to alleviate the workers' concern about child or elder care via work-sponsored programs. These programs may involve starting up a child-care center on-site, sponsoring a center in the community, joining with other companies sponsoring a center, or providing referrals or vouchers to employees for use at private centers (see Bureau of National Affairs, 1988). Problems with this solution include high start-up costs and an inability to provide the service to every employee, due to lack of space, fees for use, and age or health of the child (Aldous, 1990; Ferber & O'Farrell, 1991). According to the ideology behind the segmentative policies, the expected benefits are a decrease in absenteeism and tardiness by providing convenient sites for dropping and picking up dependents and a decrease in anxiety and psychological withdrawal by providing high-quality environments for loved ones. These two benefits, increased convenience and decreased anxiety, should also impact turnover rates and work performance.

Few empirical studies have assessed if these expectations are warranted. Much of the support for organizations' adopting child-care services has drawn on survey or interview data. For instance, one survey reported that 88% of the organizations surveyed thought that providing child-care programs increased attraction or recruiting ability, 72% thought they decreased absenteeism, and 65% thought they improved attitudes toward the organization (Perry, 1982). Auerbach (1990) interviewed hospitals in the Midwest that had recently implemented child-care programs. She reported that before the center was opened, turnover rates for parents eligible to use the service was 40%. Two years after opening, parents using the center had a turnover rate of 24%. Over 5 years, there was a company-wide annual decrease in turnover of 7.8%. This same hospital also experienced a decrease in absenteeism from these parents, from 6% to 1%. The economic benefit of the child-care program was calculated to be $250,000 annually (Auerbach, 1990). Survey and case studies provide interesting data, but any conclusions are tenuous due to the possibility that other factors are influencing the outcomes, or that the findings are specific only to this organization.

Empirical studies have found some of the predicted relations between segmentative policies and the expected outcomes, although other studies dispute the favorable findings. The supposition that providing child-care centers directly affects the work performance of employees does not seem warranted (Milkovich & Gomez, 1976; Kossek & Nichol, 1992). One study found that the use of a child-care center was related to lower absenteeism and turnover (Milkovich & Gomez, 1976), although other work did not find relations with either (Goff et al., 1990; Grover & Crooker, 1995). One of those contradictory papers found that providing child-care information had a significant relation with turnover intentions, whereas actually providing child-care assistance was not related (Grover & Crooker, 1995). Another empirical study assessing the effectiveness of an on-site child-care center reported no reduction in absenteeism (Goff et al., 1990). Rather, employees who felt satisfied with child-care arrangements in general, whatever those might be, had lower work–family conflict, which was related to lower absenteeism. It may be that each site has very specific needs, so that it is difficult to draw general conclusions about the effectiveness of any policy across companies. This chapter draws some inferences about these contradictory results in a following section.

Integrative Policies. An integrative policy is one that encourages employees to restructure their work time to cope with family demands. Programs include providing personal or parental leave, part-time employment, flexible scheduling, a compressed work week, telecommuting, and job sharing (see Bureau of National Affairs, 1988; Lechner & Creedon, 1994). These policies do not separate work from family needs, but rather the organization directly helps with family needs. However, this lack of separation of the work and family domains can also lead to disruption at work. Supervisors are not always supportive of flextime because they cannot supervise work if it is not done on-site, plus the work flow may be disrupted if certain employees are not present (Lechner & Creedon, 1995; Patridge, 1973). Especially in today's team-based environments, this might be a noteworthy downfall of integrative policies. This issue is discussed further in later sections of this chapter.

It is expected that if employees have more control over their hours and can request time to deal with their family needs they will have more positive feelings about the organization, lower work–family conflict and tension, lower turnover rates, and better work performance because they are not as distracted by family demands. Work withdrawal (absenteeism, tardiness, leaving early) is also expected to decrease if these policies are implemented, although most of the policies involve the employee not being present at work. This is because the employee has control over his or her own scheduling, so theoretically there is no need to withdraw during scheduled hours.

Most of the research on integrative policies has focused on flextime rather than the other integrative options. The findings seem fairly positive in terms of the organizational outcomes of absenteeism, turnover, and performance. In a time series field study with hourly, white-collar service employees, absenteeism was greatly decreased for employees who were allowed flexible scheduling versus a control group that did not schedule their own hours (Dalton & Mesch, 1990). In a study involving county welfare agency employees, Kim and Campagna (1981) employed experimental and control groups to assess the effects of flexible hours on absenteeism. They found that flextime's relation to absenteeism depended on the type of absences one inspected. Flextime decreased unpaid absences and short-term (2 or fewer hours a day) absenteeism. This makes sense because employees could schedule their hours around the events that may have caused them to have to leave the workplace before. However, employees using flextime used just as many paid absences (sick time) as nonusers. Work–family conflict is related to poor health (i.e., Grandey & Cropanzano, 1999), so if family policies are related to work–family conflict it would be reasonable to expect less sick leave from those using these policies. Kim and Campagna's findings suggest that flextime and paid sick leave offer two means to fulfill family needs, rather than flextime having a buffering effect on the use of sick leave.

One study found that one-half of the cases examined experienced decreased turnover rates and also improved productivity (Nollen & Martin, 1978), but others did not find that flextime interventions had any effect on turnover (Dalton & Mesch, 1990; Pierce & Newstrom, 1983). However, Dalton and Mesch (1990) proposed that flextime may have an indirect relation with turnover through absenteeism. A positive association was found between flexible work schedules and work performance (Kim & Campagna, 1981; Pierce & Newstrom, 1983). Overall, these findings reasonably support the positive organizational outcomes of flexible scheduling.

Individual well-being should improve when employees have the opportunity to schedule their work lives to fit better with their family lives. After flextime was implemented, lower levels of work–family conflict were reported in a few studies (Bohen & Viveros-Long, 1981; Lee, 1983) but not for others (Shinn, Wong, Simco, & Ortiz-Torres, 1989). One study's path analysis suggested that those with higher work–family conflict had a higher desire for flexible scheduling so as to have control over one's schedule (Coakley & Karren, 1996). This finding was corroborated by a study that demonstrated an indirect association between flexible schedules and work–family conflict via the feeling of control (Thomas & Ganster, 1995). Thomas and Ganster also found a direct connection between flexible schedules and somatic health, and other researchers have found reasonable evidence supporting the relation of flexible scheduling with job satisfaction (see Dunham, Pierce, & Castenada, 1987; Kossek & Ozeki, 1998; Rothausen, 1994). Overall, flexible scheduling seems to relate to positive individual outcomes. Flextime offers employees a sense of control over their lives as well as a means of meeting their family-role demands. More research needs to assess the outcomes of the other types of integrative policies, but it is possible that telecommuting, shorter work weeks, or job sharing provide similar outcomes by providing more autonomy.

So, as family needs are becoming a larger issue for a greater proportion of the workforce, some corporations are responding by adopting family friendly policies. The research suggests that this is a smart move, although some contradictions in the findings exist. It seems that simply adopting these policies may create positive outcomes; many of the aforementioned studies only looked at the availability of the policies, not the use of them. If policies are so desirable to prospective and current employees, why are more organizations not making this fringe-benefit package standard? And once the policies are adopted, what might keep the organization and employees from realizing the positive benefits, as demonstrated by some of the contradictory findings? Researchers need to ask what barriers might exist that would hinder the adoption and success of family friendly policies. One proposed barrier is the issue of fairness perceptions.

DISTRIBUTIVE JUSTICE AND FAMILY FRIENDLY POLICIES

> I'm tired of hearing these people cry about their child-care problems. Why should the company help them? It isn't helping me.—White female manager (Fernandez, 1990, p. 185)

> The company didn't help me with my four kids. Why should it help people now?—Hispanic male manager (Fernandez, 1990, p. 185)

Various barriers to policy adoption and effectiveness have been suggested by other authors, such as cost, lack of demand or knowledge, and gender bias (Fernandez, 1990; Friedman & Galinsky, 1992; Galinsky & Stein, 1990; Starrels, 1992). Equity perceptions have also been raised as a potential hindrance to the adoption and success of family friendly policies, and these perceptions are the focus of this chapter. How fair is it that some employees have access to special, nonwork-related benefits, such as flextime and leave time, whereas others do not?

Worse still, the employees who can use these policies are not necessarily the highest performers, but those who need the organization's assistance. Certainly the discretionary, need-based nature of these policies raises perceptions of unfairness if low performing employees are seen as benefitting. These perceptions might arouse resentfulness among co-workers. When employees perceive some allocations as unfair, a host of negative organizational consequences are typically found, such as poor performance, employee theft, absenteeism, and turnover (e.g., Cowherd & Levine, 1992; Greenberg, 1990b; Schwarzwald, Koslowsky, & Shalit, 1992). If unfairness perceptions exist toward family policies, and these are the consequences of those perceptions, it is easy to see why organizations may be wary of them.

Although fairness has been mentioned by those writing about family friendly policies, it has not been thoroughly explored by people familiar with the justice literature. Only two known studies have actually assessed the relation of justice perceptions with family friendly policies (Grover, 1991; Kossek & Nichol, 1992). To understand why all organizations are not in full support of these policies, and why the policies may not always be successful, family friendly policies can be considered within a justice framework. There are three ways to focus on justice and family friendly policies. First, social exchange as a mechanism by which individuals and organizations behave toward each other is used as a framework to combine fairness and family friendly policies. Second, justice theory is applied to how family friendly policies are allocated. Third, justice theory is discussed in terms of how policies are perceived as fair or unfair by co-workers. The scant research that has applied justice theory to policies is reviewed, and inferences are drawn about how justice perceptions might affect the success of these family-oriented programs.

Justice and Perceived Organizational Support

How is it that the mere presence of family friendly policies is associated with a range of organizational outcomes like attraction to the organization, turnover intentions, and commitment (Grover & Crooker, 1995; Honeycutt & Rosen, 1996; Sinclair et al., 1995)? One mechanism by which family-policy researchers might explain this relation is through the employee's perception of organizational support (POS; Grover & Crooker, 1995; Sinclair et al., 1995). However, in order to inspire POS in employees, the organizational acts must be perceived fairly. This section first explicates the POS mechanism for understanding the relation of family friendly policies to organizational outcomes. Then, organizational justice is discussed in terms of this mechanism.

Perception of organizational support (POS) occurs when employees believe that the organization cares about employees in a discretionary way (Eisenberger, Huntington, Hutchison, & Sowa, 1986). One way organizations might inspire such perceptions is by offering discretionary fringe benefits, such as paid parental leave. This policy is discretionary in the sense that it is not mandated by law and is given out to certain individuals as needed, not to everyone. It is believed that POS inspires a social exchange norm (Blau, 1964), so that employees feel they should reciprocate by acting in positive ways toward the organization (Eisenberger et al., 1986; Randall, Cropanzano, Bormann, & Birjulin, 1999). Research has found that employees with high POS are more likely to exhibit organizational citizenship behaviors and increased work effort (Eisenberger et al., 1986; Eisenberger, Fasolo, & Davis-LaMastro, 1990), and a lower intent to quit one's job (Sinclair et al., 1995). Family friendly benefits have been found to relate to POS (Sinclair et al., 1995). To reward the organization for its caring about their family needs, employees may respond with positive attitudes and behaviors toward the organization (Schiemann, 1987). This POS mechanism explains why just the presence of policies may have positive outcomes for the organization.

Some authors have suggested that perceptions of justice may change this social exchange relationship between the employee and organization (Masterson, Lewis-McClear, Goldman, & Taylor, 1997; Shore & Shore, 1995; Sinclair et al., 1995), in the sense that without justice, POS is greatly diminished. Fairness on the part of the employing firm contributes to the perception of support between the employee and the organization (Masterson et al., 1997; Organ, 1988). When an employee perceives an act by the organization as fair, the organization is perceived as positive and caring. As such, the act inspires the employee to act accordingly toward the organization. Of course, this relationship could be reversed causally, such that caring acts make the organization seem more fair; either way the point holds true. One study suggests that without perceptions of organizational fairness, POS would diminish, and the positive outcomes of organizational citizenship behaviors and decreased turnover intentions would not be realized (Masterson et al., 1997). Thus, fairness perceptions surrounding family friendly policies is a vital part of the policies' success at the organizational level. With this assumption in mind, the next sections discuss how fairness could affect whether the policies are allocated, and how others may view allocation decisions that are based on need.

Distributive Justice Rules: The Fairness of Resource Allocations

As a discretionary policy, allocation decisions about family friendly policies often fall on the shoulders of the front-line supervisor. It is up to this individual to decide if requests for the use of the formal policies are granted. Supervisory support for family needs is a major element for the success of family friendly policies (Friedman, 1987; Galinsky, Friedman, & Hernandez, 1991). However, supervisors may not view family friendly policies as fair. In the abstract, people have been found to be favorably predisposed toward family friendly policies (Friedman, 1987), although justice researchers would state that the actual allocation decisions require a specific comparison to a referent standard, or allocation rules (Cropanzano & Schminke, in press). Because supervisors receive the requests to enact the policies, and may have the power to decide if the request can be granted, it is important to understand the justice rules that the supervisor may consider beforehand.

There are three generally accepted justice rules that guide allocation decisions. With family friendly policies, the relevant decisions are twofold: Should an organization adopt the policies, and should a supervisor grant requests for these policies? The outcomes of these decisions are determined by the rules of equity, equality, and need. Research has demonstrated that each is acceptable to individuals, given specific environments. These environments can be characterized as supporting decision norms, in which there are general rules for all transactions of resources (Greenberg & Cohen, 1982). For example, environments that support allocating resources on the basis of merit are considered environments with equity norms. This section defines these three rules of distributive justice, discusses the situations in which they are often used, and relates them to family friendly policies.

Equity. Equity theory proposes that employees will perceive unfairness when they perceive that the ratio of their own job inputs to job outcomes is unequal to the ratio of a comparison other, or referent (Adams, 1965; Greenberg, 1990a). Allocation decisions are partially made by considering the individuals' input (hours worked, performance ratings) compared to the other individuals competing for the resource in question. This norm is most commonly found in environments of economic exchange and is expected to encourage effective performance on the task at hand (Deutsch, 1975; Leventhal, 1976). This is particularly true in Western culture, where individualism is rampant. Economic rewards are expected for contributions such as time and performance at work, and those who put more in should receive more than others who contribute less. Corporations are often set up with this reward structure.

Family friendly policies can provide both economic and noneconomic rewards. They can provide money, as with child-care credits, or they can provide time, autonomy, and special programs. However, these policies are not designed to reward meritous performance. They are available to those who need the resources, not those who have provided the organization more time, money, or effort. For example, if a supervisor receives a request from an employee for paid time when they will not be present to do the work, this rule would state that such an allocation would be unfair. Thus, family friendly policies may contradict equity rules, and in general, may be viewed as an unfair practice.

Supervisors may also be hesitant to encourage or allow use of policies that make their lives more complicated (Ronen, 1984) and thereby create more work for themselves. Giving workers more scheduling autonomy may not only complicate the production for which they are responsible but may strip the supervisor of some feelings of power. Supervisors may have a difficult time observing their subordinates for performance evaluations if the employees are choosing to work different hours than the supervisor. Telecommuting from home contains the same dilemma. Another way that family policies require more work from the supervisor is when an employee takes parental leave. This extended absence creates a void that the supervisor may be responsible for filling. This extra work for supervisors may be viewed as unfair: They have to increase their workload (more input) for the same pay (same output). Thus their ratio changes unfavorably, if they accommodate employees' family needs.

Equality. This rule encourages resources to be allocated equally across persons, regardless of input or performance (Deutsch, 1975). Conditions of social cooperation, where "getting along" with co-workers is important, would find this norm to be salient (Leventhal, 1976). Thus, allocation decisions would likely be motivated more by a desire to foster group harmony and cohesion than to encourage individuals' higher effort. This is not to say that performance will necessarily suffer under equality norms. The literature suggests that under certain conditions, group cohesion relates to group performance (Goodman, 1986). When these conditions are met, allocations based on the equality norm may be beneficial to team-based organizations.

According to the equality rule, family friendly policies can be considered fair when the policies are available to everyone. Benefits like sick time or health benefits are perceived as fair because they are available to all employees. However, sometimes policies are written specifically for certain groups, such as maternity leave and child-care benefits. Although anyone could apply for these policies at some point in their lives, they would only be granted to those who are new mothers or have small children, respectively. In theory, family friendly policies are equality based, but in practice, they only benefit those who have the pressing need. Even within the group that has the need, there is inequality. In practice is it difficult to provide the benefits so that everyone can use them. There are only so many spots available for children in care centers, and only so many people can take leave at one time. It is desirable to write family friendly policies in such a way that they are available to, and can be used by, all employees, but this is exceedingly difficult, as discussed later. Flex-time is one policy that has been adopted by organizations as an equal opportunity life-balancing policy; anyone can apply for flextime, not just those with families. But other family friendly policies may be seen as unfair if they contradict equality rules.

Need. The third type of the allocation rules, the need principle, is less well-researched than equity and equality rules (Kabanoff, 1991; Schwinger, 1986). Justice researchers do not know very much about what affects need-based allocation decisions. The need rule states that distributions should be made so that persons' needs are fulfilled, alleviating their difficulties (Leventhal, 1976). Allocations are made to the individual with the greatest need, even if that individual made a lesser contribution than another person (Greenberg & Cohen, 1982; Schwinger, 1986; Schwinger & Lamm, 1981). Thus, need-based decisions contradict equity rules by not considering input and output ratios, and they violate equality rules by treating individuals (with greater needs) differently than the rest of the group. On the whole, most corporations reward employees based on either the equity or equality rules (Kabanoff, 1991). Logically then, need-based allocations may be viewed negatively by those within the work setting.

Family friendly policies are typically need-based allocations. They are designed to respond to employees' needs, such as the need for the flexibility to leave work early to pick up a child from school, the need to stay at home with a new baby, or the need for affordable day care. Viewed through a justice perspective, the very nature of family friendly policies as a need-based allocation may create perceptions of unfairness. As a remedy for this potential ill-will, the justice literature suggests three situational factors that can promote the perceived fairness of need-based allocations. These include identifying with the beneficiary, perceiving the source of the need as unintentional, and a positive organizational culture toward family. Although the research on these determinants are scant, the few studies have been supportive (Greenberg & Cohen, 1982).

The first of these factors is that the person evaluating the request for a need-based resource identifies, or empathizes, with the potential beneficiary (Schwinger, 1986). Grover (1991) found that individuals identifying with persons who had the need for parental leave had a more positive attitude toward leave policies. The identity variables of gender, having children, likelihood of having children, and likelihood of taking parental leave were all significantly related to the perceived fairness of parental leave. Moreover, in Grover's study, fairness perceptions of parental leave mediated the relation between most of the identity variables and attitudes toward the beneficiaries. In other words, if one identifies with the needs of those who would benefit from the policies, then they view those policies as more fair. If they view the policies as more fair, they have more positive attitudes toward those who use the policies. Conversely, if employees cannot identify with those in need, or they view the policies as unfair, then those positive attitudes toward leave takers would diminish. Thus, identifying with those who might use family friendly policies would improve evaluations of those policies, and evaluations of the beneficiaries of the policies.

A second determinant is the intentionality, or controllability, of the source of need. When the cause of the need is beyond the potential recipient's control, allocators are more likely to provide resources than if the cause stemmed from the individual. A study testing this idea found that when resources were scarce, allocators were less likely to provide resources to individuals who were responsible for their state of need (Skitka & Tetlock, 1992). Family needs may be viewed as intentional because it would be assumed that the individual chose to have a child (Grover, 1991). Along these lines, the need for elder care may be viewed as more fair because such a need would not be viewed as intentional. Employees who sacrificed their careers to start a family may view others who intentionally choose to start a family and then still want to continue their careers as irresponsible. They may resent organizational programs that reward such behavior. On the other hand, some family-based requests may be perceived as less intentional, such a needing a day off to be with a sick child. More research is needed in this area as it relates to family policies.

Lastly, the organizational culture may affect whether need allocations are viewed as fair. Deutsch (1975) argued that need-based norms are salient when decision makers are concerned for the recipients' personal welfare and growth. Organizations are beginning to demonstrate a concern for societal needs, making family issues more acceptable within business policy. For example, The Conference Board, a forum for senior executives to discuss business policy, was formed "to enhance the contribution of business to society" (Peters at al., 1990, p. 2). If a goal of the organization is to behave in a socially responsible way, then decisions that show caring for family needs may be seen as legitimate or fair.

Although organizations with societal and personal goals are becoming more prevalent, such companies are still in the minority. Responding to personal needs is not widely considered to be within the domain of corporations. This creates a barrier to the adoption and usage of family friendly policies. A family friendly culture would encourage supporting individual needs, and encourage employees to identify with each other and appreciate each other's diverse issues. Norm-based decisions encourage interpersonal liking and social exchange (Deutsch, 1975; Schwinger, 1990). Studies acknowledge the importance of the organizational culture in supporting need-based policies. One needs assessment study found that culture was the most important job condition, predictive of a range of child-care related individual and organizational outcomes (Galinsky & Stein, 1990). Thompson and colleagues (1997) found that the relationship between family demands and use of family friendly benefits was moderated by a supportive organizational culture: If the workplace culture is not family friendly then the offered benefits may not be used by employees who need them. Therefore, in order for family friendly policies to thrive, the organization must foster a culture that will support these need-based allocations.

Summary. Family friendly benefits are need-based policies trying to survive in the equity-based world of corporations. Although some businesses may make decisions based on combinations of justice norms, typically these norms are equity and equality, not need (Kabanoff, 1991). Family friendly policies are designed to respond to family needs that some, and not other, employees have. By definition, they violate equity rules, which are considered fair rules by most decision makers in corporations. In addition, family friendly policies may violate equality rules in that not everyone is eligible for the benefits offered, or not all may have the opportunity to receive the benefits. These multiple violations of fairness rules for allocations are why family friendly policies may be perceived as unfair. This perception may bar their acceptance or limit their usage in many corporations. However, need-based allocations may be perceived by employees as a fair distribution of resources if they can relate to the need (identity), if the source of the need is perceived as beyond the individual's control (intention), or if the organization supports a need-based allocation norm within its culture.

Perceived Fairness of the Allocation Decision: Referents and Need Allocations

To determine if a decision is fair or not, persons look to referents, or to comparisons of others. These different referent sources contribute to employees' satisfaction with allocations beyond the allocation itself (Sweeney, McFarlin, & Inderrieden, 1990). In other words, receiving a benefit is more satisfying when it is fair. Conversely, not receiving a benefit is not pleasant but may be viewed as fair depending on the referent standard. For example, getting a promotion when you know someone else is more deserving is not as satisfying as when you are certain you deserve the promotion. Not getting a promotion may still be seen as fair, provided that those who have similar levels of performance to yourself do not receive a promotion either. In both cases, the individual compares his or her own input and outcome ratio with that of referent others. The referent standard provides the individual with information to judge whether the allocation decision was fair. In different situations, individuals compare themselves to different referent standards. With equity rules, persons look at others' inputs and outcomes and make sure that their own ratio is similar. Under equality rules, persons look to similar others to make sure they are getting the same allocations.

However, very little research has been done on the perceived fairness of need allocations, although quite a bit has explored equity and equality allocations (Kabanoff, 1991). Thus, no one really knows precisely how persons determine if a specific need allocation is fair. As mentioned earlier, several authors have proposed that fairness issues surround family benefits, without explaining what factors might affect the perceived fairness of these benefits. This chapter has already demonstrated why decision makers might view need-based allocations as unfair, given the equity-based nature of most organizations. It is also important to understand by what referent standards co-workers judge the fairness of need-based allocations.

This chapter proposes that need-based allocations can be judged by three types of referent standards. In each case, one individual perceives the policy to be unfair when compared to a certain referent standard. The three referent groups discussed here are employees with different needs, those with the same needs but limited access to the resource, and those with the same needs but different perceived access to the resource. If a comparison to these standards reveals a discrepancy, it is more likely that unfairness perceptions will exist. In the following section, these three referent standards are discussed in terms of family friendly policies as the need-based resource.

Employees With Different Needs. Employees who do not need family benefits might perceive those benefits as more unfair than those with the need. For example, a childless employee who has to pick up the slack may resent that an employee with children can take time off with the company's blessing. The quotes at the beginning of this section demonstrate the sentiment of this social comparison. This type of referent standard is probably the most mentioned potential source of inequity perceptions but may actually be less of an issue than is believed. Surveys have found that, regardless of their own needs, employees evaluate family friendly policies positively in general (DeMarr, 1997; Friedman, 1987). Research has not convincingly demonstrated that employees are resentful of those who have family needs and request family benefits. Although this may be good news, some resentment from nonbeneficiaries is still likely to occur, particularly when allocations based on family needs have some effect on nonbeneficiaries (i.e., must do extra work, do not receive their own resource request). As stated earlier, those who do not identify with the employees who need family benefits may have a harder time viewing the need-based allocations as fair (Grover, 1991).

Who does not identify with those who have family needs? Employees who have never had, and never plan to have, dependents may fall in this category (Grover, 1991). Employees who choose not to have children, who cannot have children, or who have very satisfactory child-care situation, such as an at-home spouse or grandparent, may not easily empathize with those who need help from family policies. Because those without family-policy needs have arranged their situation so they may focus on work, they may wonder why other employees are rewarded for poor planning. Another possibility is that employees resent that others will receive benefits that they themselves never had the option of using in the past. Perhaps a female executive had to make an agonizing decision not to have children in order to reach her status in the company, and if the organization offers family benefits later she may feel cheated. Those who view the policy as unfair may view family friendly policy beneficiaries as trying to get a free ride, which may affect how they interact with their co-worker. Thus, the beneficiary of the policy may find himself or herself coping with negative attitudes from co-workers as well as juggling family and work.

Same Needs, Different Availability. One set of authors mentioned how difficult it is for organizations to offer policies equally across all employees (Nelson & Couch, 1990). In this category, the referent has family needs just like the one doing the comparing. However, something is keeping the two individuals from receiving equal allocations, which then is perceived as unfair. The most discussed referent groups are women and men: Family policies are often assumed to be women's benefits, and in fact some parental-leave policies are specifically available only to women. However, men are becoming more involved in family re-sponsibilities (Schor, 1991). In fact, one study did not find significant differences between men and women's participation in family friendly benefits (Thompson et al., 1997), indicating a similar level of need. Another study found significant gen-der differences in parental leave availability (Marshall & Barnett, 1994), with women more likely to receive paid parental-leave benefits. Such differences be-tween groups can create unfairness perceptions.

There are two other barriers to offering family policies equally across em-ployees: the job one has and the resources available. The job one has may hinder someone from using family programs because they do not make enough money to pay the fees for the child-care center or to take an unpaid leave of absence (Fer-ber & O'Farrell, 1991). In fact, many jobs, such as the service industries, where women are the majority of employees (Hochschild, 1983), may not pay enough for the women to take advantage of these kinds of policies. In addition, some jobs do not lend themselves well to having flexible hours. Christensen and Staines (1990) remarked that assembly line manufacturing, or any type of team-based production, make flextime awkward for supervisors. Thus, there are barriers to using policies for those who may very well need them the most (Lechner & Cree-don, 1995).

Another case of same needs, different availability, is when the policy itself poses a barrier to the applicant. More specifically, child-care centers often have limits on the number of children they will accept, in order to maintain quality standards. Those on the long waiting lists may have negative attitudes toward the policy and the organization. In fact, Kossek and Nichols (1992) found that those who had the need (parents) but the policy was unavailable to them (full child-care center), rated the child-care policy as less fair than those who were using the cen-ter. The authors called this a *frustration effect*, in which the employees react neg-atively to a policy when it cannot help all persons in need. Thus, those who wait to receive the allocation compare their situation to those who have similar needs and are receiving the desired outcome. The end result is that those who cannot participate in a program, but have the need, are likely to have negative attitudes toward the organization (Ronen, 1984), especially when engaging in social com-parison.

Same Needs, Different Perceived Availability. Unfairness perceptions may exist because family friendly policies are perceived as only available to cer-tain people, when in fact they are available to everyone. They may be formally of-fered to everyone but perceived as unavailable due to the consequences one might experience for using the policies. These perceptions are proposed to stem from gender biases and work norms. These two factors are closely intertwined with the organizational culture; how do the decision makers of the organization view male and female roles, and how does the organization reward employees? If these com-ponents of organizational culture do not coexist with the tenants of family friendly policies, employees will not feel that the policies are, in actuality, available for their use.

With dual-career households, both spouses have to help out with family and household demands. The need for family policies certainly exists for both the spouses. Traditional views about women, however, still insist that home responsibilities fall on the woman's shoulders (Pleck, 1985; Starrels, 1990). Such gender bias may affect how people view both women and men who take advantage of family friendly policies. Parker and Allen (1999) found that women rated family policies as more fair than men did, suggesting that men are less likely to identify with this need, or to see it as appropriate. Grover's (1991) study found that holding conservative attitudes about women (or believing that men and women are not equal) was negatively related to perceptions of fairness about family policies, and to attitudes toward male and female beneficiaries of parental leave policies. Coworkers or supervisors who hold this traditional view may hinder employees' use of family policies, particularly male employees. Parental leave or flextime may not be seen as a viable option to men due to bias that men should not be responsible for the household responsibilities, and thus such requests risk denial and potential ridicule (Haas, 1987). Thus, men may perceive that the family friendly policies are special benefits that they are excluded from receiving.

Research in Sweden provides support for the effect of these gender biases (Moen, 1989). Sweden offers liberal family friendly policies, but men rarely take advantage of them. Men only took 14% of their total available days of parental leave in 1990 (Haas, 1992). But, those who had female co-workers (who would be more likely to identify with the need for this allocation) were more likely to take parental leave (Haas, 1992). Research by Pleck (1989) in the United States supports this finding: An unsympathetic attitude from supervisors may keep men from using family leaves.

Gender bias then may hinder men from applying for family benefits. This may leave them feeling that policies are unfairly distributed; women have access to benefits that men need but do not feel are available to them. The difficulty for changing this problem is that the unfairness is not due to the formal policy but the informal norms of the organization. Gender bias embedded in the work culture would need to be altered in order to diminish this perception of unfairness. If men perceive that family friendly policies are not available to them, these policies cannot have the individual and organizational benefits they were designed to elicit.

There is a second way that employees may perceived that family benefits are unavailable to them. Suppose an organization adopts the need-based policies of parental leave and flextime policies. The employee's expectation is that the organization will help them in time of need. However, the organization may reward certain behaviors which are incompatible with the use of family friendly policies. Organizations reward employees' commitment, which is judged by their presence (Perlow, 1995; Starrels, 1992). The use of integrative policies result in less time at work, or more specifically, less time being seen at work. Even if the employee is just as productive over time as before, using policies that take the employee out of the physical workspace may result in loss of promotions and raises: The employee does not seem as committed to the organization as someone who does not use these policies. Thus, in order to use family benefits, the employee must give up other organizational rewards. The presence of a needed policy that one cannot use without being punished may lead to another type of frustration effect. Formally, the policy exists for them, but they may become frustrated when they realize that they will be penalized if they actually make use of the policies. A quote from an engineer in a Fortune 100 company demonstrated this issue clearly:

> You really cannot leave for a few years and come back and expect to get to high levels. You have to be recommended for a manager's job. And so people look back at your record and see if you were committed, if you were willing to put the time in. And if not, well you don't go anywhere.—Engineer in Fortune 100 company (Fernandez, 1990, p. 185)

The unfairness of this situation may be perceived by men and women. The organizational loss of rewards is what may happen with the "mommy track." Many women believe the mommy track is an unequal career path for women who chose to take advantage of parental leave and flextime policies (Kessler-Harris, 1987). Women who want to advance in their careers may be surprised to find that using an organizational policy bars them from attaining their goals. Men may also fear using family friendly leave policies for fear of its impact on their careers (Haas, 1992; Moen, 1992). For men, this fear may be founded both in gender bias and work-ethic norms. For both women and men, perceiving that they must choose between the advancement of their careers and responding to their family's needs may make the formal policy seem unfair.

Providing a family friendly culture, in which family needs are valued and supported, may help with this source of injustice as well. One study found that both men and women were significantly more likely to apply for family benefits in a family friendly culture than the men or women in a nonfamily-supportive culture (Thompson et al., 1997). This would suggest that if the culture valued families and supported individual needs, then the policies would be perceived as available to all. If policies truly are equally available, and there is no culture of punishment for using them, policies have a better chance of being used and having the outcomes they were designed to have.

Family Friendly Policies and Justice: Conclusions

If perceptions of policies are not fair, it might be predicted that the positive outcomes of family friendly policies would be diminished, if not obliterated. At the organizational level, it is assumed that the presence and use of family friendly policies leads to perceived organizational support, attraction and retention, and

OCB (i.e., Sinclair et al., 1995). However, without fair perceptions of the organization, this may not occur, and thus neither do the positive outcomes (Masterson et al., 1997). Supervisors may feel need-based allocations are not fair when using the equity and equality rules as the standard. This may result in supervisors not allocating discretionary benefits to those who request them (Skitka & Tetlock, 1992; Ronen, 1984). If co-workers perceive that these need-based allocations are unfair, as compared to the referent standards discussed previously, they may not themselves request these policies. In addition, they may feel negatively toward those who do use the family friendly policies. Group cohesion may be negatively affected and morale may decrease (Cropanzano & Schminke, in press). Thus, the positive outcomes of family friendly policies may not only be erased, but replaced with new problems.

IMPLEMENTING FAIR FAMILY FRIENDLY POLICIES: RECOMMENDATIONS

What have we done? We have invested considerable time in management and supervisory training. . . . We believe the corporate culture has to change. . . . We encourage all managers to work on the tough diversity issues, including those of individual family problems.—Derek F. Harvey, Manager, Planning & Administration of Mobil Corporation (Peters et al., 1990, p. 39)

Given the potential hassles of dealing with the fairness issue of family friendly policies, some have asked whether these programs are worth the trouble (Kossek & Nichol, 1992). It certainly seems that inequity perceptions are likely when one uses need-based allocations, and inequity perceptions have been related to many negative consequences, as discussed previously. Potentially, those perceptions could eliminate the positive effects the policies were designed to produce. This issue is then a weighty one for organizations to consider before adopting these programs. The justice literature provides the means to circumvent these problems with family friendly policies. Although little research has assessed fringe benefits and justice (Folger & Greenberg, 1985), enough exists on both topics that inferences and recommendations can be made.

Because the outcomes will, by definition, be seen as inequitable, it is very important that the process be seen as fair. Research has demonstrated that if a process is fair, even if the outcome was unfavorable, the participants still tend to be positive about the organization (Van den Bos, Vermunt, & Wilke, 1997). If the process of adopting the policies is fair, employees will perceive that the organization cares about their opinions and is fair to employees in general. Thus, providing procedures that will be perceived as fair by all employees is vital for the acceptance of family friendly policies. This section contains recommendations based on the justice literature for organizations who wish to improve the perceptions of family policies within the workplace.

Do a Need Analysis and Get Participation

Although providing family friendly policies may attract people to an organization, if a need for these policies does not exist among employees the program is not going to be very successful (Lechner & Creedon, 1995). Beyond information gathering, the process of a need analysis provides employees an opportunity to voice their opinions, support, and concern about family friendly policies. In the interest of this process being perceived as fair, it is very important to get input from everyone, not just the higher status decision makers (Cobb, Wooten, & Folger, 1995).

Company-wide surveys is the most common way of requesting a large set of responses. Forming a task force, made up of employees who represent a large cross-section of hierarchical levels, departments, and demographic groups, can also be a good way to give individuals a chance to influence the process of adopting programs (Lechner & Creedon, 1995). Voicing opinions and being involved in the process have been found to be important in fairness perceptions of procedures that already exist (Thibaut & Walker, 1975), and Cobb et al. (1995) suggested it is also important to assure workers that they helped contribute to the ground rules of a new policy.

Change the Culture

Once a need is determined to exist, the organization should determine if the organization's values will allow the policies to be successful. As discussed earlier, maintaining a strong equity-based allocation norm would make need-based requests difficult to perceive fairly. In order for need-based requests to be viewed more positively, some suggest the culture of the organization must change to encourage need-based rules to be followed in allocation decisions. The need principle is a norm that guides allocation in relationships where the parties identify with each other and are highly interdependent (Greenberg & Cohen, 1982). Today's team environment in the workplace makes this context more probable. Getting along with the group is an important part of team functioning. In environments that encourage positive relationships and interdependence among co-workers, a need-based allocation such as paid parental leave might be perceived more fairly than in a strictly task-oriented workplace. However, that interdependence also makes integrative policies more difficult—a member of a team who wants to take parental leave, or to only work certain hours, may make team functioning very difficult. Policies about such situations would need to be spelled out when adopted.

Changing the culture of the organization is a messy business. Norms must be changed, values disseminated, old ways of thinking replaced. Communicating the new values of the organization is extremely important. This can be accomplished through memos, official documents, and especially group meetings led by high-status and high-profile members of the organization. Support for the changes needs to be demonstrated by decision makers, in order for the changes to take hold (Cobb et al., 1995; Thompson et al., 1999). Additionally, the reward structures need to be changed. Rewarding supervisors for helping employees balance work and family would send a strong message to employees. In a need-based culture, productivity as a desired outcome would be balanced with the outcome of personal and interpersonal harmony. A need-based culture, in which individual needs are respected and responded to beyond the person's inputs, would provide fertile soil for the family friendly policies to take hold (DeMarr, 1997) and be viewed fairly.

Communicate the Process and Changes

In order for the adoption of family friendly policies to be successful, employees need be informed about the policies and changes that will occur. Communicating how these new policies might meet the mission or values of the organization would lend credence to their adoption (Cobb et al., 1995). If the corporation is changing its culture, the new vision of the organization must be "bought" by those in power positions, and "sold" to the employees by communicating the new mission statement, organizational goals, and so forth. In addition, in order for a new policy to be successful, employees need to be aware of what is now offered. One study found that 6.9% of employees did not know if their corporation offered a child-care center, 16.3% were unaware if time off for dependent care was offered, and 20% were not sure if resource and referral services existed (Thompson et al., 1997). Other studies support the idea that employees are often unaware of their fringe benefits (Dreher et al., 1988; Sinclair et al., 1995). It is very important, as stated previously, that all employees are informed of the services available.

Organizations also need to inform employees about how things will change once the policy is adopted. When a co-worker goes on leave, who will do that person's work? This could be a large concern for nonbeneficiaries. If an employee is on parental leave, do they get their same job back when they return? How will decisions about scarce resources, such as spaces in the child-care center, be handled and by whom? Will people who utilize these policies be passed over for promotions? Concerns such as these need to be alleviated by two-way, corporation-wide discussions of the new policy. For researchers, these are areas that need to be assessed.

Provide Justification

For those who are dubious about the worth of family friendly policies, providing justification for the organizational decision is essential (Bies, 1987; Greenberg, 1990b). Leaders should provide causal, ideological, and referential accounts to employees (Cobb et al., 1995). Causal accounts would explain why family friendly policies are necessary to be competitive, perhaps in terms of the research on work–family conflict and the desirable outcomes the policies could provide. Lechner and Creedon (1995) recommended communicating to all employees that these programs are the organization's response to the issues of work stress and productivity. Ideological accounts provide the vision to employees for how adopting family friendly policies plays a role in the values and goals of the organization. These accounts help spread the norms the organization supports, such as responding to individuals' family needs. Lastly, leaders may want to provide referential accounts to employees. These provide a referent, or point of comparison, to which the employees can compare the new situation. For instance, the corporation may communicate to employees that Company X, a competitor, has installed flextime and generous family-leave policies, and now some prospective employees are choosing Company X over this company. Or the leader could discuss where the company might end up if this change was not implemented (Cobb et al., 1995).

Consider the Type of Policy to Adopt

If the need exists, the organization should determine which types of policies are more acceptable and desirable: Would people be more willing to help fund a child-care center to help co-workers be at work more, or do employees want the organization to respond to the need for family time by offering telecommuting as an option? If a survey shows that employees need child care but are ambivalent about flextime, that information should actually influence the policies chosen. Justice theory also would recommend that the type of policies adopted be ones available to everyone (whereas changing norms would make them perceived available). This is difficult to do, as discussed earlier, but necessary to avoid the inequity perceptions. On-site child-care that charges an extra fee may not be available to everyone, neither will flexible hours for those doing line work.

To respond to this inequality, one recommendation is to adopt cafeteria-style benefit packages, or flexible benefit plans (Friedman, 1985; Grover, 1991). Core benefits are offered to everyone, such as health and life insurance and vacation time. Optional benefits such as dependent care, mutual funds, or tuition may be purchased with flexible credits (Friedman, 1985). Every employee should have access to all these options, although the number of flexible credits available to each employee may depend on seniority, age, and/or salary. These provide employees with a choice, which is perceived as more fair than just providing the opportunity for voicing opinions (Folger & Greenberg, 1985). Not only do employees feel like they have a choice, but those who do not have family needs have other fringe benefit options. The need-based requests can be met, but the plan is perceived as providing equally for each individual. Although this is a nice conclusion that has been drawn by many, it is not a panacea. Employees may have to choose between needed health benefits and needed dependent care (Friedman, 1985). Cafeteria plans also require understanding about policies that may be complicated for unskilled labor (Lechner & Creedon, 1995). And as discussed earlier, segmentative programs like child care alone may not result in the positive outcomes expected. Telecommuting and flexible hours are other family friendly policies that would not appear on a benefits option list but that may serve the employee's needs. In cases like these, the supervisor who arranges the policy with the employee becomes more important.

Provide Supervisor Training

Supervisors can make or break the most well-developed organizational programs (Galinsky et al., 1991). As discussed earlier, if the supervisor perceives the policies as unfair, he or she may not grant requests or may punish those who use the policies when other allocation decisions arise. They may resent the inconvenience and lack of authority that flexible scheduling entails. If the supervisor has personal biases about male and female roles at work and at home, male subordinates may not feel comfortable requesting the family policies. From the subordinate's point of view, it is very important that supervisors are consistent with the organization's goals. If a formal policy is available but a supervisor never grants a request for it, frustration may ensue. Because employees look to their leaders to represent the organization (Eisenberger et al., 1986), employees may judge the fairness of the new policies based on how their supervisor behaves toward them. This treatment includes both the decisions the supervisors make (distributive justice) and how they treat employees (interactional justice). Thus it is vital that organizations adopting family policies make sure that the supervisors who will be distributing the policies support these policies. Supervisor training can help supervisors identify with those who request the policies, communicate justification for need-based distribution, and interact in a supportive way with those who need the policies. These types of behaviors, as discussed throughout this chapter, are related to the perceived fairness of distribution decisions.

There are several steps in which an organization needs to engage to train employees to be supportive of family policies. Policy statements from the top levels of the organization must make it clear that a family-supportive approach is expected from supervisors (Galinsky & Stein, 1990; Lechner & Creedon, 1995). The organization can demonstrate the importance of this approach by investing time and money in training seminars for supervisors. Organizations can influence the decisions that supervisors make by educating them about the nature of work–family conflict, its detrimental outcomes, on the policies available to counteract these problems, and on the values of the organization. This information also provides justification for need-based policies to supervisors who may be hesitant to accept the policies.

Training should also demonstrate how to treat employees with respectful interactional styles. Interpersonal sensitivity is vital here (Cropanzano & Greenberg, 1997); employees need to be able to communicate with beneficiaries and nonbeneficiaries in a respectful and caring manner. Even if the supervisor cannot provide the official organizational policy to an employee, he or she should listen to the employee's needs and respect the employee's situation. In fact, supportive supervisor behaviors themselves have been found to negatively relate to work–family conflict and detrimental outcomes (Thomas & Ganster, 1995). Lastly, in order to encourage the transfer of this supervisor training to the workplace, organizations need to reward supervisors who act in such a manner. This may be done by formal recognition, promotions, prime assignments, vacation time, or other valued resources.

CONCLUSIONS AND FUTURE DIRECTIONS

Family friendly policies are not a fad. They attempt to answer a real societal need. Likewise, the concern about fairness perceptions is also very real, and this chapter provides a means to understand this concern and address the issue. The changing nature of the economic market means that women at work is an economic necessity (Auerbach, 1990) for both the national economy as well as the family finances. In families with children, both spouses usually need to work to maintain a desirable level of income. These families need policies that will provide care for the children, both in ways that will allow the parents to work without worry (segmentative policies) and to be available for their children (integrative policies). Thus, it is not a question of whether organizations should provide these policies, but how. Justice literature provides some clues to why organizations have been hesitant to openly embrace family friendly policies and also what can make the policies more successful. For researchers, the lack of a theoretical framework for family friendly research is a limitation (Dalton & Mesch, 1990). This chapter provides such a framework. Future research incorporating justice theory can help organizations adopt policies that meet the needs of their employees in the most fair and effective way possible.

ACKNOWLEDGMENT

I would like to thank Dr. Cynthia Thompson for her insightful comments on an earlier version of this chapter.

REFERENCES

Adams, J. S. (1965). Inequity in social exchange. In L. Berkowitz (Ed.), *Advances in experimental social psychology* (Vol. 2, pp. 267–299). New York: Academic Press.

Adams, G. A., King, L. A., & King, D. W. (1996). Relationships of job and family involvement, family social support, and work–family conflict with job and life satisfaction. *Journal of Applied Psychology, 81*(4), 411–420.

Aldous, J. (1990). Specification and speculation concerning the politics of workplace family policies. *Journal of Family Issues, 11*(4), 355–367.

Auerbach, J. D. (1990). Employer-supported child care as a women-responsive policy. *Journal of Family Issues, 11*, 384–400.

Barnett, R. C., & Baruch, G. K. (1985). Women's involvement in multiple roles and psychological distress. *Journal of Personality and Social Psychology, 49*, 135–145.

Barnett, R. C., & Marshall, N. L. (1992). Worker and mother roles, spillover effects, and psychological distress. *Women and Health, 18*, 9–40.

Bies, R. J. (1987). The predicament of injustice: The management of moral outrage. In L. L. Cummings & B. M. Staw (Eds.), *Research in organizational behavior* (Vol. 9, pp. 289–319). Greenwich, CT: JAI.

Blau, P. M. (1964). *Exchange and power in social life.* New York: Wiley.

Bohen, H. H., & Visveros-Long, A. (1981). *Balancing jobs and family life: Do flexible work schedules help?* Philadelphia, PA: Temple University Press.

Bureau of National Affairs, Inc. (1988). 33 Ways to ease work/family tensions—An employers checklist. *The National Report on Work & Family.* Buraff.

Burke, R. J. (1989). Some antecedents and consequences of work–family conflict. In E. B. Goldsmith (Ed.), *Work and family: Theory, research and applications* (pp. 287–302). Newbury Park, CA: Sage.

Carter, B., & Peters, J. K. (1996, November/December). Remaking marriage & family. *Ms., 7*(3), 57–65.

Christiansen, K., & Staines, G. L. (1990). Flextime: A viable solution to work/family conflict? *Journal of Family Issues, 11*(4), 455–476.

Coakley, L., & Karren, R. (1996). *An analysis of work schedule autonomy and work/family conflict.* Presented at the 11th Annual Conference of the Society for Industrial and Organizational Psychology at San Diego, CA.

Cobb, A. T., Wooten, W. C., & Folger, R. (1995) Justice in the making: Toward understanding the theory and practice of justice in organizational change and development. In W. A. Pasmore & R. W. Woodman (Eds.), *Research in Organizational Change and Development* (243–295). Greenwich, CT: JAI.

Cowherd, D. M., & Levine, D. I. (1992). Product quality and pay equity between lower-level employees and top management: An investigation of distributive justice theory. *Administrative Science Quarterly, 37*, 302–320.

Cropanzano, R., & Greenberg, J. (1997). Progress in organizational justice: Tunneling through the maze. In C. L. Cooper & I. T. Robertson (Eds.), *International Review of Industrial and Organizational Psychology, 12* (pp. 317–372). New York: Wiley.

Cropanzano, R., & Schminke, M. (in press). Using social justice to build effective workgroups. In M. Turner (Ed.), *Groups at Work: Advances in Theory and Research.* Mahwah, NJ: Lawrence Erlbaum Associates.

Dailey, R. C., & Kirk, D. J. (1992). Distributive and procedural justice as antecedents of job dissatisfaction and intent to turnover. *Human Relations, 45*, 305–317.

Dalton, D. R., & Mesch, D. J. (1990). The impact of flexible scheduling on employee attendance and turnover. *Administrative Science Quarterly, 35*(2), 370–387.

DeMarr, B. J. (1997, August). *The role of stress in employee preferences for family-friendly benefits: Testing an integrated model.* Presented at the annual meeting of the Academy of Management, Boston, MA.

Deutsch, M. (1975). Equity, equality, and need: What determines which value will be used as the basis for distributive justice? *Journal of Social Issues, 31*, 137–150.

Dreher, G. F., Ash, R. A., & Bretz, R. D. (1988). Benefit coverage and employee cost: Critical factors in explaining compensation satisfaction. *Personnel Psychology, 41*, 237–254.

Dunham, R. B., Pierce, J. L., & Castaneda, M. B. (1987). Alternative work schedules: Two field quasi-experiments. *Personnel Psychology, 40*, 215–242.

Eisenberger, R, Fasolo, P., & Davis-LaMastro, V. (1990). Perceived organizational support and employee diligence, commitment, and innovation. *Journal of Applied Psychology, 75,* 51–59.

Eisenberger, R., Huntington, R., Hutchison, S., & Sowa, D. (1986). Perceived organizational support, *Journal of Applied Psychology, 71,* 500–507.

Ferber, M. A., & O'Farrell, B. (Eds.). (1991). *Work and family: Policies for a changing work force.* Washington, DC: National Academy Press.

Fernandez, J. P. (1990). *The politics and reality of family care in corporate America.* Lexington, MA: Lexington.

Folger, R., & Greenberg, J. (1985). Procedural justice: An interpretive analysis of personnel systems (pp. 141–183). In K. M. Rowland & G. R. Ferris (Eds.), *Research in personnel and human resources.* Greenwich, CT: JAI.

Friedman, D. E. (1985). Corporate financial assistance for child care. *Research Bulletin Conference Board* (pp. 10–34). New York: The Conference Board.

Friedman, D. E. (1987). Work vs. family: War of the worlds. *Personnel Administrator, 32*(8), 36–39.

Friedman, D. E., & Galinsky, E. Work and family issues: A legitimate business concern. In S. Zedeck (Ed.), *Work, Families, and Organizations* (pp. 168–207). San Francisco: Jossey-Bass.

Frone, M. R., Russell, M., & Cooper, M. L. (1992). Antecedents and outcomes of work–family conflict: Testing a model of the work–family interface. *Journal of Applied Psychology, 77*(1), 65–78.

Galinsky, E. (1990). Strategies for integrating the family needs of workers in to human resource planning. In D. B. Fishman & C. Cherniss (Eds.), *The human side of corporate competitiveness* (pp. 152–170). Newbury Park, CA: Sage.

Galinsky, E., Friedman, D. E., & Hernandez, C. A. (1991). *The corporate reference guide to work–family programs.* New York: Families and Work Institute.

Galinsky, E., & Stein, P. J. (1990). The impact of human resource policies on employees: Balancing work/family life. *Journal of Family Issues, 11*(4), 368–383.

Goff, S. J., Mount, K., & Jamison, R. L. (1990). Employer supported child care, work/family conflict, and absenteeism: A field study. *Personnel Psychology, 43,* 793–809.

Goodman, P. S. (1986). Impact of task and technology on group performance. In P. S. Goodman and Associates (Eds.), *Designing effective work groups* (pp. 120–167). San Francisco: Jossey-Bass.

Grandey, A., & Cropanzano, R. (1999). The conservation of resources model applied to work–family conflict and strain. *Journal of Vocational Behavior, 54,* 350–370.

Greenberg, J. (1990a). Looking fair versus being fair: Managing impressions of organizational justice. In Staw B. M. & Cummings, L. L. (Eds.), *Research in organizational behavior* (pp. 111–157). Greenwich, CT: JAI.

Greenberg, J. (1990b). Employee theft as a reaction to underpayment inequity: The hidden cost of pay cuts. *Journal of Applied Psychology, 75,* 561–568.

Greenberg, J., & Cohen, R. L. (1982). Why justice? Normative and instrumental interpretations. In J. Greenberg & R. L. Cohen (Eds.), *Equity and justice in social behavior,* (pp. 437–469). New York: Academic.

Grover, S. L. (1991). Predicting the perceived fairness of parental leave policies. *Journal of Applied Psychology, 76*(2), 247–255.

Grover, S. L., & Crooker, K. J. (1995). Who appreciates family-responsive human resource policies: The impact of family-friendly policies on the organizational attachment of parents and non-parents. *Personnel Psychology, 48,* 271–288.

Haas, L. (1987). Fathers' participation in parental leave. *Social change in Sweden, 37.* New York: Swedish Information Service.

Haas, L. (1992). Nurturing fathers, working mothers—Changing gender roles in Sweden. In J. Hood (Ed.), *Men, work and parenting.* Newbury Park, CA: Sage.

Hammonds, K. H. (1996). Balancing work and family: Big returns for companies willing to give family strategies a chance. *Business Week,* 74–80.

Hochschild, A. (1983). *The managed heart: Commercialization of human feeling.* Berkeley: University of California Press.

Honeycutt, T. L., & Rosen, B. (1997). Family friendly human resource policies, salary levels, and salient identity as predictors of organizational attraction. *Journal of Vocational Behavior, 50,* 271–290.

Kabanoff, B. (1991). Equity, equality, power, and conflict. *Academy of Management Review, 16*(2), 416–441.

Kessler-Harris, A. (1987). The debate over equality in the workplace: Recognizing differences. In N. Gerstel & H. E. Gross (Eds.), *Families and work* (pp. 520–539). Philadelphia, PA: Temple University Press.

Kim, J. S., & Campagna, A. F. (1981). Effects of flexitime on employee attendance and performance: A field experiment. *Academy of Management Journal, 24,* 729–741.

Kopelman, R. E., Greenhaus, J. H., & Connolly, T. F. (1983). A model of work, family, and interrole conflict: A construct validation study. *Organizational Behavior and Human Performance, 32,* 198–215.

Kossek, E. E., & Nichol, V. (1992). The effects of on-site child care on employee attitudes and performance. *Personnel Psychology, 45,* 485–509.

Kossek, E. E., & Ozeki, C. (1998). Work–family conflict, policies, and the job–life satisfaction relationship: A review and directions for organizational behavior–human resources research. *Journal of Applied Psychology, 83*(2), 139–149.

Lamm, H., & Schwinger, T. (1983). Need consideration in allocation situations: Is it just? *Journal of Social Psychology, 119,* 205–209.

Lechner, V. M., & Creedon, M. A. (1995). *Managing work and family life.* New York: Springer.

Lee, R. A. (1983). Flexitime and conjugal roles. *Journal of Occupational Behavior, 4,* 297–315.

Leib, J. (1997, July 24). Firms spend $1M on child, elderly care. *The Denver Post,* p. C1.

Lerner, M. J. (1977). The justice motive: Some hypotheses as to its origins and forms. *Journal of Personality, 45,* 1–52.

Leventhal, G. S. (1976). Fairness in social relationships (pp. 211–240). In J. W. Thibaut, J. T. Spence & R. C. Carson (Eds.), *Contemporary topics in social psychology.* Morristown, NJ. General Learning Press.

Marshall, N. L., & Barnett, R. C. (1994). Family-friendly workplaces, work–family interference, and worker health. In G. P. Keita & J. J. Hurrell (Eds.), *Job stress in a changing workforce* (pp. 253–264). Washington, DC: American Psychological Association.

Masterson, S. S., Lewis-McClear, K., Goldman, B. M., & Taylor, M. S. (1997, August). *Organizational justice and social exchange: An empirical study of the distinction between interactional and formal procedural justice.* Paper presented at annual meeting of Academy of Management, Boston.

Milkovich, G. T., & Gomez, L. R. (1976). Day care and selected employee work behaviors. *Academy of Management Journal, 19,* 111–115.

Mize, J., & Freeman, L. C. (1989). Employer-supported child care: Assessing the need and potential support. *Child & Youth Care Quarterly, 19,* 289–301.

Moen, P. (1989). *Working parents: Transformations in gender roles and public policies in Sweden.* Madison: University of Wisconsin Press.

National Commission on Working Women (1989). *Women, work and the future.* Washington, DC: Author.

Nelson, P. T., & Couch, S. (1990). The corporate perspective on family responsive policy. *Marriage & Family Review, 15*(3–4), 95–113.

Nollen, S. D., & Martin, V. H. (1978). *Alternative work schedules, part I: Flextime.* New York: AMACOM.

Organ, D. W. (1988). *Organizational citizenship behavior: The good soldier syndrome.* Lexington, MA: Lexington.

Organ, D. W., & Moorman, R. H. (1993). Fairness and organizational citizenship behavior: What are the connections? *Journal of Applied Psychology, 74,* 157–164.

Parker, L. & Allen, T. D. (1999, April). *Work/family feud: Variables influencing employees' fairness perceptions of work/family policies.* Paper presented at the 14th annual meeting of the Society of Industrial and Organizational Psychology, Atlanta, GA.

Patridge, B. D. (1973). Notes on the impact of flexitime in a large insurance company: II. Reactions of supervisors and managers. *Occupational Psychology, 47*, 241–242.

Perlow, L. A. (1995). Putting the work back into work/family [Special issue: Organizational Studies Conference: Best Papers.] *Group and Organization Management, 20*(2), 227–239.

Peters, J. L., Peters, B. H., & Caropreso, F. (Eds.). (1990). *Work and family policies: The new strategic plan.* New York: The Conference Board.

Perry, K. (1982). *Employers and child care: Establishing services through the workplace.* Washington, DC: U.S. Department of Labor, Women's Bureau.

Pierce, J. L., & Newstrom, J. W. (1983). The design of flexible work schedules and employee responses: Relationships and process. *Journal of Occupational Behavior, 4*, 247–262.

Pleck, J. H. (1985). *Working wives, working husbands.* Beverly Hills, CA: Sage.

Pleck, J. H. (1989). *Family supportive employer policies and men's participation.* Paper prepared for the Panel on Employer Policies and Working Families, Committee on Women's Employment and Related Social Issues, Commission on Behavioral and Social Sciences and Education. Washington, DC: National Research Council.

Randall, M., Cropanzano, R., Bormann, C., & Birjulin, A. (1999). Organizational politics and organizational support as predictors of work attitudes, job performance, and organizational citizenship behavior. *Journal of Organizational Behavior, 20*, 159–174.

Ronen, S. (1984). *Alternative work schedules: Selecting, implementing, and evaluating.* Homewood, IL: Dow Jones-Irwin.

Roskies, E., & Carrier, S. (1994). Marriage and children for professional women: Asset or liability? In G. P. Keita & J. J. Hurrell, Jr. (Eds.), *Job stress in a changing workforce* (pp. 269–282). Washington, DC: American Psychological Association.

Rothausen, T. (1994). Job satisfaction and the parent worker: The role of flexibility and rewards. *Journal of Vocational Behavior, 44*, 317–336.

Schiemann, W. A. (1987). The impact of corporate compensation and benefit policy on employee attitudes and behavior and corporate profitability. *Journal of Business and Psychology, 2*, 8–26.

Schor, J. B. (1991). *The overworked American: The unexpected decline of leisure.* New York: Basic.

Schwinger, T. (1986). The need principle of distributive justice. In Bierhoff, H. W., Cohen, R. L. & Greenberg, J. (Eds.), *Justice in social relations* (pp. 211–225). New York: Plenum.

Schwinger, T., & Lamm, H. (1981). Justice norms in allocation decisions: Need consideration as a function of resource adequacy for complete need satisfaction, recipients' contributions, and recipient's interpersonal attraction. *Social Behavior and Personality, 9*, 235–241.

Shinn, M., Wong, N. W., Simko, P. A., & Ortiz-Torres, B. (1989). Promoting the well-being of working parents: Coping, social support, and flexible job schedules. *American Journal of Community Psychology, 17*, 31–55.

Shore, L. M., & Shore, T. H. (1995). Perceived organizational support and organizational justice. In R. Cropanzano & K. M. Kacmar (Eds.), *Organizational politics, justice, and support: Managing the social climate of the workplace* (pp. 149–164). Westport, CT: Quorum.

Sinclair, R. R., Hannigan, M. A., & Tetrick, L. E. (1995). Benefit coverage and employee attitudes: A social exchange perspective. In L. E. Tetrick & J. Barling (Eds.), *Changing Employment Relations: Behavioral and Social Perspectives* (pp. 163–185). Washington, DC: American Psychological Association.

Skitka, L. J., & Tetlock, P. E. (1992). Allocating scarce resource: A contingency model of distributive justice. *Journal of Experimental Social Psychology, 28*, 491–522.

Starrels, M. E. (1992). The evolution of workplace family policy research. *Journal of Family Issues, 13*(4), 259–278.

Starrett, C. (1987, November/December). 20 Corporations that listen to women. *Ms.*, 45–52.

Solomon, C. (1994). Work/family's failing grade: Why today's initiatives aren't enough. *Personnel Journal*, 72–87.

Sweeney, P. D., McFarlin, D. B., & Inderrieden, E. J. (1990). Using relative deprivation theory to explain satisfaction with income and pay level: A multistudy examination. *Academy of Management Journal, 33*, 423–436.

Thibaut, J. W., & Walker, L. (1975). *Procedural justice: A psychological analysis.* Hillsdale, NJ: Lawrence Erlbaum Associates.

Thomas, L. T., & Ganster, D. C. (1995). Impact of family-supportive work variables on work–family conflict and strain: A control perspective. *Journal of Applied Psychology, 80*(1), 6–15.

Thompson, C., Beauvais, L., & Lyness, K. (1999). When work–family benefits are not enough: The influence of work–family culture on benefit utilization, organizational attachment, and work–family conflict. *Journal of Vocational Behavior, 54,* 392–415.

Thompson, C. A., Beauvais, L. L., & Carter, H. K. (1997, August). *Work–family programs: Only slow-trackers need apply? An investigation of the impact of work–family culture.* Presented at the annual meeting of the Academy of Management, Boston, MA.

Trost, C. (1987, November 30). Best employers for women and parents. *The Wall Street Journal,* p. 21.

Tyler, T. R. (1991). Using procedures to justify outcomes: Testing the viability of a procedural justice strategy for managing conflict and allocating resources in work organizations. *Basic and Applied Social Psychology, 12,* 259–279.

U.S. Bureau of the Census. (1993). *Statistical abstracts of the United States, 1992.* Washington, DC: Government Printing Office.

Van den Bos, K., Vermunt, R., & Wilke, H. (1997). Procedural and distributive justice: What is fair depends more on what comes first than what comes next. *Journal of Personality and Social Psychology, 72*(1), 95–104.

Wortman, C., Biernat, M., & Lang, E. (1991). Coping with role overload. In M. Frankenaeuser, U. Lunberg & M. Chesney (Eds.), *Women, work, & health: Stress and opportunities* (pp. 85–110). New York: Plenum.

Zedeck, S., & Mosier, K. L. (1990). Work in the family and employing organization. *American Psychologist, 45*(2), 240–251.

Zimmerman, S. L. (1995). *Understanding family policy* (2nd ed.). Thousand Oaks, CA: Sage.

Causes and Consequences of Applicant Perceptions of Unfairness

Stephen W. Gilliland
University of Arizona

Dirk D. Steiner
Université de Nice, Sophia Antipolis

> *We need to hire the best and brightest. The best and brightest are usually in high demand at other companies, so we have to make sure we treat our applicants well. That is part of our competitive advantage.*
>
> *The initial turnover rate is a major concern at [our company] due to the fact that employees receive extensive and expensive training. We want to do everything we can to make sure that each experience an employee has with our company is a positive one. This starts with the interview process because first impressions often extend through an employee's entire stay with the company.*
>
> *Our applicants are also potential customers. When we interview applicants we are not only in an assessment mode, but also in a selling mode. We strive to create a comfortable, hassle-free experience for our applicants.*

Human-resource managers from three large companies in computer software, healthcare, and manufacturing industries provided the introductory quotes. Each of these companies recognized the need for attending to applicants' perceptions of the selection process, but the reasons for this attention vary. Applicants' perceptions are considered important because they affect applicants' job acceptance decisions, perceptions of the organization and early turnover, and customer behavior and decisions.

Despite the obvious importance of applicant perceptions of selection processes to some human-resource managers, researchers have only recently turned attention toward the applicant side of the selection process. Many recent models have emerged that attempt to describe causes and consequences of applicants' perceptions of selection procedures (e.g., Arvey & Sackett, 1993; Herriott, 1989; Schmitt & Gilliland, 1992; Schuler, 1993). A number of excellent research studies have also been conducted (e.g., Macan, Avedon, Paese, & Smith, 1994; Smither, Reilly, Millsap, Pearlman, & Stoffey, 1993). One theme that emerges from these models and research is that perceptions of fairness and justice are central to applicants' perceptions of selection procedures. Based on organizational justice theories, Gilliland (1993) proposed a justice framework for studying applicant reactions to selection processes. The theoretical foundation of justice theories contributes to the accurate definition of constructs and the generation of specific hypotheses. Consequently, a number of recent studies have used the justice framework to study applicants' perceptions of selection process fairness (Gilliland, 1994; Ryan, Greguras, & Ployhart, 1996; Steiner & Gilliland, 1996).

When examining applicant fairness from a justice perspective, two important questions can be asked: What impacts applicants' perceptions of fairness?; and what are the consequences of this impact? Answering the first question requires examining research and theory that identify the determinants or causes of applicants' perceptions of fairness, including procedures and practices (e.g., type of selection procedure) that impact fairness perceptions, as well as the justice dimensions that underlie these perceptions. The second question addresses how applicants' attitudes, behavior, and decisions are affected by their experiences during the selection process. Are applicants who feel the selection process was unfair less likely to accept a job offer? Are they less committed to the organization if they do accept the offer? If they turn down the offer or if they are rejected, are they less likely to recommend the company to others or to purchase the company's products or services?

In this chapter, these issues surrounding the causes and consequences of applicants' perceptions of fairness are addressed. The literature is reviewed and gaps in our current understanding of these processes are identified. We offer suggestions for future research. However, rather than offering a comprehensive model of these issues, as was done by Gilliland (1993), or a comprehensive review of the literature, as was done by Cropanzano (1997), this chapter focuses around the following hypothesis: With regard to both the causes and consequences of applicants' fairness perceptions, unfavorable (negative) treatment is more critical than favorable (positive) treatment. By focusing on unfairness rather than fairness, we are not trying to suggest that only negative treatment is important. Indeed there are many ways in which selection procedures can enhance or promote perceptions of fairness. However, we are suggesting that the factors that lead to perceptions of unfairness are more important in determining applicants' reactions than factors that lead to perceptions of fairness.

A theoretical foundation for this hypothesis is provided by theories of impression formation and decision making. For example, interview (Schmitt, 1976) and performance appraisal research (Steiner & Rain, 1989) demonstrate that negative information is often more salient and weighs more heavily in evaluations than either neutral or positive information. In the decision-making literature, image theory suggests that decision alternatives are initially screened to evaluate the extent to which they violate the decision maker's standards (e.g., values, goals, plans). This initial screen relies exclusively on violations; positive features of the decision alternative or fit with the decision maker's standards does not weigh into the screening process. Initial research in the justice domain related to this hypothesis was presented by Van den Bos, Vermunt, and Wilke (1997). They found that when both procedural and distributive justice were unfavorable, reactions were extremely negative, but when both were positive, reactions were only slightly positive. Suggestions for future research on the asymmetry between positive and negative information are provided at various points throughout this chapter.

A second theme developed in this chapter is the extent to which environmental and individual factors moderate the causes and consequences of applicant fairness. For example, cultural norms can influence the extent to which different procedural justice determinants impact fairness perceptions (Steiner & Gilliland, 1996). Similarly, additional job offers or previous work experience may influence the extent to which fairness perceptions impact job acceptance decisions or organizational commitment. The first section of this chapter addresses the causes of perceived unfairness and conditions that may moderate these causes. The next section address consequences of applicant fairness perceptions and potential moderators of these relations. This chapter is concluded by outlining a number of "next steps" for research on applicant fairness.

CAUSES OF APPLICANT UNFAIRNESS

When talking to job applicants about their selection experiences, it is easy to gather incidents of poor treatment. Indeed, a number of researchers have used this method to identify determinants of fairness and job choice behavior (Bies & Moag, 1986; Gilliland, 1995; Rynes, Bretz, & Gerhart, 1991). In an effort to summarize the various determinants of applicant fairness, we examine fairness with respect to three aspects of the hiring process: selection procedures, hiring personnel, and hiring policies. For each of these aspects, we identify the justice dimensions that lead to applicant perceptions of unfairness when they are not respected.

Organizational justice can clearly be segmented into concerns regarding procedures (procedural justice) and concerns regarding outcomes (distributive justice). In the selection context, procedural justice reflects the selection process, personnel, and policies, whereas distributive justice reflects the outcome of the assessment and the hiring decision. Given that much of the variance in distributive justice is explained by the assessment outcome or hiring decision alone (Smither et al., 1993), an organization has less control over perceptions of distributive justice than procedural justice. Therefore, this chapter focuses predominantly on procedural justice.

Procedural justice has been segmented into formal procedures, interpersonal treatment, and explanations or information (Gilliland, 1993). Interpersonal treatment and explanations are often referred to as interpersonal and informational justice, respectively (Greenberg, 1990); alternatively, *interactional justice* is the term often used to encompass these two aspects of procedural justice (Bies & Moag, 1986). Researchers have also proposed a number of rules or determinants of these justice reactions (Gilliland, 1993; Leventhal, 1980). For example, in the selection context reactions to formal procedures are based on perceptions of job relatedness, whether or not one had the opportunity to perform or demonstrate one's abilities, consistency of administration, and opportunity for reconsideration. We now turn our consideration to how these justice rules may be violated with different selection procedures.

Selection Procedures

Selection procedures have typically been examined from a psychometric validity perspective. This prediction paradigm (Cropanzano, 1997) has led to the development of many valid selection instruments. However, recently Cropanzano pointed out that many of the selection procedures that are psychometrically valid lack perceived fairness or social validity (Schuler, 1993). A number of studies have compared different selection procedures in terms of perceived fairness, favorability, and other user reactions (e.g., Kravitz, Stinson, & Chavez, 1996; Rynes & Connerley, 1993; Steiner & Gilliland, 1996). Generally, interviews, work sample tests, and accomplishment records (e.g., resumes) are perceived most favorably. Personality tests, honesty tests, and written-ability tests get mixed evaluations, ranging from neutral to negative. Reactions to graphology (i.e., handwriting analysis) are uniformly negative. A problem with many of these comparative studies is that applicants are not asked about actual experiences but rather are asked how they would react to the various selection procedures.

Instead of discussing which selection procedures lead to perceptions of unfairness and why, this chapter focuses on three popular selection procedures that can lead to negative reactions. These include interviews, ability tests, and personality (and honesty) tests. With each procedure we discuss what can lead to negative reactions, both in terms of features of the selection method and justice dimensions (see Table 8.1 for a summary).

Interviews.   As indicated, when compared to other selection procedures, reactions toward interviews tend to be positive. However, important variation has also been found in reactions to those interviews. Interviewer behavior, degree of interview structure, and specific interview questions can all affect applicants' perceptions of interview fairness (for a review, see Gilliland & Steiner, 1999). In-

TABLE 8.1
Causes of Applicant Unfairness

Aspects of the Hiring Process	Potentially Unfair Features	Key Justice Concerns
Selection procedures		
Interviews	Interview structure	Opportunity to perform
	Situational questions	Propriety of questions
	Improper questions	
Ability tests	Applicability to the job	Job relatedness
	Information regarding the test	Opportunity to perform
		Information–communication
Personality and honesty tests	Type of questions	Job relatedness
		Invasion of privacy
		Fakability
Hiring personnel	Lack of respect	Interpersonal effectiveness
	Communication skills	Two-way communication
	Improper questions and statements	Propriety of questions
Hiring policies		
Retesting and reviewing decisions	Lack of retesting or reviewing	Opportunity for reconsideration
Communication	Delays in recruiting process	Feedback timeliness
	Generic rejection letters	Feedback informativeness

terviewer behavior is considered in a later section of this chapter that addresses the impact of hiring personnel on applicant fairness. With regard to interview structure, research has demonstrated that applicants perceive both structured and unstructured interviews to be similar in terms of job relatedness (Smither et al., 1993) but that unstructured interviews are seen as providing a greater opportunity to demonstrate one's abilities (Latham & Finnegan, 1993) and are therefore perceived to be more fair (Latham & Finnegan, 1993; Schuler, 1993).

Latham and Finnegan (1993) also considered applicant perceptions of situational versus patterned behavioral interview questions. Situational questions are future oriented ("what would you do . . ."), whereas behavioral are past oriented ("tell me about a time when . . ."). Student applicants indicated that situational questions were perceived more favorably in terms of job relatedness and consistency of administration, but that behavioral questions provided greater opportunity to demonstrate their abilities. They also indicated that job relatedness and consistency were less important than opportunity to perform. As a result, behavioral questions were perceived to be more fair and in fact, comparable to unstructured interviews on perceived fairness. To the extent that these results can be generalized, we conclude that interviews that deny applicants the opportunity to feel that they can demonstrate their abilities will be perceived negatively. The satisfaction of job relatedness and consistency rules does not compensate for a violation of the opportunity to perform rule.

Interviews can also be perceived as unfair if they include deception, improper questions, or prejudicial statements (Bies & Moag, 1986). Although much of this interview behavior is unethical or illegal, the incidence of this behavior is disturbingly common (Rynes, 1993). Gilliland (1993) suggested that applicants have a propriety of questions procedural rule that is violated by these statements and questions. In support of this suggestion, Kravitz et al. (1996) demonstrated strong relations between perceived invasiveness and perceived fairness.

It is clear that interviews can and often are perceived positively by job applicants. But it is also clear that applicants have expectations regarding how they should be treated during the interview. If they are not allowed the opportunity to demonstrate their abilities or if they are asked improper question, the interview will likely be perceived to be unfair. It should be noted that these conclusions are based on preliminary research and more thorough evaluation is needed to support the suggestion that opportunity to perform and propriety of questions are critical determinants of perceptions of interview fairness.

Ability Tests. Reactions to cognitive ability tests range from moderately positive (e.g., Macan et al., 1994; Smither et al., 1993) to moderately negative (Rynes & Connerley, 1993). Part of this variation may be explained by the job relatedness of the ability test. When job applicants were asked what made ability tests fair or unfair, Gilliland (1995) found that the majority of the issues centered on job relatedness. More directly, Rynes and Connerley (1993) found more favorable reactions toward ability tests with business related items than more general ability tests. On the other hand, Smither and colleagues (1993) manipulated the business context of ability test items but found this manipulation had no effect on fairness perceptions. Thus, it is unclear the extent to which perceptions of job relatedness influence the perceived fairness of cognitive ability tests.

Another procedural determinant that may cause cognitive ability tests to be seen as unfair is a lack of opportunity to perform. In a simulated hiring situation, Kluger and Rothstein (1993) had students complete either a cognitive ability test or biodata inventory and collected reactions to the testing situation. Regardless of feedback received regarding their performance, students perceived cognitive ability tests to be less controllable and also less fair than biodata inventories. The relation between unfairness and inability to control the situation or lack of opportunity to perform is similar to problems applicants appear to have with structured interviews.

A final cause of unfairness perceptions with cognitive ability tests may have more to do with how they are administered than with the tests themselves. Gilliland (1995) found that one of the major complaints with cognitive ability tests was the lack of information provided regarding the test itself. This problem is exemplified in the following comment: "I had no problem with the test, but they didn't provide me with any initial information before the test—no discussion of the types of scores they got or what they were looking for." Although it is probably obvious to most applicants why an interview is part of the selection process, this may not be the case with cognitive ability tests. Failure to provide an explanation or to allow questions about the test may lead to perceptions of unfairness.

Personality and Honesty Tests. Of the three types of selection procedures we examine in this chapter, reactions are generally most negative toward personality and honesty tests (Kravitz et al., 1996; Rynes & Connerley, 1993; Steiner & Gilliland, 1996). A major problem with these tests is that they are seen as lacking both face validity and scientific validity (Steiner & Gilliland, 1996). This lack of perceived job relatedness results in perceptions of unfairness. Interestingly, Rosse, Miller, and Stecher (1994) found that a standard personality test was perceived more favorably by actual job applicants when it was administered with a battery of cognitive ability tests. It is possible that the combination of personality and cognitive ability tests is seen as more job related than a personality test alone.

Personality and honesty tests can also be judged unfairly because they are perceived to invade personal privacy (Kravitz et al., 1996). Indeed the lawsuit filed by Soroka against Dayton Hudson Corporation in California was, in part, based on the belief that certain MMPI personality inventory items violating personal privacy. Further research is needed to determine whether personality and honesty tests with job related and non-invasive items are perceived to be fair.

Overt honesty tests may pose a unique procedural justice problem in that applicants perceive them to be fakable. These tests ask for admission of prior counterproductive behavior, such as theft. Gilliland (1995) found that the most salient objection applicants had to these tests was the perceived ease with which they could be faked. As one applicant indicated: "The questions were a joke because it seemed too obvious how you should respond. I think some people will lie to help themselves look better." Even if these tests are not widely faked and demonstrate validity (Ones, Viswesvaran, & Schmidt, 1993), applicants perceive them to be fakable, and therefore, perceive them to be unfair.

Hiring Personnel

Although the bulk of research on applicants' perceptions of fairness has focused on the fairness of different selection procedures, it is clear that the personnel involved in the hiring process can also have a major impact on applicant fairness. For example, anecdotes abound in which candidates complain of improper behavior by interviewers. When considering hiring personnel, we include human-resources employees who have the responsibility for such functions as collecting application blanks, administering tests, and conducting interviews, but we also consider supervisors or managers who are likely to interact with candidates at some phase in the hiring process, perhaps for a final interview.

In Gilliland's (1993) model of applicant reactions to selection systems, he noted that human-resource personnel are likely to affect reactions through the interpersonal treatment dimensions of procedural justice, including interpersonal effectiveness, two-way communication, and propriety of questions. The characteristics of hiring personnel relevant to interpersonal effectiveness examined in previous research include traits such as respect (Bies & Moag, 1986) and affect (including warmth, personableness, and empathy; Liden & Parsons, 1986; Rynes, 1991; Schmitt & Coyle, 1976). Hiring personnel may also differ in their communication skills with job candidates. Giving applicants the opportunity to actively participate in interactions with personnel and allowing them to ask questions are essential aspects of the two-way communication dimension as indicated by research regarding fairness in the performance appraisal context (Greenberg, 1986; Landy, Barnes, & Murphy, 1978). The third dimension of interpersonal treatment under the control of hiring personnel is the propriety of questions. For example, Bies and Moag (1986) found that this category includes both improper questions and prejudicial comments made by interviewers. Supporting the importance of some of these dimensions, Steiner, Gilliland, and Dew (1997) found that interpersonal treatment and asking relevant questions were the only significant predictors of recruiter effectiveness in samples of French professionals and college students.

Line managers who have the task of selecting individuals to work under their supervision and their direction may be more likely to use personal stereotypes and biases in making their hiring decisions. Whereas human-resources personnel are likely to be trained in Equal Employment Opportunity (EEO) issues and be aware of discriminatory practices, supervisors who are conducting a final interview with an applicant who will become part of their work group often state that it is important to hire someone who will fit in, whose personality will correspond well with the supervisor's and the group's. We recognize that these issues of fit are important to collegial work performance (Bretz & Judge, 1994), but to the extent that they may be based on group membership, such as sex or race, they are potentially problematic from both legal and perceived fairness points of view. Supervisors may also ask inappropriate questions when assessing an applicant's fit.

Hiring Policies

A final aspect of the hiring process that can impact applicants' perceptions of unfairness is the hiring policies that are established regarding issues of retesting and communication (see Table 8.1).

Retesting and Reviewing Decisions.   Arvey and Sackett (1993) suggested that the opportunity to retake a selection procedure and the opportunity to review test scores and scoring are important determinants of applicants' perceptions of fairness. There is certainly support for this suggestion with regard to drug testing.

Murphy, Thornton, and Reynolds (1990) found that drug testing was evaluated much more favorably if the testing policy involved retesting with a second sample or testing method. With other personnel procedures, such as performance appraisal, the opportunity for reconsideration is also a strong determinant of perceived fairness (Greenberg, 1986). Despite this related research, we know of no research that has investigated the impact of selection retesting or reviewing policies on applicants' perceptions of fairness.

Communication. One of the problems discussed with regard to cognitive-ability tests was the administration of these tests without providing adequate information on the tests' purpose and the types of scores generated. This highlights the extent to which lack of communication can lead to perceptions of unfairness. With regard to communication, both timing and informativeness are important. When Rynes and colleagues (1991) asked job applicants what made a once attractive company unattractive, a significant number of responses identified delays in the recruiting process. Additionally, the more qualified the candidates were, the more they tended to attribute these delays to problems with the organization. Similarly, Gilliland (1995) found that the failure to provide timely feedback was one of the leading contributors to perceptions of unfairness among unsuccessful applicants.

In addition to feedback timeliness, justification or explanations for decisions are important to applicants, particularly when the decision is negative. Bies and Moag (1986) found that the absence of justification was associated with perceptions of unfair recruiting practices. Scenario-based studies of rejection letters also demonstrate the importance of justification (Bies & Shapiro, 1988; Gilliland, Baker, Dew, & Polly, 1996). Providing an explanation for a rejection decision in the rejection letter improves perceptions of process and outcome fairness. Given that this justification is often easy to provide, it is surprising that so many organizations do not provide more detail in their rejection letters. One possible explanation for this behavior is a fear of litigation; from a legal perspective, information is seen as ammunition that may be used against the company. Also, in some cases informative feedback is simply not operationally feasible. The Federal Bureau of Investigation assesses approximately 80,000 applicants each year. They simply do not have the computer resources available to send out anything more than generic decision letters that contain pass–fail information (Kolmstetter, 1997).

Moderators of Fairness Determinants

We have identified salient justice determinants that arise due to the selection procedures, the hiring personnel, and the hiring policies. However, the importance of justice determinants is likely to depend both on the situation and the individuals involved. For example, an honesty test may be viewed as appropriate

TABLE 8.2
Moderators of Fairness Determinants

Environmental Factors	Industry norms
	Cultural norms
Individual Factors	Work experience
	Selection process experience
	Self-efficacy
	Protected group status

for a bank teller but be considered completely unrelated and unfair for an electrician. This section examines some environmental and individual factors that may moderate the salience of different justice dimensions (see Table 8.2 for a summary).

Environmental Factors.   Although there are many potential environmental factors that impact the salience of justice dimensions for job applicants, this section considers two specific factors: industry norms and cultural norms. Certainly industry norms can be seen to affect the perceived job relatedness of different selection procedures. For example, drug testing is seen as much more appropriate with airline pilots and air traffic controllers than with photographers and janitors (Murphy et al., 1990). Similarly, criminal records, honesty tests, and personality tests were evaluated more positively when applied to decisions for second-level managers rather than for skilled production workers (Kravitz et al., 1996). The opposite was true for physical-ability tests, which were perceived to be more invasive and less fair when used for second-level managers. Unfortunately, only limited research has examined the moderating effect of jobs on fairness evaluations of different selection methods. No research has examined whether different norms exist in terms of interpersonal treatment or timely feedback with different industries and occupational groups. This is clearly a direction for future research.

Culture is also a moderator of justice determinant salience. Steiner and Gilliland (1996) found some differences in the perceived fairness of various selection procedures in the United States and France. But, more interestingly, they also found that the justice dimensions underlying these fairness evaluations varied somewhat by culture. Americans tended to base fairness perceptions of selection techniques more on scientific evidence and the employer's right to obtain information than did French respondents. To supplement the growing body of literature indicating the importance of culture in distributive justice (e.g., Hui, Triandis, & Yee, 1991; Kim, Park, & Suzuki, 1990), it would be interesting to study how cultures also differ in terms of the importance of interpersonal treatment and justification for decisions as well as other aspects of procedural justice (see McFarlin & Sweeney, this volume).

Individual Factors.   Individual factors may also influence the salience of different justice dimensions (see Table 8.2). A mechanism that may allow for studying these individual factors are the hiring expectations of job applicants. Gilliland (1994) found that hiring expectation related positively to fairness for hired individuals and negatively for rejected applicants. In keeping with the idea that fairness reactions are stronger in response to violations of justice because they go against our expectations, work experience and experiences with selection processes are likely to create different expectations regarding the hiring process. In a very general sense, because of the authority and power of an organization in the hiring process, we might expect that individuals with little experience will be much more tolerant of violations of justice than individuals who have had a great variety of these types of experiences. As individuals gain knowledge of organizational functioning through years of work experience and are exposed to more hiring situations, a number of the justice dimensions are likely to become more important to them. For example, individuals with lots of relevant experience are likely to have little patience for selection procedures that are not job related or that provide them with little opportunity to exhibit their experience. These individuals likely have greater self-efficacy (Bandura, 1982) regarding their chances of being hired, and their variety of experiences has presumably exposed them to a variety of job-related and unrelated selection procedures. When confronted with a rather unrelated selection procedure, their high expectations of success may immediately plummet creating a strong violation of the job relatedness justice rule.

The relative importance of different types of information about the selection procedure and the decision also will likely differ based on experience. Young or inexperienced applicants are likely to value informative feedback about an unsuccessful candidacy to help orient them toward experiences or other job opportunities that may suit them better. More experienced applicants, who have received numerous rejection letters, probably have lower expectations regarding the amount of informative feedback they are likely to receive. The importance of the various factors of interpersonal treatment are also likely to be influenced by experience. The neophyte or the individual who has experienced a long period of unemployment is likely to need the interpersonal warmth and thoughtfulness of effective human-resources personnel to keep from being discouraged on the job market.

Finally, another set of individual difference factors can be identified relative to the minority or protected group status of the applicant. Individuals who are members of groups protected by equal employment opportunity legislation might be particularly sensitive to propriety of questions issues that surround their protected status (age, marital status, organizational affiliations, etc.). Consistent with our theme of justice violations going against expectations, questions that seem related to a particular group status may signal to applicants that a company desires to avoid hiring members of their group. Such inappropriate questions may also reduce their self-efficacy beliefs about their chances of being hired.

CONSEQUENCES OF APPLICANT FAIRNESS

The quotes at the beginning of this chapter suggest that attention to applicant fairness is important for a variety of reasons. Research on the consequences of applicant fairness has identified attitudes, decisions, and behavior that are related to fairness perceptions. The following sections discuss consequences of applicant fairness that are related to applicant decisions and attitudes, as well as legal challenges and spillover effects. Table 8.3 provides a summary of these consequences.

Applicant Decisions

In the selection domain, one of the most immediate consequences of justice violations may be on the applicant's decision to continue with the selection process and to accept a job offer. In a study of applicant withdrawal from consideration for police officer positions, Schmit and Ryan (1997) reported that 11.7% of the applicants who withdrew prior to the selection exam stated that perceived unfairness of hiring practices was the reason. However, in a follow-up study, Ryan and McFarland (1997) found that perceptions of fairness were unrelated to withdrawal behavior. At least two possible explanations for this lack of relation exist. First, if unfairness is only a concern for a limited number of applicants (i.e., approximately 12% of the 40% who withdrew), a strong relation between fairness and

TABLE 8.3
Consequences and Moderators of Applicant Unfairness

Consequences	
1. Applicant Decisions	• Applicant withdrawal
	• Job offer acceptance
2. Attitudes	• Organizational commitment
	• Job satisfaction
	• Supervisor–subordinate relationship
3. Legal Challenges	• Discrimination
	• Invasion of privacy
	• Defamation
4. Spillover Effects	• Applicant recommendations
	• Customer purchase behavior
Potential Moderators	
1. Environmental Factors	• Job Market
	• Legal environment
	• Cultural norms
2. Individual Factors	• Alternative job offers
	• Self-efficacy
	• Work experience
	• Knowledge of legal protection

withdrawal across all applicants (including those who do not withdraw) is not likely to be observed; fairness is not expected to be related to withdrawal for greater than 90% of applicants at this early stage of selection. However, as Murphy (1986) demonstrated, the utility of selection can be seriously reduced to the extent that the best applicants turn down job offers. Given that the best applicants are likely to have the most alternatives, unfairness during selection could be crucial to their decision to refuse an offer.

Second, the previous discussion of the causes of applicant unfairness identified selection procedures, hiring personnel, and hiring policies as potential sources of unfairness. Prior to taking the selection exam, applicants really do not have much except publicized hiring policies on which to base fairness perceptions. It would be expected that unfairness have a greater impact on later applicant decisions, such as the decision to accept a job offer. Research relevant to this possibility has indicated that one aspect of the selection process, interviewer affect, is related to applicant attraction to the firm (Turban & Dougherty, 1992) and likelihood of job acceptance (Schmitt & Coyle, 1976). Similarly, Macan et al. (1994) reported that job applicants who reacted unfavorably to the selection procedures indicated that they were less likely to accept the job. It is important to note that both Macan et al. (1994) and Rynes (1991) found that job attributes are more important than perception of the selection process in predicting these outcomes. Cropanzano (1997) reviewed other studies that are consistent with the impact of unfairness on the acceptance of job offers, although further research on actual applicant decisions to accept offers is still needed.

Applicant Attitudes

Toward the Company. At times, individuals will accept jobs even when they feel they were treated unfairly during the selection process, when it is a high-paying job or when they only have one offer, for example. But even in these situations, unfair hiring practices appear to have residual effects. Both Singer (1992) and Gilliland and Troth (1997) reported negative attitudes in such areas as satisfaction and organizational commitment by individuals treated unfairly in the selection process. Given the existing research, it is unclear how long these initial attitudes persist, but there is evidence that initial fairness experiences are more important in shaping reactions than later experiences (Van den Bos et al., 1997).

Toward the Supervisor. Another way in which unfair treatment can have lingering effects on organizational behavior is in the case where the hired individual's supervisor was involved in the hiring process. Here, unfair treatment could influence the work relationship that develops between the supervisor and subordinate (cf. the leader–member exchange model of leadership, Graen, 1976). Only a few studies have examined the role of the initial interaction between subordinates and supervisors, such as in a selection interview, in the development of high-quality relationships. The supervisor's impressions of ability and initial liking for the subordinate, for example, have been found to relate to relationship development (Dockery & Steiner, 1990). Furthermore, in so far as these relationships are based on exchanges between supervisors and subordinates (Sparrowe & Liden, 1997), injustices in the treatment of a potential work-group member during the hiring process may be viewed as violating this exchange, thereby creating a poor environment when the applicant accepts the job despite the mistreatment.

Legal Challenges

Organizations are facing an increasing number of legal challenges from job applicants. These challenges include discrimination charges, invasion of privacy claims, and defamation claims against the applicant's former employer. Some research has identified characteristics of selection practices that tend to withstand legal challenges (e.g., Williamson, Campion, Malos, Roehling, & Campion, 1997), but no research has linked unfair treatment during the selection process to the likelihood of filing legal challenges. Nonetheless, it is likely that the reason applicants try to get justice in the courts is because they do not feel they have received justice in the hiring process. As with other consequences of applicant fairness, legal challenges may have more to do with what the organization has done wrong, than with what it has done right.

There are a number of ways in which subsequent research could examine the relationship between applicant justice and legal challenges. One method would involve collecting retrospective reports from individuals who have filed discrimination and other legal challenges about the reasons for those challenges. It would be important to try to distinguish the legal basis for the challenge from the perceptual basis. For example, an applicant may decide to hire a lawyer because of the incredible disrespect with which he or she was treated. However, the lawyer may then build a legal challenge around discriminatory questions and comments. A quantitative approach to studying the relationship between applicant justice and legal challenges could involve nonlinear logistic regression, which would indicate the extent to which unfairness along different procedural justice dimensions increases the probability of a legal challenge.

Spillover Effects

In addition to influencing an applicant's attitudes and decisions regarding the selection process and job, unfairness in the selection process can influence other behavior and decisions, such as whether or not the applicant recommends the organization to others or whether or not the applicant continues to purchase the organization's products and services. A number of recent studies have found that applicants' perceptions of fairness are related to their intentions to recommend the job to others (Bauer, Maertz, Dolen, & Campion, 1997; Gilliland, 1994; Smither et al., 1993). The extent to which these intentions are related to actual behavior could impact the quality and success of an organization's recruiting efforts. Unfortunately, no research has examined the impact of fairness perceptions on actual recommendation behavior.

It is also possible that applicant's perceptions of fairness may influence their customer purchase behavior. This was the concern expressed by the human-resource representative at the beginning of this chapter and is also captured in the following quote from an human-resource manager in the auto industry: "Regardless of whether or not we hire these people, we want to make sure they continue to buy our cars." Macan and colleagues (1994) assessed purchase intentions among applicants who were assessed by cognitive ability tests and found a weak relation between perceptions of fairness and purchase intentions. However, conceptually, we would not expect the linear relation between perceptions of fairness and purchase intentions to be very strong. The application process and purchase setting are distinct enough that it would probably take relatively strong instances of application process unfairness to change purchase behavior. Rather than investigating linear relationships between fairness and purchase intentions, we recommend that future research examine the impact of clearly unfair treatment on changes in purchase intentions. How much unfairness will an applicant endure before they refuse to have anything further to do with the organization? Answering such questions will require different research methods than the typical correlational approaches.

Moderators of Fairness Consequences

This chapter has discussed various of consequences to individuals and organizations in situations where applicant justice is violated. However, a number of situational factors are likely to mitigate or moderate the occurrence or severity of these consequences. We consider external, environmental factors and individual difference variables that may play this moderating role between justice violations and consequences (see Table 8.3).

Environmental Factors. Environmental factors include such things as the job market, the legal environment, and cultural norms. When the job market is tight and few alternative opportunities are available to individuals, we can imagine that justice violations will play a limited role on job acceptance decisions—the individual feeling obligated to accept any rare offer—although the negative consequences on subsequent work-related attitudes and job performance as presented previously are still likely to result. On the other hand, when unemployment is relatively low and many job are available, justice violations should play a significant role in job acceptance decisions. In the United States, the current economy is strong, unemployment is very low, and organizations are struggling to attract the best job applicants (Saltzman, 1997). Given these economic conditions, organizations should carefully consider the justice of their hiring practices.

The salience of the legal environment is also likely to moderate the severity of consequences following some justice violations. If the violations are due to protected group membership and a discrimination case or sexual harassment case has been the subject of a great deal of media attention, minority or female job applicants may be especially sensitive to hiring decisions that are unfavorable to them or to questions that seem related to their group membership. For example, 8 months after the widely publicized sexual harassment allegations during confirmation hearing of Clarence Thomas, complaints of sexual harassment filed with the EEOC increased by more than 50% (Bennett-Alexander & Pincus, 1995).

Considering these justice–consequence relationships from a more international perspective, it seems obvious that the legal issues, protected groups, and ease of prosecuting discrimination violations are likely to be quite different from country to country. Cultural norms are also likely to play a role here. In France, for example, it is common practice in employment advertising to specify the desired age of an applicant (usually less than 35). Where such practices are common, older individuals may be less likely to be sensitive to hiring practices that are age-related.

Individual Factors. Several individual difference variables are also likely to moderate the severity of consequences following violations of justice (see Table 8.3). The individual's decision to accept a job offer in conjunction with the degree to which the individual has alternatives in the job market is the first of these factors. Imagine a scenario in which an individual accepts a job despite poor treatment during the hiring process. Several responses seem plausible once this employee accepts the job. If the decision to accept was due to the lack of alternatives, this individual is likely to experience little commitment toward the organization and job initially and seek other alternatives at the first available opportunity. Of course, once inside the organization, positive treatment could mitigate the negative experiences of the selection process. If on the other hand an individual accepts a job given perceived alternatives or because other positive aspects of the job largely outweighed the negative treatment during hiring, dissonance theory might predict that this individual will be even more committed to the organization: "I suffered so much to get here, it must be a great place" (cf. the initiation experiments of Aronson & Mills, 1959). Of course, this series of events is only plausible to the extent that the individual chose to accept the job freely and was not constrained by the lack of alternatives, thereby allowing the rationalization of the job acceptance.

Self-efficacy (Bandura, 1982) with regard to the job market is another individual difference variable that likely moderates the consequences of justice violations in hiring. More specifically, individuals who feel confident that they will get other job offers will be more likely to turn down jobs for which the selection process has seemed unfair. Similarly, an applicant armed with lots of work experience will have a more realistic view of life in work organizations and may be more choosy regarding different opportunities. In particular, individuals who have already experienced many injustices are more likely to respond negatively to new ones than those with few such past experiences (Sheppard, Lewicki, & Minton, 1992).

Many individuals, particularly those with less education, less work experience, and less experience on the job market, are unaware of the legal protection that is available to them in the selection situation. That is, they are unaware of the various protected groups and the legislation that protects individuals against certain kinds of hiring practices. Thus, they are less likely to be sensitive to justice violations related to protected group status and less likely to pursue a discrimination case when a violation occurs.

Summary

This review of consequences of applicant unfairness suggests many potential effects of violating justice during the application process. However, with a few exceptions (e.g., applicant recommendation intentions) existing research has not found strong relation between perceptions of fairness and consequences. Rather than suggesting that applicant fairness is not practically important, we suggest that research has not examined this issue from the right perspective. Rather than looking for correlations between perceptions of fairness and various consequences, research should examine the influence of unfair treatment on various consequences. How poor does the treatment have to be before applicants pursue legal challenges or decide to not purchase the companies products or services? When research questions are reframed in this way, it becomes essential to consider moderators of these consequences.

CONCLUSIONS

This chapter has examined a variety of causes and consequences of applicant fairness reactions during the selection process and have indicated a number of areas where more research needs to be done. In addition, we have discussed some potential moderating variables, most of which have not yet been the subject of much research. Attention to these moderating variables is important to help us understand why, how, and when reactions of unfairness occur and produce serious consequences.

Research on organizational justice in the personnel selection process must continue to use a variety of methods. Some methods will be focused more on process issues, for example to understand the development of expectations, and other methods will need to be more field based to attempt to understand the reality for individuals and organizations of selection fairness. The research by Van den Bos et al. (1997), in which they manipulated the order of presentation of information on justice violations, exemplifies the first of these concerns regarding process issues. Research by Ryan and her colleagues (e.g., Ryan & McFarland, 1997; Schmit & Ryan, 1997), on applicant withdrawal from the selection process, provided a good example of the second approach, which concerns individual and organizational reality. Their correlational evidence suggests that there is little if any relation between perceptions of fairness and applicant withdrawal. However, more than 10% of withdrawing applicants cited fairness issues as the reason for their withdrawal. By focusing on and trying to explain the outcome this research has uncovered important information regarding the relation between fairness and applicant withdrawal. A similar approach could be used to study the influence of fairness on job acceptance decisions, legal challenges, and even changes in customer purchase behavior. Although there is only a weak correlation between applicant fairness perceptions and customer purchase intentions (Macan et al., 1994), research may discover that a majority of applicants who are treated very unfairly during the selection process refuse to recommend the company or purchase their products.

Finally, research can begin to focus on remedies to unfairness. When mistakes are made, what can organizations do to correct them? What needs to be done to prevent future injustices? Research in other domains of fairness may provide direction in answering these questions. For example, Baron (1993) has addressed steps to counter the effects of destructive criticism. Additionally, research from the service marketing literature on fairness in service delivery (e.g., Clemmer, 1993) and service recovery (Tax, Brown, & Chandrashekaran, 1996) may be applied to human resources functions such as selection. A better understanding of the hows and whys of applicant reactions to unfairness should provide direct links to preventing future problems and for developing antidotes for mistakes.

REFERENCES

Aronson, E., & Mills, J. (1959). The effect of severity of initiation on liking for a group. *Journal of Abnormal and Social Psychology, 59,* 177–181.

Arvey, R. D., & Sackett, P. R. (1993). Fairness in selection: Current developments and perspectives. In N. Schmitt & W. Borman (Eds.), *Personnel Selection in organizations* (171–202). San Francisco, CA: Jossey-Bass.

Bandura, A. (1982). Self-efficacy mechanism in human agency. *American Psychologist, 37,* 122–147.

Baron, R. A. (1993). Criticism (informal negative feedback) as a source of perceived unfairness in organizations: Effects, mechanisms, and countermeasures. In R. Cropanzano (Ed.), *Justice in the workplace: Approaching fairness in human resource management* (155–170). Hillsdale, NJ: Lawrence Erlbaum Associates.

Bauer, T. N., Maertz, C., Dolen, M. R., & Campion, M. A. (1997). *Applicant reactions to employment testing: A longitudinal assessment.* Unpublished manuscript.

Bennett-Alexander, D. D., & Pincus, L. B. (1995). *Employment law for business.* Chicago, IL: Irwin.

Bies, R. J., & Moag, J. S. (1986). Interactional justice: Communication criteria of fairness. *Research on Negotiation in Organizations, 1,* 43–55.

Bies, R. J., & Shapiro, D. L. (1988). Voice and justification: Their influence on procedural fairness judgments. *Academy of Management Journal, 31*, 676–685.

Bretz, R. D. Jr., & Judge, T. A. (1994). Person–organization fit and the theory of work adjustment: Implications for satisfaction, tenure, and career success. *Journal of Vocational Behavior, 44*, 32–54.

Clemmer, E. C. (1993). An investigation into the relationship of fairness and customer satisfaction with services. In R. Cropanzano (Ed.), *Justice in the workplace: Approaching fairness in human resource management* (pp. 193–207). Hillsdale, NJ: Lawrence Erlbaum Associates.

Cropanzano, R. (1997). *A tale of two paradigms: Psychometrics meets social justice in the conduct of psychological assessment.* Unpublished manuscript.

Dockery, T. M., & Steiner, D. D. (1990). The role of the initial interaction in leader–member exchange. *Group and Organization Studies, 15*, 395–413.

Gilliland, S. W. (1993). The perceived fairness of selection systems: An organizational justice perspective. *Academy of Management Review, 18*, 694–734.

Gilliland, S. W. (1994). Effects of procedural and distributive justice on reactions to a selection system. *Journal of Applied Psychology, 79*, 691–701.

Gilliland, S. W. (1995). Fairness from the applicant's perspective: Reactions to employee selection procedures. *International Journal of Selection and Assessment, 3*, 11–19.

Gilliland, S. W., Baker, R. C. III, Dew, A. F., & Polly, L. M. (1996, April). *Rejection letter fairness: Process and outcome explanations for negative decisions.* Presented at the 11th annual conference of the Society for Industrial and Organizational Psychology, San Diego, CA.

Gilliland, S. W., & Steiner, D. D. (1999). Applicant reactions to interviews: Procedural and interactional justice of recent interview technology. In R. W. Eder & M. M. Harris (Eds.), *The employment interview: Theory, research, and practice* (2nd ed., pp. 69–82). Sage.

Gilliland, S. W., & Troth, M. A. (1997). *Consequences of employee selection system justice.* Manuscript under review.

Graen, G. (1976). Role making processes within complex organizations. In M. D. Dunnette (Ed.), *Handbook of industrial and organizational psychology* (pp. 1210–1259). Chicago: Rand McNally.

Greenberg, J. (1986). Determinants of perceived fairness of performance evaluations. *Journal of Applied Psychology, 71*, 340–342.

Greenberg, J. (1990). Organizational justice: Yesterday, today, and tomorrow. *Journal of Management, 16*, 399–432.

Herriott, P. (1989). Selection as a social process. In M. Smith & I. Robertson (Eds.), *Advances in selection and assessment* (pp. 171–187). Chichester, England: Wiley.

Hui, C. H., Triandis, H. C., & Yee, C. (1991). Cultural differences in reward allocation: Is collectivism the explanation? *British Journal of Social Psychology, 30*, 145–157.

Kim, K. I., Park, H., & Suzuki, N. (1990). Reward allocations in the United States, Japan, and Korea: A comparison of individualistic and collectivistic cultures. *Academy of Management Journal, 33*, 188–198.

Kolmstetter, E. C. (1997, April). *Practical considerations for giving upfront information and feedback in a large-scale pass/fail selection system.* Paper presented at the 12th annual conference of the Society for Industrial and Organizational Psychology, St. Louis, MO.

Kluger, A. N., & Rothstein, H. R. (1993). The influence of selection test type on applicant reactions to employment testing. *Journal of Business and Psychology, 8*, 3–25.

Kravitz, D. A., Stinson, V., & Chavez, T. L. (1996). Evaluations of tests used for making selection and promotion decisions. *International Journal of Selection and Assessment, 4*, 24–34.

Landy, F. L., Barnes, J. L., & Murphy, K. R. (1978). Correlates of perceived fairness and accuracy of performance evaluation. *Journal of Applied Psychology, 63*, 751–754.

Latham, G. P., & Finnegan, B. J. (1993). Perceived practicality of unstructured, patterned, and situational interviews. In H. Schuler, J. L. Farr & M. Smith (Eds.), *Personnel selection and assessment: Individual and organizational perspectives* (pp. 41–55). Hillsdale, NJ: Lawrence Erlbaum Associates.

Leventhal, G. S. (1980). What should be done with equity theory? New approaches to the study of fairness in social relationship. In K. J. Gergen, M. S. Greenberg & R. H. Willis (Eds.), *Social Exchange: Advances in Theory and Research* (pp. 27–55). New York: Plenum.

Liden, R. C., & Parsons, C. K. (1986). A field study of job applicant interview perceptions, alternative opportunities, and demographic characteristics. *Personnel Psychology, 39*, 109–122.

Macan, T. H., Avedon, M. J., Paese, M., & Smith, D. E. (1994). The effects of applicants' reactions to cognitive ability tests and an assessment center. *Personnel Psychology, 47*, 715–738.

Murphy, K. R. (1986). When your top choice turns you down: Effect of rejected offers on the utility of selection tests. *Psychological Bulletin, 99*, 133–138.

Murphy, K. R., Thornton, G. C. III, & Reynolds, D. H. (1990). College students' attitudes toward employee drug testing. *Journal of Applied Psychology, 43*, 615–631.

Ones, D. S., Viswesvaran, C., & Schmidt, F. L. (1993). Comprehensive meta-analysis of integrity test validities: Findings and implications for personnel selection and theories of job performance. *Journal of Applied Psychology, 78*, 679–703.

Rosse, J. G., Miller, J. L., & Stecher, M. D. (1994). A field study of job applicants' reactions to personality and cognitive ability testing. *Journal of Applied Psychology, 79*, 987–992.

Ryan, A. M., Greguras, G. J., & Ployhart, R. E. (1996). Perceived job relatedness of physical abilities testing for firefighters: Exploring variations in reactions. *Human Performance, 9*, 219–240.

Ryan, A. M., & McFarland, L. (1997). *Predicting applicant withdrawal from selection processes.* Unpublished manuscript.

Rynes, S. L. (1991). Recruitment, job choice, and post-hire consequences: A call for new research directions. In M. D. Dunnette (Ed.), *Handbook of industrial and organizational psychology* (2nd ed., Vol. 2, pp. 399–444). Palo Alto, CA: Consulting Psychologists' Press.

Rynes, S. L. (1993). Who's selecting whom? Effects of selection practices on applicant attitudes and behaviors. In N. Schmitt & W. Borman (Eds.), *Personnel Selection in organizations* (pp. 240–274). San Francisco, CA: Jossey-Bass.

Rynes, S. L. Bretz, R. D. Jr., & Gerhart, B. (1991). The importance of recruitment in job choice: A different way of looking. *Personnel Psychology, 44,* 487–521.

Rynes, S. L., & Connerley, M. L. (1993). Applicants reactions to alternative selection procedures. *Journal of Business and Psychology, 7*, 261–272.

Saltzman, A. (1997). Making it in a sizzling economy. *U.S. News and World Report, 122*(24), 50–58.

Schmit, M. J., & Ryan, A. M. (1997). Applicant withdrawal: The role of test-taking attitudes and racial differences. *Personnel Psychology, 50*, 855–876.

Schmitt, N. (1976). Social and situational determinants of interview decisions: Implications for the employment interview. *Personnel Psychology, 29*, 79–101.

Schmitt, N., & Coyle, B. W. (1976). Applicant decisions in the employment interview. *Journal of Applied Psychology, 61*, 184–192.

Schmitt, N., & Gilliland, S. W. (1992). Beyond differential prediction: Fairness in selection. In D. M. Saunders (Ed.), *New approaches to employment management: Fairness in employee selection* (pp. 21–46). Greenwich, CT: JAI.

Schuler, H. (1993). Is there a dilemma between validity and acceptance in the employment interview? In B. Nevo & R. S. Jager (Eds.), *Educational and psychological testing: The test taker's outlook* (pp. 239–250). Toronto, Canada: Hogrefe & Huber.

Sheppard, B. H., Lewicki, R. J., & Minton, J. W. (1992). *Organizational Justice: A search for fairness in the workplace.* New York: Lexington.

Singer, M. S. (1992). Procedural justice in managerial selection: Identification of fairness determinants and associations of fairness perceptions. *Social Justice Research, 5*, 49–70.

Smither, J. W., Reilly, R. R., Millsap, R. E., Pearlman, K., & Stoffey, R. W. (1993). Applicant reactions to selection procedures. *Personnel Psychology, 46*, 49–76.

Sparrowe, R. T., & Liden, R. C. (1997). Process and structure in leader–member exchange. *Academy of Management Review, 22*, 522–552.

Steiner, D. D., & Gilliland, S. W. (1996). Fairness reactions to personnel selection techniques in France and the United States. *Journal of Applied Psychology, 81*, 134–141.

Steiner, D. D., & Gilliland, S. W., & Dew, A. F. (1997). *Applicant attitudes toward selection techniques and recruiters: Student and professional points of view in France.* Unpublished manuscript.

Steiner, D. D., & Rain, J. S. (1989). Immediate and delayed primacy and recency effects in performance evaluation. *Journal of Applied Psychology, 74*, 136–142.

Tax, S. S., Brown, S. W., & Chandrashekaran, M. (1996). *Customer evaluations of service complaint experiences: Implications for relationship marketing.* Unpublished manuscript.

Turban, D. B., & Dougherty, T. W. (1992). Influences of campus recruiting on applicant attraction to firms. *Academy of Management Journal, 35*, 739–765.

Van den Bos, K., Vermunt, R., & Wilke, H. A. M. (1997). Procedural and distributive justice: What is fair depends more on what comes first than on what comes next. *Journal of Personality and Social Psychology, 72*, 95–104.

Williamson, L. G., Campion, J. E., Malos, S. B., Roehling, M. V., & Campion, M. A. (1997). *The employment interview on trial: Linking interview structure with litigation outcomes.* Unpublished manuscript.

9

▼▼▼▼▼▼▼▼

A Passion for Justice:
The Rationality and Morality
of Revenge

Robert J. Bies
Georgetown University

Thomas M. Tripp
Washington State University

> *But if injury ensues, you shall give life for life, eye for eye, tooth for tooth, hand for hand, foot for foot, burn for burn, wound for wound, stripe for stripe.*
> *Old Testament* (Exodus 21:23–25)

> *You have heard the commandment, "an eye for an eye, a tooth for a tooth." But what I say to you is: offer no resistance to injury. When a person strikes you on the right cheek, turn and offer him the other.*
> *New Testament* (Matthew 5:38–39)

Revenge is a phenomenon that both fascinates us and leaves us fearful. At some moment in our lives, we have all felt the primal urge to get even when harmed, and the passion of that moment makes revenge feel like the right thing to do. It is not only when we are harmed personally that revenge feels like the righteous response; for, we vicariously experience that righteous feeling when others are harmed or when swift vengeance is dealt the perpetrator of harm (Bies & Tripp, 1998a; Jacoby, 1983). Indeed, witness the audience's applause and approval of acts of revenge in such films as *Dirty Harry* and *The First Wives Club*.

But we are also afraid of revenge. We are fearful of the sometimes uncontrollable power of the passion of revenge (Tripp & Bies, 1997), when such emotions can cause events to escalate out of control, as in a feud or physical violence (Bies & Tripp, 1996). Our fears about revenge are further magnified when we witness how revenge has shaped the centuries of hatred and hostility in nations around the world, as in the case of the Balkans (Pomfert, 1995).

Our conflicted feelings about revenge are also reflected in the introductory biblical quotations, the first that provides a rationality and a morality for revenge and the second that provides an alternative moral vision and rationality for not engaging in revenge. Whether fearful or fascinated, there is no denying that revenge is intertwined in the social fabric of our human condition; indeed, revenge has been a powerful social force that has shaped the history of the world.

Recently, amidst the growing scholarly research on revenge in the workplace, there is an emerging view of revenge as justice (Bies & Tripp, 1996; McLean Parks, 1997). Although it is true that revenge is typically viewed as an irrational, if not evil, response, it is also true that the motivation for revenge is often rooted in the perception of undeserved harm and feelings of injustice (Tripp & Bies, 1997). Given the concept of deservingness is central to both normative formulations of justice (Feinberg, 1974) and social psychological theories of justice (e.g., Adams, 1965; Crosby, 1976), attempts to get even or evening the score (i.e., to receive what one rightfully deserves) are also central to justice. Moreover, there is a tradition in philosophy (e.g., Solomon, 1990) and legal theory (e.g., Cahn, 1949) that recognizes that passion and the emotions of injustice are central to understanding the justice process. Yet, the dominant models of organizational justice do not view revenge as central to the justice process.

This chapter argues that revenge is central to the process of justice in organizations, as it reflects a response to remedy or prevent injustice. In focusing on revenge as justice, passion and emotions become figural in understanding responses to injustice (Bies, 1987, 2000). Although this chapter highlights the importance of the passions of justice, it argues that there is a rationality and morality to revenge. Needless to say, this perspective that revenge is central to a theory of justice is a radical departure from current models.

REVENGE AS JUSTICE?: OVERCOMING THE MYTHS AND BIASES

Until recently, viewing revenge as justice received very little academic support or legitimacy. This lack of support and legitimacy is not by accident. For, there are myths and biases surrounding the topic of revenge that have created a distorted image of revenge as a motive and behavior (Bies & Tripp, 1996, 1998a; Bies, Tripp, & Kramer, 1997; McLean Parks, 1997; Tripp & Bies, 1997).

First, there is the powerful myth about revenge in which an act of vengeance is viewed only as a destructive and antisocial act, as in the case of employee theft (Greenberg, 1997) or workplace aggression (O'Leary-Kelly, Griffin, & Glew, 1996). Indeed, this myth perpetuates the view of revenge as a form of organizational deviance (Robinson & Bennett, 1995), an aggressive behavior that must be controlled or prevented (Neuman & Baron, 1997).

But revenge has many faces and not just bad or ugly ones (Bies & Tripp, 1998a). For the reality is that revenge can be good (i.e., constructive and prosocial; Bies & Tripp, 1996; Tripp & Bies, 1997). For example, there is evidence that revenge can restore self-esteem victims of abusive management practices (Bies & Tripp, 1998b), lead to corrections in an unfair resource allocation (Tripp & Bies, 1997), and act as a powerful deterrent against power abuse by authority figures and organizational decision makers (Bies & Tripp, 1995).

If revenge can be good, and not just bad and ugly, then why does this myth about revenge continue to persist? The answer to that question must begin with an examination of the prevailing ideological foundation of management and organization theory (Treviño & Bies, 1997; Tripp & Bies, 1997). Specifically, organization and management theory is rooted in the ideology of the *organizational imperative* (Scott & Hart, 1979). The organizational imperative is based on a primary and absolute proposition: "Whatever is good for the individual can only come from the modern organization" (p. 43), and the related secondary proposition: "Therefore, *all behavior must enhance the health of such organizations* (italics added)" (p. 43). Indeed, as Scott and Hart concluded, "the organizational imperative is the sine qua non of management theory and practice . . . the metaphysic of management: absolute and immutable" (p. 46).

The ideology of the organizational imperative has important implications for the study of revenge, for, as we know, ideological assumptions shape theory building and empirical research (Scott & Hart, 1971). First, and foremost, the ideology of the organizational imperative leads researchers to view revenge typically as a threat to the well-being of the organization (e.g., Neuman & Baron, 1997; Skarlicki & Folger, 1997). Furthermore, revenge is characterized as a violation of organizational norms, and, as such, a form of deviance (Robinson & Bennett, 1995). The ideology perpetuates a biased and incomplete portrayal of revenge, one that is not consistent with empirical reality.

There is growing body of research that paints a richer, more complete picture of revenge. For example, some organizations recognize revenge as a powerful tool of informal social control (Morrill, 1992)—one that can regulate social behavior in organizations—and thus is functional (Bies & Tripp, 1995, 1996, 1998b). Furthermore, if we look to how revenge impacts the avenger or bystanders, there is evidence that revenge can be constructive for the individual and bystanders. For example, Tripp and Bies (1997) found that avengers report revenge solved the problem at hand, and, in some cases, the revenge protected the powerless bystanders who were being victimized by others in the organization.

The organizational imperative ideology also leads researchers to focus on revenge only in its extreme forms, as in violence (Folger & Skarlicki, 1998), for that is where the threat of revenge is greatest. We do not dispute that feuds and violence occur and can be acts of revenge, but there is empirical evidence that revenge can take a variety of forms, and often it is mundane, informal, and nonviolent (Neuman & Baron, 1997; Skarlicki & Folger, 1997). For example, although revenge can take the form of feuding or physical violence, it more often takes the form of a revenge fantasy, or a private confrontation with the perpetrator, or social withdrawal (e.g., avoidance, withholding support or help), or even forgiveness (Bies & Tripp, 1996).

Fourth, the ideology leads those who study organizational justice to focus primarily on how the fairness of structures and processes can serve management interests (Treviño & Bies, 1997). In fact, many justice researchers could be characterized as apologists for management. Even a cursory examination of academic books and articles on justice finds that organizational researchers have focused almost exclusively on explaining how the justice concept can serve management interests, such as organizational citizenship behaviors (Organ, 1988), organizational commitment (Folger & Konovsky, 1989), and productivity (Greenberg, 1996).

Let us be quite clear that we are not arguing that management does not need excuse makers and apologists, for clearly they do. Rather, we claim that, as justice researchers, we are falling short of our moral responsibility to question how our efforts may unwittingly contribute to perpetuating, not ameliorating, injustice in the workplace. In so doing, we would correctly broaden the research focus to examine how people endure and cope with injustice and become more critical of management practices that motivate revenge (O'Leary-Kelly et al., 1996). For, there is growing recognition that there may be situational events or organizational practices that can precipitate, and even justify, acts of revenge (Bies & Tripp, 1996, 1998a, 1998b; McLean Parks, 1997).

The ideology of the organizational imperative still maintains its stranglehold and influence on organizational justice research (Treviño & Bies, 1997). But, the growing empirical research suggests a more enlightened view of revenge, a view that will reshape our theories of justice. It is to those findings that we turn our attention, beginning with an exploration of the sense of injustice.

THE JUSTICE PROCESS: IT BEGINS WITH THE SENSE OF INJUSTICE

Our analysis begins with the premise that to understand justice in organizations, one must understand the events that arouse the sense of injustice, which are the emotions and passion motivating revenge (Bies, 1987, 2000). Choosing the sense of injustice as the starting point for analyzing justice dynamics has its intellectual roots in the seminal legal theory of Edmond Cahn (1949). In his book, *The Sense of Injustice*, Cahn asked "Why do we speak of the 'sense of injustice' rather than the 'sense of justice'?" (p. 13). Cahn answered:

> Because 'justice' has been so beclouded by natural-law writings that is almost inevitably brings to mind some ideal relation or static condition or set of perceptual standards, while we are concerned, on the contrary, with what is active, vital, and experiential in the reactions of human beings. (p. 13)

For Cahn (1949), justice was "not a state, but a process; not a condition, but an action. 'Justice,' as we shall use the term, means the *active process* of remedying or preventing that which would arouse the sense of injustice" (p. 13). He defined the sense of injustice as "the sympathetic reaction of outrage, horror, shock, resentment, and anger, those affections of the viscera and abnormal secretions of the adrenals that prepare the human animal to resist attack. Nature has thus equipped all men to regard injustice to another as personal aggression" (p. 24).

Building on Cahn's (1949) argument, the sense of injustice is aroused by the provocation of another person. The sense of injustice is a response to a perceived harm or wrongdoing by another party (Tripp & Bies, 1997). It is this provocation that elicits the passion, which motivates the revenge (Bies & Tripp, 1996). Indeed, across a series of studies, those who engage in revenge always report taking action in response to the provoking action of another person (see Tripp & Bies, 1997, for a review of this evidence). As such, revenge is not a random response but an intentional and directed response to perceived harm or wrongdoing. To elaborate, not only was revenge rooted in an intuitive sense of injustice, but it usually reflects a self-controlled response that may not be immediate to the harm. Indeed, in many cases, revenge is a cool and calculated, response (Tripp & Bies, 1997).

OUR MODEL OF REVENGE: TOWARD A NEW THEORY OF JUSTICE

Our model of revenge (Bies et al., 1997) conceptualized a revenge episode in terms of: the specific event that sparked feelings of revenge, arousing the sense of injustice; an interplay of revenge cognitions and emotions, which involves a heating-up process; and the enactment of revenge. Our model will be discussed in more detail later in this section.

Provocation of Justice: Sparking Events

One category of sparking events involves violations of explicit rules, norms, or promises (Bies & Tripp, 1996). Employees are motivated to seek revenge when the formal rules of the organization are violated. One such example is organizational decision makers who change the rules or criteria of decision making after the fact to justify a self-serving judgment (Bies & Tripp, 1996). Another example of rule violation involves a formal breach of a contract between an employee and employer, which can lead to litigation (Bies & Tyler, 1993).

Violations are not limited to formal rules but also include breaches of social norms and etiquette. For example, when bosses or co-workers make promises but then break them, or even lie outright, the victims may be motivated to avenge such wrongs (Bies & Tripp, 1996). More broadly, any perceived inequities on the job or violations of fairness norms can motivate revenge (cf. Skarlicki & Folger, 1997). Examples of such inequities and violations include bosses or co-workers who shirk their job responsibilities, or take undue credit for a team's performance, or outright steal ideas (Bies & Tripp, 1996). The revenge motive may also be salient when private confidences or secrets are disclosed to others inside or outside the organization—that is, when people feel betrayed by someone they trusted (Bies, 1993).

Another category of sparking events centers around status and power derogation (Bies & Tripp, 1996). Several studies suggest that attempts to derogate a person's status or power can motivate revenge. For example, bosses who are hypercritical, overdemanding, and overly harsh—even cruel—in their dealings with subordinates over time, can spark revenge cognitions and emotions (Bies & Tripp, 1996, 1998b). Other revenge-provoking incidents include destructive criticism (Baron, 1988), public ridicule intended to embarrass a subordinate or co-worker (Morrill, 1992), or when the employee is accused wrongly by boss or peer (Bies & Tripp, 1996).

Heating Up: Revenge Emotions and Cognition

The experience of injustice is "hot and passionate," reflecting the intense and personal pain of a violated psyche and sense of self (Bies, 2000). Until the recent research on revenge, the sense of injustice has received little empirical study, although Adams and Freedman (1976) highlighted the need for this type of research. The notable exception is the innovative and insightful work of George Mikula (Mikula, 1986; Mikula, Petri, & Tanzer, 1990).

In our research, we found that the initial revenge emotions are often quite intense, characterized by expressions of pain, anger, and rage. For example, respondents in the Bies and Tripp (1996) study reported that, after they were harmed, they were "mad, angry, and bitter," and felt engulfed in "white-hot" emotions. One participant in the Bies and Tripp study described herself as "inflamed and enraged," and "consumed by the thought of revenge," whereas another participant "needed to satisfy the burning desire of revenge." At the time of these initial emotions, a heating-up process may begin, where emotions and desire for revenge intensify. This process will be shaped by cognitive processes.

Whether the sense of injustice is transformed into revenge depends on how one makes sense of or cognitively processes the harm or wrongdoing. As part of this sense-making process, the assignment of blame is critical. If one can place blame on another person, pain and confusion converts to anger and determination, and thus revenge becomes more likely. It is the assignment of blame that is at the foundation of the rationality and morality of revenge.

One important cognitive process is the attribution process. When people make overly personalistic attributions about the behavior of other organizational members (Kramer, 1994), such judgments can motivate revenge (Bies et al., 1997).

Bies and Tripp (1996) identified two kinds of motives in personalistic attributions: selfishness and malevolence. A selfish harmdoer causes harm for personal profit, picking the victim or avenger purely based on opportunity. A malevolent harmdoer causes harm for the sake of hurting a particular victim. When individuals overattribute sinister and malevolent motives to others' actions, they may perceive harmful intent or believe they are being belittled even in their otherwise seemingly benign social encounters.

A second important cognitive dynamic contributing to individuals' perceptions that they are being intentionally harmed or singled out unfairly is the *biased punctuation of conflict* (Bies et al., 1997). Biased punctuation of conflict refers to a tendency for individuals to construe the history of conflict with others in a self-serving and provocative fashion. Bies et al. (1997) provided this example:

> In an interpersonal conflict with a manager M, a disgruntled employee E may reinterpret the history of interpersonal conflict between them as a sequence of exchanges M-E, M-E, M-E, M-E, in which the initial hostile or aggressive move was made by M (e.g., "She passed me over for promotion just because I was a white male, even though I was clearly the most qualified candidate"). From E's perspective, each of his reactions are legitimate and proportionate responses to a malicious, provocative act by the other.
>
> However, the manager M may punctuate the same history of interaction between them as E-M, E-M, E-M, E-M, in which the roles of "offender" and "responder" are reversed. Thus, for her, their conflict began because he was always late in completing his assignments and seemed passive aggressive towards her, resulting in her decision to select someone else for the management trainee position. (p. 23)

In short, the biased punctuation of conflict contributes to self-justificatory motives: It allows each feuding disputant to believe that the other disputant started it and that revenge is required to, not only even the score, but to stop it, or deter future aggressions. In other words, both sides view their own actions as purely defensive behaviors made in response to the other's unwarranted actions (Kahn & Kramer, 1990). Such beliefs, even when erroneous, provide a rationality and morality for revenge. Indeed, as Frank (1987) perceptively observed, "to defend against a powerful and evil enemy . . ." one must invent justifications to ". . . [shift] responsibility for one's own aggressive actions to the opponent" (p. 340). Consistent with Frank, Bies and Tripp (1996) found that avengers would justify their actions as morally right and in service of justice.

The phenomenon of biased punctuation reminds us that, although revenge behavior often appears to be a response to a specific precipitating event (e.g., a dismissal that is perceived as unjust), such acts are almost always embedded in a protracted history of perceived injustices or conflict (Tjosvold & Chia, 1989; Wall & Callister, 1995). As a result, acts of revenge within organizations are seldom bolts from the blue. Instead, managers and co-workers usually report, especially with the advantage of hindsight, that there had been a protracted history of behaviors and exchanges suggesting something was seriously wrong with the individual (e.g., mutterings, withdrawal, veiled threats, etc.). From the perspective of outsiders, these events often seem minor and unrelated. In the avenger's mind, however, they form a coherent and cumulative pattern of egregious insult and injury, necessitating a proportionate retaliatory response against the organization or one or more of its members. What seems to outsiders like a minor insult becomes perceived as the "straw that broke the camel's back" to the aggrieved avenger (Morrill, 1992).

Doing Justice: Types of Revenge

Our research program has identified a variety of revenge responses (cf. Skarlicki & Folger, 1997). Bies and Tripp (1996; Tripp & Bies, 1997) found that, although not all revenge is motivated by justice, many types of revenge are rooted in the justice motive. Drawing on our research, we identify types of revenge that serve the interests of justice.

A quite common response to revenge-provoking incidents is to do nothing. Such inaction was due to a variety of reasons including giving the perpetrator the benefit of the doubt (Bies & Tripp, 1996). Others did nothing out of fear of retaliation, especially when the perpetrator had been their boss; in other cases, victims did nothing because they rationalized revenge just was not worth it, or that karma would take care of the perpetrator (Tripp & Bies, 1997).

Doing nothing does not necessarily mean resignation; for, often the enactment of revenge occurred intrapsychically (Bies & Tripp, 1996). For example, people reported satisfying their revenge impulses by fantasizing about the painful and sordid revenge they will inflict on the perpetrator but with no intention of acting on those feelings. Sometimes such fantasies were shared publicly, even with co-workers. Thus, in the avenger's mind, justice is served through these fantasies. At least, fantasizing serves as coping response that allows one to blow off steam (Bies et al., 1997) or vent the emotions associated with injustice. Such relief may be all that is required for an avenger to get over it and continue on in productive work relationships.

What also might appear as inaction may also be construed by the avenger as justice served. Some people serve justice when they, the victims, forgive their perpetrators (Bies & Tripp, 1996). In forgiving, avengers reported that when they let go, it released the anger and desire for revenge.

Beyond inaction, there are several types of revenge whose objective is behaviorally to deliver justice or remedy injustice (Bies & Tripp, 1996; Tripp & Bies, 1997). Some avengers seek justice by working harder. For example, in response to humiliating public criticism of their work performance, people might work harder to prove the critic, often their boss, wrong. This action would restore their own status while tarnishing their critic's credibility. Tripp and Bies (1997) reported about one respondent who discovered that her boss lied to her about her qualifications for a promotion. She later discovered that she was qualified and that her boss believed women should not work in that kind of job. She confronted her boss on the lie, then continually worked harder to overcome the obstacles her boss threw at her. Not only did she overcome the obstacles, but she later quit working for him to take the promotion. From the avenger's perspective, justice is served when people, whose work is slighted by their bosses, get even by working harder and publicizing their successes, thus making the boss look bad in the process, and getting their deserved outcomes (Bies & Tripp, 1996).

Some avengers prefer a more direct approach such as private confrontations with the perpetrators to problem solve and negotiate fair resolutions to their situations. Thus, justice can also be served when the perpetrators of harm receive feedback that particular behaviors or attitudes hurt others or are inappropriate (Bies & Tripp, 1996). Often, the perpetrators are unaware of the harms they commit against co-workers and being made aware is sufficient for them to correct their behaviors. In these situations, the avengers seek to restore justice by eliminating the source of the injustice, but do they do not necessarily seek recompense beyond the discomfort such private confrontations inflict on the perpetrators.

Other avengers seek more: Not only do they want to eliminate the source of the injustice but they focus on retributive justice (Hogan & Emler, 1981)—they want to harm the perpetrator. In Bies and Tripp (1996) and Tripp and Bies (1997), we found retributive elements in the following types of revenge: public complaints designed to humiliate another person, public demands for apologies that are intended to embarrass the perpetrator, bad-mouthing the perpetrator, whistleblowing, and litigation.

Other forms of revenge resembled inequity reduction responses. For example, people might avoid the perpetrators for a short period of time, refusing to greet them or even acknowledge their presence. Or, people might withhold effort or work (Bies & Tripp, 1996; Tripp & Bies, 1997, such as deliberately not supporting the perpetrator when support is needed, or intentionally turning in poor work performance. Other people sometimes transfer out of the job or department, as the ultimate act of withholding support and friendship. In all these acts, the benefit the perpetrator receives from the avenger is reduced or eliminated, thus restoring equity in the relationship.

It is worth noting that, no matter in what type of revenge avengers engage, avengers are aware of the effects of their actions on others beyond themselves and their perpetrators: Bystanders may also benefit or get caught in the crossfire. Bies and Tripp (1998a) collected data on how avengers evaluate their acts of revenge. From this data emerged a multiple-stakeholder taxonomy. Avengers identified three groups of people who their revenge helps or hurts: the avengers themselves, the perpetrators, and bystanders. Avengers justified revenge that not only helped themselves, or that restored equity between an avenger and perpetrator but that also helped bystanders. In the Bies and Tripp (1998a) study, some respondents claimed that in getting even with corporate bullies, they stood up for others who could not stand up for themselves. Correcting an injustice done to innocent bystanders, and particularly done for those who are powerless, can be a sufficiently motivating principle for revenge (Bies & Tripp, 1998b).

CONCLUSION

In a nutshell, there is clear and consistent empirical evidence that revenge has its own moral imperative. First, revenge is, in many cases, a response to a perceived injustice. Second, revenge is most often intended to restore justice. For instance, while engaging in revenge, people reported their strong belief that they were doing the right thing and that they were doing justice. Third, although the act of revenge may have served self-interest, it often serves other interests, and it is usually justified in moral terms. The justice rationality can be a powerful motivation and justification for revenge.

In assessing the morality of revenge as an observer, one must use not just the organization's interests. One must look also at revenge through the eyes of the avenger and innocent bystanders in assessing the morality of revenge. In other words, the morality of revenge must be evaluated in terms of three different stakeholders who may be affected: the avenger, the perpetrator, and bystanders (Bies & Tripp, 1998a). There may be times where revenge does more good than harm, even if the good is to the employees and the harm is to (some members of) the upper management. Certainly, that is the way the avengers often view it and justify it.

If researchers wish to understand when and why people in organizations become avengers and to understand what form and level of vengeance they seek, then they must understand the avengers' perspectives. This means that goals and viewpoints other than those prescribed by top management must be considered. Furthermore, it must also be assumed that avengers are rational, moral beings: They are goal directed, respond to their environment, often cooly calculate the costs and benefits of their actions, and justify their actions. They are not necessarily random, crazed, impetuous, petulant, or otherwise stupid or evil, as portrayed by the popular stereotypes of vengeance seekers and their acts of revenge (Barreca, 1995, Jacoby, 1983).

ACKNOWLEDGMENT

We owe a debt of gratitude to Rod Kramer for his contribution in stimulating and enriching our analysis of revenge.

REFERENCES

Adams, J. S. (1965). Inequity in social exchange. In L. Berkowitz (Ed.), *Advances in experimental social psychology* (pp. 267–299). New York: Academic.

Adams, J. S., & Freedman, S. (1976). Equity theory revisited: Comments and annotated bibliography. In L. Berkowitz (Ed.), *Advances in experimental social psychology* (pp. 43–90). New York: Academic.

Baron, R. A. (1988). Negative effects of destructive criticism: Impact on conflict, self-efficacy, and task performance. *Journal of Applied Psychology, 73,* 199–207.

Barreca, R. (1995). *Sweet Revenge: The wicked delights of getting even.* New York: Harmony Books.

Bies, R. J. (1987). The predicament of injustice: The management of moral outrage. In L. L. Cummings & B. M. Staw (Eds.), *Research in organizational behavior* (pp. 289–319). Greenwich, CT: JAI.

Bies, R. J. (1993). Privacy and procedural justice in organizations. *Social Justice Research, 6,* 69–86.

Bies, R. J. (2000). Interactional (in)justice: The sacred and the profane. In J. Greenberg & R. Cropanzano (Eds.), *Advances in organizational behavior.* San Francisco: New Lexington.

Bies, R. J., & Tripp, T. M. (1995). The use and abuse of power: Justice as social control. In R. Cropanzano & M. Kacmar (Eds.), *Organizational politics, justice, and support: Managing social climate at work* (pp. 131–145). New York: Quorum.

Bies, R. J., & Tripp, T. M. (1996). Beyond distrust: "Getting even" and the need for revenge. In R. M. Kramer & T. Tyler (Eds.), *Trust in organizations* (pp. 246–260). Newbury Park: Sage.

Bies, R. J., & Tripp, T. M. (1998a). The many faces of revenge: The good, the bad, and the ugly. In R. W. Griffin, A. O'Leary-Kelly & J. Collins (Eds.), *Monographs in organizational behavior and industrial relations* (Vol. 23: Dysfunctional behavior in organizations: Part B: Non-violent dysfunctional behavior, pp. 49–67). Greenwich, CT: JAI.

Bies, R. J., & Tripp, T. M. (1998b). Two faces of the powerless: Coping with tyranny. In R. M. Kramer & M. A. Neale (Eds.), *Power and influence in organizations* (pp. 203–219). Thousand Oaks, CA: Sage.

Bies, R. J., Tripp, T. M., & Kramer, R. M. (1997). At the breaking point: Cognitive and social dynamics of revenge in organizations. In R. A. Giacalone & J. Greenberg (Eds.), *Antisocial behavior in organizations* (pp. 18–36). Thousand Oaks, CA: Sage.

Bies, R. J., & Tyler, T. (1993). The "litigation mentality" in organizations: A test of alternative psychological explanations. *Organization Science, 4,* 352–366.

Cahn, E. (1949). *The sense of injustice.* New York: New York University Press.

Crosby, F. (1976). A model of egoistic relative deprivation. *Psychological Review, 83,* 85–113.

Feinberg, J. (1974). Noncomparative justice. *The Philosophical Review, 83,* 297–338.

Folger, R., & Konovsky, M. A. (1989). Effects of procedural and distributive justice on reactions to pay raise decisions. *Academy of Management Journal, 32,* 115–130.

Folger, R., & Skarlicki, D. P. (1998). A popcorn metaphor for employee aggression. In R. W. Griffin, A. O'Leary-Kelly & J. Collins (Eds.), *Monographs in organizational behavior and industrial relations* (Vol. 23: Dysfunctional behavior in organizations: Part A: Violent and deviant behavior, pp. 43–81). Greenwich, CT: JAI.

Frank, J. D. (1987). The drive for power and the nuclear arms race. *American Psychologist, 42,* 337–344.

Greenberg, J. (1996). *The quest for justice on the job: Essays and experiments.* Thousand Oaks, CA: Sage.

Greenberg, J. (1997). A social influence model of employee theft: Beyond the fraud triangle. In R. J. Lewicki, R. J. Bies & B. H. Sheppard (Eds.), *Research on negotiation in organizations* (Vol. 6, pp. 29–51). Greenwich, CT: JAI.

Hogan, R., & Emler, N. P. (1981). Retributive justice. In M. J. Lerner & S. C. Lerner (Eds.), *The justice motive in social behavior* (pp. 125–143). New York: Plenum.

Jacoby, S. (1983). *Wild Justice: The Evolution of Revenge.* New York: Harper & Row.

Kahn, R. L., & Kramer, R. M. (1990). Untying the knot: De-escalatory processes in international conflict. In R. L. Kahn & M. N. Zald (Eds.), *Organizations and nation-states: New perspectives on conflict and cooperation* (pp. 139–180). San Francisco: Jossey-Bass.

Kramer, R. M. (1994). The sinister attribution error. *Motivation and Emotion, 18,* 199–231.

McLean Parks, J. (1997). The fourth arm of justice: The art and science of revenge. In R. J. Lewicki, R. J. Bies & B. H. Sheppard (Eds.), *Research on negotiation in organizations* (pp. 113–144). Greenwich, CT: JAI.

Mikula, G. (1986). The experience of injustice: Toward a better understanding of its phenomenology. In H. W. Bierhoff, R. L. Cohen & J. Greenberg (Eds.), *Justice in interpersonal relations* (pp. 103–123). New York: Plenum.

Mikula, G., Petri, B., & Tanzer, N. (1990). What people regard as just and unjust: Types and structures of everyday experiences of injustice. *European Journal of Social Psychology, 20,* 133–149.

Morrill, C. (1992). Vengeance among executives. *Virginia Review of Sociology, 1,* 51–76.

Neuman, J. H., & Baron, R. A. (1997). Aggression in the workplace. In R. A. Giacalone & J. Greenberg (Eds.), *Antisocial behavior in organizations* (pp. 37–67). Thousand Oaks, CA: Sage.

O'Leary-Kelly, A. M., Griffin, R. W., & Glew, D. J. (1996). Organization-motivated aggression: A research framework. *Academy of Management Review, 21,* 225–253.

Organ, D. W. (1988). *Organizational citizenship behavior: The good soldier syndrome.* Lexington, MA: Lexington Books.

Pomfert, J. (1995, December 18). Atrocities leave thirst for vengeance in Balkans. *The Washington Post,* A1.

Robinson, S. L., & Bennett, R. J. (1995). A typology of deviant workplace behaviors: A multidimensional scaling study. *Academy of Management Journal, 38,* 555–572.

Scott, W. G., & Hart, D. K. (1971). The moral nature of man in organizations: A comparative analysis. *Academy of Management Journal, 14,* 255+.

Scott, W. G., & Hart, D. K. (1979). *Organizational America: Can individual freedom survive within the security it promises?* Boston: Houghton Mifflin.

Skarlicki, D. P., & Folger, R. (1997). Retaliation in the workplace: The roles of distributive, procedural, and interactional justice. *Journal of Applied Psychology, 82,* 434–443.

Solomon, R. C. (1990). *A passion for justice: Emotions and the origins of the social contract.* Reading, MA: Addison-Wesley.

Tjosvold, D., & Chia, L. C. (1989). Conflict between managers and workers: The role of cooperation and competition. *The Journal of Social Psychology, 129,* 235–247.

Treviño, L. K., & Bies, R. J. (1997). Through the looking glass: A normative manifesto for organizational behavior. In C. L. Cooper & S. E. Jackson (Eds.), *Creating tomorrow's organizations: A handbook for future research in organizational behavior* (pp. 439–452). London: Wiley.

Tripp, T. M., & Bies, R. J. (1997). What's good about revenge? The avenger's perspective. In R. J. Lewicki, R. J. Bies & B. H. Sheppard (Eds.), *Research on negotiation in organizations* (pp. 145–160). Greenwich, CT: JAI.

Wall, J. A. Jr., & Callister, R. R. (1995). Conflict and its management. *Journal of Management, 21,* 515–558.

Organizational Justice
in Strategic Decision Making

M. Audrey Korsgaard
Harry J. Sapienza
David M. Schweiger
University of South Carolina

You are the CEO of an international manufacturing firm considering major opportunities in the United States, South America, and China. Your strengths are in the American markets, but the less stable Asian market is growing more rapidly. New, fiercer competitors are emerging on all fronts and pursuing one opportunity may foreclose the others. You are under considerable pressure from investors and your board to continue increasing earnings per share, while growing revenue and improving margins. You have received critical input from your top managers representing various functions and regions, but you fear their positions may too strongly reflect their parochial interests. Nevertheless, you will need their commitment to carry out whatever is decided. What do you do?

This short scenario is not unlike those being faced by many CEOs and division presidents (hereafter referred to as CEOs) today. CEOs and their top-management teams must make and implement strategic decisions that deliver both short-term financial results and position the firm for future success.[1] Neither one alone is an easy task. This chapter addresses the challenges faced by top-management teams in making and implementing strategic decisions and the role organizational justice can play in dealing with these challenges. This chapter is divided into three sections. The first section discusses the challenges and determinants of effective

---

[1]Early on, theorists tended to focus on the functions of the chief executive in making strategic decisions (e.g., Barnard, 1938; Selznick, 1957), but more recently theorists have recognized that strategic decision making involves a group or "team" of top decision makers rather than being the sole responsibility of the CEO (Hambrick & Mason, 1984). Therefore, it should be kept in mind that when we speak of "top management" in the following sections we are referring to this group.

strategic decision making. The second section addresses how organizational justice can impact strategic decisions. The final section provides practical recommendations and directions for future research.

THE NATURE OF STRATEGIC DECISIONS AND STRATEGIC DECISION MAKING

Simply put, strategic decisions are decisions on issues most important to the overall welfare of the firm (Mintzberg, Raisinghani, & Theoret, 1976). Strategic decisions are likely to be the sole province of top management, involve large amounts of the firm's resources, tend to be long-term in orientation, have multifunctional or multibusiness consequences, and require consideration of the firm's external environment (Pearce & Robinson, 1997). For example, strategic decisions may involve such issues as entry into a new market or exit from an existing market, diversification into new businesses, or the development of new core competencies and competitive weapons. Clearly, what strategy a firm determines to pursue is critical to its long-term survival and performance. Although considerable research and theory exist on what strategies are most effective under various circumstances, less well understood is the process by which optimal strategic decisions might be reached and implemented (Eisenhardt & Zbaracki, 1992). Therefore, the process of making strategic decisions is currently a major area of inquiry in the field of strategic management.

The effectiveness of the strategic decision making can be evaluated against three criteria: quality, commitment, and continuity (Amason, 1996). First, an effective decision-making process should yield high-quality decisions. High-quality strategic decisions are well-reasoned and formulated on sound assumptions and facts (Schweiger, Sandberg, & Rechner, 1989). Research and theory suggests that the decision-making process, particularly the process of gathering and evaluating information, plays a role in determining decision quality (Wooldridge & Floyd, 1989). Second, an effective decision should result in outcome consensus among members of the senior management team. Outcome consensus refers to the extent to which senior managers understand the strategy and are committed to carrying it out (Dess, 1987; Wooldridge & Floyd, 1990). Research suggests that the decision-making process itself affects the degree of outcome consensus among management team members (Schweiger et al., 1989; Wooldridge & Floyd, 1989). Finally, effective decision processes ensure the continuance of the team as a trusting and cohesive unit. That is, to be successful over time, the strategic decision processes should reinforce the interpersonal relationships among team members so that the team can continue to work together cooperatively in formulating and implementing new strategy. The process of strategic decision making can serve to strengthen or undermine the decision-making team's social structure (Amason, 1996).

The Challenges of the Strategic Decision-Making Process

Several characteristics of the strategic decision-making context make the process of strategic decision making unique and challenging. First, because strategic decisions unfold in an unpredictable future, they are marked by high uncertainty. The pace and depth of change in many industries and technologies today (D'Aveni, 1994) render accurate forecasting difficult, if not impossible. Additionally, because of the inherent uncertainty, often, the top management team cannot confidently distinguish accurate assumptions and forecasts from inaccurate ones.

Second, strategic decisions require the consideration of a complex array of variables. For example, many industries are facing multiple environmental demands such as deregulation (e.g., electric power, banking, telecommunications), emerging international markets (e.g., China), and globalization (e.g., branded footwear). Moreover, as the number of external factors increases, so does the number of internal factors. For example, as a firm pursues more international markets, it will have to manage more geographically dispersed functions, product lines, or subsidiaries.

Third, the high stakes involved in strategic decisions place top managers under a great deal of pressure to make the right decisions and to make them quickly. By definition, such decisions may affect the future direction, value, or even survival of a firm. For example, a poor acquisition or move into a new market can have a lingering financial impact on a firm and preclude it from pursuing future opportunities. Top managers are under tremendous economic pressure from vigilant shareholders and employees dependent on the financial success of the firm. They also face great competitive pressure to produce high-quality goods economically and on time. And they face social pressure to meet community, government, and interest group standards. All of these are managed in the face of ever-narrowing windows of opportunity and product development times.

Fourth, because of the inherently political nature of the process, it is often difficult to reach agreement on what the optimal course of action will be. Although there are shared interests among top managers (e.g., survival of the firm, bonuses), there also may be personal interests (e.g., power and position) that may or may not be aligned with those of other executives or the good of the firm. When such interests are not aligned, executives are likely to engage in political behavior that furthers their own, or their organizational unit's, interests (Cyert & March, 1963). Such behavior may include attempting to influence strategic decisions to their favor, withholding or filtering the information other executives receive, or failing to support the implementation of strategic decisions. The very uncertainty and complexity of the situation facing top managers often means that no one position is clearly and obviously superior. As a result, it is unclear whether positions held by various members of top management reflect an honest evaluation of evidence or disguised self-interests.

Finally, strategic decisions typically involve an ongoing process. Strategic decisions are often a series of interrelated decisions that are made and implemented over a period of time (e.g., months or years). They may be based on a clear articulation of the firm's strategic direction (e.g., to consolidate a fragmented market through acquisition), followed by a series of supporting decisions (e.g., to make a particular acquisition). Or, they may be the net result of a series of seemingly unrelated discrete decisions (e.g., a series of new product introductions) that cumulate to have a major strategic impact (Bower, 1970; Lindblom, 1959). Thus, top managers often need to revisit, revise, and append strategic initiatives.

These five challenges illustrate the importance of and difficulty in achieving quality, consensus, and continuity in strategic decision processes. The uncertainty and complexity inherent in strategic issues strain top managers' ability to make high-quality decisions, whereas the high (and often conflicting) stakes of top managers render consensus difficult to achieve. Conflict of interests may also lead to infighting and factionalism that, given the on-going nature of the strategic management process, can prove fatal to the long-term viability of strategic initiatives as well as the team itself.

Antecedents of Quality, Consensus, and Continuity in Strategic Decision Making

This section reviews research regarding the factors contributing to decision quality, outcome consensus, and team continuity. As illustrated in Fig. 10.1, these factors can be grouped into two main aspects of the strategic decision-making process: cognitive aspects and social–political aspects.

Cognitive Aspects of the Decision-Making Process

The cognitive aspects most often studied have been the extent or comprehensiveness of information processing (including the amount of information seeking, information sharing, and information analysis used to reach decisions), the speed with which such decisions are reached and the amount of debate or conflict in the process. The extent of information processing is thought to have a direct and positive impact the quality of strategic decisions. This view is based on the assumption that the high levels of uncertainty and complexity characteristic of strategic problems require extensive information search, analysis, and generation of ideas to reach the required level of decision quality (Galbraith, 1973; Schweiger & Sandberg, 1989; Schweiger, Sandberg, & Ragan, 1986; Schweiger et al., 1989). In support of this view, Bourgeois and Eisenhardt (1988) found in in-depth case studies that the best performing firms had top-management teams that considered a greater range of alternatives more thoroughly. Kim and Mauborgne (1995) also found that subsidiary performance was higher among firms that engaged in more extensive information processing in the strategic decision-making process.

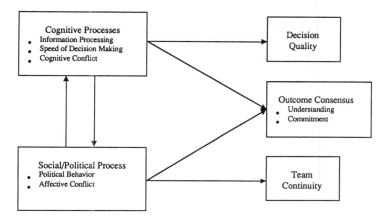

FIG. 10.1.   Antecedents of decision quality, outcome consensus, and team continuity in strategic decision making.

Greater information processing is also predicted to have a positive impact on outcome consensus (Kim & Mauborgne, 1995), although the evidence is not clear. The more information seeking, sharing, and evaluating team members do, the more they should understand both the prioritization of organizational goals and the means intended to achieve them. Wooldridge and Floyd (1990) found that greater involvement in the strategic decision process led to greater understanding of the decision. However, they found no relationship between involvement and commitment to the decision. They concluded that involvement alone was not enough to secure managers' commitment, rather that substantive involvement would enhance both understanding and commitment only when the participants play a substantive role in the process.

The speed of decision making is another cognitive aspect of the strategic decision-making process thought to affect decision quality, although the relationship is not well-established in the literature. On the surface, fast decision making suggests less comprehensiveness, and thus, potentially lower quality decisions. Kim and Mauborgne (1995), for example, argued that processes requiring greater information processing would necessarily result in slower decisions. However, of two factors expected to increase information processing, they found that one (opportunity to refute others' ideas) led to slower decisions whereas the other (familiarity with context) hastened decision making. Bourgeois and Eisenhardt (1988) challenged the idea that comprehensiveness and decision integration are negatively associated with decision speed. In fact, they found that top-management teams making more integrated decisions and considering more alternatives made faster decisions than those considering a smaller, less integrated set. They argued that the very comprehensiveness and integration of information allowed such teams to reach decisions in a more efficient manner. It should be noted, however, that their study included only eight top-management teams and that the high-performing teams were those also beset by the least amount of political behavior and infighting.

Another cognitive aspect of the decision-making process is the amount of debate or cognitive conflict in the decision procedure. A conflict procedure uses active debate and surfacing of differences of views as a technique for generating diverse opinions, preferences, and assumptions among managers (Schweiger et al., 1986). This approach is often contrasted with consensus approaches, which focus on identifying similarities of views as a vehicle by which to reach decisions. (Note that consensus as a process is distinct from outcome consensus: Consensus processes refer to the decision rules top-management teams use to reach strategic decisions). A series of studies examining the relative efficacy of conflict (e.g., devil's advocacy and dialectical inquiry) versus consensus processes found that groups using conflict techniques produce higher quality decisions (Schweiger et al., 1986; Schweiger et al., 1989; Schweiger & Sandberg, 1989). Thus, conflict techniques may help tap the diverse knowledge of decision participants as well as the latent creativity in the group (Amason & Schweiger, 1997).

Although conflict processes increase decision quality, research suggests that they negatively affect outcome consensus and team continuity. Studies by Schweiger and colleagues (Schweiger et al., 1986; Schweiger et al., 1989 Schweiger & Sandberg, 1989) showed that groups using consensus techniques were more satisfied with their decisions and more inclined to wish to work together in the future than were groups using conflict techniques. Furthermore, in their review of the strategic decision-making literature, Finkelstein and Hambrick (1996) concluded that heterogeneous top-management teams that produced high-quality decisions via debate are also likely to be ill-structured for implementation. That is, the high levels of conflict observed in such groups are seen to undermine the outcome consensus and team continuity necessary for high-performing top-management teams.

Social–Political Aspects of the Decision-Making Process

The outcomes of strategic decision processes have also been shown to be influenced by the social–political elements in the strategic decision-making process. Two elements in particular are relevant: the degree of political behavior and affective conflict occurring during the decision-making process.

Broadly conceived as the use of power or influence to create unity of strategic direction, politics has at times been depicted as an endemic, necessary, or even useful element of strategic decision making (Cyert & March, 1963; Selznick, 1957). However, more narrowly defined as activities aimed at steering the strategy process toward the achievement of personal or subgroup goals without regard to the welfare of the organization as a whole, political activities such as hard influence tactics (e.g., coalition formation), bargaining, and secrecy or obstruction have generally been seen as dysfunctional (Pearce, 1997).

Political behavior is likely to have a direct negative impact on outcome consensus and team continuity. When top managers perceive that others are attempting to manipulate the process for their own gain, they distrust the individuals, end up uncommitted to decisions reached, and are disinclined to work together on future decisions. Moreover, because political tactics can involve obstruction and secrecy, the top-management team as a whole is less likely to understand and accept decisions or one another. For example, Tjosvold and Field (1983) found that when subgroups lobby for their own goals (rather than global ones), they have relatively less understanding of and commitment to goals actually selected. Similarly, Eisenhardt and Bourgeois (1988) found the use of political tactics in decision-making processes related to dissatisfaction with decisions and with one another.

Recent evidence also indicates that social or affective conflict among top-management teams is likely to undermine outcome consensus and team continuity. Affective conflict is emotional conflict involving interpersonal friction and disputes, whereas cognitive conflict is intellectual disagreement over task-related ideas (Amason, 1996). Amason found that strategic decision processes marked by affective conflict resulted in lower commitment to the decisions reached and less satisfaction in working with the group. Amason noted that cognitive conflict and affective conflict were highly correlated with one another and speculated that affective conflict may be a by-product of cognitive conflict.

Social–political aspects of the decision-making process are also likely to adversely affect decision quality. Research indicates that both political behavior (Eisenhardt & Bourgeois, 1988) and affective conflict (Amason, 1996) are associated with lower quality decisions. Social–political processes are thought to affect the quality of strategic decision by hindering the cognitive aspects of the process. For example, Whitney and Smith (1983) found that subgroup friction resulted in less information sharing. Similarly, Guth and MacMillan (1986) found political activity associated with misrepresentation of information and stalling tactics. Moreover, both Eisenhardt and Bourgeois (1988) and Tjosvold and Field (1983) found competition and political activity among group members associated with slower decision making.

An Unresolved Dilemma: Achieving Quality, Commitment, and Continuity

The literature previously reviewed suggests how decision-making processes affect quality, commitment, and continuity. Specifically, cognitive processes marked by high levels of information processing and cognitive conflict appear to enhance decision quality and outcome consensus, and political behavior and affective conflict appear to adversely affect decision, outcome consensus and continuity, and, indirectly, quality. However, the literature also indicates that the effects of social and cognitive processes are complex and potentially noncomplementary.

Although cognitive conflict is a positive process for enhancing decision quality, it may indirectly have an adverse effect on outcome consensus and team continuity. As Amason (1996) suggested, cognitive conflict may stimulate affective conflict, which will negatively impact outcome consensus and team continuity. Furthermore, research suggests that enhancing the information processing capability of the group (e.g., through team membership diversity), may directly hinder consensus and continuity (Cho, Hambrick, & Chen, 1994; Priem, 1990; Smith, Smith, Olian, Sims, O'Banna & Scully, 1994). Moreover, political behavior and affective conflict may inhibit information sharing and the team's ability to reach a decision in a timely manner. Thus, techniques that focus only on enhancing cognitive processes may ensure decision quality in the short run, but without attention to social–political aspects, the information processing capability of the team may decline over time.

In summary, the current literature poses a dilemma. Specifically, how does a top-management team (or its CEO) promote diverse views, active debate, and choose the best decision regardless of the preferences of some team members without undermining consensus and threatening the long-term viability of the team? Researchers have argued that the problems associated with conflict among team members may be addressed by establishing a team culture that encourages open debate as well as supportive behavior among team members (Amason & Sapienza, 1997; Schweiger & Sandberg, 1991). Yet current research offers little in the way of explanation as to how such teams develop the openness and sense of mutuality associated with high-cognitive conflict and low-affective conflict.

Procedural justice theory may provide a solution to this dilemma. Because procedural justice theory addresses the process of decision making independent of the decision outcomes, this approach can help disentangle the dilemma of balancing cognitive and social–political processes. Specifically, as proposed in the following, procedural justice theory provides a framework for decision processes that can promote outcome consensus and team continuity without sacrificing decision quality. Furthermore, we suggest that adhering to the principles of fair decision processes will enhance quality over time through its effects on the willingness of team members to share information.

PROCEDURAL JUSTICE IN STRATEGIC DECISION MAKING

Principles of Procedural Justice

Organizational justice concerns the fairness in decision making. The theory suggests that individuals are highly sensitive to the fairness of both the process and outcomes of decision making. Two main classes of fairness perceptions are important: *distributive justice*, the fairness of the distribution of resources; and *procedural justice*, the fairness of the procedures used to make the distribution. Distributive justice perceptions are thought to be governed by norms of fair exchange or equity. Specifically, individuals want decisions to result in outcomes that are commensurate with the contributions they provided (Walster, Walster, & Berscheid, 1978) or are consistent with what they expected to receive (Crosby, 1976; Folger, 1986). That is, when a decision outcome is consistent with an individual's beliefs or expectations, the individual is likely to perceived the outcome as distributively just.

In contrast, procedural justice addresses control over the decision-making process; as such, procedural justice perceptions are determined by various aspects of the decision-making procedure. One of the most important procedural factors is process control or voice, which refers to the opportunity for affected parties to voice their opinions or present evidence in the process of decision making (Lind & Tyler, 1988). In addition, Leventhal (1980) identified six principles that promote procedural justice: consistent application of criteria, bias suppression, utilization of accurate information, correctability of error, representativeness, and ethics. More broadly, formal rules and procedures that are consistent with principles of due process (e.g., adequate forewarning, opportunity for appeal) are generally viewed as more procedurally just (Folger, Konovsky, & Cropanzano, 1992; Sheppard & Lewicki, 1987). In addition to formal rules, the conduct of the decision maker influences perceptions of procedural justice; this form of procedural justice is termed *interactional justice* (Tyler & Bies, 1990).[2] Unlike institutionally sanctioned formal procedures, interactional factors are under the discretion of the decision maker. Bies and colleagues (Tyler & Bies, 1990; Folger & Bies, 1989) identified two main dimensions of interactional justice: *proper enactment of procedures* and *proper interpersonal treatment*. Proper enactment of procedures refers to behavior that demonstrates the decision maker's integrity, such as the suppression of personal biases, timely feedback, and justification for the decision. Proper interpersonal treatment refers to behavior that demonstrates the decision maker's interpersonal sensitivity, such as being truthful in communication and treating people with courtesy and respect.

Lind (1997) noted that procedural justice perceptions are pivotal cognitions in determining organizational attitudes and behavior, many of which are pertinent to strategic decision making. Individuals are more apt to find the decision acceptable and satisfactory if they believe that they were treated fairly in the process. Procedural justice also affects the quality of relationships individuals have with the leader, the group, and the organization. Specifically, procedural justice has a positive impact on trust in the decision maker, social harmony, and organizational commitment (Alexander & Ruderman, 1987; Folger & Konovsky, 1989; Korsgaard & Roberson, 1995). Procedural justice is also positively associated with cooperative behavior (Konovsky & Pugh, 1994; Moorman, Niehoff, & Organ, 1993). Furthermore, research indicates that procedural justice can have an impact

---

[2]Unless otherwise indicated, we use the term *procedural justice* throughout the remainder of this section to encompass both just rules–procedures and interactional fairness.

on reactions beyond the impact of distributive justice. That is, regardless of the perceived fairness of outcomes, individuals who perceive the decision procedures or treatment as fair are more apt to find the decision acceptable, trust the decision maker and be committed to the organization (Folger & Konovsky, 1989). Moreover, procedural justice often interacts with distributive justice (Brockner & Wiesenfeld, 1996). Specifically, the effect of procedural justice tends to be stronger the more unfair or unfavorable the outcomes are perceived to be. Thus, procedural justice can ameliorate the negative effects of an unfavorable or unfair allocation of resources.

A premise of this research is that procedural fairness operates through the dual mechanisms of self-interest and relational concerns (Lind & Tyler, 1988; Tyler & Lind, 1992). Fair procedures and treatment assure individuals that there is a structure (or key decision maker) in place that will fairly serve them, even if the outcome of particular decision was unfavorable. Thus, in the long run, their interests will be protected. The relational model of organizational justice (Tyler & Lind, 1992) suggests that justice is also important for what it signals regarding an individual's status. That is, individuals value procedural justice because it helps define and validate one's status and worth in the group or organization.

Implications for Strategic Decision Making

The earlier review of strategic decision making posed a dilemma of balancing cognitive and social–political processes in strategic decision-making processes. As outlined in Fig. 10.2, we argue that procedural justice theory provides a framework for understanding how strategic decision-making processes can be managed to allow for maximal use of the team's cognitive capabilities while sustaining the social fiber of the team. Specifically, we propose that procedural justice will promote positive social interactions during the strategic decision-making process and, consequently, positively impact outcome consensus and team continuity. We further argue that by enhancing the flow of information among team members, adhering to the principles of fair decision processes will enhance decision quality. We discuss these proposed relationships in the following sections.

Procedural Justice in Strategic Decision Processes

As Fig. 10.2 suggests, we expect procedural justice to benefit quality, consensus, and continuity through its effect on social and cognitive processes. With respect to social processes, interactional justice is likely to be particularly relevant in managing affective conflict. One main aspect of interactional fairness is proper treatment (Tyler & Bies, 1990) or interpersonal sensitivity (Greenberg, 1993), which involves showing concern for affected parties and treating them with dignity and respect. These actions preserve an individual's standing in the organization (Tyler & Lind, 1992). Research suggests that actions that threaten one's standing or identity may lead to personalizing the conflict (Bies & Tripp, 1996;

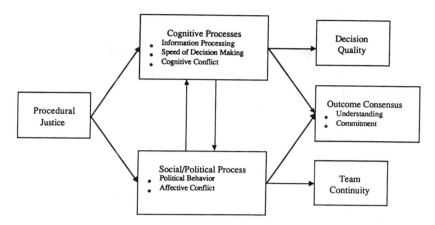

FIG. 10.2. A framework for the impact of procedural justice on strategic decision making.

Bies, Tripp, & Kramer, 1997). Conversely, a high degree of interpersonal sensitivity may minimize affective conflict, even when the outcome is unfavorable. For example, Baron (1993) found that when managers received unfavorable feedback in an interpersonally sensitive manner, they considered it fair and believed it was motivated by the critic's desire to help them. These findings suggest that in the context of strategic decision making, affective conflict can be managed by following principles of interactional justice, specifically, by displaying interpersonal sensitivity.

Another important aspect of interactional justice, social accounts or informational justice (Greenberg, 1993), may also be instrumental in managing affective conflict. Social accounts involves providing an explanation of the procedures used to make decisions (Bies & Shaprio, 1988). As noted previously, Amason (1996) suggested that cognitive or task-based conflict among team members can lead to or degrade into affective or personal conflict. Amason and Sapienza's (1997) work suggests that one reason why cognitive conflict may lead to affective conflict is that team members may misinterpret the meaning or intent of intellectual debate. Team members are particularly likely to make such a misinterpretation when inadequate explanation is provided for opposing views. Thus, when a team member makes an effort to provide a reasonable explanation for an opposing view, such opposition is likely to be viewed as rational and just by other members of the team. In this way, social accounts may limit the extent that cognitive conflict spills over into affective conflict.

Procedural justice is likely to have a positive impact on the cognitive aspects of the strategic decision-making processes in two ways. First, research and theory suggest that procedural justice is likely to directly affect the degree of information processing in team decision making. Certain aspects of formal and informal procedures, such as voice, timely feedback and justification, involve information sharing and should thus have a positive impact on the amount of information exchanged. Additionally, procedural justice may indirectly enhance cognitive aspects of decision making through its affect on social–political aspects. As noted previously, interactional justice is likely to promote more positive social interactions among team members. Social interactions characterized by a high degree of affective conflict and political behavior are apt to result in withholding or distorting information, thereby disrupting the cognitive aspects of the decision process (Bourgeois & Eisenhardt, 1988; Guth & MacMillan 1986; Pearce, 1997; Whitney & Smith, 1983).

Decision Quality

Through its impact on cognitive processing, procedural justice may enhance the quality of decisions. To the extent that informational aspects of procedural justice are followed, such as soliciting input and providing timely feedback, more information is likely to be exchanged. Furthermore, to the extent that the decision process is conducted with interpersonal sensitivity, team members should be more willing to share information. As a result of this greater information flow, decision quality should be enhanced.

Evidence regarding the impact of procedural justice on decision quality is presently underdeveloped. Using global learning, balance between local and global concerns, organization renewal and decision speed as indicators of decision quality in multinationals, Kim and Mauborgne (1995) obtained mixed results regarding the impact of procedural justice. Our own study (Korsgaard et al., 1995) showed that leaders could manage processes fairly without undermining decision quality; in fact, our results suggested that when leaders had the opportunity to incorporate team members' input into the decision, decision quality was enhanced. Furthermore, Johnson (1997) found that procedural justice in strategic decision making was positively correlated with successful implementation of decisions. We cannot say that this result demonstrates a causal effect of fair processes on decision quality. However, consonant with our own study it suggests at a minimum that fair processes do not undermine decision quality.

Procedural Justice and Outcome Consensus

The positive effects of procedural justice on social and cognitive aspects of the decision-making process should result in greater understanding of and commitment to strategic decisions. Information flow is likely to be enhanced when the decision process is conducted in a procedurally just manner. As a result, team members should have greater understanding of the decision. Moreover, when principles of procedural justice are followed, strategic decisions should be resolved with less acrimony; consequently, team members should be more accepting of the decision.

Research and theory on procedural justice also suggests a positive impact on outcome consensus. As noted previously, justice is a powerful determinant of individuals' acceptance of a decision, even when the decision is unfavorable. Thus, proper attention to procedures and interactions should help build outcome consensus by enhancing team members' commitment to and acceptance of a strategic decision, regardless of whether the decision is one that team members initially preferred. Furthermore, procedural and interactional factors can mitigate against adverse reactions to unfair or unfavorable outcomes. Thus, these factors may be particularly important to building outcome consensus to unpopular strategic decisions.

Although empirical work examining the effects of procedural and interactional justice on strategic decision making is sparse, the existing evidence strongly supports these assertions. Kim and Maubourgne (1991) investigated these issues in a study of 145 subsidiaries of 19 multinational corporations competing in various industries. They found that subsidiary managers' perceptions of headquarters' procedural justice in strategic decision making had a positive impact on their satisfaction with the decision. In a follow-up study of 119 of these subsidiaries 10 months later, Kim and Maubourgne (1993) found greater procedural justice associated with greater compliance with the strategic decision. In both studies, the impact of procedural justice existed beyond any effects of distributive justice. Similar findings were obtained in a recent study of 56 international joint ventures (IJVs). Johnson (1997) examined the effects of the procedural and distributive justice in strategic decision making finding teams' perceptions of procedural justice were positively related to their commitment to the strategy, independent of the distributive justice of decisions.

Research also supports the impact of interactionally fair behaviors on attitudes toward strategic decisions. We examined one interactional factor, consideration of input, in a field experiment of 20 intact, fast-track teams in a Fortune 500 company (Korsgaard et al., 1995). We manipulated the consideration leaders gave to team members' input and the control-team members had over the final decision. The findings indicated that consideration had a positive impact on team members' commitment to the strategic decision. This effect was moderated by decision control such that consideration of input had a greater impact when team members lacked influence. Sapienza & Korsgaard (1996) examined the reactions of 118 investor–board members to the timeliness of feedback (another interactional fairness factor) from entrepreneurial CEOs. Results indicated that timely feedback had a positive and unique impact on board members' commitment to strategic decisions beyond the impact of board members' influence over these decisions. In sum, the findings of these four studies strongly indicate that procedural justice contributes to outcome consensus.

Justice and Team Continuity

Our model also suggests that procedural justice, by promoting positive social interactions, helps maintain or enhance team continuity. That is, when the process of strategic decision making is procedurally justice, there should be less affective conflict and disruptive political behavior. Consequently, trusting and cooperative relationships between team members should be maintained or strengthened.

The relational model of procedural justice also suggests that there may be long-term effects of procedural justice on team functioning and decision quality (Tyler & Lind, 1992). According to this model, individuals' beliefs about their standing and worth in a group or organization are strongly influenced by the fairness of decision-making procedures and interactions with decision makers. These beliefs, in turn, define the quality of relationships individuals have with the organization and its members and their willingness to trust authorities and cooperate with other members of the organization (Konovsky & Pugh, 1994). Thus, this theory suggests that procedural justice will help build trust in leadership and cooperative relationships among group members.

The effects of procedural justice on team-member relationships have been observed in studies on strategic decision making. In their study of subsidiaries' reaction to headquarters strategic decision making, Kim and Maubourgne (1991) found that procedural justice had a positive impact on social harmony and on trust in the headquarter's leadership. In a follow-up study, Kim and Maubourgne (1993) found that managers of these subsidiaries cooperated with strategic directives to the extent that they viewed the decision-making process as fair. Similarly, Korsgaard et al. (1995) found that fair treatment in the form of consideration of input had a positive impact on trust in the leader and attachment to the team, and Korsgaard and Sapienza (1996) found investors' trust in CEOs to be greater the more feedback they received.

CONCLUSION

Ultimately, strategic decision-making processes have a profound effect on firm success (Amason, 1996; Dean & Sharfman, 1996) for they shape the most important and long-reaching decisions of the firm. This chapter suggests that following principles of procedural justice will enhance the effectiveness of these processes and thereby foster better quality decisions, greater consensus, and greater team continuity. Although it would be naive to suggest that such practices can eliminate political infighting, research does suggest that procedural justice can help minimize the divisive social and political processes that undermine consensus and continuity and can facilitate the information flow needed to make high-quality decisions (Johnson, 1997; Kim & Maubourgne, 1991; 1993; Korsgaard et al., 1995; Sapienza & Korsgaard, 1996).

The high-stakes environment facing top managers makes for a highly political, hard-nosed game played by powerful, motivated individuals. In such settings, fair processes may be the exception rather than the norm. The model we developed suggests that leadership should consciously intervene to establish norms of procedural and interactional fairness. In essence, the leader should create an environment wherein managers are encouraged to fight fair and to respect the duty of others to do the same (Schweiger & Sandberg, 1991). Curtailing cognitive conflict would undermine decision quality. However, evidence is beginning to emerge that the best CEOs are able to elicit significant debate while maintaining a healthy, committed team (Amason & Sapienza, 1997; Eisenhardt, 1989). We posit that such top-management teams are headed by CEOs with a keen appreciation of procedural and interactional fairness.

The unique aspects of strategic decision making may qualify the impact of procedural justice and warrant further research. First, because outcomes of strategic decisions involve greater uncertainty and a longer time frame do the outcomes of more discrete and well-defined decisions (e.g., layoffs, grievance appeals, or pay-raise decisions), the interpretation of the favorableness of the outcomes is more open to subjectivity. Thus, procedural factors may have an especially potent impact on perceived distributive justice. Second, in addition to the substantial personal (i.e., career) and parochial (i.e., department or division) stakes involved, strategic decisions have consequences for top managers' power and standing within the senior-management team. Therefore, group status concerns may carry more weight in strategic decision making than in other sorts of decisions.

Moreover, there may be multiple layers of justice in the strategic decision-making process. Whereas justice is typically concerned with individuals' reactions to the actions and decisions made by an authority, such as the CEO (Tyler & Lind, 1992), members of a top-management team are likely to evaluate the fairness of their fellow team members as well as the CEO. Fair treatment by peers may serve as a strong signal of a team member's status within the team and the trustworthiness of the peers. If team members are attentive to the interactional fairness of other members, more complex, reciprocal effects may occur as team members assess and react to the fairness of others.

Finally, adhering to norms of fairness at the very top of the organization may also trickle down through the organization to create a more widespread support for strategic initiatives and preserve or strengthen employees' attitudes toward the organization (Wiesenfeld & Thibault, 1997). When senior managers are procedurally fair, middle managers are likely to behave in kind; outcome consensus and organizational attitudes should thereby be enhanced throughout the workforce. That is, procedural justice in strategic decision making may foster a culture for fairness throughout the organization. The prospect of developing a culture for fairness raises several questions. Are there conditions (e.g., team history, the firm's administrative history) that preclude or delay the introduction of fairness principles in top-management teams? Furthermore, because strategic decision making is an on-going process, what are the implications of occasional violations for sustaining norms of fairness? That is, if a CEO or team member occasionally falters, will trust disappear?

Top managers are under tremendous pressure to make effective strategic decisions. Such decisions must be made well before the contingencies within which they will be implemented can be known. Furthermore, their success requires unity of action, commitment, and follow through at all levels in the organization. Although considerable theory has evolved in strategic management that prescribes strategy content, relatively little theory has evolved to guide the strategic decision-making process. The CEO is faced with the challenge of managing the strategic decision-making process in a manner that will spur debate among top managers yet minimize the acrimony, distrust, and lack of commitment that can accompany such conflict. We argue that procedural justice theory provides a framework for understanding and dealing with these challenges. As such, we hope this chapter stimulates thinking on this topic and encourages others to pursue research in this promising area of inquiry.

REFERENCES

Alexander, S., & Ruderman, M. (1987). The role of procedural justice and distributive justice in organizational behavior. *Social Justice Research, 1*, 177–197.

Amason, A. C. (1996). Distinguishing the effects of functional and dysfunctional conflict on strategic decision making: Resolving a paradox for top management teams. *Academy of Management Journal, 39*, 123–148.

Amason, A. C., & Sapienza, H. J. (1997). The effects of top management team size and interaction norms on cognitive and affective conflict. *Journal of Management, 23*(4), 495–516.

Amason, A. C., & Schweiger, D. M. (1997). The effects of conflict on strategic decision making effectiveness and organizational performance. In C. De Dreu & E. Van de Vliert (Eds.), *Using conflict in organizations* (pp. 101–115). London: Sage.

Baron, R. A. (1993). Criticism as a source of perceived unfairness. In R. Cropanzano (Ed.), *Justice in the Workplace: Approaching Justice in Human Resource Management* (pp. 79–103). Hillsdale, NJ: Lawrence Erlbaum Associates.

Bies, R. J., & Shapiro, D. L. (1988). Voice and justification: Their influence on procedural fairness judgments. *Academy of Management Journal, 31*, 676–685.

Bies, R. J., & Tripp, T. M. (1996). Beyond distrust: "Getting even" and the need for revenge. In R. M. Kramer & T. Tyler (Eds.), *Trust in organizations* (pp. 246–260). Thousand Oaks, CA: Sage.

Bies, R. J, Tripp, T. M., & Kramer, R. M. (1997). At the breaking point: Cognitive and Social dynamics of revenge in organizations. In R. A. Giacalone & J. Greenberg (Eds.) *Antisocial behavior in organizations* (pp. 18–36). Thousand Oaks, CA: Sage.

Bourgeois, L. J., & Eisenhardt, K. M. (1988). Strategic decision processes in high velocity environments: Four cases in the microcomputer industry. *Management Science, 34*, 816–835.

Bower, J. L. (1970). *Managing the resource allocation process: A study of corporate planning and investment.* Boston, MA: Harvard University Press.

Brockner, J., & Wiesenfeld, B. M. (1996). An integrative framework for explaining reactions to decisions: Interactive effects of outcomes and procedures. *Psychological Bulletin, 120*, 189–208.

Cho, T. S., Hambrick, D. C., & Chen, M. (1994). Effects of top management team characteristics on competitive behaviors of the firms. *Best Paper Proceedings of the Academy of Management,* 12–16.

Crosby, F. (1976). A model of egotistical relative deprivation. *Psychological Review, 83*, 85–113.

Cyert, R. M., & March, J. G. (1963). *A behavioral theory of the firm.* Cambridge, MA: Blackwell.

D'Aveni, R. A. (1994). *Hyper-competition.* New York: The Free Press.

Dean, J. W., & Sharfman, M. P. (1996). Does decision process matter? A study of strategic decision-making effectiveness. *Academy of Management Journal, 39*, 368–396.

Dess, G. G. (1987). Consensus on strategy formulation and organizational performance: Competitors in a fragmented industry. *Strategic Management Journal, 8,* 258–277.

Eisenhardt, K. M. (1989). Making fast decisions in high velocity environments. *Academy of Management Journal 32,* 543–576.

Eisenhardt, K. M., & Bourgeois, L. J. III. (1988). Politics of strategic decision making processes in high-velocity environments: Toward a midrange theory. *Academy of Management Journal, 31,* 737–770.

Eisenhardt, K. M., & Zbaracki, M. J. (1992, Winter). Strategic decision making. *Strategic Management Journal, 13,* 17–37.

Finkelstein, S., & Hambrick, D. C. (1996). *Strategic leadership: Top executives and their effect on organizations.* West/Wadworth.

Folger, R. (1986). Rethinking equity theory: A referent cognitions model. In H. W. Bierhoff, R. L. Cohen & J. Greenberg, (Eds.), *Justice in social relations* (pp. 145–162). New York: Plenum.

Folger, R., & Bies, R. J. (1989). Managerial responsibilities and procedural justice. *Employee Responsibilities and Rights Journal, 2,* 79–90.

Folger, R., & Konovsky, M. A. (1989). Effects of procedural and distributive justice on reactions to pay raise decisions. *Academy of Management Journal, 32,* 115–130.

Folger, R. Konovsky, M. A., & Cropanzano, R. (1992). A due process metaphor for performance appraisal. In B. M. Staw & L. L. Cummings (Eds.), *Research in Organizational Behavior,* (vol 14, pp. 129–177). Greenwich, CT: JAI.

Galbraith, J. (1973). *Designing complex organizations.* Reading, MA: Addison-Wesley.

Greenberg, J. (1993). The social side of fairness: Interpersonal and informational classes of organizational justice. In R. Cropanzano (Ed.), *Justice in the Workplace: Approaching Justice in Human Resource Management* (pp. 79–103). Hillsdale, NJ: Lawrence Erlbaum Associates.

Guth, W. D., & MacMillan, I. C. (1986). Strategy implementation versus middle management self-interest. *Strategic Management Journal, 36,* 844–863.

Johnson, J. P. (1997). *Strategic decision making, commitment, and organizational justice: Implications for the control and performance of international joint ventures.* Unpublished Doctoral dissertation, University of South Carolina.

Kim, W. C., & Maubourgne, R. A. (1991). Implementing global strategies: The role of procedural justice. *Strategic Management Journal, 12,* 125–143.

Kim, W. C., & Maubourgne, R. A. (1993). Procedural justice, attitudes, and subsidiary top management compliance. *Academy of Management Journal, 36,* 502–526.

Kim, W. C., & Mauborgne, R. A. (1995). A procedural justice model of strategic decision making: Strategy content implications in the multinational. *Organization Science, 6*(1), 44–61.

Konovsky, M. A., & Pugh, S. D. (1994). Citizenship behavior and social exchange. *Academy of Management Journal, 37,* 656–669.

Korsgaard, M. A., & Roberson, L. (1995). Procedural justice in performance evaluation. *Journal of Management, 21,* 657–699.

Korsgaard, M. A., Schweiger, D. M., & Sapienza, H. J. (1995). Building commitment, attachment and trust in strategic decision-making teams: The role of procedural justice. *Academy of Management Journal, 38,* 60–94.

Leventhal, G. S. (1980). What should be done with equity theory? In K. J. Gergen, M. S. Greenberg & H. R. Willis (Eds.), *Social exchange: Advances in theory and research* (pp. 27–55). New York: Plenum.

Lind, E. A. (1997). Litigation and claiming in organizations: Antisocial behavior or quest for justice? In R. A. Giacalone & J. Greenberg (Eds), *Antisocial behavior in organizations* (pp. 150–171). Thousand Oaks, CA: Sage.

Lind, E. A., & Tyler, T. (1988). *The social psychology of procedural justice.* New York: Plenum.

Lindblom, C. E. (1959). The science of muddling through. *Public Administration Review, 19,* 79–88.

Mintzberg, H., Raisinghani, D., & Theoret, A. (1976). The structure of "unstructured" decision processes. *Administrative Science Quarterly, 21,* 246–275.

Moorman, R. H., Niehoff, B. P., & Organ, D. W. (1993). Treating employees fairly and organizational citizenship behavior: Sorting the effects of job satisfaction, organizational commitment and procedural justice. *Employee Responsibilities and Rights Journal, 6,* 209–225.

Pearce, J. A., & Robinson, R. B. (1997). *Strategic management: Formulation, implementation, and control* (6th ed.). Chicago, IL: Irwin.

Pearce, R. J. (1997). Toward understanding joint venture performance and survival: A bargaining and influence approach to transaction cost theory. *Academy of Management Review, 22,* 203–225.

Priem, R. L. (1990). Top management team group factors, consensus, and firm performance. *Strategic Management Journal, 11,* 469–478.

Sapienza, H. J., & Korsgaard, M. A. (1996). Procedural justice in entrepreneur–investor relations, *Academy of Management Journal, 39,* 544–574.

Sapienza, H. J., Korsgaard, M. A., & Hoogendam, J. (1997). What do new venture boards do? *Frontiers of entrepreneurship research,* 118–130.

Schweiger, D. M., & Sandberg, W. R. (1989). The utilization of individual capabilities in group approaches to strategic decision-making. *Strategic Management Journal, 10,* 31–43.

Schweiger, D. M., & Sandberg, W. R. (1991). The team approach to making strategic decisions. In H. E. Glass (Ed.), *Handbook of business strategy* (pp. 6–20). Boston, MA: Warren, Gorham & Lamont.

Schweiger, D. M., Sandberg, W. R., & Ragan, J. W. (1986). Group approaches for improving strategic decision making: A comparative analysis of dialectical inquiry, devil's advocacy, and consensus. *Academy of Management Journal, 29,* 51–71.

Schweiger, D. M., Sandberg, W. R., & Rechner, P. L. (1989). Experimental effects of dialectical inquiry, devil's advocacy, and consensus approaches to strategic decision making. *Academy of Management Journal 32,* 745–772.'

Selznick, P. (1984). *Leadership in administration.* Berkeley: University of California Press.

Sheppard, B. H., & Lewicki, R. J. (1987). Toward general principles of managerial fairness. *Social Justice Research, 1,* 161–176.

Smith, K. G., Smith, K. A., Olian, J. D., Sims, H. P., O'Bannon, D. P., & Scully, J. A. (1994). Top management team demography and process: The role of social integration and communication. *Administrative Science Quarterly, 39,* 412–438.

Tjosvold, D., & Field, R. H. G. (1983). Effects of social context on consensus and majority vote decision making. *Academy of Management Journal, 26,* 500–506.

Tyler, T., & Lind, E. A. (1992). A relational model of authority in groups. *Advances in experimental social psychology, 25,* 115–191.

Tyler, T. R., & Bies, R. J. (1990). Beyond formal procedures: The interpersonal context of procedural justice. In J. Carroll (Ed.), *Applied social psychology and organizational settings* (pp. 77–98). Hillsdale, NJ: Lawrence Erlbaum Associates.

Walster, E., Walster, G. W., & Berscheid, E. (1978). *Equity: Theory and research.* Boston, MA: Allyn & Bacon.

Whitney, J. C., & Smith, R. A. (1983). Effects of group cohesiveness on attitude polarization and the acquisition of knowledge in a strategic planning context. *Journal of Marketing Research, 20,* 167–176.

Wiesenfeld, B. M., & Thibault, V. (1997, August). *Managers are employees, too: Exploring the relationships between procedural fairness, managers' self-perceptions, and managerial behaviors following a layoff.* Paper presented at the 1997 meeting of the Academy of Management, Boston, MA.

Wooldridge, B., & Floyd, S. W. (1989). Strategic process effects on consensus. *Strategic Management Journal, 10,* 295–302.

Wooldridge, B., & Floyd, S. W. (1990). The strategy process, middle management involvement, and organizational performance. *Strategic Management Journal, 11,* 231–241.

LOOKING TO THE FUTURE

Are Flexible Organizations the Death Knell for the Future of Procedural Justice?

Maureen L. Ambrose
Marshall Schminke
University of Central Florida[1]

> *A commercial world where everything has "gone soft," "gone fickle," "gone fashion," . . . is to most of us a world gone bonkers. How do you deal with a bonkers world other than with bonkers organizations, peopled with bonkers folk? My answer is, in short: You can't!* (Peters, 1994, p. 8)

Recently organizations have faced increasingly unpredictable environments and technologies and have struggled to find ways to deal effectively with this turbulence. One response has been to eliminate traditional hierarchies and bureaucracies and create more fluid and flexible structures. During this same period, organizational justice researchers have continued to explore the antecedents and consequences of justice perceptions. However, an implicit assumption in most of this justice work is that organizations are stable, static, hierarchical organizations, with a focus on stable rules, procedures, and situations. Although this assumption was appropriate when early work on procedural justice was conducted, both anecdotal and empirical evidence suggest today's organizations are moving away from stable, hierarchical structures. This chapter explores how these changing organizational forms may affect perceptions of justice. Specifically, this chapter suggests that changes in organizational structures will lead individuals to rely more heavily on the procedural justice rule of ethicality and less heavily on other rules like consistency and representativeness. We describe how this increased emphasis on ethicality may lead individuals to focus more on outcomes as an indi-

---

[1]This work was completed while the first author was at the University of Colorado at Boulder and the second author was at Creighton University.

cator of fairness. Thus, ironically, a shift in what individuals focus on in procedural terms leads perceptions of justice to become more outcome oriented.

First the movement toward more flexible organizations is examined. Next, how this shift in structure may affect individuals' expectations of procedural fairness and how ethics may provide a framework by which to evaluate fairness is considered. Then Kohlberg's (1981, 1984) model of cognitive moral development (CMD) is discussed and how the application of this model leads to an increased emphasis on outcomes. Finally, the implications of this shift and how and why organizations might manage this process are considered.

CHANGING ORGANIZATIONAL STRUCTURES

In 1987, Tom Peters noted that the successful firm of the 1990s and beyond would be:

- flatter
- populated by more autonomous units
- oriented toward differentiation
- more responsive
- much faster at innovation
- a user of highly trained, flexible people

The 1990s saw Peters' predictions fulfilled. Evolution and revolution in technology, manufacturing, international competition, and consumer tastes have changed the face of today's corporate structures. They are decentralized, less formal, more responsive, more innovative, and more adaptable than those of only 10 years ago. Consider the following cases:

In the late 1980s, Campbell Soup was in trouble. Earnings were falling, marketing efforts were weak, and political battles and feuds flared among the members of the Dorrance family, which owned 58% of the company's stock. In 1990, the firm hired CEO David Johnson. Of his vision for the company, Johnson said, "I want to rip out the bureaucracy, the pretense, the corridors-of-power syndrome, the games that are played. I want us to think like a small company" (Grant, 1996, p. 80). Under his direction, by 1995, return on sales had increased from 0.1% to 9.6% and the stock price had more than doubled.

In 1992, Sears lost $3.9 billion. The same year it hired Arthur Martinez to head its retail operations. Under Martinez's reign, Sears focused on its core business as a moderate-priced department store—divesting itself of its nonretailing operations (e.g., brokerage services, credit cards, real estate, and insurance). In 1995, Sears earned over $1.0 billion, and Martinez became CEO. Of his policies for success, Martinez said,

We're replacing 29,000 pages of policies and procedures with two very simple booklets. We call them "Freedoms" and "Obligations." We're trying to tell our managers what they're responsible for, what freedoms they have to make decisions, and where to turn if they need help. But we don't want to codify every possible situation. (Sellers, 1995, p. 98)

Movement to more flexible structures has not been limited to U.S. firms. Honda, a model of automotive success in the 1980s, suffered from Japan's recent prolonged recession, strengthening yen, and increased competition from other automakers—a triple threat to its prosperity. Additionally, Honda missed the sport-utility vehicle boom of the early 1990s. CEO Nobuhiko Kawamoto led Honda back to prosperity with a focus on breaking with traditions that had guided the firm for over 40 years. He moved manufacturing and research and development (R&D) closer together to better share ideas and fix problems. Kawamoto also placed more emphasis on individual responsibility and initiative (Taylor, 1996). Painful as some of his initiatives have been, he also believes the battles have only just begun. "The real competition to survive in the world is starting now. Now that we have turned the corner, we have to accelerate" (Taylor, 1996, p. 100).

MECHANISTIC AND ORGANIC STRUCTURES

These changes in organizational structures reflect classic organization theory descriptions of rigid, bureaucratic (mechanistic) structures giving way to smaller, flexible (organic) structures when facing increased technological or environmental uncertainty (Burns & Stalker, 1961; Khandwalla, 1977; Lawrence & Lorsch, 1967). Burns and Stalker provided standard descriptions of each. Traditional mechanistic structures, efficient and appropriate in stable business conditions, are characterized by:

- a high degree of functional specialization and narrow view of task
- clear lines of authority
- precisely defined methods for accomplishing each task
- hierarchical structures and controls
- a highly centralized command structure
- vertical communication
- focus on firm specific knowledge and expertise

On the other hand, organic structures are flexible and adaptive to changing situations. They are characterized by:

- a broader view of task
- continual adjustment and redefinition of individual tasks

- shedding narrow interpretations of responsibility
- broad concern for and commitment to task
- network-based systems of control, authority, and communication
- decentralized knowledge and expertise
- lateral communication focusing on information and advice rather than orders
- importance and prestige attached to knowledge and expertise beyond that which is firm and specific

It is important to note that these two structural forms represent ends of a continuum, not a dichotomy. No organization is perfectly organic or mechanistic. Rather, they may display characteristics of one or the other (or both), and intermediate stages exist between the two archetypes.

That today's organizations are becoming more organic in an attempt to cope with an increasingly unpredictable world is clear. What is also clear is that they are doing so with good reason. Evidence supporting the advantages of organic structures in turbulent times is not just anecdotal or limited to research from the 1960s and 1970s. Recent research demonstrates the positive effects of organic structures. For example, Parthasarthy and Sethi (1993) studied 87 firms (primarily in the machinery, motor vehicles and parts, aircraft and parts, and electronic equipment production industries) that employ flexible manufacturing systems. They found that firms with organic structures outperformed their mechanistic counterparts.

Jennings and Seaman (1990) demonstrated similar findings in a study of savings and loan (S&L) institutions. Prior to the 1980 deregulation of S&Ls, S&Ls were primarily limited to financing residential mortgages. After deregulation their environment became more complex and uncertain; they were allowed to participate in a much wider variety of financial undertakings and instruments, including consumer loans, credit cards, equity positions in real estate, commercial loans, and governmental loans. Jennings and Seaman reported that Texas S&Ls with organic structures were able to be more aggressive in pursuing new business ventures in their new deregulated environment (after 1980) than their mechanistic counterparts.

The benefit of organic structures also was demonstrated by Covin and Slevin (1989), who examined the performance of smaller firms and found that those facing hostile environments (risky, stressful, with strong competitive and technological forces), performed better with organic structures. Those facing benign environments performed better with mechanistic structures.

Within-organization evidence also supports the effectiveness of organic structures in turbulent environments. For example, McDonough and Leifer (1983) found that within firms that employ both mechanistic and organic structures simultaneously, less effective work units were more mechanistic than more effective units.

It is clear why firms have moved to more organic structures as their technologies, markets, and general operating environments have become more complex and less predictable. In such settings, organic structures outperform mechanistic structures on a number of dimensions. However, the effect of organic structures goes beyond organizational outcomes; individual-level outcomes also are affected. For example, Meadows (1980a, 1980b) found that organic structures led to both greater employee satisfaction and innovation. The next section considers how these dynamic, nonhierarchical organizations might affect another individual level variable: the perception of procedural justice.

ORGANIZATIONAL JUSTICE IN THE 20TH CENTURY

Figure 11.1 shows the progression of research interests on organizational justice issues since the 1970s. This research makes a clear distinction between process and outcome concerns. Early justice research focused on outcome concerns—distributive fairness—the perceived fairness of outcome distributions (Brockner, Greenberg, & Brockner, 1986; Greenberg, 1988; Mowday, 1983; Oldham, Kulik, Ambrose, Brand, & Stepina, 1986; Oldham et al., 1982). In general, this research shows that individuals' perceptions of the fairness of outcomes affect those individuals' attitudes and behaviors.

Research on fairness shifted to an emphasis on procedural fairness in the 1980s. Much of this research stemmed from Thibaut and Walker's (1975) finding that, even when individuals received unfavorable outcomes, they evaluated the outcome more positively when they believed the process by which it was determined was fair. Also influential on subsequent organizational justice research was work by Leventhal (1980; Leventhal, Karuza, & Fry, 1980), who identified six rules of procedural justice (consistency, bias suppression, accuracy, correctability, representativeness, and ethicality).

Thibaut and Walker's (1975) and Leventhal's (1980; Leventhal et al., 1980) work focused on structural attributes of procedures, and investigations of structural attributes dominated justice work through the mid-1980s. More recently research has distinguished between structural and social aspects of procedural justice (Bies & Moag, 1986; Brockner & Wiesenfeld, 1997; Cropanzano & Greenberg, 1997; Greenberg, 1990a; Tyler & Bies, 1990). The social side of justice has two components—procedural explanations (i.e., a rationale for why a decision was made) and interpersonal sensitivity (i.e., the quality of treatment the target receives). Research demonstrates that both procedural explanations and interpersonal sensitivity influence perceptions of fairness (Bies & Moag, 1986; Greenberg, 1990b, 1991, 1993a, 1993b; Konovsky & Cropanzano, 1991).

A final body of work that warrants note, but that is not captured in the aforementioned review, is the work by Lind and Tyler (1988; Tyler & Lind, 1992) on

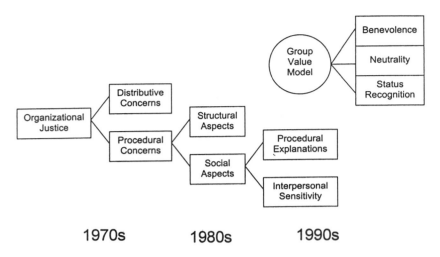

FIG. 11.1.   Three decades of procedural justice research.

the *Group Value Model*. Lind and Tyler maintained that procedures are important primarily because they provide information about an individual's standing within a group or relationship to authorities. A group-value approach maintains the importance of the attributes of procedures identified in procedural justice research but suggests that these attributes are important because they convey information about an individual's position within the group. Critical to a group value approach are three perceptions: benevolence, neutrality, and status recognition. These ideas are discussed later in the chapter.

PROCEDURAL JUSTICE IN THE 21ST CENTURY

Since the 1980s, there has been substantial research on procedural justice that demonstrates the importance of the perceived fairness of procedures in organizations. This research focuses on how attributes of the procedures affect individuals' perceptions of fairness and how these fairness perceptions affect individuals' affective and behavioral reactions. However, little research examines how contextual attributes affect perceptions of fairness. This lack of interest in contextual factors is surprising, as influential work on procedural justice suggests that context may have an important effect on perceptions of procedural justice (Leventhal, 1980; Lind & Tyler, 1988). For our analysis, we revisit Leventhal's (1980) seminal work and explicitly consider the role of organizational structure on the way individuals assess procedural justice.

Leventhal (1980) identified six procedural rules that guide an individual's thinking about procedural fairness: consistency, bias suppression, accuracy, correctability, representativeness, and ethicality. Leventhal suggested that when an individual assesses the fairness of a procedure, he or she considers each of these rules. However, Leventhal maintained that the different rules may be given different weights and the "relative weight of procedural rules may differ from one situation to the next" (p. 46). Leventhal noted:

> The following analysis assumes that an individual applies procedural rules selectively and follows different rules at different times. The basic criteria used to evaluate the fairness of procedures change with circumstances. In some situations, one procedural rule may be considered much more relevant than others, in which case judgments of procedural fairness may be dominated by that rule. In other situations however, several procedural rules may be applicable. The influence of a rule on the individual's judgments of procedural fairness is defined as its weight. (p. 39)

There has been little discussion of the factors that affect the relative weight of these rules. We suggest that organizational structure may influence how individuals weight these procedural rules. Specifically, we suggest that in flexible organic structures, the relevance of some rules may decrease, whereas others will increase.

Recall Burns and Stalker's (1961) description of mechanistic and organic structures. Mechanistic organizations are slow to respond to change; they possess precisely defined methods for accomplishing tasks, clear lines of authority, and hierarchical structures and control. Organic organizations respond quickly to change; they exhibit a continual adjustment and redefinition of individual tasks and decision-making authority is decentralized. Justice researchers have implicitly assumed a mechanistic organizational structure describes organizations. Mechanistic structures provide stable procedures that remain consistent over time. However, organizations are becoming more organic, and organic organizations are characterized by fluidity: fluid tasks, fluid structures, fluid procedures. The following section describes how the movement to more organic structures might affect the relative importance of Leventhal's six procedural justice rules.

Consistency

The consistency rule suggests that procedures need to be consistent across time and people. For example, Leventhal (1980) noted that leaders of a workgroup should set performance expectations in advance and once such standards are established, a marked deviation from them will be perceived as a violation of fair procedure. If changes are made too frequently and easily, procedures will be seen as less fair. However, in a rapidly changing environment, consistency over time may be impossible. Consider the role of changing technologies, as illustrated in the automobile service industry. As automotive mechanical and electronic systems became more complex in the 1970s and 1980s, service turnaround times often increased proportionately; greater complexity in systems led naturally to greater difficulty in diagnosing and solving problems. Performance standards that reflected earlier (and simpler) tasks were no longer appropriate and thus, required change. Ironically, even more sophisticated onboard computer diagnostic systems ("black boxes") have changed the rules yet again, as complicated problems that previously required hours or days to diagnose may now become clear in a matter of minutes. More rapid technological changes require more rapid rules changes, rendering consistency a less relevant aspect of procedures.

Accuracy

The accuracy rule states that allocative procedures need to be based on as much good information and informed opinion as possible. Information and opinion must be gathered and processed with minimum error. In dynamic environments, the need for rapid decisions may decrease the relevance of accuracy. Anyone who has ever needed to finish a rush job knows that speed often leads to errors. However, enough speed may more than compensate for raw statistical accuracy. For example, we have a friend who worked as a demand forecaster for a major soap manufacturer. For 5 years she won company awards for her contributions to the forecasting group. She was the first to admit that her forecasts were almost never as accurate as those of her co-workers. In fact, she did none of the sophisticated computer modeling favored by the rest of the group, and weeks might pass without her computer even being turned on. However, she had a rare ability to take in vast quantities of seemingly raw and unrelated data (trade reports, consumer surveys, weather reports, etc.) and make sense of information others saw as "noise." Often, she had already forecast significant shifts in soap demand days before regional sales figure results (and other such data that lend themselves to regression analysis) were even available to her colleagues for analysis. On average, her forecasts were approximately 90% as accurate as her colleagues'. However, in a business that requires moving high-bulk, low-value product across large geographical regions, a day or two advantage in forecasts far more than compensates for some loss in accuracy. Thus, the accuracy rule may be less important in organic organizations. Indeed, Leventhal et al. (1980) noted that "when speed is essential less accurate methods for gathering information . . . will be seen as fair" (p. 197).

Representativeness

The representativeness rule suggests that all phases of procedures must reflect the basic concerns, values, and outlook of important subgroups. Representativeness is similar to voice. Individuals generally perceive situations as more fair when they are allowed input to decisions, either by having total control or through participative decision making or consultation with management. One might expect opportunities for voice to increase in decentralized organizations, as decisions are made at the local level. However, gathering input from all relevant subgroups can be complicated, cumbersome, and time consuming. As with the accuracy rule, Leventhal et al. (1980) noted that when decisions need to be made quickly (e.g., in times of change) representativeness may be less important. Political-polling organizations understand this. In the race to project winners on election night, they seek to identify critical samples whose voting patterns historically predict those of the larger electorate. Note that these samples need not be representative, of the ethnic, gender, or religious makeup of the general public—nor should they be expected to be. Is it fair that the rest of us are not heard in these preresult polls? Maybe not. But, in their high-stakes, high-pressure environment, what the polling organization values is speed, not true representativeness.

Correctability

We expect that correctability will also receive less weight in an organic organization. The correctability rule dictates that there must be opportunities to modify and reverse decisions. Leventhal (Leventhal et al., 1980) suggested that the ability to review and modify decisions at various stages of the process through some sort of (informal or formal) appeal procedure is important for procedural fairness. However, appeals are time consuming and the importance of rapid decisions may preclude an effective appeals process. Moreover, in fluid environments, the circumstances surrounding the appeal may change. For example, a large eastern power company, facing declining sales, declining customer satisfaction, and increased pressure from shareholders and regulators, hires a new CEO. On this CEO's arrival, over 900 employee grievances lie unresolved at various points in the company's appeal process. A significant portion involves dysfunctional relationships between supervisors and subordinates. Four months later, after a broad and deep reorganization, many of these supervisors are no longer with the firm. Clearly, the company has significantly limited options to correct the bad situations now, because the foci of many of the grievances are no longer employees. Thus, we expect correctability to be less relevant in organic organizations.

Bias Suppression

The bias suppression rule suggests that self-interest or devotion to doctrinaire views should not influence procedures. We suggest that the importance of bias suppression remains unchanged; regardless of organizational structure, employees will require that decision makers be bias free in determining allocations. Unlike the previous procedural rules, employees are not expected to see the need to trade off bias suppression against other desirable attributes (e.g., speed) in an organic organization. Thus, employees will still consider bias suppression an important attribute of procedural fairness. However, it may be more difficult for managers to behave unbiasedly in rapidly changing environments. In novel situations and situations with limited time, individuals tend to regress to well-learned responses and rely more heavily on stereotypes (Gilbert & Hixon, 1991; Perry, Kulik, & Bourhis, 1996). Thus, although bias suppression may be equally important to employees, it may be more difficult for managers to eliminate bias from their decision processes. For example, consider a manager who has to assign additional work to a subordinate because of a tight deadline. She may choose the subordinate who came through last time and who she has categorized as *responsible* or *hard working* or *dependable*, although these particular duties require no special skills or expertise. On closer reflection, the manager may realize that it is not fair to require additional work of the same employee and that she has not considered relevant details in making this decision. However, under pressure the manager's decision is biased by the salience of the employee and her own self-interest (her need to easily find someone she knows will do the job).

Ethicality

Leventhal's (1980) final rule, ethicality, suggests that procedures must be compatible with the fundamental moral and ethical values of the individual. We suggest that as consistency, accuracy, representativeness, and correctability decrease in times of rapid change, the ethicality rule will receive increased emphasis. Thus, individuals will rely less on the structural rules outlined previously and more on their basic values and moral beliefs. The following describes how procedural justice judgments might change as a result of this shift in the weighting of Leventhal's procedural rules.

How might perceptions of procedural justice change if individuals rely on the ethicality rule rather than consistency, accuracy, representativeness, correctability, and bias suppression? What do ethical procedures look like? Unfortunately, Leventhal's (1980) description of the ethicality rule is vague. The rule is based on an assumption that "judgments of fairness and justice are related to a larger intrapsychic system of moral and ethical values and standards" (p. 46). Although Leventhal provided several examples of ethical violations that might lead procedures to be perceived as unfair (e.g., observation techniques that violate one's privacy, allocation procedures that involve deception, bribery, or trickery), he did not provide a clear description of what the system of moral and ethical values looks like. In the next section, we draw on research on ethics to explore one such system and consider the role it might play in individuals' assessments of the fairness of organizational procedures. Specifically, we examine how individuals' cognitive moral development affects their assessments of fairness. We suggest that, counterintuitively, an increased weighting of the ethicality rule—a rule of procedural justice—will lead most individuals to focus on the fairness of outcomes—increasing concerns about distributive justice.

A MODEL OF ETHICALITY

One useful way of examining ethics is to consider how individuals think about what is right and what is wrong. Probably the best-known model in this area is Kohlberg's (1981) *stages of cognitive moral development* (CMD). CMD describes the level of maturity or sophistication of an individuals' moral reasoning. Kohlberg identified six stages of moral development through which individuals may progress, two at each of three levels: preconventional, conventional, and postconventional (see Table 11.1). The first two stages (the preconventional level) reflect egocentric views of what constitutes ethical behavior. What is right is what produces the best consequences for me or what an authoritarian power dictates. The next two stages (the conventional level) reflect more peer- or social-based views of what is ethical. What is right is what is expected of me by relevant others (peer group, family, or society) or what is in the collective best interest of society. The fifth and sixth stages (the postconventional level) reflect a more universalistic view of what is ethical. Stage 6 in particular is based on ethical principles that are independent of specific authority figures. What is right is what is right according to natural or universal laws or principles.

These three stages of moral development reflect a shift in the focus of individuals' ethical concerns from maximizing self interest (the egocentric approach of the preconventional level) to maximizing joint interests (the utilitarian approach of the conventional level) to applying universal laws or principles of behavior (the deontological approach of the postconventional level; Fritzche & Becker, 1984; Victor & Cullen, 1988; Williams, 1985). In other words, the preconventional and conventional levels reflect ethical reasoning based on outcomes whereas the postconventional level reflects reasoning based on rules, principles, or procedures. Individuals at the first two levels consider the outcomes of actions to be moral or not (rather than the actions themselves), whereas individuals at the third level consider actions or procedures to be moral or not, independent of their outcomes.

TABLE 11.1
Kohlberg's Stages of Moral Development

Preconventional Level
    Stage 1: Punishment and obedience orientation
    Stage 2: Instrumental relativist orientation
Conventional Level
    Stage 3: "Good boy–nice girl" orientation
    Stage 4: Law and order orientation
Postconventional Level
    Stage 5: Social contract legalistic orientation
    Stage 6: Universal ethical principle orientation

THE DEATH OF PROCEDURAL JUSTICE?

We argue that in dynamic environments, individuals will decrease their reliance on traditional procedural rules like consistency and increase their reliance on the procedural rule of ethicality. Here lies an interesting irony. Research demonstrates that most adults operate at the conventional level (Stages 3 and 4) of Kohlberg's (1981) model (Blasi, 1980; Kohlberg, 1984; Rest, 1986; Trevino, 1986). (Indeed, Weber [1990] found that 86.4% of managers operated at the conventional level.) This suggests that when most individuals focus on ethics, they focus on outcome-related issues. If so, as their evaluations of procedural fairness become oriented toward ethicality, they also move away from a focus on the procedures themselves and toward a focus on the outcomes of those procedures. These outcomes reflect distributive fairness issues, not procedural. Thus, as the ethicality rule becomes more important in procedural justice judgments, most individuals will focus more on distributive fairness as an indicator of procedural fairness. In essence, this suggests that as the ethicality rule grows in importance, procedural concerns will fade away, leaving only distributive fairness. This shift suggests that the field may have come full circle, back to a primary focus on distributive rather than procedural fairness issues; distributive justice will become increasingly important and procedural justice will be less important in the new organizations of the next century.

Now, the reader may respond to this prediction—that an increased focus on ethics implies, in practice, an increased focus on outcomes—with a resounding "So what? Why not just pay particular attention to making sure that outcomes are fair and let it go at that?" The answer lies in the normative position of Kohlberg's (1981) formulation; he argued—from both cognitive and moral perspectives— that higher, more principled stages represent better moral reasoning.

Kohlberg (1981) argued that cognitively, higher stages are better than lower stages. First, higher stages are more cognitively complex than lower stages, and second, they are more cognitively inclusive than lower stages. By more cognitively complex, Kohlberg meant that individuals typically have difficulty understanding moral arguments framed in terms of stages higher than their own, but show little difficulty understanding arguments at their own or lower levels. By more cognitively inclusive, he meant that Stage 5 ideas include Stage 4 ideas as fundamental elements, Stage 4 ideas include Stage 3 ideas as elements, and so on.

Additionally, Kohlberg (1981) asserted that morally, higher stages are better than lower stages. That is, their terms more accurately reflect the criteria of morality as principles of justice (cf., Rawls, 1971).[2] He asserted that moral reasoning requires

---

[2]Kohlberg (1981) stated that "no principle other than justice has been shown to meet the formal conception of a universal prescriptive principle" (p. 176) and that "no philosopher ever has seriously attempted to demonstrate that an alternative substantive principle to justice could function in a universal prescriptive fashion in a satisfactory way" (p. 177). For a more complete description of these arguments, see Kohlberg's essays "From *is* to *ought*: How to commit the naturalistic fallacy and get away with it in the study of moral development" (Kohlberg, 1981, chap. 4) and "Justice as reversibility: The claim to moral adequacy of a highest stage of moral judgment" (Kohlberg, 1981, chap. 5).

individuals to construct judgments of justice, of which the six stages reflect increasingly sophisticated views. His arguments rest on both theoretical and empirical arguments. Theoretically, his framework is based on Piaget's (cf., 1948) work on the cognitive–developmental moral stages of children. Kohlberg asserted that:

> an adequate psychological theory of [moral] stages and stage movement presupposes a normative theory of justice . . . the normative theoretical claim that a higher stage is philosophically a better stage is one necessary part of a psychological explanation of a sequential stage movement. (Kohlberg, 1984, p. 223)

Kohlberg also stressed that moral philosophers have long argued that morally adequate judgments must be both universal and prescriptive and argued that both increase at higher stages of moral reasoning (Kohlberg, 1981).

Empirical results also suggest that higher levels reflect more ethical reasoning. For example, individuals evaluate higher stages as more morally adequate, although they may not fully understand reasoning at stages higher than their own (Kohlberg, 1981). Additionally, reviews by Blasi (1980), Rest (1986), and Rest and Narvaez (1994) all suggested that higher stages of moral reasoning translate to more ethical behavior. Put simply, both cognitively and morally, "each stage is able to do things that prior stages could not" (Kohlberg, 1981, p. 147). But does this higher moral reasoning translate to important outcomes for organizations? We believe it does. In the following section we identify why organizations should be interested in the cognitive moral development of their employees.

ETHICAL TRAINING AND PROCEDURAL JUSTICE

The ethical development of employees is important primarily because it affects decision making and behavior. In the more unpredictable environments of tomorrow's organizations, there will be fewer rules to govern behavior. Under these conditions, the ethical norms of the organization will play a larger role in guiding behavior. With this increased importance of ethics, organizations will benefit from enhancing the ethical thinking of their members, thereby enhancing both the quality of ethical reasoning and the quality of ethical actions (Blasi, 1980; Rest 1986; Rest & Narvaez, 1994).

The question is whether ethical reasoning is malleable, responsive to ethics education or training. The answer is yes (e.g., Rest, 1986, 1994). In particular, programs lasting several weeks or more, which involve dilemma discussion and active participation, create the most lasting effects. Interestingly, programs aimed at adults (24 years and older) seem to be more effective that those aimed at younger individuals, so training may be most effective in adult work situations. Therefore, ethics education and training may be expected to result in more employees that reflect postconventional ethical reasoning. Consider what this shift means in terms of how individuals interpret ethical behavior. For example, Stage 5 individuals determine what is right by recognizing values and rules relative to one's group, and recognizing that these rules should be upheld in the interest of impartiality and as part of one's social contract with the group (Kohlberg, 1984). Stage 6 individuals determine what is right by developing and adhering to self-chosen ethical principles that reflect universal principles of justice like "the equality of human rights and respect for the dignity of human beings as individual persons" (Kohlberg, 1984, p. 176).

The universal values articulated by Kohlberg (1984) as providing the ethical framework by which decisions are evaluated is remarkably similar to those values embraced by the Group Value Model. For example, Tyler and Lind (1992) identified neutrality as central to judgments of procedural fairness. They noted that people focus on whether there is "a level playing field," and "lack of bias" in decisions (p. 141). This concern about neutrality is similar to Kohlberg's Stage 5 focus on impartiality in the application of rules. The Tyler and Lind focus on status recognition is related to Kohlberg's Stage 6 focus on human rights and dignity. Tyler and Lind noted that individuals assess their standing in the group (status recognition) by paying particular attention to the interpersonal quality of treatment they receive. "In particular, if one is treated politely and with dignity . . . feelings of positive social standing are enhanced" (p. 141). Thus, the principles Kohlberg explicates as guiding the highest levels of ethical decision making—the ones organizations would seek to develop through training—reflect those values Lind and Tyler described as guiding perceptions of procedural justice. For individuals at higher levels of moral reasoning, the shift to the procedural justice rule of ethicality would not lead to a focus on outcomes. Rather, the shift would increase the importance of the forces within the Group Value Model that drive perceptions of procedural fairness—benevolence, status recognition, and neutrality.

So, are flexible organizations the death knell for procedural justice? Yes and no. In the short run, yes. As long as individuals are utilitarian (outcome focused) in their ethical thinking, the shift toward the ethicality rule in the evaluation of procedures will reduce procedural justice perceptions to assessments of distributive justice. However, in the long run, no. If we are able to train individuals to reason ethically at higher, more process-oriented levels, the increased importance of ethicality will be reflected in the increased importance of those aspects of procedural justice emphasized by the Group Value Model. With sophisticated, ethical decision makers, the balanced focus on outcomes and procedures will re-emerge.

REFERENCES

Bies, R. J., & Moag, J. S. (1986). Interactional justice: Communication criteria of fairness. In R. J. Lewicki, B. H. Sheppard & B. H. Bazerman (Eds.), *Research on negotiation in organizations* (vol. 1, pp. 43–55). Greenwich, CT: JAI.

Blasi, A. (1980). Bridging moral cognition and moral action: A critical review of the literature. *Psychological Bulletin, 88,* 1–45.

Brockner, J., Greenberg, J., & Brockner, A. (1986). Layoffs, equity theory, and work performance: Further evidence of the impact of survivor guilt. *Academy of Management Journal, 29,* 373–384.

Brockner, J., Grover, S., Reed, T., & DeWitt, R. L. (1992). Layoffs, job insecurity and survivors' work effort: Evidence of an inverted-U relationship. *Academy of Management Journal, 35,* 413–425.

Brockner, J., & Wiesenfeld, B. M. (1996). An integrative framework for explaining reactions to decisions: The interactive effects of outcomes and procedures. *Psychological Bulletin, 120,* 189–208.

Burns, T., & Stalker, G. M. (1961). *The Management of Innovation.* London: Tavistock.

Covin, J. G., & Slevin, D. P. (1989). Strategic management of small firms in hostile and benign environments. *Strategic Management Journal, 10,* 75–87.

Cropanzano, R., & Greenberg, J. (1997). Progress in organizational justice: Tunneling through the maze. In L. T. Robertson & C. L. Cooper (Eds.), *International review of industrial and organizational psychology* (pp. 317–372). New York: Wiley.

Fritzche, D. J., & Becker, H. (1984). Linking management behavior to ethical philosophy. *Academy of Management Journal, 27,* 166–175.

Gilbert, D. T., & Hixon, J. G. (1991). The trouble of thinking: Activation and application of stereotype beliefs. *Journal of Personality and Social Psychology, 60,* 509–517.

Grant, L. (1996, May 13). Stirring it up at Campbell. *Fortune, 134,* 80–86.

Greenberg, J. (1988). Equity and workplace status: A field experiment. *Journal of Applied Psychology, 73,* 606–613.

Greenberg, J. (1990a). Organizational justice: Yesterday, today, and tomorrow. *Journal of Management, 16,* 399–432.

Greenberg, J. (1990b). Employee theft as a reaction to underpayment inequity: The hidden cost of pay cuts. *Journal of Applied Psychology, 75,* 561–568.

Greenberg, J. (1991). Using explanations to manage impressions of performance appraisal fairness. *Employee Responsibilities and Rights Journal, 4,* 51–60.

Greenberg, J. (1993a). The social side of fairness: Interpersonal and informational classes of organizational justice. In R. Cropanzano (Ed.), *Justice in the workplace: Approaching fairness in human resource management* (pp. 79–103). Hillsdale, NJ: Lawrence Erlbaum Associates.

Greenberg, J. (1993b). Stealing in the name of justice: Informational and interpersonal moderators of theft reactions to underpayment inequity. *Organizational Behavior and Human Decision Processes, 54,* 81–103.

Jennings, D. F., & Seaman, S. L. (1990). Aggressiveness of response to new business opportunities following deregulation: An empirical study of established financial firms. *Journal of Business Venturing, 5,* 177–189.

Khandwalla, P. N. (1977). *The Design of Organizations.* New York: Harcourt, Brace, Jovanovich.

Kohlberg, L. (1981). *Essays in moral development, Volume I: The philosophy of moral development.* San Francisco: Harper & Row.

Kohlberg, L. (1984). *Essays in moral development, Volume II: The psychology of moral development.* San Francisco: Harper & Row.

Konovsky, M., & Cropanzano, R. (1991). The perceived fairness of employee drug testing as a predictor of employee attitudes and job performance. *Journal of Applied Psychology, 76,* 698–707.

Lawrence, P. R., & Lorsch, J. W. (1967). *Organization and Environment.* Homewood, IL: Irwin.

Leventhal, G. S. (1980). What should be done with equity theory? In K. J. Gergen, M. S. Greenberg & R. H. Willis (Eds.) *Social exchange: Advances in theory and research* (pp. 27–55). New York: Plenum.

Leventhal, G. S., Karuza, J., & Fry, W. R. (1980). Beyond fairness: A theory of allocation preferences. In G. Mikula (Ed.), *Justice and social interaction* (pp. 167–218). New York: Springer-Verlag.

Lind, E. A., & Tyler, T. R. (1988). *The social psychology of procedural justice.* New York: Plenum.

McDonough, E. F., III, & Leifer, R. (1983). Using simultaneous structures to cope with uncertainty. *Academy of Management Journal, 26,* 727–735.

Meadows, I. S. G. (1980a). Organic structure, satisfaction, and personality. *Human Relations, 33,* 383–392.

Meadows, I. S. G. (1980b). Organic structure and innovation in small work groups. *Human Relations, 33,* 369–382.

Mowday, R. T. (1983). Equity theory predictions of behavior in organizations. In R. Steers & L. Porter (Eds.), *Motivation and work behavior* (3rd ed., pp. 91–113). New York: McGraw-Hill.

Oldham, G. R., Kulik, C. T., Ambrose, M. L., Stepina, L. P., & Brand, J. F. (1986). Relations between job facet comparisons and employee reactions. *Organizational Behavior and Human Decision Processes, 38,* 28–47.

Oldham, G. R., Nottenburg, G., Kassner, M. K., Ferris, G., Fedor, D., & Masters, M. (1982). The selection and consequences of job comparisons. *Organizational Behavior and Human Performance, 29,* 84–111.

Perry, E. L., Kulik, C. T., & Bourhis, A. C. (1996). Moderating effects of personal and contextual factors in age discrimination. *Journal of Applied Psychology, 81,* 628–647.

Peters, T. (1987). *Thriving on chaos.* New York: Harper & Row.

Peters, T. (1994). *Liberation management.* New York: Knopf.

Piaget, J. (1948). *The moral judgment of the child.* Glencoe, IL: Free Press.

Parthasarthy, R., & Sethi, S. P. (1993). Relating strategy and structure to flexible automation: A test of fit and performance implications. *Strategic Management Journal, 14,* 529–549.

Rawls, J. A. (1971). *A theory of justice.* Cambridge, MA: Harvard University Press.

Rest, J. R. (1986). *Moral development: Advances in theory and research.* New York: Praeger.

Rest, J. R. (1994). Background: Theory and research. In J. R. Rest & D. Narvaez (Eds.), *Moral development in the professions: Psychology and applied ethics* (pp. 1–26). Hillsdale, NJ: Lawrence Erlbaum Associates.

Rest, J. R., & Narvaez, D. (1994). Summary: What's possible? In J. R. Rest & D. Narvaez (Eds.) *Moral development in the professions: Psychology and applied ethics* (pp. 213–224). Hillsdale, NJ: Lawrence Erlbaum Associates.

Sellers, P. (1995, October 16). Sears, in with the new . . . out with the old. *Fortune, 133,* 96–98.

Taylor, A., III. (1996, September 9). The man who put Honda back on track. *Fortune, 134,* 92–100.

Thibaut, J., & Walker, L. (1975). *Procedural justice: A psychological analysis.* Hillsdale, NJ: Lawrence Erlbaum Associates.

Treviño, L. K. (1986). Ethical decision making in organizations: A person–situation interactionist model. *Academy of Management Review, 11,* 601–617.

Tyler, T., & Bies, R. (1990). Beyond formal procedures: The interpersonal context of procedural justice. In J. S. Carroll (Ed.), *Applied social psychology and organizational settings* (pp. 77–98). Hillsdale, NJ: Lawrence Erlbaum Associates.

Tyler, T. R., & Lind, E. A. (1992). A relational model of authority in groups. In M. Zanna (Ed.), *Advances in Experimental Social Psychology, 25,* 115–191. San Diego, CA: Academic.

Victor, B., & Cullen, J. B. (1988). The organizational bases of ethical work climates. *Administrative Science Quarterly, 33,* 101–125.

Weber, J. (1990). Managers' moral reasoning: Assessing their responses to three moral dilemmas. *Human Relations, 43,* 687–702.

Williams, B. (1985). *Ethics and the limits of philosophy.* Cambridge, MA: Harvard University Press.

Emerging Justice Concerns in an Era of Changing Psychological Contracts

Russell Cropanzano
Cynthia A. Prehar
Colorado State University

Organizational justice research developed in the second half of the 20th century and came of age in the 1980s and 1990s. One might suspect that, perhaps, scholars of justice would be devoted futurists. Because fairness research evolved near the end of one century, its proponents might naturally look to the next. Although this speculation has an intuitive appeal, one could also argue that organizational justice researchers have not spent enough time looking ahead and may have to play catch-up with their colleagues in other specialties (cf., Cascio, 1995; Goldstein & Gilliam, 1990; Offermann & Gowing, 1990). If we, as justice researchers, have been slow to examine our future, it may be that such an examination is especially difficult for us given the nature of our topic. For justice researchers, looking to the future is fraught with both theoretical and applied problems.

Theoretically speaking, organization justice is concerned with the perceptions people form about their work outcomes and the procedures by which these outcomes are allocated. In general, justice perceptions are defined relative to some referent. (In)justice perceptions result from comparing an actual event to some imagined standard (Cropanzano & Ambrose, in press; Cropanzano & Schminke, in press; Kulik & Ambrose, 1992). As the standards change, perceptions of fairness change accordingly. The answer to the question, "What is fair?," alters across people, situations, and times. This aspect of justice theory is appealing: Changing standards of fairness makes the theory flexible enough to account for differences in justice perceptions. However, this flexibility is also the source of our dilemma in extrapolating justice research into the future. If standards are constantly changing, how can we predict what will be perceived as fair (or unfair) into the future? What we lack in current theory is an understanding of how standards change from one time to the next. Justice is dynamic, not static. Lacking an understanding of these dynamics, we can ascertain neither the trajectory nor velocity of changing justice perceptions. Unfortunately, empirical theories of justice have seldom dealt with its fluid nature, and this is a conspicuous omission if we wish to foretell the future.

Practically speaking, the real-world situations that engender a contemporary sense of unfairness are likely to change. Almost all observers agree that in the next century the work economy will become more global and more competitive (e.g., Greider, 1997; Massachusetts Institute of Technology Commission on Industrial Productivity, 1989; Thurow, 1996). These changes may exacerbate existing concerns over such issues as downsizing, but they may also create new challenges such as the increased use of temporary workers and rising workloads.

To look to the future, therefore, justice researchers will need to overcome two problems: How to think about changing perceptions and changing standards of fairness; and to identify which aspects of the work environment will require out attention in the future. The first problem is one of theory; the second is one of application. The goal of this chapter is to navigate a route through these twin dilemmas. As such, this chapter is organized into two distinct parts, each corresponding to one of the two problems we have identified.

In the first part, we address the theoretical concerns by offering a preliminary framework for thinking about how standards of fairness evolve. Our framework is based on the idea of psychological contacts. We argue that justice perceptions are defined relative to psychological contracts negotiated between individuals and between individuals and organizations. These contracts define the acceptable standards on which justice is predicated. As the contracts change, so do standards of fairness. Thus, if justice is defined relative to the standards embodied in contracts, and contracts exhibit development over time, then justice standards should change accordingly. Fortunately, although the justice literature has not yet addressed how standards change, the psychological contracts literature has (e.g., Morrison, 1994; Robinson, Kraatz, & Rousseau, 1994; Rousseau, 1995, chap. 6, this volume). We illustrate the link between contracts and justice by first providing a brief overview of contracts and how they change. Then, we will pose a prefatory structure for integrating the two literatures.

In the second part of the chapter, we turn our attention away from these theoretical concerns and examine the work environment from the perspective of global economic changes. Based on this examination, we identify several issues that we believe will require the attention of justice researchers in the 21st century. These include downsizing, the temporary workforce, wage concerns, and rising workloads. All of these will likely become salient concerns in the years ahead.

PART I: A THEORETICAL EXAMINATION
OF PSYCHOLOGICAL CONTRACTS
AND ORGANIZATIONAL JUSTICE

What is fair now might not be fair in the future; few would dispute this point. However, the challenge that confronts us is how to anticipate and understand shifting standards of fairness. In projecting justice into the next century, the key theoretical problem one encounters is understanding the dynamics of fairness perceptions. By dynamics, we refer to changing standards regarding what is fair. Neither our obligations nor the obligations of others are sacrosanct. As obligations shift, so to do our perceptions of fairness. For example, the American judiciary once viewed organizations as the exclusive property of their owners (usually shareholders). Because a private firm belonged to certain individuals, then those individuals had the right to hire and fire their employees more or less at will. Because the job was the property of the owners, it could be granted or taken away at the owners' behest (Youngblood & Bierman, 1985). More recently, U.S. courts have begun to view jobs as, at least in part, the property of the job incumbent. When an individual has done his or her job well for an extended period of time, then he or she obtains a sort of "squatter's rights" that obligate owners to provide a minimum of protection from capricious discharge (Gordon & Lee, 1990). Arbitrary dismissal was more likely to be fair historically and less likely to be fair today. What was just changed over time. As our perceptions of commitments change, so do our perceptions of justice.

Often theories of organizational justice are not explicit as to how standards of justice change. These dynamics have not been fully articulated. Fortunately, a related body of research exists to help us address this problem. The literature on psychological contracts has examined how standards of right and wrong evolve in various work settings. Consequently, if research on psychological contracts were integrated with research on organizational justice, then the former could inform the latter as to the dynamics of fairness. As a preliminary inquiry into this possibility, we examine psychological contracts in the following two sections. First, we review the literature on contracting and contract change. Following this review, we discuss organizational justice in light of psychological contracts, posing a potential model for integrating the two constructs.

What Are Psychological Contracts
and How Are They Negotiated?

Research on psychological contracts is predicated on the fact that people form agreements about their mutual responsibilities. Very loosely, we might say that a contract is a shared belief that one person will perform (or withhold) some actions in return for a reciprocal gesture by another individual. Contracts facilitate behavior, defining what is right in a particular situation and thereby making social coordination possible (for reviews see Rousseau, 1989; Shore & Tetrick, 1994). A complete discussion of the different types of psychological contracts is well beyond the scope of this chapter. The reader is referred to excellent reviews by Rousseau (1989; 1995), Rousseau and Parks (1993) and Shore and Tetrick (1994). Suffice it to say, however, that all contracts are not explicit. Many are implied but never formalized or concretely explicated. Relatedly, many contracts are abstract and open ended. For example, employees may believe that their employer has an obligation to treat them respectfully, without specifying precisely what respectfully means. As the reader will readily observe, the sometimes implicit and open-ended nature of contracts provides fertile ground for misunderstandings and perceived injustice.

Although contract terms are not always clearly explicated, we can still define the basic elements of most contracts. Rousseau and Parks (1993, pp. 6–7; for a related discussion see also Rousseau, 1995, pp. 16–21) maintain that contracts have at least three attributes. First, there is a *promise*. Individuals (or other social entities such as work organizations) agree to behave in a certain fashion. Second, there is a *payment* or *consideration*; in return for the promise, another individual or social entity provides something in return. This need not be financial compensation but could be a reciprocal set of actions. For instance, a firm may guarantee job security (a promise) and in return, an employee may be willing to master specialized skills that are useful for her employer but are not transferable to other organizations (a payment). Third is *acceptance*. Both parties must give their voluntary and informed consent. Failing this, a fair deal cannot be struck. Promise, payment, and acceptance delineate three stages at which fairness concerns could arise should any of these factors be breached.

One advantage that psychological contract researchers have over justice researchers is that the former have addressed the nature of changing psychological contracts. Contract researchers have articulated, albeit at a primarily theoretical stage, the ways in which and reasons why perceptions of promises, payments, and acceptances may change. Psychological contracts evolve at many stages in the employment relationship and between many individuals (Kissler, 1994; Shore & Tetrick, 1994). For instance, at the hiring stage, recruiters explicitly and implicitly communicate expectations to potential employees, thereby creating a set of implied promises (e.g., "Most people who start in this job end up in upper level management within 5 years"). As new employees are socialized into an organization, their perceptions might be further shaped by conversations with or observations of co-workers and their supervisors. For example, although the recruiter may have promised the employee that his or her weekends would definitely be free, he or she may soon come to realize from watching his or her co-workers that he or she will need to work overtime and on the weekends to achieve the promise of an upper level management position. Therefore, contracts are fluid and are often revised throughout one's employment with a company. Likewise, as these contracts change, so do standards of fairness. What was fair according to one contract may well be unfair according to another. Thus, one can glean an understanding of the dynamics of justice perceptions by understanding the dynamics of changing contracts.

Rousseau and Parks (1993) offered a taxonomy of reasons as to why psychological contracts might change. Factors internal to the workers and external in the work environment might precipitate change over the course of the employment relationship. The first potential reason for change is *contract drift*. This is largely an internal phenomenon that occurs when the passage of time alters one's understanding of the contract terms, perhaps as a function of personal values or general cognitive psychological phenomenon (e.g., self-serving bias). For instance, new managerial hires might willingly put in a lot of unpaid overtime to impress their supervisors at the start of the job. They feel obligated to do so and the employer comes to expect such behavior. However, after a few years, these employees may feel they have "paid their dues" and should be able to work regular hours. Consequently, they may come to see unpaid overtime as unfair and attempt to change their payment to the organization.

Maturational change is another explanation for how contracts are altered. This phenomenon is closely related to contract drift and occurs when time changes the meaning and stimulus values of job characteristics and other work experiences. For instance, an employee who has invested 10 years in an organization may feel more invested in his job than an employee who has only worked there 1 year. A seasoned employee is more likely to have a close network of acquaintances and more formal and informal obligations to others. For this reason, he or she may think it unfair to pull up stakes and find a new position. When compared to a newer hire, the veteran employee may feel that justice demands more loyalty and commitment to her employer.

Third, *social cues* offer a venue for contract change. Group norms and beliefs affect individual perceptions of the organization. If a work group is cohesive, the way they interpret changes (e.g., job redesign, downsizing) may affect the way individuals within the group negotiate their contracts with the organization. For example, a work group may have a good relationship with their immediate supervisor but not be very trustful of upper level management. When rumors of a layoff begin to circulate, the group may begin to associate their supervisor with one of them and individuals may become suspicious of once seemingly normal requests from the supervisor (e.g., "Business is slow today, would you like to leave early?"). What were once considered fair exchanges between the supervisor and subordinates are no longer considered so, as group norms influence perceptions of the psychological contract.

Finally, contracts may be altered due to an all-encompassing label of *organizational change*. Rousseau and Parks (1993) argued that policy and procedural changes (e.g., changes in compensation), changes in leadership, and reactions to economic pressures (e.g., shutting down a plant and relocating employees across the country) sends new messages to employees and thus, affects perceptions of old contracts. For instance, a sales division, in an effort to motivate its employees to sell more aggressively, might move from a base-salary plus commission-compensation plan to a 100% commission-only plan. Some employees may prefer this system and exert more effort to achieve their desired salaries. However, others who are not as sure about their ability to maintain previous salary levels, may feel the change was radically unfair. In both cases, the changed compensation practice has affected the implied contract between organization and employee.

In summary, we can see from this cursory review that there are several stages and several reasons why psychological contracts might change during an employment relationship. These changes are likely to provide signals for emerging justice concerns. In the section that follows we further explicate the relation between organizational justice and psychology contracts. In particular, we maintain that contracts provides referent standards against which we can ascertain fairness and unfairness. This observation allows for an integration of the contract and justice literatures.

Organizational Justice and Psychological Contracts

Returning to our original definition of contracts, we can see that they are perceptions of obligation between individuals or between an individual and the organization. When we believe that these obligations are met, we are likely to perceive that justice exists—even when the outcomes are not to our best advantage (e.g., Brockner & Wiesenfeld, 1996; Cropanzano & Folger, 1991; Folger & Cropanzano, in press). However, when we believe that those obligations are breached, then we are likely to perceive that an injustice exists. For example, in conducting a performance review, we might presume that a supervisor is obliged to take our opinions into account. When this anticipated voice is not allowed, we feel very strongly that we have been treated unfairly (Taylor, Tracy, Renard, Harrison, & Carroll, 1995).

In large measure, social justice and psychological contract researchers are talking about the same phenomenon but from a different point of view. Contract researchers begin with the terms of the agreement and look forward to the consequences of violation and fulfillment. Justice researchers, on the other hand, begin with the consequences of the agreement and look backward to the standards that originally gave rise to fairness perceptions. The simplest way to understand the relation between justice and contracts is to treat the terms of the contract as a predictor and justice as an outcome. In this model, a contract exists, one party acts in a way that is perceived to be inconsistent with the terms of the contract, and the other party feels a sense of injustice and moral outrage. Although not necessarily stated as such, research evidence is quite consistent with this perspective (Alexander, Sinclair, & Tetrick, 1995; Folger & Cropanzano, in press; Morrison & Robinson, 1997; Robinson, 1996; Robinson & Morrison, 1995; Robinson & Rousseau, 1994; Rousseau & Anton, 1988, 1991; Taylor, Masterson, McClear, & Goldman, 1996).

The relation between contracts and justice does not end with perceptions of injustice and moral outrage, however. Fairness perceptions carry over into the formation of new psychological contracts once the old ones are broken. In this sense, justice perceptions now act as a predictor and (new) contracts as the outcome. If individuals feel they have been treated unfairly, this will probably affect the negotiation and acceptance of new contracts. Promises and payments may be renegotiated, or acceptance may not come as easily.

What we are, in essence, proposing is a reciprocal relation between fairness and contracts. The terms of an accepted contract—what we perceive to be the explicit or implicit promises and payments—are the standards by which we evaluate fulfillment of the contract. If the terms are met, a sense of justice is maintained. If the terms change, however, then a breach of contract may be perceived and injustice perceptions may ensue. Violations of contracts lead to feelings of injustice which, in turn, affect the forging of new contracts. In this way, the two research literatures are intimately related (for a similar perspective see Alexander et al., 1995).

Summary

As argued in this chapter, justice perceptions result, at least in part, from one's perceptions of the psychological contract. Generally speaking, when the terms of a contract are met, one is being treated fairly. When they are violated, one is being treated unfairly. The advantage of this integration is that there is a sizable literature examining the causal variables that change psychological contracts. As these causes impact the terms of contracts, then perceptions of fairness should shift accordingly. This provides a means, however tentative, of understanding the dynamics of justice standards.

PART II: ECONOMIC CHANGES AND EMERGING JUSTICE CONCERNS

At the outset of this chapter, we identified two problems confronting researchers who desire to understand the emerging justice concerns of the next century. The first concern was a theoretical one. Part I of this chapter argues that psychological contracts offer a conceptual framework for comprehending potential shifts in justice standards. In this section, however, we leave this more academic concern and turn our attention to practical and applied issues.

As discussed, several economic trends and societal forces are leading to the breaking and re-negotiation of psychological contracts. Organizations are changing their promises; workers are changing their payments. These adjustments define the terrain of injustice perceptions. Organizational change has been prompted by the need to raise productivity in order to increase competitiveness. The solution to this goal, at least in principle, is straightforward: Do more with less. Other things being equal, productivity increases when costs drop or when output rises. In recent years, business has used three strategies for cutting personnel costs: downsizing (retaining fewer workers), using more contingent workers (who are less expensive and sometimes can be discarded more easily), and curtailing wage increases. At the same time, workloads have been increased. Thus, we anticipate that there will be four flashpoints for contact violation: downsizing, contingent workforce, wage stagnation and distribution, and rising workloads. These trends could continue to generate ill-will for as long as the current economic climate persists or until workers accept or forge new agreements. As such, each of these could be engines of injustice during the next century.

Downsizing and the Emergence of New Employment Contracts

Since the early 1980s, a business practice commonly termed *downsizing* has proliferated in U.S. companies. Several studies illustrate this trend. For example, between 1987 and 1991, more than 85% of Fortune 1000 companies downsized their white-collar staffs (The Wyatt Company, 1993). The American Management Association found that 39% of the 1,084 companies surveyed in 1988 had reduced their workforce (American Management Association, 1994). Experts also agree that downsizing is far from over (McKinley, Sanchez, & Schick, 1995). What has led U.S. companies to adopt this practice and what implications might this have for justice researchers? Given that downsizing does not always lead to gains in productivity (The Wyatt Company, 1993) and almost invariably contributes to work stress (Ornstein & Isabella, 1993), answers to the questions seem particularly urgent for today's workforce.

A Brief History of Downsizing and the Old Employment Contract. Downsizing has a relatively recent history, with the practice really only coming into popularity in the late 1970s and early 1980s. But what did the old employment contract look like before then? To begin answering this question, we need to examine the post World War II economy. After the Second World War, the U.S. economy flourished. America was technologically more advanced than many other nations. In addition, the country had not suffered the devastating effects of war on its own soil (MIT Commission on Industrial Productivity, 1989). Business was predictable and stable. As a consequence, the United States enjoyed a significant portion of the market share and could afford large organizations with several layers of management (Gottlieb & Conkling, 1995). The "bigger is better" philosophy was taught in business schools and embodied in large companies like IBM and General Motors. Firms that accepted this philosophy tended to have large payrolls and several layers of management (Holland, 1989; Tomasko, 1987; Whetten & Cameron, 1994).

Accompanying this economic success, many organizations explicitly or implicitly promised full employment and job security. Employment relationships were perceived to be long term and career progression traditionally happened via within-company promotions. Compensation practice and benefits were awarded based on tenure and hard work. Organizations offered these perks and workers expected the terms to continue in exchange for their loyalty and commitment. Samuelson (1995) argued that Americans developed a sense of entitlement during these times, feeling that certain rights should be guaranteed, including secure jobs, rising living standards, and satisfying work. Until the early 1970s, organizations seemed willing and able to fulfill these demands. But several trends converged to change the nature of what organizations could promise workers.

The recession of the 1970s was the first warning that business practices needed to change (Gottlieb & Conkling, 1995). Slow economic growth curtailed feelings of invincibility, as corporations were no longer witnessing steady gains in profit. Commensurate with this trend, international competition flourished, leading to product and service redundancy among competitors (Buch & Aldridge, 1991). U.S. companies were forced to get products to market faster in order to remain competitive. Accompanying these economic changes were advances in technology, which streamlined many work processes, making production faster but requiring fewer human workers (Appelbaum, 1991; Gottlieb & Conkling, 1990).

As these trends converged, U.S. companies were forced to reevaluate how they did business. In response to the rapidly changing market place and need for stronger financial bases for international competition, mergers and acquisitions became common business practices. Acquiring or taking over companies, however, often lead to duplication of layers and positions. One way to eliminate this redundancy, of course, was to eliminate the duplicated workers (Appelbaum, 1991; Offerman & Gowing, 1990). Downsizing had become a common method for dealing with the economic reality facing many companies.

Economic conditions have since improved, yet the practice of downsizing has not waned. Although many earlier downsizing initiatives were reactive, short-sighted responses to economic pressures, reductions in force have become strategic and intentional efforts adopted by even the healthiest of companies to improve productivity, efficiency, and competitiveness (Hitt, Keats, Harback, & Nixon, 1994). Downsizing and its consequences for workers do not appear to be diminishing soon. As a consequence, a new psychological contract has emerged between workers and organizations.

Justice Concerns and the New Employment Contract. McGregor and Tornow (1990) described some of the elements of the new contracts that have emerged since downsizing has been adopted as a common business practice. Job security and predictable career paths are less common, and workers must be flexible to meet to ups and downs of business cycles. Skills and requirements are more dynamic, and employees need to have a range of up-to-date skills, demanding life-long learning. Employee commitment is shifting more from the company to oneself; that is, today's workers are encouraged to think of themselves as self-employed even when they are employed with only one organization (Arnold, 1997).

Given this new state of contracting, where might fairness concerns arise? In addressing this question, we need to consider two stages of the downsizing effort: the actual duration when workers are laid-off and the aftermath and residual effects for the surviving workforce. First, any downsizing effort embodies fairness concerns for two groups of people: the victims and the survivors. Justice research has been slow to follow the victim's fate, but we do know that victims of involuntary job loss experience much stress during and after the loss of their jobs (Leana & Feldman, 1988; Ornstein & Isabella, 1993). It could be that procedurally fair downsizing policies (e.g., providing explanation, treating victims with dignity and respect) might help mitigate the negative effects of job loss, although this is in need of investigation. Other recommended human-resource policies could also be examined by justice researchers. For example, providing generous severance pay and outplacement counseling may influence perceptions of fairness as well.

But there is a more fundamental question. Why should organizations care about the opinions of people they let go? First, any employee should be considered a consumer. If a large number of employees are let go and feel they were treated with gross injustice, they may be a source of negative publicity for the company. In addition, there is a more immediate reason why organization should be concerned about how downsizing victims are treated: Their treatment effects the survivors attitudes and behaviors. Several studies have shown that procedural fairness is related to survivor's subsequent organizational commitment and trust in the organization (e.g., Brockner, 1994; Martin, Parsons, & Bennett, 1995). Perceptions of control during the downsizing effort also appear to affect survivors' perceptions of fairness and job satisfaction (Davy, Kinicki, & Schneck, 1991). Thus, organizations are encouraged to attend to justice issues during a downsizing effort as perceptions of fairness appear to affect multiple constituencies.

Justice research could be applied to other aspects of the surviving workforce. Downsizing efforts often lead to increased workloads and less satisfying work (Hitt, Keats, Harback, & Nixon, 1994). Another critical concern is defining career success (Arnold, 1997). A downsizing initiative may fundamentally change the career path for managers and other employees. Opportunities for advancement are often fewer as many middle- and upper level management positions are eliminated (London, 1987; O'Neill & Lenn, 1995). If promotions are no longer the way by which success if defined, how will employees react to new reward systems? These are areas that to date have not been addressed by justice researchers but offer a fertile ground for more investigation.

In conclusion, the business practice of downsizing has fundamentally changed the nature of psychological contracts between workers and organizations. Workers are less trustful and organizations are not guaranteeing the benefits they used to. As argued in the first part of this chapter, the changing contract should be accompanied by changing standards of fairness. Therefore, the links between contracts, justice, and downsizing deserves the attention of researchers and practitioners alike.

The Rise of a Temporary Workforce

Around 1990, only 100 temporary employment agencies and approximately 470,000 temporary employees existed in the United States (Feldman, 1995). Since the 1990s, however, the United States has witnessed a rapid growth in the temporary employment industry, with more than 1.6 million employees employed by over 1,500 agencies (Fierman, 1994). Employment of a temporary workforce has been adopted as a business strategy for many of the same reasons as downsizing was in the last part of this century. In response to ebbing economic cycles, increased labor costs, and the shift from manufacturing to service and retail industries, organizations have turned to the temporary workforce to meet their production and staffing needs (Beard & Edwards; 1995, Feldman, 1995). von Hippel, Magnum, Greenberger, Heneman, and Shokglind (1997) delineated more specific strategical reasons as to why organizations adopt temporary workforces. These include cutting costs (e.g., recruitment, training, wages, and benefits), increased flexibility (e.g., meet cyclical production demands), and avoiding restrictions and consequences (e.g., liabilities associated with hiring and firing employees, unions, etc.). Instead of using temporary employees as replacements for the occasional sick or vacationing permanent employee, many organizations now have positions that are permanently staffed by temporary workers. Given the sharp rise of this form of employment, a closer look at the psychological contracts between these workers and organizations is warranted.

The "New" Temporary Employment Contract and Employee. Twenty years ago, temporary workers were traditionally used as replacements for permanent employees who themselves were temporarily absent, perhaps due to vacation or illness (von Hippel et al., 1997). The typical temporary employee was a married woman with children, or a student in high school or college. These employees were willing to accept lower wages and fewer benefits in exchange for a more flexible work schedule and shorter term commitments (Feldman, 1995). In general, temporary employees seemed happy with this arrangement.

The profile of temporary employees in today's workforce is quite different, however. Today's temporary worker, in addition to the married woman and college student, may very well be a downsized worker looking for permanent employment, a retired worker looking for supplemental income to make ends meet, a recent college graduate who is unable to find satisfying full-time work, or a woman looking to retool her portfolios before reentering the labor market after an absence from full-time employment (Feldman, 1995). Although some of these workers are, in fact, looking only for short-term arrangements (commonly called permanent temps), many are hoping to find permanent work and income to support their families (temporary temps). When compared to permanent work, temporary work usually pays less, comes with fewer benefits, has little to no job security, and offers few opportunities for growth. Given this, it should come as no surprise to find that employees in the *temporary temps* category are often very dissatisfied with the employment arrangement (Beard & Edwards, 1995; Parks & Kidder, 1994).

Over 70% of temporary employees fall in the temporary temps category (von Hippel et al., 1997). Although they are looking for permanent work, their experiences as a temporary employee differ quite dramatically from the typical permanent employee (Feldman, 1995). Wages are often lower, although their work contribution relative to permanent employees may be equivalent once the temporary employee has learned the job. Few fringe benefits, if any, exist, and the absence of health insurance is a large source of stress for workers who may find themselves in temporary work arrangements for several months ongoing. Finally, temporary workers are not guaranteed employment. The organization employing their services can terminate them at will and the temporary employee has little recourse if their dismissal happens earlier than the original terms stated. In short, the psychological experience of temporary workers searching for permanent work is often fraught with stress and uncertainty.

Effects of Temporary Work and Areas of Concern for Justice Research.
Beard and Edwards (1995) offered several psychological links between temporary workers and job attitudes including job satisfaction, job involvement, and commitment. The job insecurity surrounding temporary work results in a psychological experiences of powerlessness. Not knowing when an employment contract will end, not having a regular paycheck to rely on, and other feelings of unpredictability could lead to decreased job satisfaction, involvement, and well-being. Other links to these outcomes include a loss of control over one's work environment and employment terms, more transactional–economic psychological contracting as opposed to relational contracting, and social comparisons between their outcomes and those with permanent positions. Beard and Edwards concluded that temporary workers are employees at risk and that more attention needs to be paid to the potentially negative outcomes of contingent work.

The temporary worker is not the only employee affected by temporary work arrangements, however. Full-time, permanent employees are affected by these arrangements as well (Feldman, 1995; Pearce, 1993). Some employees may feel like supervisors assign temps the easy work, whereas they are left with harder assignments at no additional pay. Pearce (1993) found that permanent employees who worked with contract laborers had less organizational trust than permanent employees who worked alone. She also noted that permanent employees may feel the organization is exploiting contract laborers. Therefore, although temporary workers may seem like an ideal short-term remedy for many employment situations, long-term effects on the core workforce demand further attention (Feldman, Doerpinghaus, & Turnley, 1994).

Given this discussion of how temporary work arrangements may affect temporary and permanent workers, how might justice research contribute to our understanding of these work arrangements? Equity evaluations seem germane to the study of contingent work. Most of the research reviewed here implies that comparisons are made between temporary and permanent employees: Do I get paid as much? Is my work less (or more) challenging? Do I get the same benefits? Furthermore, procedural and distributive justice issues come into play. If a temporary temp knows that a position will end (i.e., it is not a temp-to-hire arrangement), can being let go in a procedurally fair manner lessen the psychological blow of these experiences? Answers to these questions could contribute considerably to our understanding of temporary workers as this segment of the workforce has been relatively untouched by justice researchers.

Wages: Slower Growth Rates and Uneven Distributions

Wage Stagnation. It has, or had, become almost a truism in America that each generation would live better than the one that preceded it. In part, this was reflected in the expectations that wages would continue to rise (Samuelson, 1995). Unfortunately, wage growth has not continued apace with expectations. The income of working families has been relatively flat since the early 1970s. In 1973 the median family earned $30,663 per year. In 1987 this figure was $30,853 (Phillips, 1990). Similar conclusions appear if we examine the change in weekly earnings per worker during the same period. If we equate all earnings in 1987 dollars, then between 1972 and 1987, the median weekly wages dipped from $366 to $312. Mostly, this trend has been due to the frozen wage rates for many middle-class and working-class men. Upper and upper middle-class workers have fared somewhat better, continuing the income growth of previous decades (Peterson, 1994). As seen in the next section, this has led to a greater wage polarization, as the relatively wealthy have become wealthier and the relatively poor have become poorer (Frank & Cook, 1995; Philips, 1990).

Fortunately, earnings for female workers have grown somewhat more than earnings for their male counterparts, reducing (although not eliminating) the gender gap and rescuing family incomes (Schor, 1991; Thurow, 1996). By 1987, women were earning about 70% as much as their male co-workers (Philips, 1990). Although women were still relatively underpaid, this was certainly an improvement from 62.5% in 1979. Male wage earners, on the other hand, watched their incomes drop somewhat. Within two-parent household, women were able to off-set the decline in male wages. This not only protected overall family earnings, it also served to keep the U.S. per capita income rising (Philips, 1990; Schor, 1991). The downside, however, is that this rescue could only take place in intact families with two wage earners. Single parent families, the vast majority of which are headed by women, are over-represented among the poor (Bennett, 1994; Peterson, 1994).

The causes of these stagnant wages are complex and not easily understood. As Greider (1997) observed, global capitalism gives organizations a much stronger bargaining position vis-a-vis their workforce. For example, U.S. firms in many industries, such as automobiles and steel, need to remain competitive with foreign competitors. Many of these competitors have a lower wage workforce. Depending on the skill level required to produce the product, businesses can relocate to other nations and export their products back into the United States. Thus, fewer U.S. workers are needed and those that remain have less clout for demanding pay increases. Likewise, low-productivity growth, of course, must almost inevitably flatten wage growth. If firms are not producing more, than their profits are apt to lag and there will be less to distribute to employees (Prichard, 1992). Thus, faster productivity growth could be one tool for improving flagging wages.

Women are over one half of the U.S. population. As they have entered the workforce in greater and greater numbers, women have inevitably expanded the pool of potential employees. Through a simple process of supply and demand, therefore, the dollar value of a given worker may have fallen. This is an intriguing possibility to consider from a justice perspective. Is it unfair to men that they must now compete with women? The answer depends on whether one views justice from a normative perspective (e.g., as a philosopher trying to answer a "should" question) or from a phenomenological perspective (e.g., as a justice researcher trying to anticipate who will feel unfairly treated during the next century).

From a normative perspective, the fact that women's earnings have risen relative to men does not show that men were unfairly treated. In fact, it demonstrates the exact opposite. Higher wages illustrate that women are valuable workers. This suggests that the previous underemployment was due to something that artificially restricted women's access to jobs and opportunities. Societal norms of sexism were probably the principal culprit. Looked at from this perspective, it is difficult to sympathize with an aggrieved male worker, especially given that women's earnings still lag behind. In fact, one might even argue that male workers were overpaid relative to what they should have been earning in a fair-labor market. On the other hand, justice judgments are not always rational. They can be biased by self-interest. For this reason, one could predict a tendency to blame female workers. This would not be normatively correct, of course, but it could become a problem if present trends continue. One might hope, instead, that a growing economy will produce opportunity for all.

The relative changes in female versus male earnings might create a future dilemma for justice researchers. Implicitly, many justice researchers have advocated giving people those things that they see as fair, such as greater voice and equitable pay. How might we respond, however, if promoting (subjectively perceived) justice for one group comes at the disadvantage of another? Perhaps justice researchers should investigate ways of persuading people that they are not being treated unfairly. The literature on social accounts (Tyler & Bies, 1990) would be a good place to begin.

Before concluding, we should ask one final question: How serious is the problem of wage stagnation? In this regard, there are some hopeful signs. Part of the problem might be statistical, lying in the way the government calculates inflation. Every month the U.S. Bureau of Labor Statistics (BLS) calculates the Consumer Price Index (CPI). The CPI is based on a metaphorical basket of many goods and services. The BLS surveys a sample of 4,800 households as to which items they purchase and how much they spend on each. The CPI has become an extremely popular way of measuring inflation (for an introductory discussion of the CPI, see Moore, 1985).

However, the CPI has various potential pitfalls. Some economists have recently argued that it overstates the amount of inflation by as much as 1.5% (Miller, 1996). A lower CPI means that real incomes are higher than is commonly realized. The value of money changes with the inflation rate. As inflation increases, a dollar is worth less because it takes more of them to purchase a particular good or service. For this reason, when incomes are compared over time, the earnings must be represented in constant dollars. The dollars are constant in the sense that they are standardized for a particular year. Using constant dollars adjusts for inflation, but inflation is estimated with the CPI. If the CPI overestimates inflation, then the constant dollars are, in a manner of speaking, overcorrected. The value of the dollar has decreased less than would be apparent. In other words, the dollar can purchase more commodities than the CPI-adjusted estimates tell us it can. Consequently, it is quite possible that income figures used in this chapter actually understate the growth in earnings. This is an encouraging possibility, because it would mean that the American dream may not be so far away as some commentators have suggested. Justice researchers may be (mercifully) spared this research topic.

Rising Pay Inequality. Regardless of this vicissitudes of the CPI, another economic trend remains. Wealth in the United States has become more and more unevenly distributed (Peterson, 1994; Sheppard, Lewicki, & Minton, 1993; Thurow, 1996). Although scholars hotly debate the size and cause of this wage polarization, few dispute its existence (see Frank & Cook, 1995, for an excellent discussion). Some telling statistics are provided by Philips (1990). In the period between 1977 and 1987, the after-tax family income of the top 1% of the U.S. population leaped from $174,498 to $303,900. By comparison, the bottom 10% of the U.S. population saw their earnings slid from $3,528 to $3,157. There was a big gap to begin with, and it became even bigger. Data reviewed by Peterson (1994) shows that since the early 1970s, the rate of earnings growth is highly correlated with one's starting position. In particular, the wealthiest quintile in the early 1970s saw the largest income gains, the next wealthiest quintile saw the second largest income gains, and so forth—down to the poorest quintile, which showed slight losses (see also Phillips, 1990). These differences are dramatic. Between 1977 and 1989, the wealthiest 1% garnered a full 70% of the growth in personal income (Frank & Cook, 1995). Affluence has become so concentrated in the United States that the top 1% of household control a full 37% of the nation's wealth (Frank & Cook, 1995).

The extent of the problem varies by nation. Some regions, such as Latin America, are perennial bastions of inequality (Skidmore & Smith, 1992). Elsewhere the record is more mixed. For instance, during the 1980s, the United Kingdom underwent growing wage polarization (Moore & Sinclair, 1995). The top 20% of British wage earners earned 22% more in 1985 than they did in 1979. The bottom 10%, on the other hand, saw there earnings slip by 9.7% (Philips, 1990). Although perhaps less dramatic, rising inequality has also been observed in Japan (Philips, 1990). These global trends are important because they suggest that wider economic forces probably explain part of the growth in inequality. Nevertheless, it remains significant that U.S. incomes are relatively more unequal than elsewhere in the industrialized world. For example, Mishel and Bernstein (1993) found more wage polarization in the United States than in Australia, Canada, Germany, or Sweden. These cross-national differences suggest that economic policy choices are partially responsible for the rise in income inequality that has been observed in the United States.

The implications of these cross-national comparisons are complex. We can illustrate this by juxtaposing the United States and France. Relative to the United States, France has a more comprehensive social-welfare system, higher wages, and considerable worker protections against discharge and dismissal. As one might expect given these differences the growth in inequality has been less in France and more in the United States (Moore & Sinclair, 1995; Philips, 1990). However, before suggesting that Americans imitate the French system, we need to look more closely at the economic trade-offs. Relative to France, the United States has a lower unemployment rate, lower taxes, a stronger record of job creation and is more competitive internationally (e.g., Thurow, 1996). It is plausible, therefore, that French record of wealth redistribution, as well as the American record of economic growth, has come as a trade-off.

It may be too simple to assert that some nations are right and others wrong. Instead, it could be that some have chosen to err on the side of job creation and growth, whereas others have elected to err on the side of equality and worker protection. Societies seek to balance partially competing economic goals; they come to different conclusions about the requisite trade-offs. Although wage inequality could, in principle, be eliminated, to do so might carry heavy costs. A justice researcher might summarize this conundrum in the form of a question: Is it better for everyone to be poorer so that there is less inequality? Or alternatively, is it better for everyone to be richer but with more inequality? There is no easy yes–no answer to this question. The particulars depend on the amount of wealth and the size of the inequality, as well as on the values of the respondent. In the next century, it will be important for justice researchers to help society strike a balance between growth and equality.

Although we emphasize economic trade-offs, it is not our position that high levels of wage polarization are preferable to lower levels. We can illustrate this by considering the implications of American inequality within the context of our earlier discussions of contingent workers and downsizing. Bringing these three trends together, Peterson (1994) cautioned that a two-tiered wage system could emerge in the United States. In the upper tier would be those professional "knowledge workers" whose extensive education allows them to command high salaries and perhaps even a modicum of job security (although as we have seen even college-educated managers have been vulnerable to downsizing). The analyses of wage inequality presented here could suggest that these types of jobs will only be available to those in the upper income tier. For the rest, maintaining current living standards may become a more urgent concern. Many workers could see their earnings stagnate, or continue to stagnate, creating a smaller middle class and a growing chasm between the rich and the poor (for similar arguments see Philips, 1990).

It is sobering to consider how our national culture might change if this two-tiered wage system becomes a reality. When wealth is unequally distributed within in a society, there is likely to be more unrest (Thurow, 1996). Indeed, both Philips (1990) and Peterson (1994) suggested that this growing wage polarization in the United States may have something to do with the various social pathologies that have been observed, such as broken homes, urban decay, and a pervasive sense of cynicism (see also Kanter & Mirvis, 1989). This litany of social ills suggests the need for a closer look.

Violated Contracts and Implied Parties.   Many observers have maintained that stagnant wages or rising inequity are among the defining economic facts of the last generation (Peterson, 1994) and perhaps of the next (Samuelson, 1995). However, it is still an open question whether not psychological contracts shed any new light on these issues. In particular, a skeptic might argue that we have not answered the most fundamental question of all: In the case of unfavorable wage distributions, with whom does a contract exist? Answering this question requires extending our concept of psychological contracts.

Generally speaking, a contract is an agreement between two are more parties. However, in the case of disadvantageous wages, there may not be two parties as such. Instead, American workers may simply have a sort of generalized expectation—an imprecise sort of agreement—with society at large. If we accept this reasoning, then one party to the contract is the individual, but the other party is implied and not fully specified. Society is an indeterminate affiliation of individuals and groups. It is at best difficult and at worse impossible to fully specify what the term means. For this reason, any contract between an individual and society stretches the definition of a contract to the breaking point. We have already seen that contracts can involve tacit or implied agreements, but we now argue for the existence of tacit or implied partner.

A critic could reasonably argue that the incorporation of an implied party to an agreement renders the notion of a contract theoretically superfluous, or at least too vague to do provide any utility. This is an empirical question that cannot be definitely resolved here. However, we maintain that the concept of a tacit party may not be as unusual as it might first appear. In fact, evidence suggests that individuals frequently form agreements with large, ill-defined social entities. For example, Rousseau (1995) observed that workers form contracts with organizations and not just with other individuals. Likewise, individuals perceive that organizations can treat them with injustice (Cropanzano, Kacmar, & Bozeman, 1995) and support (Shore & Shore, 1995). In light of these findings, it may not be extraordinary to propose that people have contracts with the larger society, as they do with other social groupings.

Unfavorable Wage Distributions and Emerging Justice Concerns.   When we consider matters from a social justice perspective, the utility of a psychological contracts approach becomes more conspicuous. There are at least two reasons for this; one is theoretical and the other is practical. First, psychological contracts provide a sense of why we feel injustice, rather than simply disappointment, in the face of declining economic opportunities. Second, the idea of a tacit party may have predictive utility. In particular, it may afford us a fuller understanding of why disadvantaged people lash out at innocents.

It has been widely observed that Americans have come to expect a rising standard of living and may respond negatively if this expectation is not fulfilled (e.g., Peterson, 1994; Philips, 1990; Samuelson, 1995). However accurate these two observations may be, they are insufficient for our understanding of psychological contracts and justice because they do not necessarily follow from one another. Breached expectations will sometimes cause a sense of unfairness, but at other times they will not (Folger & Cropanzano, in press). Not receiving some benefit that one expected will no doubt engender disappointment, but for a sense of unfairness to result, an expectation must be transgressed in a manner that is morally wrong or ethically inappropriate. Thus, the fact that Americans might expect rising living standards should not promote unfairness unless those violated expectations are attributed to some (immoral) source. Put loosely, people need someone to blame. The idea of broken psychological contracts nicely captures this sense of moral violation, even if the tacit party is indefinite.

The idea of an implied or tacit party has practical advantages as well. It may help us to understand the peculiarly misdirected manner in which some individuals respond to wage stagnation and inequality. When workers see their opportunities diminish, they sometimes have a sense that someone or something has done something wrong. However, because the other party to the contract is as faceless as an entire society, upon whose doorstep does the rest blame? This example high-lights a problem that has not been investigated in either the organizational justice or the psychological contracts literature: There is a sense of rage and injustice that may have no precise target against which it can be directed.

We suggest that this pent-up animosity is in need of expression and will go off as soon as a suitable target is found. This idea might explain the seemingly ran-dom anger that comes from declining economic prospects. Those who have a sense that their contract has been violated, but who lack an explicit party to blame, may be especially susceptible to ideologies that attribute their travails to some powerless group, such as immigrants. This provides the wronged person with a safe (for him or her) target. Of course, this anger could easily be misdi-rected. For example, White Americans might blame African Americans although the latter have less wealth than the former (Loury, 1998). These observations also raise the possibility for the deliberate manipulation of people's emotions. A per-son who sees their economic prospects declining, may be induced to blame inno-cents. Such unscrupulous manipulation is, unfortunately, not unheard of in human history.

Rising Workloads

In a landmark book, Schor (1991) presented considerable evidence that the hours worked by Americans has steadily increased since the Second World War. Schor (1991) stated the matter bluntly: "Just to reach their 1973 standard of living, they [American employees] must work 245 more hours, or six extra weeks a year" (p. 81). This particular figure applies to production and supervisory workers. Schor's estimates vary depending on sundry factors, such as the job class in question, the particular method of estimating work hours, and the gender of the person being considered. Overall, however, Schor (1991) concluded that from 1969 to 1987, the average person worked an additional 163 hours per year. These figures are for so-called market hours and do not include hours worked to maintain one's house-hold. In addition, Americans have far fewer vacation days than are available in other industrialized nations (Schor, 1991). If one accepts Schor's thesis, then it would seem that the new psychological contract has demanded that subordinates simply do more.

How Serious is the Problem?   However, Schor's (1991) ideas are contro-versial in light of the issues this chapter has already considered. The most impor-tant concerns are in regard to such trends and downsizing and contingent work (i.e., part-time and temporary workers). If more and more people are being down-sized or are working part-time, it could be argued that work loads should be de-creasing. This possibility runs directly counter to Schor's thesis. The challenge for economists is to rectify these seemingly disparate trends. In a recent analysis of these issues, Bluestone and Rose (1997) suggested a resolution. If we examine the broken contracts closely, it seems possible that the putative trends toward over and underwork are actually closely related. Paradoxically, they could even be reinforcing one another.

First, as Bluestone and Rose (1997) noted, we need to distinguish between people and jobs. A job is a position of paid employment. People hold jobs. Schor (1991) was interested in people. In her research, Schor was exploring the number of hours worked, on average, by different persons. However, contingent work is about jobs. This research investigates the number of jobs that were once full-time (or potentially could be full-time) and are now part-time. Now, consider the fact that many individuals work multiple jobs. If one asks people to report their hours worked, the method preferred by Schor (1991), then each respondent will aggregate his or her hours across the jobs that the individual is current holding. This produces a fairly high estimate of hours worked. On the other hand, if one polls employers, a method used by other economists, then these respondents will answer in terms of jobs. Because a given part-time job allows for fewer hours than a full-time position, these estimates are fairly low. Like Schor, this chapter is more concerned with people than with jobs. Thus, the job-based estimates are probably less relevant for our purposes.

However, according to Bluestone and Rose (1997), the second issue is the more important one. As a result of downsizing and the limited security of contingent jobs, many Americans find themselves in a cycle of "feast and famine" (p. 58). Paid work comes in intermittent waves, punctuated by intervals of down time in which no money is earned. To carry them through these lean periods, individuals often put in extra hours whenever work is available. For many, paid employment is "boom and bust." During a boom, people work a good deal; during a bust, many hardly work at all. Thus, many Americans seem to have the worst of both worlds. Depending on the time period in question, they may be both underworked and overworked.

After taking into account the number of hours worked by persons and the intermittent cycles of available employment, as well as adjusting for some reporting biases, Bluestone and Rose (1997) concluded that Americans are indeed working more hours than they used to, although Schor's (1991) estimates are probably somewhat inflated. More notably, the variability in hours worked may be more consequential than the mean number. The feast and famine cycle seems to be a characteristic of many people's work lives. Justice researchers have not begun to consider the implications of this.

Workloads and Justice Concerns. In his classic formulation of equity theory, Adams (1965) reminded us that when we ascertain fairness, both outcomes and inputs matter. Indeed, according to equity theory, it is our outcomes relative to our inputs that make the difference. If we earn less than a comparison other, we might still perceive fairness so long as we also contribute less (for a review, see Greenberg, 1982). It is equitable to pay high contributors more than low contributors, at least in some situations (Cropanzano & Schminke, in press). So far this chapter has only considered the outcome side of the equation. We have been concerned with what people expect to get from their psychological contracts, such as job security, stable employment, and a rising rate of pay. To complete this analysis we also need to reflect on employee inputs. These inputs are captured in the idea of workloads. When individuals form a psychological contract with an organization, they agree to contribute a certain amount of effort. Thus, rising workloads would seem to transgress this contract.

However, if we accept Bluestone and Rose's (1997) analysis, we have a problem. If a single organization unilaterally raised its employees' work hours, then we would obviously expect individuals to experience feelings of injustice and reduce their inputs, perhaps by working less. Yet, according to Bluestone and Rose, this is not what is occurring. Instead, individuals are working harder because they have taken on multiple jobs. It is conceivable, therefore, that no single employer is at fault. More properly, individuals will have a choice as to where they rest blame.

Because downsizing and contingent work seem to be partially driving the trend toward more work hours, then this problem could reduce to the types of contract violations that we reviewed in earlier sections. As we discussed in the case of downsizing, they might blame the organization that took their job, whereas in the case of contingent work they might blame the organization that refuses to hire them on a full-time and permanent basis. These transgressions would involve reasonably well-articulated contracts between individuals and their (potential) employers.

However, in the case of rising workloads, it is not always easy to ascertain who is accountable. For one thing, blame may be spread among multiple organizations. If one holds two jobs, for example, are both firms liable? For another, it is not always clear who violated what. For instance, consider the case of an individual who disdains unemployment. Let us stipulate that he or she accepts contingent work but maintains his or her preference for a full-time job. If the position is with a firm with which he or she has had no prior relationship, then they have no one-to-one contract that can be violated. Can the employer be seen as unfair for giving him or her only part of what he or she wanted? In these situations, it is simply not clear how blame would be assigned.

According to Bluestone and Rose (1997), these examples are not atypical. Given the trend toward rising work loads, it would be useful to understand more about these circumstances. Unfortunately, there is only limited theory and data to guide us. It is possible that individuals will invoke a contact with a tacit society and declare the nation as a whole to be responsible. Another possibility is that, lacking anyone to blame, people might shrug and accept their fate. Clearly, more research is needed to investigate how people understand contract violations when the state of affairs is particularly complicated.

SUMMARY AND CONCLUSIONS

Organizational justice researchers need to look to the future. Unfortunately, we have so far been stymied by this task. In this chapter, we argue that difficulties in forecasting our future are the result of two different problems. In Part I, we maintain that it would be easier for us to look ahead if we had conceptual paradigms that described the nature of changing standards of fairness. In the first half of this chapter, we attempt to address this problem by integrating the justice literature with research on psychological contracts. Standards of justice can be viewed as terms embodied in psychological contracts. When the contracts change, injustice will often follow. In Part II, we change our focus from theoretical concerns toward applied issues. We consider four trends that may lead to changing psychological contracts and, therefore, are potential flashpoints for justice research: downsizing, the rise of a contingent workforce, uneven pay distributions, and (arguably) higher work loads.

The thesis of this chapter—that justice researchers need a method for understanding changing standards of fairness—is tenuous if one considers a final caveat. Since the dawn of the industrial revolution, has there ever been a static period? When was the hypothetical golden age that did not see change? Contemporary scholars, for example, are fond of pointing out that modern businesses operate in a far more fluid environment than did their predecessors in the 1950s and 1960s, but in what sense is this true? That stable period, as we have seen, was characterized by a good deal of productivity and economic growth. Likewise, the decades proceeding this era witnessed a major depression and a world war. The types of changes vary from decade to decade, but the reality of change seems to be constant.

In the final analysis, perhaps the task of organizational scientists is less novel than we sometimes realize. Our era is typical in one respect: Change remains a defining attribute of modern capitalistic societies. The particular modifications and adjustments vary but change per se is omnipresent. However, it is for this reason that the task of looking ahead is so fundamental. If change is systematic, then any perspective on organizational justice that does not deal with change is inherently limited. Outside the confines of a few safe decades, the application of a static paradigm would be suspect. If justice researchers want to continue influencing theory and practice, then we need to investigate the ebb and flow of our ideas as the future unfolds.

REFERENCES

Adams, J. S. (1965). Inequity in social exchange. In L. Berkowitz (Ed.), *Advances in experimental social psychology* (Vol. 2, pp. 267–299). New York: Academic.

Alexander, S., Sinclair, R. R., & Tetrick, L. E. (1995). The role of organizational justice in defining and maintaining the employment relationship. In L. E. Tetrick & J. Barling (Eds.), *Changing employment relations: Behavioral and social perspectives* (pp. 61–89). Washington, DC: American Psychological Association.

American Management Association. (1994). *AMA survey on downsizing and assistance to displaced workers.* New York: American Management Association.

Appelbaum, S. H. (1991). How to slim successfully and ethically: Two case studies of "downsizing". *Leadership and Organization Development Journal, 12*(2), 11–16.

Arnold, J. (1997). The psychology of careers in organizations. In C. L. Cooper & I. T. Robertson (Eds.), *International review of industrial and organizational psychology* (Vol. 12, pp. 1–38). New York: Wiley.

Beard, K. M., & Edwards, J. R. (1995). Employees at risk: Contingent work and the psychological experience of contingent workers. In C. L. Cooper & D. M. Rousseau, *Trends in organizational behavior* (Vol. 2, pp. 109–126). New York: Wiley.

Bennett, W. J. (1994). *The index of leading cultural indicators: Facts and figures on the state of American society.* New York: Touchstone.

Bluestone, B., & Rose, S. (1997, March–April). Overworked *and* underemployed. *The American Prospect, 58*–69.

Brockner, J. (1994). Perceived fairness and survivors' reactions to layoffs, or how downsizing organizations can do well being good. *Social Justice Research, 7*(4), 345–363.

Brockner, J., & Wiesenfeld, B. M. (1996). An integrative framework for explaining reactions to decisions: The interactive effects of outcomes and procedures. *Psychological Bulletin, 120*, 189–208.

Buch, K., & Aldridge, J. (1991). O. D. under conditions of organizational in decline. *Organization Development Journal, 9*(1), 1–5.

Cascio, W. F. (1995). Whither Industrial and Organizational Psychology in a changing world of work. *American Psychologist, 50*, 928–939.

Cropanzano, R., & Ambrose, M. L. (in press). Procedural and distributive justice are more similar than you think: A monistic perspective and a research agenda. In J. Greenberg & R. Cropanzano (Eds.), *Advances in organizational justice.* Lexington, MA: New Lexington.

Cropanzano, R., & Folger, R. (1991). Procedural justice and worker motivation. In R. M. Steers & L. W. Porter (Eds.), *Motivation and work behavior* (5th Ed., pp. 131–143). New York: McGraw-Hill.

Cropanzano, R., Kacmar, K. M., & Bozeman, D. P. (1995). The social setting of work organizations: Politics, justice, and support. In R. Cropanzano & K. M. Kacmar (Eds.), *Organizational politics, justice, and support: Managing the social climate of work organizations* (pp. 1–18). Westport, CT: Quorum.

Cropanzano, R., & Schminke, M. (in press). Using social justice to build effective work groups. In M. Turner (Ed.), *Groups at work: Advances in theory and research.* Mahwah, NJ: Lawrence Erlbaum Associates.

Davy, J. A., Kinicki, A. J., & Schneck, C. L. (1991) Developing and testing a model of survivor responses to layoffs. *Journal of Vocational Behavior, 38*, 302–317.

Feldman, D. C. (1995). Managing part-time and temporary employment relationships. In M. London (Ed.), *Employees, careers, and job creation.* San Francisco, CA: Jossey-Bass.

Feldman, D. C., Doerpinghaus, H. I., & Turnley, W. H. (1994, Autumn). Managing temporary workers: A permanent HRM challenge. *Organizational Dynamics,* 49–63.

Fierman, J. (1994, January 24). The contingency workforce. *Fortune,* 30–36.

Folger, R., & Cropanzano, R. (in press). Accountability. In J. Greenberg & R. Cropanzano (Eds.), *Advances in organizational justice.* Lexington, MA: New Lexington.

Frank, R. H., & Cook, P. J. (1995). *The winner-take-all society.* New York: The Free Press.

Goldstein, I. L., & Gilliam, P. (1990). Training systems in the year 2000. *American Psychologist, 45*, 134–143.

Gordon, M. E., & Lee, B. A. (1990). Property rights in jobs: Workforce, behavioral and legal perspectives. In G. R. Ferris & K. M. Rowland (Eds.), *Research in personnel and human resources management* (Vol. 8, pp. 303–348). Greenwich, CT: JAI.

Gottlieb, M. R., & Conkling, L. (1995). *Managing the workplace survivors: organizational downsizing and the commitment gap.* Westport, CT: Quorum.

Greenberg, J. (1982). Approaching equity and avoiding inequity in groups and organizations. In J. Greenberg & R. L. Cohen (Eds) *Equity and justice in social behavior* (pp. 389–435). New York: Academic.

Greider, W. (1997). *One world, ready or not: The manic logic of global capitalism.* New York: Simon & Schuster.

Hitt, M. A., Keats, B. W., Harback, H F., & Nixon, R. D. (1994). Rightsizing: Building and maintaining strategic leadership and long-term competitiveness. *Organizational dynamics, 23*(2), 18–32.

Holland, M. (1989). *When the machine stopped: A cautionary tale from industrial America.* Boston, MA: Harvard Business School Press.

Kanter, D. L., & Mirvis, P. H. (1989). *The cynical Americans: Living and working in an age of discontent and disillusion.* San Francisco, CA: Jossey-Bass.

Kissler, G. D. (1994). The new employment contract. *Human Resource Management, 33,* 335–352.

Kulik, C. T., & Ambrose, M. L. (1992). Personal and situational determinants of referent choice. *Academy of Management Review, 17,* 212–237.

Leana, C. R., & Feldman, D. C. (1988). Individual responses to job loss: Perceptions, reactions, and coping behaviors. *Journal of Management, 14,* 375–389.

London, M. (1987). Employee development in a downsizing environment. *Journal of Business and Psychology, 2,* 60–73.

Loury, G. C. (1998). Unequalized. *The New Republic, 218*(14), 10–12.

Martin, C. L., Parsons, C. K, & Bennett, N. (1995). The influence of employee involvement program membership during downsizing: Attitudes toward the employer and the union. *Journal of Management, 21,* 879–890.

McKinley, W., Sanchez, C. M., & Schick, A. G. (1995). Organizational downsizing: Constraining, cloning, and learning. *Academy of Management Executive, 9*(3), 32–44.

Miller, M. (1996). Grow up. *The New Republic, 214*(20), 20–22.

Mishel, L., & Bernstein, J. (1993). *The state of working America.* Washington, DC: Economic Policy Institute/M. E. Shapre.

MIT Commission on Industrial Productivity (1989). *Made in America: Regaining the productive edge.* New York: Harper Perennial.

Moore, D. S. (1985). *Statistics: Concepts and controversies* (2nd ed.). New York: Freeman.

Moore, S., & Sinclair, S. P. (1995). *Sociology.* London: Hodder Headline.

Morrison, D. E. (1994). Psychological contracts and change. *Human Resource Management, 33,* 353–372.

Morrison, E. W., & Robinson, S. L. (1997). When employees feel betrayed: A model of how psychological contract violation develops. *Academy of Management Review, 22,* 226–256.

O'Neill, H. M., & Lenn, D. J. (1995). Voices of survivors: Words that downsizing CEO's should hear. *Academy of Management Executive, 9*(4), 23–34.

Offerman, L. R., & Gowing, M. K. (1990). Organizations of the future: Changes and challenges. *American Psychologist, 45,* 95–108.

Ornstein, S., & Isabella, L. A. (1993). Making sense of careers: A review 1989–1992. *Journal of Management, 19*(2), 243–267.

Parks, J. M., & Kidder, D. L. (1994). "Till death do us part . . ." Changing work relationships in the 1990s. In C. L. Cooper & D. M. Rousseau (Eds.), *Trends in organizational behavior* (Vol. 1, pp. 111–136). Chichester, England: Wiley.

Pearce, J. L. (1993). Toward an organizational behavior of contract laborers: Their psychological involvement and effects on employee co-workers. *Academy of Management Journal, 36,* 1082–1096.

Peterson, W. C. (1994). *Silent depression: Twenty-five years of wage squeeze and middle-class decline.* New York: Norton.

Philips, K. (1990). *The politics of rich and poor: Wealth and the American electorate in the Reagan aftermath.* New York: Harper Perennial.

Prichard, R. D. (1992). Organizational productivity. In M. D. Dunnette & L. M. Hough (Eds.), *Handbook of Industrial and Organizational Psychology* (2nd Ed., Vol. 3, pp. 443–471). Palo Alto, CA: Consulting Psychologists Press.

Robinson, S. L. (1996). Trust and breach of the psychological contract. *Administrative Science Quarterly, 41,* 574–599.

Robinson, S. L., Kraatz, M. S., & Rousseau, D. M. (1994). Changing obligations and the psychological contract: A longitudinal study. *Academy of Management Journal, 37*, 137–152.

Robinson, S. L., & Morrison, E. W. (1995). Psychological contracts and OCB: The effect of unfulfilled obligations on civic virtue behavior. *Journal of Organizational Behavior, 16*, 289–298.

Robinson, S. L., & Rousseau, D. M. (1994). Violating the psychological contract: Not the exception but the norm. *Journal of Organizational Behavior, 15*, 245–259.

Rousseau, D. M. (1989). Psychological and implied contracts in organizations. *Employee Responsibilities and Rights Journal, 2*, 121–139.

Rousseau, D. M. (1995). *Psychological contracts in organizations: Understanding written and unwritten agreements.* Thousand Oaks, CA: Sage.

Rousseau, D. M., & Anton, R. J. (1988). Fairness and implied contract obligations in job terminations: A policy-capturing study. *Human Performance, 1*, 273–289.

Rousseau, D. M., & Anton, R. J. (1991). Fairness and implied contract obligations in job terminations: The role of contributions, promises, and performance. *Journal of Organizational Behavior, 12*, 287–299.

Rousseau, D. M., & Parks, J. M. (1993). The contracts of individuals and organizations. In L. L. Cummings & B. M. Staw (Eds.), *Research in organizational behavior* (Vol. 15, pp. 1–43). Greenwich, CT: JAI.

Samuelson, R. J. (1995). *The good life and its discontents: The American dream in the age of entitlement, 1945–1995.* New York: Times.

Schor, J. B. (1991). *The overworked American: The unexpected decline of leisure.* New York: Basic.

Sheppard, B. H., Lewicki, R. J., & Minton, J. W. (1993). *Organizational justice: The search for fairness in the workplace.* Lexington, MA: Lexington.

Shore, L. M., & Shore, T. H. (1995). Perceived organizational support and organizational justice. In R. Cropanzano & K. M. Kacmar (Eds.), *Organizational politics, justice, and support: Managing the social climate of work organizations* (pp. 149–164). Westport, CT: Quorum.

Shore, L. M., & Tetrick, L. E. (1994). The psychological contract as an explanatory framework in the employment relationship. In C. L. Cooper & D. M. Rousseau (Eds.), *Trends in organizational behavior* (Vol. 1, pp. 91–109). Chichester, England: Wiley.

Skidmore, T. E., & Smith, P. H. (1992). *Modern Latin America* (3rd Ed.). New York: Oxford.

Taylor, M. S., Masterson, S. S., McClear, K. L., & Goldman, B. M. (1996, April). *Restoring the faith: Using procedural justice interventions to rebuild the psychological contract.* Paper presented at the annual meeting of the Society for Industrial and Organizational Psychology. San Diego, CA.

Taylor, M. S., Tracy, K. B., Renard, M. K., Harrison, J. K., & Carroll, S. J. (1995). Due process in performance appraisal: A quasi-experiment in procedural justice. *Administrative Science Quarterly, 40*, 495–523.

Thurow, L. C. (1996). *The future of capitalism.* New York: Penguin.

Tomasko, R. M. (1987). *Downsizing.* New York: American Management Association.

Tyler, T. R., & Bies, R. J. (1990). Beyond formal procedures: The interpersonal context of procedural justice. In J. S. Carroll (Ed.), *Applied social psychology and organizational settings* (pp. 77–98). Hillsdale, NJ: Lawrence Erlbaum Associates.

von Hippel, C., Magnum, S. L., Greenberger, D. B., Heneman, R. L., & Skoglind, J. D. (1997). Temporary employment: Can organizations and employees both win? *Academy of Management Executive, 11*(1), 93–104.

Wyatt Company. (1993). *Best practices in corporate restructuring.* Washington DC: Wyatt.

Youngblood, S. A., & Bierman, L. (1985). Due process and employment-at-will: A legal and behavioral analysis. In K. M. Rowland & G. R. Ferris (Eds.), *Research in personnel and human resources management* (Vol. 3, pp. 185–230). Greenwich, CT: JAI.

13

▼▼▼▼▼▼▼▼

Organizational Justice as Proaction and Reaction: Implications for Research and Application

Jerald Greenberg
Carolyn Wiethoff
Ohio State University

As Greenberg (1982, 1987) chronicled, when social psychologists and organizational psychologists first became interested in matters of justice in organizations, their focus was reactive in orientation. That is, they paid attention to the manner in which people responded to conditions they believed to be unfair. The most influential approach to embrace this orientation was Adams's (1965) theory of inequity, which examined the ways in which people sought to escape the aversive internal state of inequity they experienced when confronted with perceived imbalances between work-related outcomes and contributions. Then, beginning with Leventhal (1976), social scientists expanded their focus to proactive attempts to create equity (i.e., the way people seek to maintain fair distributions of resources between people). This launched a popular research approach examining people's adherence to various norms of justice (Greenberg, 1982; Greenberg & Cohen, 1982). These orientations not only complement each other, but together, they have provided considerable insight into the topic of organizational justice that is well represented in this book.

It is instructive to revisit the reactive–proactive distinction in justice research because of the important, but largely unrecognized, implications that is has for both research and application. We say "largely unrecognized" because justice scholars have so thoroughly blended both approaches in their work in such seamless fashion that for all practical purposes the reactive–proactive distinction is now little more than a historical footnote. However, we believe that several key insights for researching and applying organizational justice principles come to light by examining the manner in which the reactive–proactive distinction is addressed in contemporary research and theory. In short, we argue that each perspective focuses on a unique set of processes that need to be understood if we are to investigate and apply organizational justice principles to organizational practice (Greenberg & Lind, 2000). This chapter examines the issues underlying this argument.

Specifically, we begin by describing in more detail some fundamental distinctions on which our arguments are based. In doing so, we introduce a six-step framework outlining the basic processes by which justice judgments and efforts to promote justice are made in organizations. The remainder of this chapter describes each of these steps by highlighting the psychological processes and research questions associated with it. As seen later, this exercise is useful not only in suggesting some potentially valuable areas of future research but also as a tool for organizing the various themes addressed in this book.

A GENERIC JUSTICE FRAMEWORK

As a prelude to our analysis we propose a generic framework for organizing the various processes and steps that occur in addressing matters of organizational justice. In introducing this framework, we elaborate on the distinction between proaction and reaction on which the approach is predicated. We then outline the framework that guides our analyses in the rest of this chapter.

Reaction and Proaction: A Fundamental Distinction

Beneath the simplicity of the proactive and reactive approaches to organizational justice (Greenberg, 1987) lies a fundamental distinction that has guided the way justice research has been conducted for 25 years (for reviews, see Bartle & Hayes, 1999; Colquitt, Conlon, Wesson, Porter, & Ng, in press; Cropanzano & Greenberg, 1997). Essentially, the reactive orientation approaches justice as a percept: People experience situations, which they then perceive, and toward which they react (hence, the term *reactive*). This approach is based on studying justice perceptions as a consequence of environmental conditions, and these perceptions constitute the dependent variables used in our research. A typical focal question utilizing this orientation is: How do people respond to fair and unfair conditions?

By contrast, the proactive approach treats justice as a motive: People motivated to be fair do various things to achieve this state. Instead of considering the consequences associated with certain states, this approach examines the way people create those states. Conceptually, justice is treated as a cause, rather than a consequence. Concerns about justice are then treated as independent variables in our research. A typical focal question is: How can fair conditions be created?

It is easy to imagine how confusion may result by studying justice from both proactive and reactive orientations. If nothing else, approaching justice as an antecedent or as a consequence has profound implications for the research we do. After all, questions about whether and how to manipulate justice perceptions in the lab, or how to tap its predictive power in survey research, are central to the proactive approach. Likewise, questions about how to assess justice perceptions in an attitude survey, or how to make inferences about justice perceptions based on behavioral observations, are fundamental to the reactive approach. The way we address these research questions is an indication of the approach that guides our research. Moreover, as this chapter explains, it ultimately also has implications for the applying justice principles in organizations. To set the stage for this analysis, we describe a simple approach to organizational justice predicated on the sequence of generic processes that may be followed in an organizational setting.

Organizational Justice: A Process Sequence

The steps outlined here summarize a general sequence of psychological processes that are likely to be triggered in organizations. Although this sequence is logical, we readily acknowledge that in actual practice the various steps might not occur in the order we propose. Also, because our approach is generic and skeletal, we are aware that it ignores many of the rich factors that promise to complicate the processes we are describing. Indeed, we do not intend to be comprehensive. Rather, we offer this framework as a heuristic for organizing a series of processes that become salient when reactive and proactive approaches to justice are taken. We present this approach graphically in Fig. 13.1.

Our framework embraces the familiar *stimulus-organism-response* (i.e., S-O-R) approach that has become hegemonic in cognitive psychology (Solso, 1998). In general, we refer to an event (S) that occurs, which a focal person perceives (O), and to which he or she responds (R). Specifically, as it applies to organizational justice, we begin with a salient occurrence (e.g., a change in organizational policy, or the addition of new job responsibility). This event is then assessed (Step 1: Assessment), resulting in a perception (e.g., the event was fair or unfair). Next, the focal person decides how to respond (Step 2: Reaction), and then responds in some fashion (e.g., the person resigns from the job). These three processes and the two steps that connect them constitute the core of the reactive approach to organizational justice (i.e., responding to conditions of justice or injustice).

Assuming that the focal person's response is undesirable, and that this reaction is not dismissed as idiosyncratic, organizational policy-makers are likely to begin the process of assessing the consequences of the triggering event (Step 3: Response Feedback). This may lead an organizational official, such as a manager, to take steps to bring about certain conditions (e.g., to make the workplace desirable) that will lead employees to behave in some intended fashion. This triggers Step 4: Creation, which is intended to bring about a certain perceptual state—in our case, cultivating the impression that the organization or its agents acted fairly. Following this, the manager has to make the decision to take the actions pre-

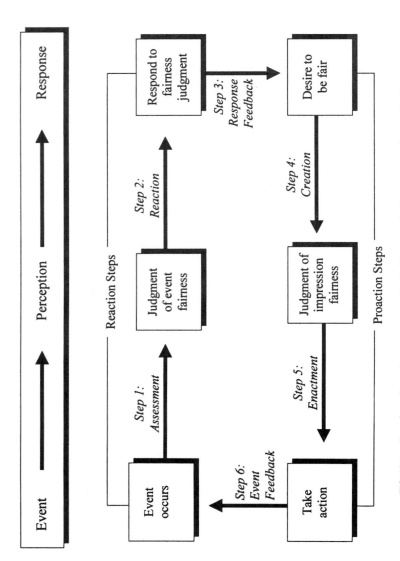

FIG. 13.1. Overview of generic processes associated with creating justice and responding to injustice.

viously identified or to revise them as needed (Step 5: Enactment). Finally, once the action has been taken, organizational policy-makers are then likely to once again assess the consequences of their actions (Step 6: Event Feedback).

Steps 4 and 5 represent the core of the proactive approach to organizational justice (i.e., organizational agents doing what is necessary to promote justice). Steps 3 and 6, the two feedback steps, also are carried out by organizational agents. They are distinguished from the other steps insofar as they focus more on organizational realities than on underlying psychological processes.

In the six sections that follow, we explain this approach in a way that promises to make it far less abstract. Specifically, we describe each of the various steps outlined here and highlight several key theoretical and applied issues that emanate from them. Specifically, we assert that different focal questions of justice application arise at each step in the process.

STEP 1: ASSESSMENT

Jay has been working for Just-Us Corp. as a machinist for three years, during which time he has developed an excellent record. His productivity has been outstanding, and he is hardly ever late or absent. Both his manager and his co-workers always can count on him. In fact, many consider Jay an exemplary employee. By contrast, Jay's colleague Tim, who came to the company at the same time, has struggled. Tim often fails to meet performance goals. His work has not been so poor as to warrant dismissal, but it's clear that Tim is not a star. One day, it is announced that the company will change the formula it uses to compute machinists' wages: Base pay will be lowered, but the piece-rate will be raised. As a result, more productive employees, like Jay, stand to make more money for doing the same work, whereas less productive employees, like Tim, can expect to make less.

In this situation, both Jay and Tim are expected to assess their situations vis-à-vis the new organizational reality they face. Assuming each is capable of making accurate projections, and that they are willing to do so, these two men are likely to reach different conclusions about how the new pay system is likely to impact them. This underscores a key point that is basic to the study of organizational justice—namely, organizational justice is based on individual perceptions and is inherently subjective. People perceive their subjective experience of a situation as reality; this experience drives their interpretation of, and their response to, the things they encounter (Pinkley, 1992). Every person's perception of a situation is uniquely shaped by the cognitive vantage point, or frame, from which he or she views it. Tannen (1979) described a frame as the way a person "organizes knowledge about the world and uses this knowledge to predict interpretations and relationships regarding new information, events, and experiences" (pp. 138–139). Frames define and order the relevance of particular information contained in a situation, creating normative expectations that form the basis of value judgments (Mather & Yngvesson, 1981).

The question of what prompts individuals to frame events as violations of justice principles is central to the field of organizational justice. This framing process is highly likely to occur during the assessment step. Questions of assessment focus on how and why justice issues become salient to individuals in a particular situation. People receive outcomes and are governed by procedures on a daily basis, but only in some of these instances do they evaluate the fairness of these occurrences. In this case, for example, the revision of the pay system is likely to prompt Jay and Tim to consider how the change affects them, and to assess the fairness of that change.

In this regard, several fundamental research questions emerge, each of which deals with determining antecedents of justice perceptions. For example, what components of a situation trigger justice-related concerns? Are some individuals more sensitive to justice issues than others are? And, in general, what prompts people to judge situations as being fair or unfair? Our current knowledge of what prompts people to engage a justice frame can be grouped into three general categories: context cues, information cues, and individual differences. Findings in each area are discussed in turn.

Context Cues

Considerable empirical evidence supports the claim that the relative significance of justice judgments is affected by the context in which events occur (e.g., Lowe & Vodanovich, 1995). Because justice judgments typically involve assessments of others' actions, the primary source of contextual information is social in nature. In examining social context, researchers have sought to identify those components of human interaction that contribute to the initiation of justice perceptions.

For example, Lind and his colleagues (see van den Bos, Lind, & Wilke, this volume) have presented fairness heuristic theory as a step in this investigation. These researchers view fairness frames as a tool people use to seek the information they need to feel socially secure in unfamiliar or unstable situations. Fairness is most salient, they claim, when individuals are not sure whether they can trust authority figures in their work environment (van den Bos, Wilke, & Lind, 1998). Consistent with the group-value model (Lind & Tyler, 1988), researchers have found that workers' beliefs about their inclusion in a particular group are shaped by the treatment they receive from their supervisors (Huo, Smith, Tyler, & Lind, 1996). Judgments about the fairness of this treatment are heuristics used to determine the overall trustworthiness, neutrality, and perceived respect individuals can expect in the work environment (Lind & Tyler, 1988). The group value model suggests that justice assessments are likely to be made when people need additional information to determine their place and status within a group.

Justice perceptions also are colored by the referent others chosen for outcome and process comparison. Social comparison is one of the primary techniques of allocation fairness judgments (Adams, 1965; Crosby, 1976; Folger, 1987). Although we know relatively little about how and why individuals select particular reference points for comparison (Grienberger, Rutte, & van Kippenberg, 1997), it is likely that the physical presence or absence of likely targets impacts their choice (for a review, see Suls & Wills, 1991). Indeed, this may be the case among Jay and Tim in our example. Because they were hired at the same time and work together on the job, each is likely to be a salient comparison person for the other. In this case, of course, making the comparison to Jay paints a bleak picture for Tim.

Justice judgments also depend on the rules and norms that have been established for a particular environment. Once rules and norms are established, violations of them can trigger perceptions of injustice (Bies & Tripp, this volume). This is precisely what appears to have happened in the case of Jay and Tim. These violations are salient because they violate established expectations of how interactions in the particular environment will occur. Research has demonstrated that failure to receive expected or promised outcomes can trigger perceptions of injustice (Greenberg, 1987). The violation of patterns of behavior or rewards that people have come to associate with certain behaviors or situations is perhaps one of the more salient triggering devices that prompts assessments of justice.

Information Cues

Some events are known to prompt justice frames across a variety of situations. For example, in addition to comparing their treatment to that of referent others, people also evaluate processes and outcomes relative to internalized standards of justice: their own beliefs about what is fair (Folger, 1987). When such standards are used, the type and timing of information presented can influence the initiation of justice-based framing across a variety of situations.

First, the order in which situationally relevant information is presented has implications for individual assessments of justice. For example, people may experience, or at least learn about, a procedure before they become aware of the personal outcomes it will yield. In this connection, recent research has demonstrated a primacy effect: People pay attention to information that is presented first (van den Bos, this volume), and that relates to procedures, particularly when believed to be unfair (Steiner, Guirard, & Baccino, 1999). If the initial information someone receives about a situation raises justice-related questions, it is likely that fairness assessments will continue to be made throughout the individual's interaction in that situation.

Second, the source of justice-related information also can affect perceptions. For example, many researchers have noted that the credibility of authority figures is enhanced when they communicate decisions in a thorough manner, and when they show dignity and respect in doing so (especially when the impact of the decisions is negative; Greenberg, 1990, 1993b; McFarlin & Sweeney, 1996). On the other hand, managers who deliver negative information without providing sufficient explanation or displaying interpersonal sensitivity are viewed as rude and demeaning, and their actions are more likely to be categorized as unjust (Greenberg, 1993a).

Individual Differences

Another class of factors that may influence the way Jay and Tim respond to the organizational change they encounter is the individual differences between them. For example, according to research on equity sensitivity (e.g., O'Neill & Mone, 1998), it is possible that one of these men will be more inclined to perceive inequities than the other (Huseman, Hatfield, & Miles, 1987). It also is possible that if either Jay or Tim were female, there might be differences in the way they react, although the evidence is less clear in this regard (Hartman, Yrle, & Galle, 1998; Sweeney & McFarlin, 1997).

Still another determinant may be differences in their personalities and individual predispositions (Major & Deaux, 1982), such as endorsement of the Protestant work ethic (Greenberg, 1979). Identification with a particular occupation, preferences for egalitarianism or proportionality, self-efficacy, and personal ethical frameworks also are likely to affect how and when people are sensitive to the fairness of situations they face (Ployhart & Ryan, 1997; Rasinski, 1987; Schminke, Ambrose, & Noel, 1997; Witt & Broach, 1993).

Because the literature on individual differences in justice perceptions has been scattershot, it is difficult to develop a clear profile of how various people will perceive (and respond to) the events in their environment. Despite this inherent complexity, it is apparent that individual differences do, in fact, play a key role in determining the way people assess the fairness of the situations they face.

Challenges for Research and Application

The various issues raised previously in this chapter regarding the assessment step are important insofar as they raise several key questions about organizational justice that are relevant to theory and research.

Measurement Bias. Studies of organizational justice that focus on the assessment step have to tap people's perceptions of the fairness of an event they experienced. A key question in this regard is methodological in nature (namely, Does asking questions about perceived injustice lead to biased or misleading responses?). Indeed, it is critical to recognize the possibility that measurement effects may result from the procedures we use. In keeping with standard research logic, experimental studies of justice manipulate certain elements of a situation (e.g., process, outcome, or interpersonal treatment) and then measure participants' perceptions of fairness. A problem with doing this is that our research questions may be reactive (Webb, Campbell, Schwartz, Sechrest, & Grove, 1981). That is, the research questions themselves may prime concerns about justice that otherwise may have gone unnoticed.

A related problem is that although such research may tell us how people perceive the fairness of various manipulations, it does not explain how and when justice perceptions become salient in everyday life. Direct questions about fairness perceptions trigger justice frames, making it difficult, if not impossible, to determine whether frames were enacted a priori or whether they are triggered by research probes. Less intrusive measures, such as open-ended interviews or focus groups, would allow researchers to determine the naturally occurring perceptions of justice that may occur in a variety of environments (Folger & Belew, 1985). However, insofar as such studies are time consuming and require careful interpretation of data, they are difficult to perform.

Perceptual Salience.   Even if this methodological issue is adequately addressed, another fundamental question bearing on the assessment step arises: When do justice perceptions become salient? One answer to this question is suggested by research on the relationships between members of in-groups and out-groups (Allen & Wilder, 1965). For example, people's willingness to attribute unfair characteristics to an individual may be greater when responding to the actions of a member of a rival group, whereas more flattering attributions may be made toward in-group members who behave identically. In this regard, assessments of justice may be subject to various inaccuracies, such as the self-serving bias (Greenberg, 1983), and the fundamental attribution error (Ross, 1977).

A second answer to this question is provided by fairness heuristic theory (van den Bos et al., this volume). This approach suggests that justice becomes salient whenever people are concerned about potential problems of social interdependence and their social identity. Not surprisingly, justice judgments are likely to be made at the initial stages of relationships, when people first meet, rather than during the later stages, when social identities are more clearly established.

Judgment Formation.   Once justice becomes salient, people are likely to make judgments about it, although precisely how they do so is unclear. Accordingly, we may ask: How are justice judgments formed? Some insight into this question is provided by Petty and Cacioppo's (1986) elaboration likelihood model.

This approach distinguishes between two modes of information processing—central and peripheral—that are likely to be activated when people assess the fairness of the situations they confront. In the central mode, information is actively synthesized with current knowledge. Listeners rely on logical analyses of the content of a message to reach conclusions, and these conclusions are likely to be strongly held and resistant to change. On the other hand, peripheral processing relies on heuristics or cues from the message source or situation to form a conclusion in the listener's mind. Conclusions reached as a result of peripheral processing are more weakly held and susceptible to change if central processing of a contrary viewpoint can be encouraged.

Bobocel, McCline, and Folger (1997) theorized that when employees receive and process their managers' messages centrally (as opposed to peripherally) it affects their justice perceptions positively. Future research should expand on these findings to identify those variables that prompt listeners to engage in central processing in workplace situations. It also would be helpful to identify and explore those cues provided by the situation, the source, and the messages themselves that are likely to serve as justice-related heuristics, or peripheral cues. In situations where peripheral processing is likely, use of these heuristics may further encourage positive justice perceptions.

The Possibility of Context Effects.   A fifth basic question in need of investigation has to do with the nature of the organizational settings in which justice research is conducted: How are assessments of justice and injustice affected by the settings in which they occur? In some cases, applied justice researchers may be so pleased to have access to an organizational research site, that they overlook the manner in which their findings may be qualified by the nature of the setting studied. Although studies of organizational justice have been conducted in a wide variety of organizations (Greenberg & Lind, 2000), no clear picture has emerged of the extent to which the results may be qualified by these settings.

In large part, this is so because our research on assessments of justice in organizational settings is just beginning. However, even as this research matures, we fear that unless a framework is introduced for organizing and categorizing possible contextual differences, attention to the possibility of contextual differences in justice assessments are likely to go unnoticed. Although we believe it currently may be premature to introduce any such taxonomy, we acknowledge the possibility that different structural forms and cultural norms may influence the way people assess the fairness of various situations they confront. As such, we encourage future justice researchers to pay attention to these and other contextual variables that may moderate the results of organizational justice studies. With prolonged attention to such variables, what now seems like only background noise, may tomorrow be recognized as a key figural determinant of justice assessments.

STEP 2: REACTION

As expected, Just-Us Corp.'s new pay policy brought significantly higher pay to the more productive employees, like Jay. On the other hand, less productive employees, like Tim, saw their compensation substantially reduced. Helen, Jay and Tim's supervisor, noticed some changes in both men. Jay frequently remarked about how very fair he believed the new compensation system was as he cheerfully made coffee and cleaned the break room, a chore he assumed on his own initiative. Tim, on the other hand, started coming to work so late that Helen was forced to issue a written reprimand. One day, she approached Tim at quitting time to discuss the problem, and found him grumbling about how unfair the new system was. She also found a startling surprise: Tim was holding three of the company's power drills, appearing as if he was planning on taking them home without permission.

The new compensation system has triggered very different reactions from Jay and Tim. Jay perceives the new pay system as fair, and is responding in positive fashion by assuming extra duties. Tim, on the other hand, sees the system as unfair, prompting withdrawal and retaliatory behavior toward the company. Although their reactions are quite different, Jay and Tim are both reacting to their perceptions of justice or injustice.

This idea is in keeping with equity theory (Adams, 1965), which claims that people will take action aimed at redressing feelings of inequity they experience. These reactions can be viewed on a continuum ranging from positive, constructive attempts to change the situation on one end, through doing nothing in the middle, to disruption or sabotage on the other (Bies & Tripp, this volume) and are moderated by the way individuals cognitively process information about the situation (Kickul, Neuman, & Parker, 1999). The fact that people express their feelings of inequity behaviorally is fundamental to research bearing on the Reaction step, to which we now turn our attention.

Determinants of Reactions to Perceived Injustice

Research has revealed several key factors that influence the way people respond to perceived injustice. We now consider several such variables that appear to be especially important in this regard.

History of Unjust Treatment.   When making a decision about if and how to respond to injustice, people are likely to take into account the history of the injustice they realize. Specifically, people are more likely to respond to injustices that have been ongoing than those that are believed to be one-time events (Wall & Callister, 1995). Although even some single unfair events may trigger extreme retaliatory behavior (see Bies & Tripp, this volume), people often respond to such occurrences by mentally dismissing them as aberrations. However, insofar as repeated injustices may be systemic—and therefore, more serious—responses may be deemed not only appropriate, but necessary.

Form of Injustice.   Recent evidence (for a review, see Brockner & Wiesenfeld, 1996) suggests that although people sometimes fail to react behaviorally in response to distributive injustices (e.g., pay cuts, layoffs, undesired policy changes), they will respond in dramatic fashion when these outcomes are presented in a socially insensitive, uncaring manner (e.g., when interactional justice in violated; Bies & Tripp, 1996). It appears that the insult of interpersonal personal insensitivity may be necessary to trigger adverse reactions instigated by the insult of unfair outcomes. This idea has manifested itself in several ways, including stealing from one's employer (Greenberg, 1990), failing to follow organizational policy (Greenberg, 1994), suing one's former employer for wrongful termination (Lind, Greenberg, Welchans, & Scott, in press), and even acting in violent or aggressive fashion (Greenberg & Alge, 1998).

The Use of Justifications. Research has shown that people react less negatively to situations they perceive to be unfair when they receive adequate justifications for these occurrences than they receive either no justification or inadequate justification (e.g., Greenberg, 1993a, 1994, 1997; Konovsky & Folger, 1991; Schaubroeck, May, & Brown, 1994). Reactions may be influenced by justifications because retaliation or revenge is a likely frustration-based response to undeserved injustice (Tripp & Bies, this volume). Justifications or explanations provide a rationale for the undesirable event, which may mitigate the reaction in some way, such as by explaining that the actor had no control over the outcome (i.e., externalization), or that the consequences are not as severe as they appear (i.e., minimization; on the uses of these and other such techniques, see Greenberg, 1990).

Social accounts moderate perceptions of injustice by providing the information necessary for people to understand processes and outcomes (Brockner, DeWitt, Grover, & Reed, 1990). This information reduces uncertainty, particularly when negative outcomes are salient to workers. By providing a rationale for the outcome or procedure, organizational officials may be reducing the frustration experienced by those employees who are most adversely affected by their practices. This implies that had Tim been told the reason for the company's change to piece-rate compensation, he may not have been prompted to withdraw from Just-Us Corp., as he did, or be tempted to steal from it. Instead, providing a rationale for the pay-system change may lead Tim to accept both the process and its outcomes, although they affect him negatively, because he understood the necessity and rationale for the company's action. Thus, although Tim might not like the outcome, the fact that he understands it better may limit his adverse reactions to it.

Opportunities for Expression. Tim's reaction was influenced, no doubt, by the opportunities he had to express his feelings of inequity. He did this by explaining to Helen how he felt, and by preparing to steal company property. In short, he was able to identify appropriate response outlets.

Studies of ethical behavior have determined that people's willingness to engage in questionable activities varies in proportion to their ability to identify an anonymous and appropriate mechanism for the behavior (Loch & Conger, 1996). Similarly, fear of being caught, or lack of knowledge about how to carry out various dysfunctional behaviors may thwart desired reactions. This suggests that the way people will respond to feelings of injustice may depend on the knowledge they have about opportunities for expressing themselves with impunity. Indeed, theorists have noted that underpaid workers may refrain from expressing their feelings of inequity by withholding job performance insofar as doing so may threaten their job security (Greenberg, 1982).

Challenges for Research and Application

It is clear that many central issues regarding behavioral and cognitive reactions to perceptions of justice and injustice are not well understood. We have identified several such questions relevant to the Reaction step, the answers to which promise to benefit both research and practice in organizational justice.

Direct Versus Vicarious Injustice Experiences. Suppose, over the years, Tim has observed other employees at Just-Us suspected of taking home company property not getting into trouble. This may have taught Tim vicariously that he can get away with expressing feelings of inequity by stealing, thereby exposing him to a viable mode of inequity reduction. Although Tim may not have experienced this directly, he learned how to respond by observing others and experiencing vicariously what happens to them. This raises a key question that is not well understood: Do reactions to injustice depend on personal experiences with it?

Research has shown that even when observers are aware of injustices, they may fail to take behavioral action because they respond cognitively by derogating the victims (Skarlicki, Ellard, & Kellin, 1998). With this in mind, it is not surprising that social movements predicated on widespread societal injustice sometimes fail to stimulate action even among people who are sympathetic with the cause. It is clear that people may experience feelings of injustice vicariously, in situations that do not affect them directly. Suppose a friend of Tim's, Kathleen, sympathizes with his situation and joins him in acknowledging its unfairness. Yet, it is not clear if she will take steps to help Tim. If Kathleen works elsewhere in the company, leading her to believe that the company is introducing unfair policies, she may be inclined rise to the occasion by coming to Tim's aid by adopting the cause of the unfairness herself. Unfortunately, direct evidence bearing on this possibility is lacking. To appreciate the full range of responses to inequity, researchers would be well advised to explore the manner in which people react to those perceptions of injustice that have little or no direct impact on them.

Finding Effective Justifications. As noted earlier, the tendency for interpersonally fair treatment to mitigate reactions to injustice is robust. This is determined, in large part, by the adequacy of the information used to explain undesirable outcomes. However, precisely what exactly makes an explanation adequate? In other words, we may ask: What justifications most effectively thwart negative behavioral impulses?

Although current research provides some insight into the kind of excuses most palatable to listeners, we currently do not know much about the power of these accounts to modify behavioral reactions to perceived injustice. It is unclear, for example, whether information merely satisfies a need to know and reduces stress (Vermunt & Steensma, this volume) or if it actually enhances perceptions of justice in the mind of the listener. We need studies that examine workers' perceptions of accounts and excuses in light of their planned behavioral reaction to the perceived injustice. Do excuses mitigate reaction plans? If so, under what circumstances does this occur? Our understanding of the cycle of perceiving and reacting to injustice will be enhanced when answers to these questions are found.

Trust Between Worker and Supervisor. It is likely that Jay's positive perceptions of justice are prompted by the feelings of trust he has for Just-Us as an employer. Indeed, research suggests that trust develops over time and that, as it does so, expected patterns of behavior emerge (Lewicki & Wiethoff, 2000). When expectations are violated, people who trust the violator may make different attributions about the cause of the behavior than those who are not in a trusting relationship, leading them to respond differently.

For example, if Tim trusts Helen and other managers at Just-Us, Kelley's (1972) theory of causal attribution suggests that he will recognize the company's undesirable policy as inconsistent and distinctive, prompting him to believe that it may not have been volitional. As such, it may be readily forgiven, and may not trigger an adverse reaction. However, if he does not trust the company to be fair, he probably will show less restraint when it comes to behaviorally expressing the negative emotions he feels. This logic suggests that future research would be well served by asking: How does trust influence perceptions of justice? Further exploration of the link between trust-based expectations and justice perceptions promises to enhance our understanding of when and how people are willing to respond in accordance with their perceptions of justice or injustice.

STEP 3: RESPONSE FEEDBACK

Helen pondered the actions of her two subordinates, Jay and Tim. She decided that the new compensation plan had been a good idea because it provided more rewards for Jay—a good worker and a nice guy. But Tim had always seemed like a good guy too, and it was hard for Helen to come up with a good reason for him to be stealing tools from Just-Us. "He is making less money now," Helen acknowledged and decided she would talk to Tim about how his reduced wages might be affecting him.

The Response Feedback step occurs when managers recognize certain critical employee behaviors, such as Jay's good organizational citizenship or Tim's theft and then interpret those behaviors as a response to employees' assessments of justice or injustice. It might be helpful to view this step not as the manager's reaction to voiced employee perceptions of injustice but as attributions that managers make about specific employee behaviors. A less perceptive manager than Helen—and we admit that there are some—might either fail to notice Tim and Jay's behaviors or miss the opportunity to put them into context. In essence, this step focuses on managers' reactions to their employees' reactions to justice and injustice. This is why the diagram in Fig. 13.1 depicts the Response Feedback step as a bridge between reactive and proactive approaches rather than part of either one.

When do Managers Respond to Employees Reactions to Injustice?

Unfortunately, relatively little work has been done on the question of when managers make the attribution that employee behaviors are motivated by perceptions of justice or injustice. Research in this area focuses on identifying the processes and cues that prompt managers to view actions through a justice-related lens. Two questions have become most salient: First, how are attributions about employee behaviors created? And second, what contextual cues should trigger justice-related attributions?

Justice-Based Attributions. As discussed in the previous section, much of Helen's assessment of Jay and Tim's behavior is going to be based on what she knows about them and has come to expect from them. In this case, Jay's and Tim's behavior was salient to Helen because it violated her expectations, albeit in different directions. Kelley's (1972) theory of causal attribution suggests that Helen will evaluate Jay's and Tim's behavior in three areas: consensus, consistency, and distinctiveness. Because both Jay's and Tim's behavior is clearly different from that of other machinists in the company, Helen will note that consensus is low for both. Neither man is behaving in a manner that appears to be typical for machinists in the Just-Us Corp. work environment.

However, Helen will find differences between the two men on the latter two dimensions. Because Jay has established a pattern of punctuality on the job, Helen has come to view his early arrivals as personally consistent. And, because she has seen Jay's conscientiousness both in the coffee room and on the shop floor, where he has taken special care to ensure that his machines are clean and functioning well, Helen does not view Jay's actions as particularly distinctive. Kelley's (1972) theory suggests that because consistency is high and distinctiveness is low, Helen will make internal attributions about Jay's behavior. Thus, rather than seeing Jay's perception of the new salary program as a cause for his good organizational citizenship behaviors, she is likely to believe that Jay is simply behaving in this way because he is, as she noted, "a good guy." Helen may be delighted that the company now pays Jay more money each month, but she probably will not interpret his behaviors as a reaction to that pay raise.

On the other hand, Tim's behavior ironically may send a more correct signal to Helen. Although the act is consistent with his current behavioral patterns on the job, Tim has never before been caught stealing from Just-Us, and Helen has never had reason to suspect that he would. The distinctiveness of Tim's action is very high. Despite the moderating effect of low consensus, the fact that Tim's action is a shock to Helen may, in fact, prompt her to seek an external cause for his behavior. In this instance, she correctly assumes that Tim's reaction to the pay plan is motivating his theft. This, of course, would be the first step toward doing something about it.

Lack of Voice. Conventional wisdom dictates that listening to employees and encouraging feedback is simply good management, and ample research has demonstrated that providing individuals with a voice in establishing procedures or distributing outcomes enhances perceptions of fairness (Greenberg, Bies, & Eskew, 1991). Because Tim and Jay are now subject to a pay plan that they had no voice in selecting, Helen should immediately be prompted to investigate justice perceptions as a potential culprit for observed negative behaviors. As Vermunt and Steensma (this volume) illustrate, paying careful attention to, and showing appreciation for, employee feedback reduces stress and encourages positive views of justice. This tactic has the added advantage of mitigating reactions to perceived injustice: When employees faced with injustice communicate assertively, managers are more likely to respond with fair treatment (Korsgaard, Roberson, & Rymph, 1998).

Challenges for Research and Application

Although social scientists have spent a great deal of time determining how people make attributions for others' behavior, this knowledge has not been applied to the realm of organizational justice (for an exception, see Cohen, 1982). Significantly more research is needed to determine when people believe that others are reacting in response to perceived injustice. Future studies should examine two important questions. First, how can a manager's ability to make justice-related attributions be improved? Second, how do employees describe perceptions of injustice, and can managers accurately interpret this information? The following provides some guidance in each of these areas.

Sensitizing Managers to Justice Issues. A question critical to the Response Feedback step is: Can managers be sensitized to their employees' perceptions of fairness? Although preliminary, recent research suggests that the answer is yes. For example, both Latham (Cole & Latham, 1997; Skarlicki & Latham, 1996, 1997) and Greenberg (1999a, 1999b) found that various organizational outcomes were improved when managers were trained (e.g., using lectures, role-playing scenarios, and case studies). Indeed, the employees whose managers receive such training came to recognize that their managers have become more sensitive to the injustices they face.

Future efforts along these lines may be well informed by Bies, Tripp, and Kramer's (1997) description of biased punctuation of conflict (see also Bies & Tripp, this volume). According to this view, conflict continues when people make cognitive attributions that cast other parties at fault instead of stopping to evaluate their own contributions to the conflict. Indeed, applied scientists have found it difficult to convince managers that their own behavior may be contributing to the very problems they seek to solve (Greenberg & Lind, 2000). However, we suspect that managers trained in perspective taking and conflict management will be better equipped to recognize when justice-related concerns are responsible for aberrant employee behavior.

Describing Injustices.   As social scientists, we are well-equipped to make highly sophisticated distinctions between concepts—particularly abstract ones, such as justice. However, it may be naïve to expect lay people to share our sensitivity to matters of justice. In this connection, the key question is: Do employees interpret justice in the same way as scientists have conceived of it? Both Greenberg (1986) and Sheppard and Lewicki (1987) analyzed the open-ended responses of managers to questions about what determines fairness in their workplaces, and found generally good fit between participants' open-ended responses and scientific ideas of justice. However, this should not be taken as an indication that practicing managers share organizational scientists' sensitivity to matters of justice—at least, not in the same way.

Although we know perceptions of injustice when we see them as survey results, it is unclear whether we would recognize them if they were phrased in the employee's own words in a naturally occurring conversation. Future studies would benefit from incorporating qualitative methodology that examines the text of employee conversations with an eye toward determining the kinds of utterances that reflect concerns about injustice. Being able to identify key phrases would aid managers in determining when they should look to justice as a potential cause of destructive and positive employee behaviors. As such, efforts toward this goal would be very useful.

STEP 4: CREATION

Helen became suspicious that Tim's behavior might have resulted from his dissatisfaction with the new pay plan, so she arranged a meeting with Tim. She began that session by respectfully asking him why he was taking the drills and what was prompting his tardiness and absenteeism. As Tim began to express his feelings about the new pay system, Helen realized that he felt betrayed by Just-Us. "From the day I got here, I was told that what I did was OK and that I was paid pretty much the same as the other guys. I didn't really understand some of the new procedures we used when the line was retooled last year, but I thought that if the company wanted me to do something different, they would tell me. No one did; they just took money away." The more they talked, the clearer it became to Helen that Tim needed two things—more information about why the company changed its policy, and additional training that will enable him to raise his income. Both struck Helen as reasonable. She then spent the next hour sharing information about the company's financial position with Tim, answering his questions about the link between Just-Us's wage structure and its profitability. Then, she and Tim selected a series of training programs they thought would help Tim improve his job skills, enabling him to make more money under the new pay system. Tim and Helen both left the meeting feeling better than they had in weeks.

In the Creation step we focus attention on the proactive creation of justice perceptions. The primary research question is: How can managers create perceptions of justice? Research has revealed several viable strategies for creating justice perceptions in the workplace.

Strategies for Promoting Impressions of Justice

Although managers might do many things to promote the impression that they are being fair, three especially important ones are identified here. They are referred to as compensation, justification, and mitigation.

Compensation.   Employees frequently feel that they are being asked to do more than should be expected of them given what they are paid. The challenge faced by the managers of such individuals is to find ways of enhancing employees' outcomes, usually without raising pay, which is not feasible economically. Research testing equity theory (Adams, 1965) has found that perceptions of justice may be promoted by providing some offsetting benefit, such as granting a high-status job title (Greenberg & Ornstein, 1983) or by enhancing desirable features of the physical environment (Greenberg, 1988b, 1989), each of which provides compensation for extra job demands. In general, managers may be able to enhance the fairness perceptions of employees enduring hardships by offering them some offsetting benefit.

In our example, Tim now has the benefit of attending training sessions that will enhance his ability to make money at Just-Us Corp. and, perhaps, to get another job should the need arise. The company-paid training serves as compensation for Tim, both directly (insofar as admission into training programs is taken as a sign of status within the company) and indirectly (insofar as it may be a path to a more lucrative position). We expect that Tim now will have more positive feelings about the compensation plan because he has been compensated (at least partially) for the loss in wages that it cost him.

Justification.   Considerable research has shown that perceptions of fairness may be promoted by providing clear explanations for of the manner in which resources have been allocated (see Folger & Skarlicki, this volume). Again, Helen and Tim's conversation served this purpose well. Helen helped Tim understand why Just-Us Corp. implemented the new policy, and how it served the company's needs and goals. She provided Tim with this justification in a highly respectful way: face-to-face, with attention to his questions and concerns. There is good reason to believe that this tactic will enhance Tim's perceptions of justice (which, as noted previously, may be considered responsible for his dysfunctional behavior.

Impression Management.   There are various things that managers can do to promote the impression that they have behaved in a fair manner. Considering what these may be, Greenberg (1988a) explicitly asked managers to report the things they could do to make their subordinates think they treated them fairly. Among the most popular responses were: publicly announcing all pay raises and promotions, allowing workers to participate in decision making, explaining why certain work assignments must be made, and explaining how pay raises are determined. Greenberg (1990) explained that the techniques for managing impressions of fairness generally fall into two categories: *entitlings* (i.e., attempts to gain responsibility for positive events) and *enhancements* (i.e., attempts to augment the positive implications of one's actions).

These techniques are applicable to our case. For example, it may be in Helen's best interest to let it be known to others that she took steps to help Tim, particularly if he becomes a successful employee, thereby promoting her image as a fair manager in the eyes of others. Although excessive self-marketing efforts may backfire, a few carefully placed self-promotional remarks tempered with a dose of modesty may be a wise investment.

Challenges for Research and Application

The goal of the Creation step is to determine how managers can enhance their employees' perceptions of fairness. Although the work we cite provides some guidance in this area, managers also may be able to intervene in employees' perception–reaction cycle in other ways. This possibility raises three interesting questions that are now addressed. First, can companies suggest comparison standards that prompt employee perceptions of justice? Second, how can justice principles be routinely incorporated into change management efforts? And third, what role should cultural sensitivity play in manager's attempts to create perceptions of justice?

Manipulating Referent Comparisons.   When people evaluate outcomes and procedures through a justice lens, they often compare their situation to that of others to determine whether, in comparison, their treatment has been fair (Kulik & Ambrose, 1992). As noted previously, research has revealed relatively little about how people identify relevant comparison others. However, a question arises: Can and should companies recommend positive comparison standards?

It is a good possibility that managers can shape workers' choices of referent others by framing the company's treatment in a positive light. For example, pay surveys can compare an organization's compensation policies in a variety of different markets, such as a geographic area, within a particular industry, or by virtue of a worker's job category. By strategically choosing the referent with which the company's employees compare most favorably, managers may be able to shape their choice of referent other for comparison. So, if Tim compares his salary to that of others in his high school class, he may believe that he is unfairly compensated. However, when Helen told him about the salary rates of other machinists in their city, Tim's perception of being unfairly paid may be lessened. Although this is a logical possibility, its effectiveness has not been tested empirically. As such, we are unsure how individuals might incorporate new referent others into their cognitive schemas about justice.

Adapting to Organizational Change.   Research has shown that employees are likely to accept new management procedures to the extent they believe the changes were developed and implemented in a fair manner (for reviews, see Cobb, Wooten, & Folger, 1995; Novelli, Kirkman, & Shapiro, 1995). As noted previously, one of the ways this perception can be cultivated is by sharing relevant information in a sensitive and caring manner. However, it is unclear how much information, and what kind of accounts, need to be presented to employees to assuage suspicions of injustice in times of change. In other words, we may ask: What is the role of justice concerns in change management efforts?

The evidence is convincing that the explanations used to justify organizational changes enhance acceptance of those changes as fair. This is seen, for example, in such contexts as: relocations (Daly & Geyer, 1994), electronic control systems (Kidwell & Bennett, 1994), changes in corporate policy (Parker, Bales, & Christensen, 1997), the introduction of self-managed work teams (Kirkman, Shapiro, Novelli, & Brett, 1996; Shapiro & Kirkman, 1999) and new human resource information systems (Eddy, Stone, & Stone-Romero, 1999). Unfortunately, it is unclear precisely what needs to be said to help people accept the fairness of organizational change and whether there are differences between settings regarding what should be said. However, insofar as several recent conceptualizations provide good insight into this issue (e.g., Cobb et al., 1995; Novelli et al., 1995), we are optimistic that answers are on the horizon.

The Role of National Culture.   The idea of synergy between culture and justice has emerged only recently in the justice literature (see Bies & Greenberg, in press; McFarlin & Sweeney, this volume). This raises the question: How does culture influence the manner in which justice is created?

We know that justice concerns are, to a certain degree, specific to the cultural context in which they are enacted (Giacobbe-Miller, Miller, & Victorov, 1998). It is necessary for managers, particularly expatriates operating abroad, to take cultural norms and expectations into account when creating policies and procedures. Although the impact of cultural norms on reactions to perceived injustice has been to be examined in a variety of settings and cultures (e.g., Leung & Park,

1986; Meindl, Cheng, & Jun, 1990), the overall pattern of results is inconclusive (Miles & Greenberg, 1993). Moreover, the current literature shows a strong, only recently acknowledged bias toward American expectations and norms. As a result, we are currently not in a good position to understand the extent to which practices aimed at promoting justice in one culture are generalizable to others. However, the reality of the global economy provides a good incentive for researchers to make the study of this issue a major priority.

STEP 5: ENACTMENT

Helen felt that she had learned a great deal from her encounter with Tim. So, when she was told the following day that Just-Us Corp. planned changes in its work schedule for machinists, she immediately began to lobby for modifications in the way the new schedules would be developed and presented to workers. With her superiors' blessings, Helen recruited Jay and Tim, along with several of their colleagues, to participate in a task force to discuss the proposed schedule changes. Together, they devised a system whereby each employee would have a say in determining the shift he or she would work. Although neither Jay nor Tim was entirely pleased with his work schedule under the new program, they each accepted the program and worked hard to make it successful. The transition was accomplished with minimal grumbling and difficulty.

Helen's experience with Tim made her sensitive to justice issues. So, when faced with a need to implement a new program, she was careful to enact the change in a manner that would maximize her employees' perceptions of justice. Sure enough, this change at Just-Us Corp. was much more successful than the compensation program revision had been. As researchers in organizational justice, and presumably believers in the inherent and practical values of fairness, we focus significant attention on the enactment of organizational justice. Our goal is to encourage leaders and managers to use justice friendly procedures and policies.

Incorporating Justice Into Organizational Activities

Two types of research questions have guided our investigation into the issues surrounding the enactment of justice. Some research has focused on questions of omission. We have been primarily interested in those circumstances in which managers fail to incorporate principles of organizational justice into their activities and have learned that managers may neglect to share information when they feel personally threatened (Kim & Mauborgne, 1997). Researchers also have sought to identify organizational practices that make it easier for managers to be sensitive to justice issues. Two such practices have been identified: giving employees voice in the decisions affecting them and reciprocating justice, indicating a sort of trickle-down effect of justice perceptions in organizations.

Sharing Information.   The traditional, "old-school" managers of yesteryear were reluctant to share information with their employees, believing that "what they don't know won't hurt them." Today's more enlightened managers tend to be willing to share information, believing that it promotes teamwork. Also, sharing information enhances people's perceptions of fairness. In fact, employees who are given information about undesirable outcomes they face are better equipped to weather the resulting storms (e.g., Greenberg, 1994; Shapiro & Brett, 1993; Tyler & Bies, 1990). This results from the power of the information itself (an instrumental benefit), but also because of the value-expressive benefit of deciding to share this information. Indeed, Helen appears to have reaped both these benefits in deciding how to develop the new work schedule. Unfortunately, not all managers are as quick a study as Helen. Fear of what may result when they relinquish power may keep them from taking this very useful step.

Granting Employee Voice.   In much the same manner as sharing information may be useful in promoting justice, so too is granting employees voice into decisions affecting them. That is, employees are more likely to accept decisions they have had a voice in formulating, and they may feel positively disposed to organizational authority figures who have given them this opportunity. Specifically, employees who have a role in decisions affecting them tend to take responsibility for the results of these decisions and to be satisfied with the resulting outcomes (for a review of the voice effect, see Greenberg & Folger, 1983).

Additionally, managers who give their employees a voice in decisions stand to reap an important political benefit as well—namely, they can reduce their liability for questionable decisions (see Grandey, this volume). After all, when employees are given a voice in determining the processes and outcomes they experience, managers are no longer singly responsible for negative outcomes, leading them to lower their feelings of vulnerability (Folger & Skarlicki, this volume).

Reciprocating Fairness.   Managers often are advised to "walk the talk" when it comes to behaving fairly in the workplace. That is, they are expected to serve as role models of acceptable behavior. This advice seems especially valid when the acceptable behavior in question has to do with being fair. In fact, ostensibly fair managers may set a standard that proves central to forming organizational culture. Interestingly, the influence process also appears to work the other way around. Notably, a manager's fairness has been found to be related to the fairness of the treatment received from his or her own subordinates (Wiesenfeld & Thibault, 1997). Although there appear to be some important influences going on in these situations, we know little about the dynamics underlying their occurrence. Examining these modeling processes seems to be a wise investment for future researchers. This appears to be especially valuable in view of the successes in training managers to be fair, as described previously (e.g., Cole & Latham, 1997).

Challenges for Research and Application

It is clear that more questions than answers can be raised regarding the Enactment Step. First, what kind of interventions successfully encourage managers' incorporation of justice-based management into their daily routine? Second, although the effects of justice are well documented in the academic literature, what impact do these findings have on practitioners? Third, what role might employees play in encouraging managerial sensitivity to justice? We address each of these questions below.

Programmatic Efforts at Enacting Justice.   Applied social scientists and practitioners reading this chapter may be tempted to ask: What programs enhance managers' sensitivity to justice issues? In this connection, we note that some managers embrace justice as a terminal value (Folger, 1998). For them, it may be necessary only to point out the perception of injustice to prompt behavior change. For others, justice is important only insofar as it is a means to an end—an impression that should be cultivated because it is instrumental in bringing about other desired ends.

From a practical perspective, this distinction does not matter insofar as managers trained in ways of being fair on the job are not only perceived to be fair, but this also promotes various desired goals, such as lowering employee theft (Greenberg, 1999b) and raising organizational citizenship (Skarlicki & Latham, 1996). It appears that when managers are encouraged, such as through training or intervention, to view their actions through a justice frame, the desire for fairness may motivate them to change their behavior. We recognize, of course, that a wide variety of factors may influence the enactment of justice-enhancing behaviors. For example, even managers who are interested in doing things to promote justice may be kept from doing so by various organizational policies and norms that may discourage such actions.

Selling Justice Concepts to Organizations.   It is evident that there is a wide gap between the knowledge that scientists have about justice and the willingness of practitioners to put this knowledge to use in organizations (Greenberg & Lind, 2000). Although several training programs and interventions have closed this gap somewhat, it continues to prevail. This raises the following question: How can scientists promote their ideas for enhancing justice among organizational practitioners?

Unfortunately, that there is an inherent difficulty in imparting scientific information to the organizational public. For managers to make an effort at enacting justice, they must first acknowledge that their actions have caused the very problems they are attempting to solve. For example, before managers incorporate justice principles in their managerial practices, they first must admit that they created the injustices that motivated the theft to begin with. Not surprisingly, selling this concept to most managers is incredibly difficult, and the methods by which our results can be presented without posing a threat to a manager's self-esteem have yet to be developed.

Employee Training. Although, as noted previously, scientists have implemented training programs designed to make supervisors more sensitive to justice issues, we wonder about the impact of training lower level employees. After all, insofar as managers may model the fairness behavior of their subordinates (Wiesenfeld & Thibault, 1997), there seems to be merit in training these individuals. As such, we ask: Should subordinate employees be trained in ways to promote organizational justice?

We believe that the answer is a resounding "yes." But, how? There is no reason to doubt that the battery of role-playing exercises, cases, and lectures used to train managers cannot also be used (albeit with some alterations) to train lower level employees. For example, employees who are taught to use voice mechanisms available to them in a respectful and effective manner may be contributing to the overall climate of fairness experienced in the organization. However, in the absence of evidence supporting this practice, we are left to label this suggestion as only reasonable speculation.

STEP 6: EVENT FEEDBACK

> Helen and her superiors now routinely use employee focus groups before new policies are initiated. Open communication about the company's financial performance is the norm at Just-Us Corp. Maybe not-so-coincidentally, the company has enjoyed its best-ever year on the machine shop floor where Jay and Tim work. No safety problems have been reported, productivity continues to rise, and job satisfaction is at an all-time high. Although Tim still has not reached Jay's level of proficiency and productivity, his tardiness problem has all but disappeared and he shows real commitment to improving his work. For many, Just-Us Corp. has become an employer of choice—a "good place to work."

Our final step, the Event Feedback Step, focuses on the specific company policies through which justice is incorporated routinely in the daily, mundane tasks performed in organizations. The key research questions here are largely practical in focus. Studies that investigate the various ways that justice principles are enacted in specific organizational programs help us understand the mechanisms through which justice concerns become routine.

Justice as Organizational Routine

Research has demonstrated that concerns about promoting justice in such areas as employee selection (Gilliland & Steiner, this volume), drug testing (Crant & Bateman, 1990; Harris, Dworking, & Park, 1990), dispute resolution (Sheppard,

Blumenfeld-Jones, Minton, & Hyder, 1994), performance appraisals (Greenberg, 1986), and layoffs (Brockner, 1994; Brockner & Greenberg, 1990; Konovsky & Brockner, 1993) can have profoundly positive effects on present and future employees of organizations. This is not to say, however, that the behaviors that enhance justice perceptions have become incorporated in the daily activities of organizations. In fact, for the most part, they probably have not.

For good managers, providing voice, treating people equally, and sharing the reasons behind their decisions are not motivated by concerns about justice, but by what they believe is sound organizational practice. Indeed, they are correct: Treating people fairly, in these and the many other ways identified in this book, is in keeping with the foundations of good management. What, we may ask, makes justice so special? Our answer is simple: Justice is the central organizing heuristic around which these managerial practices are framed, helping us understand the mechanisms that make them work. The study of organizational justice provides insight to the specific kinds of behaviors that define good management practice, some of which already appear to be known, although some others may prove to be discovered. To those who claim that "this is really all just common sense," we ask why it is not yet common practice?

Challenges for Research and Application

As the reader might imagine, the prospect of incorporating justice principles in daily organizational practice is challenging. It raises two key questions.

Riding on the Coat Tails of Other Training Programs. Because of its obvious value to practitioners, efforts to incorporate justice principles into existing managerial programs should be undertaken. The question arises of how this can be done. In other words, we ask: How can justice principles be incorporated in management training programs?

We believe that the answer lies in piggybacking justice principles on training programs designed to address issues of more ostensible concern to management. Greenberg (1999b), for example, did this in the case of employee theft. The managers in his training program learned about promoting organizational justice although they did not know it; they thought they were learning about ways to manage so as to curtail theft among employees. The same thing also may be done in training programs designed to promote diversity and equal treatment of employees (Bobocel et al., this volume) and changes in human resources policies (Grandey, this volume).

A Cautionary Note. Our closing question is a humbling one: Can managers' preoccupation with justice backfire? In all honesty, the answer is yes. Indeed, research has shown that managers who attempt to promote justice by being manipulative and ingenuine run the risk of getting caught, effectively cultivating a negative impression (Greenberg & Ornstein, 1983, found this among managers who bestowed unearned job titles to workers in an effort to raise their rewards). Those who try to fake it by promulgating what Greenberg (1990) referred to as *hollow justice*, are not doing themselves a favor.

We recognize that changing organizational behavior in the ways outlined in this chapter may be considered manipulative by some. And, of course, we acknowledge the painful irony of being unethical about matters of justice. However, the practices we preach can only be thought of as ethical. Indeed, they promise to benefit everyone, from the lowest level employee struggling to earn a living, to stockholders focusing on the bottom line. Whether one's focus is on labor or management, it is clear that promoting organizational justice is a valuable, albeit illusive, goal. However, we believe—and we dare say that the other contributors to this book will agree—that the potential benefits of organizational justice readily justify the efforts to attain it.

CONCLUSION

The picture of the theoretical and applied value of organizational justice painted by contributions to this book fill a broad canvas with images that both inform and are informed by the framework presented in this chapter. For example, some authors help us understand the way people respond to feelings of injustice that is basic to our framework—both in the feelings that are aroused and assessed (see Vermunt & Steensma, on stress) and in the manner in which people respond to those feelings (see Bies & Tripp, on revenge). In this regard, there seems to be disagreement about the extent to which behaviors that appear to be responsive to perceptions of injustice are, in reality, well-rehearsed cognitions (see van den Bos, Lind, & Wilke, on fairness heuristic theory). Cognitions also play a role in the decisions people make about precisely how to treat others fairly (see Folger & Skarlicki, on the Churchill effect; and Cropanzano & Prehar, on changing referent standards in organizations).

Although several authors have ignored the contextual variables in which justice judgments are made and in which justice-motivated actions are performed, others purposely have focused on special issues that are likely to arise in specific organizational settings (or in regard to specific organizational issues)—a key issue whose importance we have identified. These include various contemporary human-resources policies, such as affirmative action programs (Bobocel, Davey, Hing, & Zanna), family-friendly organizational policies (Grandey), and job applicants' assessments of prospective organizations (Gilliland & Steiner). Still other contributors to this volume have taken a more macro approach by examining the changing nature of organizations (see Korsgaard, Sapienza, & Schweiger, on strategic decision making; and Ambrose & Schminke, on flexible organizations), and even the cultural milieu in which justice judgments are made (McFarlin & Sweeney).

Several authors have pointed us in new directions, such as by explaining how justice concepts help explain reactions to family-friendly policies (Grandey) and how they apply to the making of strategic organizational decisions (Korsgaard et al.), both of which are areas that are only just beginning to receive guidance from justice theorists (e.g., on family friendly policies, see Grover, 1991; on strategic decision making, see Kim & Mauborgne, 1995). Still other contributors have revisited established themes in the field of organizational justice, albeit in a manner that sheds new light on established issues. For example, Vermunt and Steensma's analysis of justice and stress is reminiscent of equity theory's discussion of the role of inequity distress (see Greenberg, 1984). Likewise, Cropanzano and Prehar's analysis of psychological contracts provides interesting new insight in the classic question of the role of social comparison in assessing fairness, also fundamental to equity theory.

Taken together, we cannot help but be impressed with the wide variety of important contributions that this volume appears to have made to the organizational justice literature. Although only time will tell the extent to which this volume proves noteworthy, we strongly suspect that its influence will be considerable. We can only hope that our own remarks prove to be as valuable.

REFERENCES

Adams, J. S. (1965). Inequity in social exchange. In L. Berkowitz (Ed.), *Advances in experimental social psychology* (Vol. 2, pp. 267–299). New York: Academic.

Allen, V. L., & Wilder, D. A. (1975). Categorization, belief similarity, and intergroup discrimination. *Journal of Personality and Social Psychology, 32*, 971–977.

Bartle, S. A., & Hayes, B. C. (1999, April). *Organizational justice and work outcomes: A meta-analysis.* Paper presented at the annual meeting of the Society for Industrial and Organizational Psychology, Atlanta, GA.

Bies, R. J., & Greenberg, J. (in press). Justice, culture, and corporate image: The swoosh, the sweatshops, and the sway of public opinion. In M. Gannon & K. Newman (Eds.), *Handbook of cross-cultural management*. Oxford, England: Blackwell.

Bies, R. J., & Tripp, T. M. (1996). Beyond distrust: "Getting even" and the need for revenge. In R. M. Kramer, & T. Tyler (Eds.), *Trust in organizations* (pp. 246–260). Newbury Park, CA: Sage.

Bies, R. J., Tripp, T. M., & Kramer, R. M. (1997). At the breaking point: Cognitive and social dynamics of revenge in organizations. In R. A. Giacalone & J. Greenberg (Eds.), *Antisocial behavior in organizations* (pp. 18–36). Thousand Oaks, CA: Sage.

Bobocel, D. R., McCline, R. L., & Folger, R. (1997). Letting them down gently: Conceptual advances in explaining controversial organizational policies. *Journal of Organizational Behavior, 4*, 73–88.

Brockner, J. (1994). Perceived fairness and survivors' reactions to layoffs, or how downsizing organizations can do well by doing good. *Social Justice Research, 7*, 345–363.

Brockner, J., DeWitt, R. L., Grover, S., & Reed, T. (1990). When it is especially important to explain why: Factors affecting the relationship between managers' explanations of a layoff and survivors' reactions to the layoff. *Journal of Experimental Social Psychology, 26*, 389–407.

Brockner, J., & Greenberg, J. (1990). The impact of layoffs on survivors: An organizational justice perspective. In J. S. Carroll (Ed.), *Applied social psychology and organizational settings* (pp. 45–75). Hillsdale, NJ: Lawrence Erlbaum Associates.

Brockner, J., & Wiesenfeld, B. (1996). An integrative framework for explaining reactions to decisions: The interactive effects of outcomes and procedures. *Psychological Bulletin, 120*, 184–208.

Cobb, A. T., Wooten, K. C., & Folger, R. (1995). Justice in the making: Toward understanding the theory and practice of justice in organizational change and development. In W. A. Pasmore & R. W. Woodman (Eds.), *Research in organizational change and development* (Vol. 8, pp. 243–295). Greenwich, CT: JAI.

Cohen, R. L. (1982). Perceiving justice: An attributional perspective. In J. Greenberg & R. L. Cohen (Eds.), *Equity and justice in social behavior* (pp. 119–160). New York: Academic.

Cole, N. D., & Latham, G. P. (1997). Effects of training in procedural justice on perceptions of disciplinary fairness by unionized employees and disciplinary subject matter experts. *Journal of Applied Psychology, 82*, 699–705.

Colquitt, J. A., Conlon, D. E., Wesson, M. J., Porter, C .O. L. H., & Ng, K.Y. (in press). Justice at the millennium: A meta-analytic review of 25 years of organizational justice research. *Journal of Applied Psychology*.

Cropanzano, R., & Greenberg, J. (1997). Progress in organizational justice: Tunneling through the maze. In C. L. Cooper & I. T. Robertson (Eds.), *International review of industrial and organizational psychology* (Vol. 12, pp. 317–372). London: Wiley.

Crosby, F. (1976). A model of egoistical relative deprivation. *Psychological Review, 83*, 83–112.

Daly, J. P., & Geyer, P. D. (1994). The role of fairness in implementing large-scale change: Employee evaluations of process and outcomes in seven facility relocations. *Journal of Organizational Behavior, 15*, 623–638.

Eddy, E. R., Stone, D. L., & Stone-Romero, E. F. (1999). The effects of information management policies on reactions to human resource information systems: An integration of privacy and procedural justice perspectives. *Personnel Psychology, 52*, 335–358.

Folger, R. (1987). Reformulating the preconditions of resentment: A referent cognitions model. In J. Masters & W. Smith (Eds.), *Social comparison, social justice, and relative deprivation: Theoretical, empirical, and policy perspectives* (pp. 183–215). Hillsdale, NJ: Lawrence Erlbaum Associates.

Folger, R. (1998). Fairness as a moral virtue. In M. Schminke (Ed.), *Managerial ethics: Morally managing people and processes* (pp. 13–34). Mahwah, NJ: Lawrence Erlbaum Associates.

Folger, R., & Belew, J. (1985). Nonreactive measurements: A focus for research on absenteeism and occupational stress. In L. L. Cummings & B. M. Staw (Eds.), *Research in organizational behavior* (Vol. 7, pp. 129–170). Greenwich, CT: JAI.

Giacobbe-Miller, J. K., Miller, D. J., & Victorov, V. I. (1998). A comparison of Russian and U.S. pay allocation decisions, distributive justice judgments, and productivity under different payment conditions. *Personnel Psychology, 51*, 137–163.

Greenberg, J. (1979). Protestant ethic endorsement and the fairness of equity inputs. *Journal of Research in Personality, 13*, 81–90.

Greenberg, J. (1982). Approaching equity and avoiding inequity in groups and organizations. In J. Greenberg & R. L. Cohen (Eds.), *Equity and justice in social behavior* (pp. 389–435). New York: Academic.

Greenberg, J. (1983). Overcoming egocentric bias in perceived fairness through self awareness. *Social Psychology, 46*, 152–156.

Greenberg, J. (1984). On the apocryphal nature of inequity distress. In R. Folger (Ed.), *The sense of injustice* (pp. 167–188). New York: Plenum.

Greenberg, J. (1986). Determinants of perceived fairness of performance evaluations. *Journal of Applied Psychology, 71*, 340–342.

Greenberg, J. (1987). Reactions to procedural injustice in payment distributions: Do the means justify the ends? *Journal of Applied Psychology, 72*, 55–61.

Greenberg, J. (1988a). Cultivating an image of justice: Looking fair on the job. *Academy of Management Executive, 2*, 155–158.

Greenberg, J. (1988b). Equity and workplace status: A field experiment. *Journal of Applied Psychology, 73*, 606–613.

Greenberg, J. (1989). Cognitive re-evaluation of outcomes in response to underpayment inequity. *Academy of Management Journal, 32*, 174–184.

Greenberg, J. (1990). Employee theft as a reaction to underpayment inequity: The hidden cost of pay cuts. *Journal of Applied Psychology, 75*, 561–568.

Greenberg, J. (1993a). Stealing in the name of justice: Informational and interpersonal moderators of theft reactions to underpayment inequity. *Organizational Behavior and Human Decision Processes, 54*, 81–103.

Greenberg, J. (1993b). The social side of fairness: Interpersonal and informational classes of organizational justice. In R. Cropanzano (Ed.), *Justice in the workplace: Approaching fairness in human resource management* (pp. 79–103). Hillsdale, NJ: Lawrence Erlbaum Associates.

Greenberg, J. (1994). Using socially fair treatment to promote acceptance of a work site smoking ban. *Journal of Applied Psychology, 79*, 288–297.

Greenberg, J. (1997). The STEAL motive: Managing the social determinants of employee theft. In R. Giacalone & J. Greenberg (Eds.), *Antisocial behavior in the workplace* (pp. 85–108). Thousand Oaks, CA: Sage.

Greenberg, J. (1999a). *Comparing the fairness of single-source and multi-source performance evaluations.* Unpublished data. Columbus: Ohio State University.

Greenberg, J. (1999b). *Interpersonal justice training (IJT) for reducing employee theft: Some preliminary results.* Unpublished data. Columbus: Ohio State University.

Greenberg, J., & Alge, B. J. (1998). Aggressive reactions to workplace injustice. In R. W. Griffin, A. O'Leary-Kelly, & J. M. Collins (Eds.), *Dysfunctional behavior in organizations: Violent and deviant behavior* (pp. 83–118). Stamford, CT: JAI.

Greenberg, J., Bies, R. J., & Eskew, D. E. (1991). Establishing fairness in the eye of the beholder: Managing impressions of organizational justice. In R. Giacalone & P. Rosenfeld (Eds.), *Applied impression management: How image making affects managerial decisions* (pp. 111–132). Newbury Park, CA: Sage.

Greenberg, J. & Cohen, R. L. (1982). Why justice? Normative and instrumental interpretations. In J. Greenberg & R. L. Cohen (Eds.), *Equity and justice in social behavior* (pp. 437–469). New York: Academic.

Greenberg, J., & Folger, R. (1983). Procedural justice, participation, and the fair process effect in groups and organizations. In P. B. Paulus (Ed.), *Basic group processes* (pp. 235–256). New York: Springer-Verlag.

Greenberg, J., & Lind, E. A. (2000). The pursuit of organizational justice: From conceptualization to implication to application. C. L. Cooper & E. A. Locke (Eds.), *Industrial/organizational psychology: What we know about theory and practice* (pp. 72–107). Oxford, England: Blackwell.

Greenberg, J. & Ornstein, S. L. (1983). High status job title as compensation for underpayment: A test of equity theory. *Journal of Applied Psychology, 68*, 285–297.

Grienberger, I. V., Rutte, C. G., & van Kippenberg, A. F. M. (1997). Influence of social comparisons of outcomes and procedures on fairness judgments. *Journal of Applied Psychology, 82*, 913–919.

Harris, M. M., Dworkin, J. B., & Park, J. (1990). Preemployment screening procedures: How human resource managers perceive them. *Journal of Business and Psychology, 4*, 279–292.

Hartman, S. J., Yrle, A. C., & Galle, W. P., Jr. (1998). Equity in a university setting: Examining procedural and distributive justice. *International Journal of Management, 15*, 3–13.

Huo, Y. J., Smith, H. J., Tyler, T. R., & Lind, E. A. (1996). Superordinate identification, subgroup identification, and justice concerns: Is separatism the problem; is assimilation the answer? *Psychological Science, 7*, 40–45.

Huseman, R. C., Hatfield, J. D., & Miles, E. W. (1987). A new perspective on equity theory: The equity sensitivity construct. *Academy of Management Review, 12*, 222–234.

Kelley, H. H. (1972). Attribution in social interaction. In E. E. Jones, D. E. Kanouse, H. H. Kelley, R. E. Nisbett, S. Valins & B. Weiner (Eds.), *Attribution: Perceiving the causes of behavior* (pp. 1–26). Morristown, NJ: General Learning Press.

Kickul, J. R., Neuman, G., & Parker, C. (1999, April). *Broken promises: Consequences of psychological contract breach and organizational injustices.* Paper presented at the annual meeting of the Society for Industrial/Organizational Psychology, Atlanta, GA.

Kidwell, R. E. Jr., & Bennett, N. (1994). Employee reactions to electronic control systems: The role of procedural fairness. *Group and Organization Management, 19,* 203–218.

Kim, W. C., & Mauborgne, R. A. (1995). A procedural justice model of strategic decision making: Strategy content implications in the multinational. *Organizational Science, 6,* 44–61.

Kim, C. W., & Mauborgne, R. (1997). Fair process: Managing in the knowledge economy. *Harvard Business Review, 75*(4), 65–75.

Kirkman, B. L., Shapiro, D. L., Novelli, L., & Brett, J. M. (1996). Employee concerns regarding self-managing work teams: A multidimensional justice perspective. *Social Justice Research, 9,* 47–67.

Konovsky, M. A., & Brockner, J. (1993). Managing victim and survivor layoff reactions: A procedural justice perspective. In R. Cropanzano (Ed.), *Justice in the workplace: Approaching fairness in human resource management* (pp. 133–153). Hillsdale, NJ: Lawrence Erlbaum Associates.

Konovsky, M. A., & Folger, R. (1991). The effects of procedures, social accounts, and benefits level on victims' layoff reactions. *Journal of Applied Social Psychology, 21,* 630–650.

Korsgaard, M. A., Roberson, Q., & Rymph, R. D. (1998). What motivates fairness? The role of subordinate assertive behavior on managers' interactional fairness. *Journal of Applied Psychology, 83,* 731–744.

Kulik, C. T., & Ambrose, M. L. (1992). Personal and situational determinants of referent choice. *Academy of Management Review, 17,* 212–237.

Leung, K., & Park, H. J. (1986). Effects of interactional goal on choice of allocation role: A cross-national study. *Organizational Behavior and Human Decision Processes, 37,* 111–120.

Leventhal, G. S. (1976). The distribution of rewards and resources in groups and organizations. In L. Berkowitz & E. Walster (Eds.), *Advances in experimental social psychology* (Vol. 9, pp. 91–131). New York: Academic.

Lewicki, R. J., & Wiethoff, C. (2000). Trust, trust development and trust repair. In M. Deutsch & P. Coleman (Eds.), *Theory and practice of conflict resolution* (pp. 86–107). San Francisco: Jossey-Bass.

Lind, E. A., Greenberg, J., Scott, K. S., & Welchans, T. D. (in press). The winding road from employee to complainant: Situational and psychological determinants of wrongful termination lawsuits. *Administrative Science Quarterly.*

Lind, E. A., & Tyler, T. R. (1988). *The social psychology of procedural justice.* New York: Plenum.

Loch, K. D., & Conger, S. (1996). Evaluating ethical decision making and computer use. *Association for Computing Machinery, 7,* 74–86.

Lowe, R. H., & Vodanovich, S. J. (1995). A field study of distributive and procedural justice as predictors of satisfaction and organizational commitment. *Journal of Business and Psychology, 10,* 99–114.

Major, B., & Deaux, K. (1982). Individual differences in justice behavior. In J. Greenberg & R. L. Cohen (Eds.), *Equity and justice in social behavior* (pp. 42–76). New York: Academic.

Mather, L., & Yngvesson, B. (1981). Language, audience, and the transformation of disputes. *Law & Society Review, 15,* 775–822.

McFarlin, D. B., & Sweeney, P. D. (1996). Does having a say matter only if you get your way? Instrumental and value-expressive effects of employee voice. *Basic and Applied Social Psychology, 18,* 289–303.

Meindl, J. R., Cheng, Y. K., & Jun, L. (1990). Distributive justice in the workplace: Preliminary data on managerial preferences in the PRC. In B. B. Shaw, J. E. Beck, G. R. Ferris & K. M. Rowland (Eds.), *Research in personnel and human resources management* (Suppl. 2, pp. 221–236). Greenwich, CT: JAI.

Miles, J. A., & Greenberg, J. (1993). Cross-national differences in preferences for distributive justice norms: The challenge of establishing fair resource allocations in the European Community. In J. B. Shaw, P. S. Kirkbride & K. M. Rowland (Eds.), *Research in personnel and human resources management* (Suppl. 3, pp. 133–156). Greenwich, CT: JAI.

Novelli, L., Jr., Kirkman, B. L., & Shapiro, D. L. (1995). Effective implementation of organizational change: An organizational justice perspective. In C. L. Cooper & D. M. Rousseau (Eds.), *Trends in organizational behavior* (Vol. 2, pp. 15–36). New York: Wiley.

O'Neil, B. S., & Mone, M. A. (1998). Investigating equity sensitivity as a moderator of relations between self-efficacy and workplace attitudes. *Journal of Applied Psychology, 83*, 805–816.

Parker, C. P., Bales, B. B., & Christensen, N. D. (1997). Support for affirmative action, justice perceptions, and work attitudes: A study of gender and racial–ethnic group differences. *Journal of Applied Psychology, 82*, 376–389.

Petty, R. E., & Cacioppo, J. T. (1986). The elaboration likelihood model of persuasion. In L. Berkowitz (Ed.), *Advances in experimental social psychology* (Vol. 19, pp. 123–205). New York: Academic.

Pinkley, R. L. (1992). Dimensions of conflict frame: Relation to disputant perceptions and expectations. *International Journal of Conflict Management, 3*, 95–113.

Ployhart, R. E., & Ryan, A. M. (1997). Toward an explanation of applicant reactions: An examination of organizational justice and attribution frameworks. *Organizational Behavior and Human Decision Processes, 72*, 308–335.

Rasinski, K. A. (1987). What is fair is fair—or is it? Value differences underlying public views about social justice. *Journal of Personality and Social Psychology, 53*, 201–211.

Ross, M. (1977). The intuitive psychologist and his shortcomings: Distortions in the attribution process. In L. Berkowitz (Ed.), *Advances in experimental social psychology* (Vol. 10, pp. 174–200). New York: Academic.

Schaubroeck, J., May, D. R., & Brown, F. W. (1994). Procedural justice explanations and employee reactions to economic hardship: A field experiment. *Journal of Applied Psychology, 79*, 455–460.

Schminke, M., Ambrose, M. L., & Noel, T. W. (1997). The effect of ethical frameworks on perceptions of organizational justice. *Academy of Management Journal, 40*, 1190–1207.

Shapiro, D. L. (1991). The effects of explanations on negative reactions to deceit. *Administrative Science Quarterly, 36*, 614–630.

Shapiro, D. L., & Brett, J. M. (1993). Comparing three processes underlying judgments of procedural justice: A field study of mediation and arbitration. *Journal of Personality and Social Psychology, 65*, 1167–1177.

Shapiro, D. L., & Kirkman, B. L. (1999). Employees' reaction to the change to work teams: The influence of 'anticipatory' injustice. *Journal of Organizational Change Management, 12*, 51–66.

Sheppard, B. H., Blumenfeld-Jones, K., Minton, W. J., & Hyder, E. (1994). Informal conflict intervention: Advice and dissent. *Employee Responsibilities and Rights Journal, 7*, 53–72.

Sheppard, B. H., & Lewicki, R. J. (1987). Toward general principles of managerial fairness. *Social Justice Research, 1*, 161–176.

Skarlicki, D. P., Ellard, J. H., & Kellin, B. R. C. (1998). Third-party perceptions of a layoff: Procedural, derogation, and retributive aspects of justice. *Journal of Applied Psychology, 83*, 119–127.

Skarlicki, D. P., & Latham, G. P. (1996). Increasing citizenship within a union: A test of organizational justice theory. *Journal of Applied Psychology, 81*, 161–169.

Skarlicki, D. P., & Latham, G. P. (1997). Leadership training in organizational justice to increase citizenship behavior within a labor union: A replication. *Personnel Psychology, 50*, 617–633.

Solso, R. L. (1998). *Cognitive psychology* (5th ed.). Boston, MA: Allyn & Bacon.

Steiner, D. D., Guirard, S., & Baccino, T. (1999, April). *Cognitive processing of procedural justice information: Application of the oculometer.* Paper presented at the annual meeting of the Society for Industrial/Organizational Psychology, Atlanta, GA.

Sweeney, P. D., & McFarlin, D. B. (1997). Process and outcome: Gender differences in the assessment of justice. *Journal of Organizational Behavior, 18*, 83–98.

Suls, J., & Wills, T. A. (1991). *Social comparison: Contemporary theory and research.* Hillsdale, NJ: Lawrence Erlbaum Associates.

Tannen, D. (1979). What's in a frame? Surface evidence of underlying expectations. In R. Freedle (Ed.), *New dimensions in discourse processes* (pp. 137–181). Norwood, NJ: Ablex.

Tyler, T. R., & Bies, R. J. (1990). Beyond formal procedures: The interpersonal context of procedural justice. In J. S. Carroll (Ed.), *Applied social psychology and organizational settings* (pp. 77–98). Hillsdale, NJ: Lawrence Erlbaum Associates.

van den Bos, K., Wilke, H. A. M., & Lind, E. A. (1998). When do we need procedural fairness? The role of trust in authority. *Journal of Personality and Social Psychology, 75*, 1449–1458.

Wall, J. A. Jr., & Callister, R. R. (1995). Conflict and its management. *Journal of Management, 21*, 515–558.

Webb, E. J., Campbell, D. T., Schwartz, R. D., Sechrest, L, & Grove, J. B. (1981). *Nonreactive measures in the social sciences* (2nd ed.). Dallas, TX: Houghton Mifflin.

Wiesenfeld, B. M., & Thibault, V. (1997). Managers are employees, too: Exploring the relationships between procedural fairness, managers' self-perceptions, and managerial behaviors following a layoff. In J. B. Keys & L. N. Dozier (Eds.), *Academy of Management Proceedings* (pp. 369–373). Briarcliff, NY: Pace University.

Witt, L. A., & Broach, D. (1993). Exchange ideology as a moderator of the procedural justice-satisfaction relationship. *Journal of Social Psychology, 133*, 97–103.

Author Index

Subject Index